MARKETING
IN DEVELOPING
COUNTRIES

Joanna Kinsey

MACMILLAN
EDUCATION

First published 1988

Published by
MACMILLAN EDUCATION LTD
Houndmills, Basingstoke, Hampshire RG21 2XS
and London
Companies and representatives
throughout the world

Printed in Hong Kong

British Library Cataloguing in Publication Data
Kinsey, Joanna
Marketing in developing countries.— (Macmillan
studies in marketing management).
1. Marketing — Developing countries
I. Title
658.8' 009172' 4   HF5415.12.044
ISBN 0–333–42115–9 (hardcover)
ISBN 0–333–42116–7 (paperback)

Series Standing Order

If you would like to receive future titles in this series as they are published, you can
make use of our standing order facility. To place a standing order please contact your
bookseller or, in case of difficulty, write to us at the address below with your name
and address and the name of the series. Please state with which title you wish to begin
your standing order. (If you live outside the United Kingdom we may not have the
rights to your area, in which case we will forward your order to the publisher
concerned.)

Customer Services Department, Macmillan Distribution Ltd
Houndmills, Basingstoke, Hampshire, RG21 2XS, England.

Contents

List of tables

List of figures

List of maps

Preface

Marketing in Developing Countries is written to complement present textbooks (notably *Marketing: An Introductory Text*) which are based on and written for developed countries.

The need for more marketing in developing countries is being recognised, as a means of helping minimise the effects of an increasingly competitive international climate, protectionism, plunging commodity prices, debt and numerous other difficulties which hamper economic development. For marketing offers a method of assessing whatever resources a developing country possesses and matching them with opportunities in the wider environment. It also provides the tools and techniques to ensure that modern industrial and commercial bases are built with the least disruption to local culture. Unfortunately it is usually the case that marketing is insufficiently understood or used in developing countries, while marketing training tends to be non-existent.

In order to fill this gap the Department of Marketing at Strathclyde University introduced the Master of Commerce in Marketing for Industrialising Countries degree programme in 1981. Aimed particularly at managers, government officials and academics as vocational training and applauded by Philip Kotler as an examplar for the future teaching of marketing in developing countries, it has proved extremely successful and in 1987 was made available on a Distance Learning basis. But because there was a dearth of readily-available academic textbooks covering the use of marketing in a developing country context one had to be developed.

This book is therefore aimed particularly at those who work either in the private or public sector in developing countries and who wish to develop marketing skills. Three perspectives are considered – those of the state marketer, the multinational marketer and the private sector indigenous marketer. Undoubtedly the government official plays a major role in the development of most developing countries. It is therefore essential that he or she not only understands and uses marketing him or herself but also is aware of the multinational and indigenous marketers' perspectives so that technology is acquired on the most favourable terms and the right sort of assistance is given to small firms. The private indigenous marketer has an increasingly important role to play as grand industrialisation schemes and highly capital-intensive projects have had to be shelved through shortage of finance or lack of success. His marketing abilities are likely to determine his chances of survival and growth, which in turn influence the state of the economy.

A second type of reader who may find the book of interest is the company executive in the developed world who is concerned with subsidiaries in and/or exporting to developing countries. It is more and more apparent that there is greater interdependence between developed and developing countries and that whereas developed world markets are reaching saturation point, the future market potential in many developing countries is enormous. The right sort of marketing skills must be developed. For this reason the book should also be used by students in the developed world for international marketing courses at both the undergraduate and postgraduate level.

No apology is made for the breadth of coverage or level of generalisation which, if taken out of context, would undoubtedly not apply to specific situations. Superficiality and over-generalisation are likely to be typical of any book which is written as a foundation for further literature of a narrower nature. However, it is hoped that the use of a classification of developing countries, based on their population and potential wealth resulting from their natural resources, and the inclusion of the three different marketing perspectives within developing countries will help to minimise the problems associated with attempting to cover all developing countries. Furthermore this allows readers to select parts of the book which are most relevant to them.

And because this book is written as part of a series and assumes that readers are familiar with *Marketing: An Introductory Text* other difficulties are overcome: firstly the developed world is, for the present, still the richest export market for developing countries, and in order that they may compete effectively the sophisticated marketing environment and the marketing techniques of the developed world must be understood; secondly it is a controversial point when a country moves from the 'developing' into the 'developed' category. It has already been suggested that some of the newly industrialised countries such as Singapore should be excluded from the preferential trading terms assigned to developing countries since their standard of living and other characteristics represent the developed world much more closely. But even in less fortunate developing countries the urban areas may be more akin to Western Europe or North America than to the rest of the country. In such instances marketing as practised in Western developed nations may be more appropriate and no modifications need be made. Until the range and scope of the literature increase it is again essential that the reader selects the parts of both books which are most appropriate.

Because this book has been written primarily for the M.Com. in Marketing for Industrialising Countries degree programme, a special debt of gratitude is owed to Professor J. M. Livingstone, now Professor of Management at Glasgow University. Professor Livingstone developed and directed the M.Com. programme at Strathclyde for three years. Furthermore it is his typology of large rich, large poor, small rich and small poor developing countries which is used throughout the book.

Deepest thanks are also due to Professor M. J. Baker, Deputy Principal and Head of the Department of Marketing at Strathclyde University. As series editor he offered continual encouragement and helpful advice as well as providing a basic framework for Part I of this book, since it uses as the foundation his most widely used British marketing textbook *Marketing: An Introductory Text*.

Finally Mrs Jean Davidson deserves a special mention for struggling with, and attempting to make sense out of, my appalling handwriting, in the typing of the manuscript. She succeeded admirably in presenting the meaning which was intended. Undoubtedly many weaknesses and deficiencies of my own making remain and for these I accept full responsibility. But if as a result of the remaining more meaningful parts of the book marketing principles and practices are acknowledged and used to better effect in developing countries, a very useful purpose will have been served.

Strathclyde University   JOANNA KINSEY

Acknowledgements

The author and publishers wish to thank the following who have kindly given permission for the use of copyright material:

The Advertising Association for an adapted table on advertising, 1985;

Financial Times of London for material from various supplements;

International Monetary Fund for adapted material from *International Financial Statistics*, 1982;

Penguin Books Ltd for material from *Development in a Divided World* edited by Dudley Seers and Leonard Joy, 1971. Copyright © Penguin Books Ltd, 1970;

Prentice-Hall, Inc., for adapted material from *Marketing Management* by Philip Kotler, 4th edn., © 1980;

Starch Inra Hooper, Inc., for material from *World Advertising Expenditures*, 1979;

The Trilateral Commission for material from *Trade in Manufactured Products with Developing Controls: Reinforcing the North–South Partnership* by A. Fishlow, 1981;

Unwin Hyman Ltd for material from *International Marketing* by S. Majaro, 1977;

The World Bank for material from *World Development Reports*, 1986 and 1982, Oxford University Press, Inc.

Every effort has been made to trace all the copyright-holders, but if any have been inadvertently overlooked the publishers will be pleased to make the necessary arrangement at the first opportunity.

PART I

THE ISSUES IN MARKETING IN DEVELOPING COUNTRIES

The first part of the book considers the basic issues involved in marketing in developing countries. These are many and complex, and numerous traditional assumptions about marketing must be modified. The diversity of developing countries is enormous. In terms of economic development, they range from the least developed and those now suffering large debt problems, such as Mexico, to the most successful Southeast Asian countries, which, following in the footsteps of Japan, are well on their way to becoming 'developed'. Historically, culturally and politically their backgrounds are equally varied. And whilst the marketing concept is relevant to all, *how* it is regarded, *who* applies it, and at *what level* all add to the complexity.

However, despite the heterogeneity both of developing countries and interpretations of marketing, it is possible to set down some broad definitions, outline the different perspectives, examine characteristics of developing countries' marketing environments, discuss consumer behaviour and demonstrate how marketing research and the marketing mix may best be applied. Furthermore, although there is no standard way in which to proceed, by examining and understanding all the issues involved, decision-makers are likely to make better decisions and use marketing to its best advantage, which in turn will promote economic development.

CHAPTER 1

The marketing concept and developing countries

Contents

Introduction

Few developing countries are content with the *status quo*. Most seek a better standard of living and are experiencing some degree of industrial-isation and urbanisation. Marketing, since it is concerned with the satisfaction of needs and wants and the optimum allocation of resources, if used effectively, can ensure that economic development is promoted. This can be done on many levels. Firstly on the micro level the commercial marketer (whether indigenous or multinational) can respond to and promote the increased demand for products and services. On the national level governments of developing countries can use marketing to assess opportunities and direct development so that progress is speeded up, social problems eradicated and maximum benefit achieved. Finally on a macro level multinationals, adopting a global marketing perspective, can help integrate developing countries into an interdependent world economy.

This chapter begins with some definitions and discussion of the issues involved in developing countries and economic development. After this it considers in detail what role marketing can play. Finally it briefly outlines the levels at which marketing can be applied and the perspectives of marketers applying it.

Definition of developing countries

Developing countries, industrialising countries, underdeveloped countries, less developed countries, the Third World and the South, are all terms used to describe the countries outside the Western bloc of so-called technically advanced nations (North America, Western Europe, Japan, Australia and New Zealand) and the Communist bloc. Each term tends to have certain connotations, some being more complimentary than others and some gaining popularity as others disappear from usage.

Underdeveloped suggests countries capable of economic development but which have failed to fulfil some unstated potential for development. *Less developed* is perhaps less objectionable than *Third World* or *underdeveloped*, but implies that such countries should model themselves on those which are more developed. This may prove a dangerous guide to strategy. *Developing* was a term which came into usage in the 1960s to replace the more pejorative *underdeveloped* and is now being replaced by *industrialising*. These more recent terms tend to paint on an optimistic gloss. In reality many countries may not be developing or industrialising.

A term which avoids the above controversy but which does little to clarify the issue is *the South*, an expression made popular in 1980. The Brandt Report (1980) distinguished between *the North* (or technically-advanced nations) and *the South* (all other nations, ranging from the most successful Southeast Asian states following in the footsteps of Japan to the extremely poor countries like Chad).

Developing, or whatever terms one chooses to use, means, basically, poverty. However this is extremely difficult to define and measure. In absolute terms there are hundreds of millions of people who are illiterate and inadequately clothed and nourished. Relatively, poverty can be measured by a country's per capita income. Two thirds of the world's population subsist on an inadequate income but a country is often considered to be 'developing' if income per head falls below a more or less arbitrarily stated figure – usually one-fifth of the per capita income of the United States.

However to use such a quantified definition and say that any country with a per capita income of less than one-fifth of that of the USA is 'developing', and all other countries are 'developed' is not satisfactory. By such a criterion, some countries like the oil-producing Middle Eastern states would be considered 'developed'. But when one considers other factors such as income distribution, level of available services, expectancy of life, availability of doctors per head, conditions of employment and so on, this is clearly not the case. For example, the richest 5 per cent of the population of a developing country often receive 30 to 40 per cent of the total national income before tax, while health, education, working and infrastructural conditions may be equally distorted, and usually fall short of levels achieved in developed countries. Such non-monetary indications as numbers of telephones, energy consumption, number of vehicles, life expectancy, illiteracy and unemployment are being increasingly incorporated into measurement criteria. No one indication on its own has proved to be satisfactory or universally acceptable. In broad terms one can say that developing countries are characterised by having certain similarities. As well as low per capita income they have such characteristics as these: a high percentage of the population employed in agriculture; low savings per head; high fertility and falling mortality rates, resulting in rapid population growth; high levels of illiteracy; low standards of public health and poor sanitation; a high proportion of exports concentrated in staple crops and raw materials; wealth concentrated in the hands of a few. Many other characteristics, in their most extreme form, are often as shown in Table 1.1.

Spatially developing countries comprise much of Latin America, Africa and Southeast Asia. But to group these countries together and describe them with one collective term such as the Third World or the South, is seen today to have less relevance than previously since they range from the primitive, stagnant economies to the rapidly developing dynamic economies which are likely to be considered 'developed' in the very near future. Furthermore these nations – disparate in culture and politics as well as in the level of economic development – are diverging at a bewildering rate. Consequently, while one collective term was seen to have some significance a few years ago when such organisations as the United Nations Conference on Trade and Development (UNCTAD) started expressing their grievances against the advanced world, some sub-classification is now clearly required.

Table 1.1   The characteristics of developing countries

1. *Economic characteristics*

    low output per worker
    low income per capita

2. *Conditions of production*

    small industrial sector
    few economies of scale
    primitive and crude techniques
    lack of specialisation
    low capital per worker
    small savings per head for the bulk of the population
    lack of enterprise
    inadequate physical and social infrastructure
    low agricultural output per acre
    concentration of exports on a few primary products
    low volume of international trade per head
    low efficiency

3. *Living conditions*

    large proportion of expenditure on food and necessities
    under-nutrition
    malnutrition
    high mortality rates
    bad housing and overcrowding
    bad hygiene, public health and sanitation
    inadequate cultural facilities

4. *Aptitudes*

    absence of training facilities
    inadequate education
    illiteracy
    ignorance, false beliefs and useless or harmful knowledge

5. *Attitudes to work and life*

    poor discipline and punctuality
    caste, religious or racial prejudice
    superstition
    lack of foresight
    lack of ambition
    apathy
    lack of adaptability
    unwillingness to bear risks, venture, innovate
    inability to co-operate outside the family or tribe
    contempt for manual work
    submissiveness

Table 1.1 *Cont.*

low standards of hygiene
work-spreading attitudes
absence of birth control and high fertility rates

6. *Institutions*

land tenure hostile to improvements
uneconomic division of plots
poor markets for labour, credit, capital
poor marketing facilities for products
poor information
weak government (national and local)
political uncertainty
corrupt, inefficient and inadequate administration
rigid class, caste system
inequality
absence of opportunities
arbitrary legal administration
non-enforcement of contracts
prevalence of child labour
inferiority of women's status
weak or absent middle class

Classification of developing countries

Several subdivisions of developing countries have been suggested. The World Bank identifies low income economies with a gross national product (GNP) per person of less than $400 in 1984 and middle income economies with a 1984 GNP per person of $400 or more. This latter group is subdivided into oil exporters[1] and oil importers.[2] The World Bank has an additional category not included in developing countries, but which does not fit into the other categories of Industrial Market Economies or Eastern Europe Non Market Economies either. This is the high income oil exporters category comprising Kuwait, Oman, Libya, Saudi Arabia and the United Arab Emirates (Map 1.1; see Appendix I for full listing).

---

[1] Middle income oil exporters comprise Algeria, Angola, Cameroon, Congo, Ecuador, Egypt, Indonesia, Islamic Republic of Iran, Iraq, Malaysia, Mexico, Nigeria, Peru, Syria, Trinidad and Tobago, Tunisia and Venezuela.
[2] Middle income oil importers comprise all other middle income developing countries not classified as oil exporters. In this group is a subset of major exporters and manufacturers. It includes Argentina, Brazil, Greece, Hong Kong, Israel, Republic of Korea, Philippines, Portugal, Singapore, South Africa, Thailand and Yugoslavia.

8

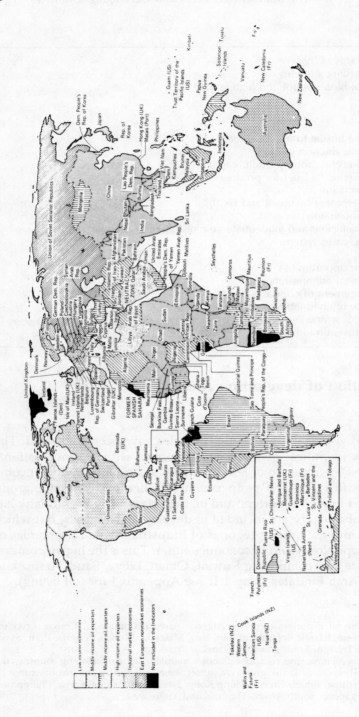

Map 1.1 The World Bank classification of countries

Source: *World Development Report 1986*, World Bank, Oxford University Press

Another more useful method is to classify developing countries by size and wealth. This classification, developed by Professor J. M. Livingstone, is useful in that it allows some indications about market size and likely industrialisation and foreign investment strategies to be acted upon by governments. Size is determined by population. Although many developing countries have rapidly expanding populations, making any precise cut-off point difficult, a country may be said to be 'large' if it has more than 30m inhabitants. If there is any disposable income such a figure permits a domestic market, and multinational corporations, often an essential stimulus to economic development, may be attracted. Wealth is even more difficult to assess, but since wealth in developing countries tends to depend on the production and sale of raw materials, a country may be considered rich (or more accurately *potentially* rich) if its earnings from these are comparable with the GNP of an advanced country. By considering whether a country is small or large, rich or poor, a fourfold classification is possible: (i) large rich (ii) large poor (iii) small rich (iv) small poor (Map 1.2 and Appendix II).

Large rich countries, for example the more populous oil exporters such as Mexico or Nigeria, have tended to be optimistic about their future development, believing that their earnings from raw materials would be sufficient for them to industrialise. They have found it easy in the past to follow import-substitution industrialisation strategies and pay their way without becoming competitive on world markets. Many have now run into problems due to any or all of the following: (i) the collapse of commodity prices or excess supply (e.g. Nigeria) (ii) high borrowing to support domestic investment and economic output (e.g. Brazil) and (iii) rapid population growth delaying real growth and causing higher unemployment (e.g. Mexico). All tend to suffer from inflation, corruption and a strain on the national infrastructure.

Large poor countries tend to fit the classic descriptions of developing countries in the most extreme form. Because there is a large population living at subsistence level, there is no domestic market for anything except basic necessities, and inadequate resources to pay for industrialisation means that such countries have little room for manoeuvre in achieving fast economic development. Political instability is common, and whilst foreign investment may be attracted by cheap labour and export incentives, it will generally seek a rapid return through assembly or licensing operations.

Small rich countries, such as the Middle Eastern oil states, with their small populations, vast natural resources, and extremely high per capita incomes, might seem to be the most fortunate, but although at present they provide rich markets for luxury products, the long-term economic prospects of such societies seem doubtful. Governments are keen to industrialise, but although more politically stable than those of large poor

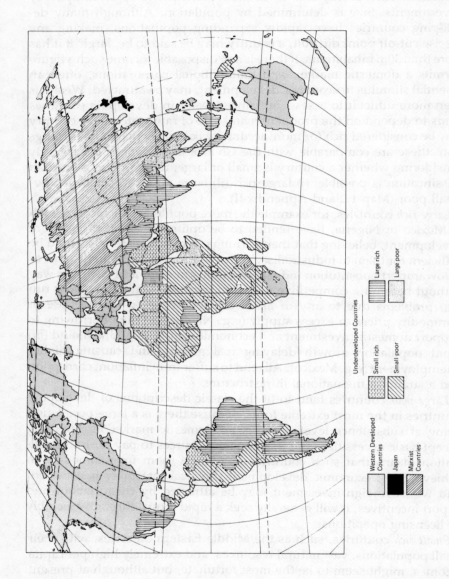

Map 1.2   Livingstone's classification of countries

Underdeveloped Countries

Large rich

Large poor

Small rich

Small poor

Western Developed Countries

Japan

Marxist Countries

countries they are handicapped simply because of the degree of wealth. Even if the home market is protected, it is unlikely to be sufficiently large for the multinational to consider operating within. And products manufactured in such states are likely to be uncompetitive on world markets due to high labour costs and inflation.

Many *small poor* countries, on the other hand, whilst appearing to hold no high cards, have been surprisingly successful in turning their disadvantages into strengths. What communities such as Singapore, Hong Kong or Taiwan arguably have (or had) is cheap labour. Together with the attractive inducements offered to incoming companies, many multinationals have set up assembly operations here. Such products as televisions and electronic equipment are built and incorporated into products sold internationally under famous brand names. The effect of increased disposable income, foreign exchange earnings and so on has been rapid economic development in such countries.

Indeed many of these small poor countries such as Hong Kong, Taiwan and Singapore have been so successful that they are now leading what have been termed the newly industrialised or newly industrialising countries (NICs). They may soon repeat Japan's success. Other countries which may have broken out of the trap of underdevelopment, and could, although more doubtfully, be put into this category include Mexico, Brazil and Argentina in Latin America, Egypt and Nigeria in Africa, Malaysia and Thailand (and to a lesser extent Indonesia and the Philippines) in the Far East. All have achieved a technological base which enables them to produce a wide range of products not requiring the most sophisticated technology, although even this has been achieved where labour costs are low and a large market is assured. All NICs are drawn from large poor, large rich or small poor countries, but not small rich ones.

Several NICs are experiencing rapid rises in the standard of living and a corresponding rise in cost. Japan, once considered a low-cost, low-quality economy, has managed to develop into a high cost, technologically innovative one. Some NICs may well be able to perform the same miracle: Singapore is currently turning itself into a high wage economy based on Japanese lines. Others, such as Mexico and Brazil may be hampered by rapidly growing populations and may prefer to postpone the rise in labour costs, preferring to employ more. Debt is another handicap for many.

Indeed the policies followed, often related to the 'size' and 'wealth' conditions existing in the NICs, have led to greater diversity within the NIC category of developing countries itself. This can easily be seen by looking at past and projected Gross Domestic Product (GDP) figures of certain countries. The International Monetary Fund (IMF) has forecast a 4.6 per cent growth rate for non-oil developing countries by 1986–90. But once individual countries are considered, the disparity is obvious.

Mexico and Brazil, with their large populations and potential wealth have tended to follow extreme policies of industrialisation through import substitution. Southeast Asian countries (note South Korea's record on Table 1.2) whose future appears much brighter, have not chosen to borrow heavily to support domestic investment and economic output, but have followed more moderate industrialisation policies based on an export orientation. Many, including Hong Kong, Singapore and Taiwan, did not even get into debt during the 1970s energy crisis. Although many observers have suggested that their proximity to Japan – the world's most dynamic industrialised nation – serves as a unifying factor for such nations, and that the current boom in the North American economy has helped these countries which already export a high percentage of their total to the States, such arguments are open to doubt.

Table 1.2   **The changing growth rate of GDP in selected NICs**

	GDP per capita annual average % change		
	1980–1	1982–3	1984–9
Mexico	3.8	− 5.2	1.4
Argentina	1.9	− 2.8	2.0
Brazil	5.1	− 2.4	Nil
South Korea	6.9	5.7	4.9
Philippines	2.8	− 0.3	− 0.4
Thailand	4.6	3.0	4.0

Source: Data Resources – quoted in *Financial Times* 25 May 1984.

What is certain is that these most successful NICs have little or no natural resources, and although oil (or any other mineral) was once considered a key to success, natural resources are now seen to create economic rents which lead to vast inequalities, which in turn make for vested political interests. The Asian NICs, on the other hand, have geared themselves to trade with the outside world. For example Hong Kong exports accounted for 26 per cent of the country's GNP in 1960. By 1980 they accounted for 70 per cent. Similarly, Taiwanese exports now account for 50 per cent GNP (approximately $50 billion in value). But despite phenomenal growth of exports in areas such as electronics, refined metals, garments, footwear and plastic products, and despite Taiwan today exporting more than Spain, Austria, Denmark, Brazil and South Africa, the Taiwanese value stability, rather than risk a repeat of the 1975–9 period of high inflation following the rise in oil prices.

What is clear, however, from the above examples is that developing countries cannot be considered as one homogeneous bloc. Furthermore no developing country is doomed to perpetual underdevelopment. Many of the most successful NICs are threatening the advanced nations. For example the Koreans and Taiwanese now hold major shares of the British home market for textiles. East Asia as a whole is beginning to dominate the automation, telecommunication and data processing fields. East Asian companies have joined the ranks of the multinationals. South Korea, for example, by 1979, had as many multinational companies listed in *Fortune 500*'s largest non-American multinationals as did Italy, a particularly striking achievement when one considers that no Korean firm appeared on the list in 1973. To correspond with such achievements consumer perceptions of some developing countries are changing. Today Pony cars from South Korea and electronic watches from Hong Kong are achieving more prestige, and even beginning to threaten the Datsuns and Seikos which have already been accepted by the Western consumer.

Thus the range of developing countries is enormous and likely to change further in the future, so that any strict classification is unlikely to remain valid for too long.

Economic development defined

Because many developing countries are considered to be more economically developed than others, it is desirable to know how economic development is defined and measured. Unfortunately, once more, there is no one universally accepted definition or yardstick. To add to the difficulty, the conceptual meaning of economic development has changed through time. The interpretation has ranged from 'economic growth' to 'modernisation' to 'distributive justice' to a 'socio-economic transformation'.

In the early post-World War II years development meant economic growth, characterised by a rapid and sustained rise in national income, or alternatively measured by increase in total GNP – that is the total capacity and volume of production of goods and services in a country. However, neither of these indices considers the individual's standard of living. And since only the total income or volume of output was examined, a country could become 'developed' almost overnight if it could rapidly generate foreign exchange, for example through the supply of a raw material such as oil. But yearly gains in total income or output could be surpassed by gains in population, leaving the individual with a lower standard of living.

Development as 'modernisation' then emerged, stressing social, psychological, political and educational changes, and since 1968 the World Bank has promoted economic development as meaning 'distributive justice' since it was realised that the benefits of growth were not reaching the poorest sections of the community. Per capita income as a whole was rising but widespread poverty and destitution were still persisting. Thus regional planning and more public goods and services were seen to be particularly relevant.

Incorporating all these changes, economic development is today considered to be more than just growth in national income or gross national product. It is now regarded as a total socio-economic transformation, which is measured in a multi-dimensional fashion. Economic growth is essential but not sufficient. There must also be changes in structure and capacity as well as output (Baxter, 1972) and attention must be paid to the quality of growth and social change. Consequently, whilst there is still much emphasis on economic indicators such as national income and gross national product, which can be easily understood, produced and compared, social indicators such as life expectancy, percentage employed in agriculture, consumption of proteins, education levels and so on are also receiving more attention.

Economic development, therefore, must include some diversification of a country's economic structure, away from primary activity and towards the manufacturing and service sectors. It must also incorporate improvements in material welfare through reduction in mass poverty, illiteracy, disease, early death and the rest and ensure more productive employment among the working age group as a whole rather than for a privileged minority. If levels of poverty, unemployment and inequality have declined over a period then some development can be said to have occurred (Sears, 1969), for it is then likely that the standard of living of the individual has improved. And by considering the typical negative characteristics of developing countries as well as total output and income levels, a more meaningful measure of economic development is possible.

The desire for economic development and difficulties involved in achieving it

All developing countries seek a better standard of living through economic development and, until recent years, have unquestioningly believed the West's experience was a desirable model to be followed as closely as possible (Kinsey, 1982). To industrialise and acquire the most up-to-date technology was thus regarded by many as the only way forward. Some countries have been better suited than others for this strategy and were consequently more successful. Others, having been made aware of what was possible, were unable to achieve their targets, especially since the rise in oil prices and world-wide economic recession. For them the gulf between the First and Third Worlds has widened.

Initially, in the 1960s, it was considered by many economists that some 'growing pains' in an economy were essential in the early stages, especially if rapid industrialisation through an unbalanced development model was the policy adopted. But as time went by, and as it was seen that only the rich were benefiting from rising national incomes, other factors began to be examined. The conditions typical of developing countries as a whole, the policies adopted by Governments and the negative spin-off effects of development have come under particular attack.

In relation to conditions, rapid population growth is frequently singled out as a factor mitigating against sustained economic development. In many countries medical knowledge has permitted a dramatic fall in the death rate without a corresponding fall in the birth rate which remains high due to cultural factors. This has upset the population equilibrium and the accelerating rate of population growth has swallowed up any increase in output and income. Culture has been responsible for many other aspects regarded as hindrances to economic development. For example what is considered a status symbol will affect the way in which people save and invest. If they hoard gold, increase land holdings or use other unproductive methods, a paucity of savings and therefore a poor base for development results. Equally, entrepreneurial ability, often considered essential for economic development, is frequently low, since many cultures encourage a tradition-bound, fatalistic outlook to life. Trade, land speculation and money-lending may be considered more profitable and less risky than entrepreneurial activity which is often left to immigrants to undertake. This in turn may cause such activity to be held in even lower esteem. Managerial skills too are usually severely under-developed, as is administrative ability, which encourages corruption. This in turn leads to cynicism and frustrates any enthusiasm and idealism qualities vital for expansion programmes.

Social factors also create more basic, but equally fundamental, barriers to economic development. Where the extended family system exists, property and income is pooled and rewards on an individual basis are therefore reduced, as is the incentive to work. Nepotism usually co-exists with such traditional attitudes, thereby reducing efficiency further.

Many policies once eagerly embraced by governments in developing countries are today being questioned. Sometimes they are considered to be the cause of continuing underdevelopment. Countries often insist on the most modern technology available, which allows them to jump several stages passed through in the West. Whilst this may be a source of prestige for the country concerned, capital-intensive machinery may be ill-adapted to the factor endowments of some countries. Equally, where Western institutions and models of organisation have been transferred wholesale, like the technology they have in some cases been found to be inappropriate. For example, trade unions developed under different social and legal systems imported from elsewhere can result in greater social injustice. And parliamentary democracies may, in some instances, be completely irrelevant. Aims of policies have sometimes been too ambitious and ill-thought out. Frequently planning incorporates several conflicting objectives at the same time, such as high growth rates in income as well as greater equality in the distribution of income, fuller employment, development of backward regions and reduction of the reliance on foreign trade. The means of achieving such objectives may be equally unclear.

The third area which sometimes handicaps the developing country's development is the area of negative spin-off consequences of advancement, such as the loss of skilled and professional manpower. Once people in developing countries have learned new skills, or been professionally trained in some field, they may choose to leave their home country permanently to seek employment elsewhere – often in more developed countries. Similarly capital can be lost through people choosing to invest elsewhere.

In addition to these three areas, which can, to some extent, be controlled by developing countries, there are the additional external, uncontrollable elements which may hamper economic development. Firstly, scientific research in the developed world has in many cases reduced the demand for traditional, foreign exchange-earning products; for example, there has been the replacement of synthetic for natural rubber. Secondly, as economic recession has spread, more protectionist measures have been adopted by the developed world, which has also reduced the amount of aid to the South. In this way developing countries have been put under additional strain.

Notwithstanding the difficulties involved, it has become abundantly clear that success is possible, as shown by the most advanced NICs. It is also evident that there is no best way in which to achieve economic development. Grand industrialisation schemes in oil-rich countries have not fulfilled their expectations, whilst many small, poor countries have advanced. In seeking to ensure that each country devises the best way to achieve a social and economic transformation *marketing* can be a powerful tool. It can ensure that society's values and environmental opportunities are taken into account, and an integrated approach to development is achieved.

The role of marketing in economic development

Marketing is generally conceived of as human activity directed at satisfying needs and wants through exchange processes (Kotler, 1984) or 'a process of exchange between individuals and/or organisations which is concluded to the mutual benefit and satisfaction of the parties' (Baker, 1983, p.4). Despite being an extremely old activity, dating from times of trade by barter, it is only since the 1950s that marketing has been recognised in the West as an orientation for business activity. In that decade the marketing concept was born.

The marketing concept is basically the idea that the entire enterprise should be orientated towards the satisfaction of consumer needs and wants. Changing social and economic conditions in the technically advanced world were fundamental in the marketing concept's evolution. From the time of the Industrial Revolution until the 1930s firms were production-orientated, demand at this time being greater than supply. Between the 1930s and the 1950s, when supply was equal to or greater than demand, firms adopted a hard-sell approach in a sales-orientation. However, as some consumer needs became satiated, and as technical and social factors altered buyers' preferences, this approach of aggressively selling what was produced failed. Supply was soon consistently greater than demand and producers were competing with each other as well as trying to combat alternative and substitute goods. In order to survive firms had to begin to consider the consumers – who they were and what they wanted – before resources were committed to production. Thus the marketing concept came into being and consumers were recognised as being at the head of the process rather than at the end, as in the sales-orientation.

The marketing concept was widely embraced over the next 20 years in Western conditions of rapid economic growth, greater affluence, important inventions, increased competition, narrower profit margins and planned obsolescence. Today some critics have called the concept inadequate and dangerous since it focuses on demand without sufficiently considering such wider issues as scarcity, environmental destruction, inflation and explosive population growth. In response the societal marketing concept has been suggested (Kotler, 1984), which means that the company must consider the welfare of society as a whole as well as satisfying consumer needs and wants.

Despite the fact that the marketing concept evolved in the advanced world, and that the boundaries of marketing have broadened considerably, in its widest sense marketing's function remains to serve and satisfy human needs and wants. By doing this it may be considered to be a strategic element in the structure of any society, since it directly allocates resources and has an important impact on other aspects of economic and social life. Consequently its relevance to economic development would seem clear.

However this is not universally accepted. In addition to the traditional problems associated with the fact that there is no one accepted definition of marketing (see Baker, 1985) and the controversy regarding the extent to which marketing boundaries should be broadened, the relevance of basic marketing principles and concepts to developing countries is disputed. There are two opposing schools of thought in this matter.

The first argues that no straight transfer of marketing principles and concepts is possible because environmental factors make them inapplicable. The conditions of a strong and strengthening buyers' market, increasing competition resulting from innovation, better education and government restriction on business for the sake of consumers, all of which led to the acceptance of the marketing concept in the advanced world, are usually lacking in developing countries. Furthermore, where there is much state planning, supply and demand relationships are controlled at the centre. This interferes with the operation of free market forces. Finally this school suggests that culture is likely to be too different to allow the transfer.

The second school of thought maintains that, whilst there must be some modifications made in response to different characteristics of the marketing environment, marketing principles and concepts can and should be applied. Thus, although the sophistication typical of marketing activities in the United Kingdom or the United States may not be required, the basic objectives and functions of marketing remain relevant.

This latter view is the one upheld in this book. It is nonsense to suggest that marketing cannot be applied to developing countries. Marketing already exists in some form in *any* society where exchange takes place. The process is the same but there may be qualitative and quantitative differences, such as fewer products moving through the system, different kinds of products, and generally a smaller variety. Used in a more active way marketing's role remains 'to ensure the continuance in growth of economies and the individual's standard of living' (Baker, 1985, p. 15). The determination of needs and wants, and the direction from management on how to maximise satisfaction in total terms, still applies. Indeed in a more difficult economic climate where stagnation, inflation and recession have resulted in less aid flowing to developing countries and more protectionist measures against them, the effective use of marketing is even more critical. And the broadening of marketing's frontiers to include social and societal marketing is as relevant, if not more so, to developing countries as it is to developed ones.

As well as matching the supply of products with consumer needs and bringing new products onto the market, marketing can bring more people into a market economy. This can easily be seen if a functional approach is adopted. This approach – first set forth by Alderson (1968) and developed by Thorelli (Thorelli and Becker, 1980) – envisages marketing as a pervasive societal activity within one large social system: the world. Each human being, each company, each society is dependent upon its environment for survival, and interdependence stems from the desire for specialisation or division of labour as a prime means of survival in a world of scarce resources. A company, society or country therefore obtains the support of the environment by disposing of its differential advantage.

This approach is particularly attractive today since effective communications have caused rapid shrinkage in international space, and the development of an interdependent world economy. A developing country can better decide which activities to develop in relation to local conditions, market structure, and resources. Trade without exploitation and global efficiency as well as economic development for the country concerned is, theoretically, likely to result. The concept of a social system existing by adapting to environmental change and maintaining a dynamic ecological equilibrium in a fast-changing world is also much more useful than static, unrealistic economic models which are often used as a rationale for development.

Furthermore marketing is useful in countering non-economic obstacles such as people's values, attitudes and ways of life which do not alter in the face of economic opportunity but instead prevent the pace of development being maintained. In this area social marketing – the design, implementation and control of social ideas (Kotler and Zaltman, 1971) – offers a powerful tool. Marketing can therefore both devise the best method of economic development and reduce the obstacles, given the resources and cultural conditions of the country. Whether strategies are inward-looking, relying on the domestic market, or outward-looking, concentrating on exports, marketing can facilitate the economic and social transformation by helping to control changes in production and demand. As well as this *developmental* role, marketing also has a *societal* role to play in economic development. Since there is no universal agreement about what are the desirable aspects involved in a social and economic transformation, marketing can ensure that a society's values are taken into account.

It is precisely because marketing is concerned with a social system and operates within it that it is able to identify opportunities and promote economic development which corresponds with a society's values. Marketing is sufficiently versatile to achieve this despite the heterogeneity of natural resources, population, culture, politics and level of development both between and within developing countries. Consequently it adds a real-world dimension which complements or provides a better alternative than traditional economic models used in development planning. In the latter, savings, capital and manufacturing are usually regarded as the only necessary preconditions for self-sustained growth whilst national and interpersonal attitudes are ignored. It is assumed that such aspects as family loyalty or intra-group harmony will be sacrificed for economic goals, with their emphasis on individuality and performance. Frequently this does not happen and initiatives fail.

Marketing can prevent this from happening by identifying cultural barriers to economic development, changing them, or adapting the method of economic development to them. For example Myrdal in 1968 listed efficiency, diligence, orderliness, punctuality, frugality, honesty, rationality in decisions, preparedness for change, alertness to opportunities, energetic enterprise, self-reliance and willingness to take a long-term view as essential modernising attitudes and ideals to promote economic development (Myrdal, 1968). But these are still often lacking in developing countries. It may be decided that some attitudes and beliefs which are incompatible with economic development can, and should, be changed. Alternatively, it could be that the method of economic development can be adapted to match existing cultural conditions.

Whatever the level of a country's development, whatever the cultural conditions or the existing opportunities, marketing provides the ideal means to understand the environment in which the social system under consideration functions, to respond to people's needs and values and thereby promote optimum economic development.

The relationship between marketing and economic development

Ideally then marketing has a fundamental role to play in the process of economic development. But in reality the relationship between the two is complex. Marketing can lead, and therefore act as a stimulus to, economic development. It can also lag behind it, acting as a response. This largely depends upon whether marketing is used actively, or whether it is allowed to evolve in a passive fashion. In some economies it has acted in both an active and a passive manner.

(a) Marketing as a stimulus for economic development

Used effectively, it is clear that marketing can lead and speed economic development through both its functions and its philosophy. Through the use of marketing research information is generated, allowing the better utilisation of resources. Efficient physical distribution enhances the productivity of the total economic system. Better storage and transport usually results in economies in distribution, expanded markets and increased production. Better standards of living can be diffused throughout the whole country just by establishing the strategic location of wholesale and retail establishments. As well as encouraging entrepreneurial initiatives and providing jobs generally, marketing stimulates wants. People are exposed to more goods. A higher level of production and a wider range of available goods follow.

The multiplier effect which marketing can set in motion is well demonstrated by the much-quoted large scale retailing introduced to Brazil by Sears Roebuck. This development introduced sales promotion, advertising and consumer credit and stimulated innovation. Output and consumption increased. Entrepreneurs and managers developed. Efficiency of distribution, an increase in the size of market and greater economic and social integration were stimulated.

Yet traditional economic models used in the formulation of development plans tend to ignore the marketing factor, considering it simply as a part of the production process. For example Rostow's stages of economic growth are based on a dynamic theory of production (Rostow, 1962). Equally, Nurske's theory of balanced growth (Nurske, 1971) describes the problems which exist on both the demand and supply side of the equation but ignores the valuable role marketing has to play. The solution to the vicious circle of poverty is seen to be the introduction of capital on the supply side, which increases productivity and creates disposable income. If, however, production were seen as an aspect of the marketing process, latent demand would first be identified. Secondly, marketing would indicate ways to convert this to effective demand, for it directs producers to develop marketable goods and improve distribution systems and ensures that products are brought to market without perishing en route. Consequently it plays an important part in effectively linking rural and urban markets, creating national markets, essential for economic development. Finally it can encourage the consumer to discriminate in order to get the greatest value for his limited purchasing power. Thus marketing ensures that the fullest use is made of whatever assets and productive capacity an economy possesses. Higher levels of economic activity are then likely to follow.

Not surprisingly, the best examples of situations in which marketing can lead economic development are provided by the multinational corporations, which are perhaps still the major method of infusing marketing into developing countries. As shown by Sears Roebuck, as well as demonstrating effective management techniques and making it necessary that more skilled management should develop locally, multinationals often provide the initial spark for development through technological transfer. Once this spark is located a multiplier effect follows. New means of production require changes in the kinds and amounts of input (energy, raw materials, parts and components, commercial services, and so on). As dependence among sectors of activity alters, the economy undergoes structural change. The multinational also brings knowledge, capital and entrepreneurship in its package of benefits. New products, product services, investment, training of workers and the purchase of materials and components from local suppliers are direct gains. Product technology, competitive pressures to modernise and the incentive to observe and imitate management techniques and marketing methods are indirect ones.

(b) Marketing as a response factor in economic development

Marketing can also be regarded as lagging behind economic development, playing an accommodating role in the development process. If measured by functions performed, institutions established and techniques applied, marketing can be seen to develop in step with the economy.

For example, in terms of distribution, barter is the first step, allowing exchange to take place. When the producer moves into a market system he acts in a dual capacity – as producer and distributor. As markets expand and output and specialisation increase full-time intermediaries develop. Distribution channels lengthen, but as producers gain financial strength, the need for separate functional middlemen declines and the number of links in the channel falls. In this sequence economic development is the motivating force which brings about changes as new institutions arise and as existing ones adapt to the changing environment.

The theory that the nature of the market system depends upon the characteristics of the trading community – for example, the size and density of the population; the size of the trading area; the level of development in transport and communications; the volume and variety of goods produced; the degree of specialisation in production and the physical constraints – is well demonstrated by the traditional sectors in many developing countries. For example, the Nigerian collective markets remain at the heart of the economy, representing 'an effective adaptation of the needs and facilities of the people to the environmental setting of the land' (Baker, 1969). Here a hot humid climate, a profusion of edible products, a high population density and low purchasing power mean that food is the basic need. The result is the rotating market of a 4-, 5- or 7-day cycle, drawing from a radius of 10–25 miles.

In relation to industrial development, the size and organisation of the firm, managerial attitudes and channel structure are expected to emerge according to the stage of development. For the firm the environment will provide the operating conditions. Such factors as disposable income, lifestyles, literacy of the population, will affect the market potential and therefore the scale of operation. Economic and social conditions such as capital, the pool of management and labour skills will influence the mode of operation, whilst distribution will be similarly affected. If there are low levels of consumer expenditure, and therefore a low market potential, together with backward technology and restricted financial resources, there will be little incentive to develop large-scale operations. Small family firms are more likely to be the norm with local but long distribution channels. As the number of affluent consumers grows and attitudes change, greater opportunities are likely to result in larger production units and wider distribution. However, whether the influence of environmental factors is so determinant has been questioned (Douglas, 1971).

(c) Marketing as first a response and then a stimulus to economic development

Under certain conditions marketing can lag behind economic development until a certain point is reached after which marketing leads economic development. This happened in the West and, more recently and more rapidly, in the Middle East, where economic development overturned marketing institutions in the space of five to ten years. The traditional 'souk' was replaced by new types of retail outlets, such as luxury shops, supermarkets and boutiques away from the centre. Public companies and multinationals developed. The infrastructure developed in response to increased demand resulting from oil income. Between 1973 and 1975 the volume and value of imports rose ten to fifteen times. Ports were congested and warehouses and the transport system were inadequate to cope. By 1978–9 demand and supply were more in equilibrium.

Middle Eastern markets are today characterised by ample supply, many private brands, a proliferation of retail outlets and changed relationships between local merchants and suppliers. Advertising and market segmentation are understood and used. The transition from a selling to a marketing orientation has come about in response to a change from a situation of product shortages and excess unsatisfied demand to conditions of ample supply and fierce competition. The typical consumer, once illiterate and with limited purchasing power is now an educated, travelled individual with considerable purchasing power and aware of all the industrialised world has to offer. A marketing orientation is now essential for all firms – manufacturing or service – and the typical market trader who once passively responded to demand must now identify genuine consumer needs and satisfy them.

There has been more change in the Middle East in the last few years than 100 years previously. The marketing era today is in full swing and is leading economic development, and, although other developing countries may not witness the same rapid transformation, it seems clear, that, whether marketing leads or lags behind economic development, the relationship is inextricable and cannot be denied.

Levels of marketing and economic development

Because of this relationship there have been many attempts to categorise countries according to the level of economic development and to describe marketing systems at each level. Fisk (1967) suggests markets pass through four historical stages according to the level of economic development: (i) fixed geographical markets (ii) open market organisations attracting buyers at scheduled times in fixed places (iii) dispersed mass markets and (iv) product differentiated markets which meet segments of demand arising when buyers exercise a wide range of choice in the products they want. Peterson's four stages are (i) subsistence (ii) surplus barter (iii) specialised and (iv) mass production and consumption (Peterson, 1977).

Marcus et al. (1975) similarly postulate four stages. In the first stage – *self sufficiency* – which occurs in 'poor, stagnant economies', exchange, if it occurs, is through barter. Marketing activities are consequently limited. In the second stage – *emerging economies* – the emphasis is on production. Barter is replaced by money and permanent local markets and trade specialists serving as intermediaries between producer and consumer begin to appear. Retailing, wholesaling, storage and transport are important marketing functions. The third stage – *industrialisation* – is typical of 'maturing nations' when modern technology extends to most areas of economic activity. Trade with other nations is encouraged and a strong and sizeable middle-class market emerges. Production and distribution networks are well organised, if complex, and marketing as a whole begins to shift from an institutional focus to a more sophisticated form of consumer satisfaction, for example, branding. The final stage – *mass consumption* – occurs when advanced technology spreads to all economic activities. Trade with other nations is regarded as essential for continued prosperity. Society has considerable discretionary income and manufacturing capacity outstrips distribution capabilities with consequent increased competition.

Finally Kotler (1973) offers a four-stage approach and describes the marketing emphasis in each. In the first stage, the *pre-industrial economy*, often a hunting, herding or farming one, capital is scarce and basic needs are all-important. Marketing exists in the form of barter or sometimes trading goods for money. *Industrialising economies* are characterised by increases in productivity through more capital and better production methods. Marketing brings goods to the urban population by a distribution system consisting of small merchants. *Industrial economies*, the third stage, have a high level of production. The problem is to generate sufficient demand, the emphasis being on market research, product design, packaging and other marketing mix elements. Finally *post-industrial economies* have societies which value the quality of life rather than materialism. Marketing must therefore identify advanced personal and social needs and develop appropriate offerings.

In all these models there is a common progression, from the most primitive stage of economic development, where marketing is at best rudimentary, to more economically developed stages which in turn require expanded markets and different and more sophisticated marketing emphases. These may be summarised as in Table 1.3.

Table 1.3   Stages of economic development and marketing emphases

Level of Economic Development	Marketing Emphasis	Extent of market
i) Self-sufficient barter economy	Exchange of basic necessities	Local
ii) Emerging, expanding economy	Distribution Development of trade, specialists and intermediaries Product-orientation	Expanding level
iii) Industrialising	Use of marketing mix Consumer orientation with product differentiation and market segmentation	National and international
iv) Industrial/post-industrial	As with (iii) but with emphasis on consumer values Societal orientation	Global

Restrictions in the use of marketing as an active force in economic development

The relationship between economic development and marketing cannot be denied. But where used actively as a stimulus to economic development marketing faces many difficulties and restrictions. Firstly the typical characterisation of developing countries cause severe constraints on the functioning of marketing. Generally the limited availability of manpower, know-how, monetary systems, transport and communications, government legislation and social norms are likely to restrain marketing from being used with the same sophistication as in Western developed countries. The emphasis is more likely to be on distributing necessities through traditional institutions and channels. Local companies are likely to have low and unpredictable sales volumes, which mitigates against the application of a central co-ordinated system of marketing typical of the United Kingdom or the United States. And whereas retail stores in the advanced world tend to operate on lower profit margins which stimulate vertical integration, the stores in developing countries tend to operate at a high level of profit because of the nature of competition. There is consequently no need for change.

To add to these factors, markets are not homogeneous. Although it is convenient to try and classify economies into stages of development and consider marketing characteristics accordingly, in reality the picture is not so clear. Most developing countries are characterised by two distinct market segments: the impoverished peasant masses who purchase the bulk of food and the affluent upper classes in the towns. Within this duality of urban and rural there is further heterogeneity, all of which hampers central marketing co-ordination and the maximum market growth of the economy as a whole.

Next the straightforward transfer of marketing methods and organisation may be difficult, because of cultural conditions. Bribery and corruption are often rife. In selecting personnel family connections may be more important than ability. Attitudes to management may therefore preclude the traditional organisation of marketing management as known in the West whilst on the broader level repercussions are likely to be more serious. Because of the absence of the right kind and quality of management to organise economic efforts and bring together resources and capabilities, and to convert self-limiting static systems into self-sustaining growth, economic development as a whole is restricted. The availability of capital, labour and so on constrains the potential rate of growth, but the ability to unlock the potential depends upon effective management which can identify opportunities and provide organisation.

Indeed marketing as a whole (functions, objectives and organisations) is generally not regarded in a favourable light. Production, capital formation, and investment are always emphasised in national plans. Marketing is undervalued and often ignored. Always consisting of intangible activities which are difficult to quantify, marketing is frequently attacked as a parasitic function, standing between the consumer and producer and draining the system of vitality. Production is consequently considered more repectable than distribution and middlemen are regarded with suspicion. This may account for large numbers of foreign traders in some developing countries. For example, Iranians form the bulk of grocers in Kuwait and Bahrain; Indians and Pakistanis own most retail stores in the United Arab Emirates. Such distrust of private enterprise leads to direct intervention by government in the form of price controls, for example, without the full implications being foreseen.

Furthermore marketing is often considered irrelevant under the product-orientation of many developing countries where there is a sellers' market and the associated characteristics of scarcity, limited price competition, monopoly or cartel conditions, tied distribution systems, low rates of product change and product differentiation. It is argued (as by the school which maintains that marketing concepts and principles cannot be applied) that until a certain point is reached, that is mature markets with supply and demand more level, marketing is unnecessary. Many of these misconceptions stem from perhaps the biggest problem – the scarcity of marketing specialists in developing countries.

Lastly, there is always this question: *should* marketing be used to promote economic development? Leaving aside the issue of whether economic development is a desirable goal with all the side-effects which may result, the *method* by which development is promoted through marketing may be questioned. For example, social marketing is a powerful force but there may be moral objections to people's attitudes being changed in order that development occurs. Acceptable if used to promote birth control, low-cost proteins and better agriculture, its impact may also be negative if it changes people's way of life and destroying traditional culture.

In conclusion, it may be that there are numerous moral, methodological, cultural and physical difficulties involved in adapting marketing as a stimulus to economic development. Nevertheless, if these are taken into account and the relevant modifications made, marketing remains a powerful, versatile tool which can be used at many levels and in many situations. Since economic development is a goal unlikely to be relinquished by developing countries, marketing remains possibly the best method to achieve it. The greatest strength of marketing is its consideration of *people* within a real-world social system. It is not constrained by economic dogma as are many of the models used in development planning. Instead it offers practical diagnostic and directive guidelines and forms the vital link between people's needs and the means of achieving them.

Perspectives of marketing in developing countries

Although the role of marketing seems clear enough in broad terms, the perspectives adopted by different types of marketers using marketing at different levels in developing countries are in no way uniform. The three major categories outlined here, and discussed in greater detail in subsequent chapters, are: (a) the indigenous marketer, that is to say nationals or permanently resident ethnic groups using marketing outside the public sector (b) the multinational marketer, and (c) the governmental marketer. As might be expected the multinational marketer is likely to be the most sophisticated and uses marketing to its fullest extent, the other two categories having less knowledge of techniques available and making very much less use of them.

(a) The indigenous marketer

If 'marketer' were taken to mean someone who understands and applies marketing in order to create, build and maintain mutually beneficial relationships with target markets, few indigenous marketers would be found in developing countries. Yet, as already discussed, wherever there is exchange some marketing, however rudimentary, can be said to occur. Most indigenous marketers, in whatever sector of activity, are passive marketers, responding to generally *local* conditions of demand rather than operating in a pro-active way, as eptomised in the above description of a marketer.

Because of the characteristics of developing countries it is likely that most indigenous marketers have limited horizons. Not being concerned with national or international markets and fierce competition but rather small local sellers' market, they are often more concerned with problems of supply rather than the effective total use of the marketing mix. Their knowledge of such tools may be limited in any case, whilst financial resources to back up any initiative, if desired, are likely to be limited. Finally, culture may dictate such negative attitudes as unwillingness to delegate authority, selection of staff according to family connection rather than ability, and so on.

As always, there will be a range of perspectives within and, especially, between developing countries, with some indigenous marketers being more marketing-orientated than others. Generally, however, effective marketing is not widely embraced. To a large extent a production-orientation dominates, with consequent limited analysis of market characteristics, growth rates, human and natural resources and even less marketing strategy. For example, product policy in manufacturing, such as it exists, tends to stress the functional qualities of the product, durability being the most important aspect. The existing product line tends to be thin with few 'new' products being added, since these tend to be imported first, after which there is little finance available for the indigenous entrepreneur to be able to compete and little inclination considering the prestige often given to imported goods. Promotion tends to be neglected, or considered unnecessary, particularly where a sellers' market exists, whilst pricing tends to be cost- rather than demand-orientated and, since large wholesalers often determine margins for distribution, control is lost immediately. Quick profits rather than long-term consumer satisfaction is the major objective.

Against a background which usually offers little inducement to the use of more effective marketing together with the general mistrust of middlemen in developing countries, the indigenous marketer tends to be somewhat negative. Yet, as has been discussed above, better use of marketing would benefit the total economic system, and marketing training to broaden horizons and improve the consciousness of the utility of marketing is clearly required. In this way the indigenous marketer could act more as a leading rather than a lagging agent in economic development. Ultimately (as witnessed in the Middle East) he may have to adopt effective marketing for his long-term survival as demand for products and service increases and as more competition enters the market.

(b) The multinational marketer

The multinational marketer stands at the other extreme to the indigenous one. Marketing concepts are well-understood and effectively used on a global scale. Indeed it is often claimed that the multinational corporation posesses additional advantages which make its objective much easier. The multinational has trademarks and patents which carry prestige with them, for they represent Western technology and advanced products which are considered superior in many developing countries. Because of this, the multinational can emphasise its 'foreignness' when this is in its favour. Through such a strategy it can introduce and promote certain products built initially for different market conditions and, assuming that tastes are converging throughout the world, adapt the market of developing countries to the product rather than produce a product having first discovered the needs and wants of the market.

Thus, whilst a multinational may have been extremely marketing-orientated in its traditional domestic market areas, in certain fields, such as cars and consumer durables, it may be much more product-orientated. There may be some adaptation by building to higher or lower standards to suit the market, but basically the product is a standardised one, sourced, produced and sold globally. Advertising in such cases receives the greatest emphasis in the marketing mix, while market research is often replaced by marketing intelligence on the political and legal situation of a country, for such a global strategy often requires total or no ownership by the multinational.

Nevertheless other aspects of marketing are promoted by multi-nationals within developing countries. Because facilitating aspects are often lacking, the multinational may develop its own. For example, in Nigeria the United Africa Company (UAC has been largely responsible for much of the established distribution network. And whilst it is sometimes argued that such developments are only partial and estab-lished solely for the organisation's benefit, even so they are usually a significant improvement on the existing infrastructure. In addition, they provide a catalyst for further development elsewhere.

Equally, in the actual organisation of the marketing function, the multinational marketer will introduce much needed principles and concepts and stimulate their use in competing companies. And because host countries are insisting more and more on some form of ownership in subsidiaries, and on the employment of nationals in executive positions, such knowledge is being introduced in a practical manner. Although the perspective and loyalty of expatriate managers will represent the parent company's policy and be different from those of managers recruited locally, nevertheless, basic marketing principles are learned and used. Since the multinational is backed by large financial resources, it has the ability to carry out marketing techniques in the most sophisticated form and demonstrate efficient marketing management.

So it can be seen that the multinational marketer is an active force of introducing marketing principles and methods and applying them to build and maintain mutually beneficial relationships with target markets. Although many multinationals may regard the world as one market segment, and therefore represent more of a product-orientation in some fields, nevertheless managerial organisation and the marketing infra-structure which is built up represent a valuable bonus for a developing country.

(c) The governmental marketer

In the past there has been very little emphasis given to marketing by the public sector. Although advertising has been used in social programmes such as birth control, generally, and especially in the field of national planning, marketing is mistrusted. To some extent this may reflect the background of public sector employers. Often they have a degree in politics or economics and are educated for a prestigious, but now out-of-date, post in the Civil Service. Not surprisingly the emphasis in planning has been on production or investment, in accordance with economic models. Marketing activities and the role of market forces are not given their due.

Too much state involvement has been the result, as is now being recognised by some developing countries. For example, in Asia generally it is being reduced. Many governments in this part of the world are collectivising agriculture, pulling out of state-owned industries and services, restoring private enterprise to its former role and finding new ways to encourage and reward businessmen. It has been seen that to allow businessmen to accept risks, organise funds and supply managerial skills to meet the needs of the market is to reduce the drain on the public purse. Consequently, in this part of the world, apart from the Philippines and India, more efficient small-scale organisations are being encouraged to replace the stifling bureaucracy of state involvement.

But within state planning too marketing has a role to play. One example which demonstrates that marketing's value has been accepted is the Kenya Tea Development Authority (KTDA). Such a state-owned authority often becomes a swollen, bureaucratic, heavily-subsidised drain on the economy. There are many examples of such bodies being unresponsive to peasant needs – as in the case of cashew-nut growers in Tanzania, tobacco farmers in Zambia and coffee producers in Angola. Yet the parastatal KTDA has been successful, due to it efficient management and its operation on strict commercial principles.

In some countries, therefore, greater emphasis is being given to marketing, and perspectives are changing elsewhere. Nevertheless, generally speaking, marketing is still not held in high esteem by government officials, and just as there are few indigenous marketers using marketing in an active way, so too there are few governmental marketers. Many states have state-run 'marketing organisations' which are simply window-dressing. The record of such bodies is poor. Certainly the lack of experienced marketers in developing countries is a handicap, but until marketing is seen in a more favourable light this situation is likely to remain.

Conclusion

This chapter began by reviewing the terminology involved in describing developing countries and economic development. Whilst it was decided that terms such as 'underdeveloped', 'less developed', 'developing', 'industrialising', 'Third World' and 'the South', may be used synonymously, depending upon how polite one wants to be, nevertheless there are identifiable basic characteristics in developing countries, taken as a whole, and a classification based on size (in terms of population) and wealth (in terms of natural resources) is possible.

All developing countries seek economic development, which is today generally considered as a socio-economic transformation, and the view put forward here is that marketing, because it deals with people and the allocation of resources, can be extremely valuable in the process. Whilst it has in many cases lagged behind economic development, it can be used to lead that development. What is not in doubt is the strong interrelationship between marketing and economic development and marketing's changing emphasis as economic development progresses.

There will always be restrictions in the use of marketing in developing countries and there will always be moral questions as to how, and whether in some cases, marketing should be used. The indigenous marketer and governmental marketer have not used marketing to the same extent or with such sophistication as the multinational marketer. They may well therefore have the most to gain. Nevertheless, because of the conditions which exist in developing countries, although marketing objectives and functions remain the same, the way in which marketing is used may have to be different. The next chapter considers this problem in its examination of the marketing environment.

CHAPTER 2

The marketing environment in developing countries

Contents

Introduction

Whoever uses marketing, at whatever level and wherever in the world, the marketing environment in which he is operating must be understood. There is an intimate relationship between the organisation (whether public, private, commerical or non-commercial) and its ever-changing environment. To be successful the marketer must understand the basic issues, especially the external uncontrollable ones, anticipate development and respond to them.

The interrelationships are many and complex, but may be summarised as shown in Figure 2.1. The organisation exists to supply needs and wants (*demand*), but in order to provide goods and services (*supply*) to satisfy these, it relies on the environment for inputs (arrow 1), such as land, raw materials, labour and capital. The organisation, in deciding what goods and services to produce and how to price, promote and distribute them, is severely affected by its environment, which offers opportunities and threats/constraints (arrow 2). Finally the organisation affects the marketing environment, both positively, for example by increasing disposable income, and negatively, for instance by destroying the landscape, which may in turn lead to greater governmental control (arrow 3).

All this may be summed up by using an ecosystem analogy. The environment of the organisation may be ragarded as its habitat, the various institutions and forces supporting the organisation constituting its ecosystem. If these institutions and forces remain in balance an ecosystem will persist without major change. Where they do not, change is inevitable.

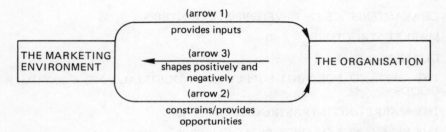

Figure 2.1   The interrelationships between the organisation and its marketing environment

Within this broad schema, it is possible to subdivide the marketing environment into distinct levels. Immediately surrounding the organisation is the task environment where the essential components of suppliers, intermediaries and the market interact. The next level is the competitive environment, which in turn is surrounded by the public environment (a public being any group that has an actual or potential interest and effect on an organisation's ability to achieve its objective). The broadest level is the macro-environment which consists of such uncontrollable elements as demography, economics, natural resources, technology, law and politics and culture (Figure 2.2).

All levels are present in developing countries, as they are in the advanced world. However the emphasis is likely to be very different. In the task environment, instead of the typical excess supply of goods and services of advanced countries, which initially led to the acceptance of the marketing concept, chronic under-supply and a different type of demand are characteristic of the market structure in many developing countries. Equally the competitive environment is likely to be more monopolistic or oligopolistic in many sectors of activity. The public environment is less pronounced in terms of pressure groups but there is likely to be a larger

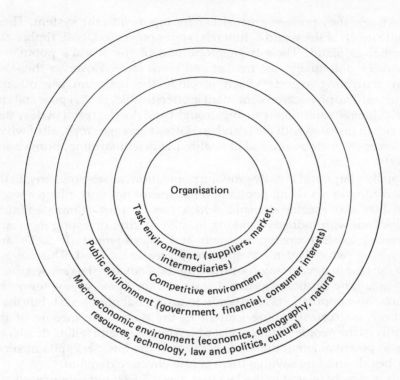

Concentric circles from centre outward:
Organisation
Task environment, (suppliers, market, intermediaries)
Competitive environment
Public environment (government, financial, consumer interests)
Macro-economic environment (economics, demography, natural resources, technology, law and politics, culture)

Figure 2.2   Components of the marketing environment

Source: Adapted from Kotler, 1980

governmental influence. However, it is the macro-economic environment which is the most influential and generally the most problematic in
developing countries. Furthermore change here is the most rapid.

These elements are discussed below in greater detail. The characteristics of developing countries which affect all components are briefly
examined, after which attention is focussed on the market structure, the
infrastructure and the impact of historical and cultural factors. Comparisons with Chapters 2 and 3 of *Marketing: An Introductory Text* (Baker, 1985)
are made wherever relevant.

Characteristics of developing countries

Taken as a whole, developing countries have certain general characteristics which have a profound effect on the marketing environment.

Collectively they possess great riches for inputs into the system. These include much of the world's minerals, water power, oil, coal, timber and potential cropland. Their large proportion of the world's population provides a potentially vast market and work-force. However there are many mitigating aspects which preclude the optimum use of such resources. The physical environment is often hostile, so that poor soil and erratic climatic conditions causing drought and floods, result in devastating human diseases with pests and predators to ravage crops, all of which reinforces the vicious circle of ill-health, inefficient farming, hunger and poverty.

Equally a large and rapidly growing population causes problems. In the United Kingdom a rising population has meant not only a larger work-force but also greater demand which has in turn stimulated mass production, with industry working to full capacity, investing more and increasing expenditure on research and development (R & D) and advertising, which again has stimulated greater demand. This has not been the case in developing countries. Medical advance has caused death rates to fall, by eradicating such diseases as smallpox, yellow fever and malaria, and populations to explode to unprecedented levels, but there has been no corresponding growth in the disposable income of the majority of the people. Thus, whilst a high birth rate and falling death rate suggest potential latent demand, because of the low per capita income, poor health and low savings there is low effective demand.

This is closely related to the fact that many developing countries have warped, highly vulnerable economies. Whereas in developed countries less than 30 per cent of the work-force are employed in agriculture, and in the United Kingdom less than 2 per cent, the primary sector having decreased significantly through time (Baker, 1985), the percentage employed in agriculture is 70–90 per cent in many developing countries. Most agriculture is for the production of subsistence crops, but within this sea of stagnating peasant economies are small islands of market-orientated production of export crops. Such exports may account for a high percentage of total exports, two-thirds of Ghana's exports being cocoa, for example and nine-tenths of Gambia's being groundnuts. But such exports are highly vulnerable to international fluctuations in price which, overall, tend downwards as market demand changes and new substitutes are found. They offer poor prospects for the long term.

This grossly inflated agricultural sector, polarised between inefficient subsistence crop production and export crops for insecure world markets, means that many of the shifts in demand, supply and market interaction which occurred in the developed countries are not happening in developing countries. For example, as agriculture became less important and manufacturing and services more so, the United Kingdom experienced greater social equality, increased disposable income and a shift to the non-essential purchases of life. But in developing countries population may be growing faster than the cultivable land, and the growing number of jobless flock to the towns faster than they can be absorbed. The socio-economic shifts typical of economic development in the advanced world remain absent, and purchasing power remains generally very low.

Other characteristics of developing countries serve as further constraints affecting all levels of the organisations's environment. Markets tend to be highly fragmented, not only between the rich minority in urban areas demanding imported luxuries and a wide range of goods and the poor elsewhere, but also between different cultural groups. For example, Nigeria has over 200 tribes. Also affecting the organisation and its task environment is the poorly developed infrastructure typical of many developing countries. Generally managerial skills are severely underdeveloped and there may be a 'brain drain' reducing those that do exist. The numerous traders usually have good financial and commercial acumen, but are likely to be poor at organising and managing productive units. Equally, operative skills are often in short supply and culture may result in more restraints. Inadequate documentary detail due to illiteracy, absence of a tradition of integrity, lack of research and advertising agencies, inadequate intermediaries and facilitating agents, poor general distribution and financial frameworks can all be further restrictive aspects.

Because monopoly or oligopoly are often the order of the day, promoted by import restrictions and scattered markets, the competitive environment of many organisations may be very different from that experienced in developed countries. Consumers are likely to suffer. Lack of quality control in manufacturing, poor storage facilities, cheating by sellers, adulterated packaged goods and approximate measures are all characteristics of consumer markets.

However consumer pressure groups are not a typical feature of the public environment in developing countries. Instead, government tends to dominate this level of the organisation's environment. Unfortunately, many developing countries are badly administered having little administrative tradition and/or rapid changes of government. Tribal, family loyalties and other cultural factors may further handicap effective administration whilst high military expenditures (often over 10 per cent of GNP and 20 per cent of the amount received in aid) indicate the order of priorities. But because many developing countries are state dominated, whether because of ideology or balance of payments problems or as a consequence of the poor managerial and commercial infrastructure, government has a profound effect on the marketing environment. It may play a regulatory role, such as in controlling prices. Alternatively, it may improve the marketing infrastructure, for example by subsidising the bureaucracy involved in distribution or even developing infrastructure

needed for industrial development (as in many southeast Asian economies) and offering support in times of recession. The governments of
Hong Kong and Taiwan spend eight times as much on projects such as
roads, harbours and airports as they do on social services. Government
may also direct entrepreneurial participation in marketing by formulating
parastatals like Corabastos (Colombia), Cobal (Brazil), Emprovit
(Ecuador) and the National Milling Corporation (Tanzania) with the aim
of supplying consumers with basic necessities at reasonable prices.
Whether acting directly, for example policing controlled prices, owning
retailing outlets and slaughter-houses, or indirectly, via legislation,
licensing of dealers, or providing advice and research services, the
influence of government cannot be ignored.

This influence is all the more significant because, along with the other
uncontrollable elements in the external environment of the organisation,
there is more dynamism and instability than that witnessed in the
developed world. Like demography, socio-economic conditions, technology and political and legal aspects are changing rapidly. Better
education means greater awareness, and more government restrictions.
Competitive forces too are increasing and some markets are becoming
more of a buyers' rather than a sellers' market. The swiftly growing urban
areas and the destruction of the balance between town and countryside
emphasise this fast-changing nature of developing countries.

However, as mentioned before, it would be wrong to regard all
developing countries as the same. There is little homogeneity either
within or between them and whilst there are general characteristics and
trends common to all, there is also a wide range of conditions experienced
by different countries. For those with the lowest levels of socio-economic
development, market potential is likely to be limited. In response,
retailing such as it is exists here is likely to be characterised by one outlet
under close and continuous supervision serving a whole community with
basic necessities. At the other extreme the newly industrialised countries
which have broken out of the trap of underdevelopment offer a much
more favourable marketing environment. Here a technological base is
established and living standards are rising. Demand is for a much wider
range of goods and the type of outlets serving it are equally varied. But
even among these countries the marketing environment will differ.

Large, rich newly industrialised countries are characterised by relatively high labour costs, industry serving primarily the domestic market,
protected by tariff barriers, a risk of indigenisation for the multinational
marketer and physical infrastructure (roads, telephones, telex, and so on)
generally under great strain. The large, poor newly industrialised
countries have a less attractive base-load domestic market and are
generally further hampered by political instability.

The small, poor newly industrialised countries, however, offer some of the most favourable marketing environments in the developing world. With more stable government, inward investment policies and constantly improving technology, they have proved particularly attractive to the multinational, especially in the field of electronics and the other 'run-away' industries. It has been claimed that many other nations benefit from 'East Asian synergy', resulting from a sense of history and the assumption that their culture is the centre of the world. This commitment to a larger culture allows motivation, a sense of direction, willingness to sacrifice the individual for the sake of the group, stable politics and a clear direction for their economies (Hofheinz and Calder, 1982).

This may be so. What is certain is that population has been kept under control. Taiwan, Singapore and South Korea have halved their net reproduction rate since the 1950s. Equally inflation, often a natural enemy to real growth, eroding the currency, undermining confidence and competitiveness and so on on world markets and encouraging the flight of capital, has also been kept in check. Massive unemployment and underemployment have therefore been avoided whilst the brain drain, typical of many developing countries, has been reversed. Southeast Asian newly industrialising countries have held on to their technologists, even when these were trained in the West, by offering strong financial and psychological incentives. Furthermore, education tends to be science-based, with science and mathematics stressed at university. Aggressive marketing is encouraged and effectively used, as shown by the success of Hyundai's Pony car in Africa and Latin America. Governments actively promote a more favourable marketing environ-ment by ensuring that the infrastructure is adequate. Even when inputs are lacking, steps are taken to ensure that this is no handicap and the gap is made good. For example, Southeast Asia lacks energy resources, but these nations are now committed to atomic power and are helped at present by finding themselves in a buyers' market.

Because many 'small, poor' Southeast Asian newly industrialising countries have used inward investment and export-led policies for economic development, the marketing environment for the multinational marketer is extremely favourable. Elsewhere it may be characterised by political uncertainties, acute shortages of qualified, competent, local nationals, host government restrictions on imports and exports, adminis-trative inefficiencies, red tape and bureaucracy, the non-availability of local finance for expansion and the difficulties of obtaining adequate raw materials from abroad in accordance with production schedules. In addition to government controls, there may be the threat of nationalis-ation, little patent or trade-mark protection, problems in remitting profits, exchange controls, wage rate and other legislation as well as many cultural handicaps. Thus the multinational marketer must assess factors over and above the general difficulties likely to affect the

indigenous or governmental marketer in developing countries. At the
same time it is the multinational which is the organisation most likely to
have influenced the marketing environment of many developing countries. The multinational has been most effective in shaping attitudes,
changing values, introducing technology and providing marketing infrastructure. Before the 1950s the early international enterprises did much
to shape the marketing environment in many developing countries. More
recently their impact has been even more significant, and on a much
wider basis spatially.

Market structure

As already noted, the demand and supply conditions in developing
countries, as a whole, are very different from those experienced in the
advanced world. And because there is not the same excess in the supply
of goods and services over demand (which led to the evolution and
acceptance of the marketing concept) or any corresponding socio-
economic shifts such as fewer people employed in agriculture, higher
disposable incomes and greater social equality, the resulting market
structure is very different. Potentially high latent demand resulting from
a growing population is reduced to low effective demand by low per
capita income, poor health, low savings and cultural lifestyles. Demand
may be further reduced by poor credit, high interest rates, inefficiency of
small agricultural holdings, poor distribution and storage resulting in
higher costs and purchasing in smaller units, and high spending by the
state on the military. Generally, therefore, there is a market for basic
necessities to satisfy the physical and safety needs of Maslow's hierarchy
(which is discussed on page 67 of Baker's *Marketing: An Introductory Text*).

Because markets in developing countries tend to be fragmented,
reflecting a scattered, relatively immobile population buying on a small
scale, the nature of goods produced, the size of production units and the
degree of specialisation are affected. Whereas in advanced economies
through time there has been increasing industrial concentration, larger
production units, increasing diversification associated with better communications and a transfer of control from owner–entrepreneur to
professional managers, the structure of the market in many developing
countries dictates otherwise for the indigenous entrepreneur. Low levels
of consumer expenditure together with illiteracy, poor technology and
low productivity provide little incentive to develop large-scale diversified
operations, while achievement motivation by management is also likely

to be lower. As well as affecting the size and organisation of firms and managerial attitudes, limited market opportunities tend to result in local but long distribution channels.

However these general observations will be tempered by government ideology, the presence of multinational operations, the level of economic development and the culture within the country being examined. For example, a relatively centrally-planned economy may result in fixed prices, government-controlled production of goods and little competition. Elsewhere, in sectors of activity where multinational corporations operate, competition may be more monopolistic and barriers to entry are likely to be high. The market structure of some of the most successful economically-advanced newly industrialising countries is fast approaching that of the United Kingdom or the United States while the least developed countries continue to stagnate.

Dualism

Whatever the stages of development, however, developing countries tend to have two distinct market structures. These are the rich urban market and the poor rural market, whose coexistence is often described as 'dualism'. The term was first used by Boeke, a Dutch economist, in 1953 to describe the modern Dutch enclave economy persisting alongside the traditional agricultural system in Indonesia. 'Dualism' used in this context was particularly strong in parts of Asia where Eastern colonies became part of the hinterland of Western capitalism. There was little incentive to develop competing industry outside the modern enclosure because the self-sufficiency of Asian subsistence economies obstructed the flow of goods to rural markets while the barter system of paying wages simply reinforced the structure.

However, the usage of the term 'dualism' has been extended, so that while the dualism promoted by colonialism still exists, dualism is now more often used to describe the (often closely related) distinction between the small rich urban market of property-owners, government officials, tradesmen, shopkeepers and other affluent individuals and the masses of rural poor. The former market, whilst consisting of a minority, nevertheless represents on average five to ten per cent of total national income and provides a high demand for modern high quality goods and luxuries, processed foods, labour saving devices and so on. The large rural market provides demand for lower quality, more essential goods.

This dualism in market structure is reflected in all aspects of the marketing function. For example, one of the first African hypermarkets was at Libreville. Covering 11 000 m^2 and employing 200, this urban store caters for one market demanding a wide variety of goods. The itinerant Gabon trader, buying 1000 fr worth of goods on credit and selling them over the next two months in tiny bazaars for 1200 fr–1300 fr, caters for the rural masses.

Dualism also exists on other levels. Even within the urban centres different market structures exist between the modern affluent sector and the inhabitants of the slums and shanty towns.

The demand for and supply of industrial and consumer goods

The relative importance of the demand for and supply of industrial and consumer goods will be dictated largely by such factors as type of developing country (according to size and wealth), its policy for industrialisation, its standard of living and the relative cultural influences.

All developing countries have a demand for industrial goods. To what extent they choose to rely on foreign investment to provide these will be determined by their industrialisation policy which in turn will be strongly influenced by their size and wealth status. A small, rich country such as Saudi Arabia will have to develop its own industry since multinationals are deterred by high labour costs and a small domestic market. Although such countries represent lucrative export markets for consumer goods, any goods they might produce here would be uncompetitive on world markets, while the small domestic market would not be sufficient to warrant a production plant. Furthermore, the cultural differences would pose an additional deterrent. A large, potentially rich country such as Nigeria is also more likely to rely on developing its own heavy industrial base, but through choice rather than necessity. It will tend to insist on the minimum amount of foreign ownership and control deemed necessary. Its demand from overseas suppliers will therefore be mainly for equipment and supplies while (especially in the present financial situation) consumer goods will be subject to import restrictions. These goods will be produced locally, although a developing country in this category having a Marxist orientation may actively suppress the demand for consumer goods.

On the other hand a small, poor (in natural resources) country such as Singapore is more likely to rely on foreign investment and adopt an export-orientated policy. It will therefore have a lower demand for industrial goods for the purpose of establishing a national diversified industrial base, and the emphasis of both supply and demand will tend to be on consumner rather than industrial goods. In addition consumers in these countries are more likely to benefit from a wider selection of lower priced but higher quality goods.

Whatever the nature of the country or its industrialisation policy, the structure of indigenous demand for consumer goods will, naturally, be related to the standard of living. Where standards are high, especially in the cities, the demand for consumer goods too will be high. But even within the affluent areas of developing countries, the market structure may still vary enormously, affected by cultural values. The Middle East provides an interesting example. Here there is a very high demand for consumer goods. For example, Kuwait provides the biggest market in the world for Philips' video-cassette recorders. This reflects the indigenous culture's emphasis on entertainment at home. Demand is further boosted by Western short-term workers buying such goods and then leaving them behind, and by poorer Arab or Indian immigrant labourers buying them to take home. The motive for buying consumer goods in the Middle East, however, may sometimes be indistinct. A product is often purchased because it is new and has Western technology, while brand loyalty is strong, reflecting the Arab's desire to personalise products. But notwithstanding these characteristics, a product may fail if it does not fit in with the local culture. Automatic dishwashers – which incorporate newness, Western technology and brand names – initially were not very successful because firstly they were not suited to traditional Arab crockery, and secondly they were seen as unimportant where hired help was available.

Conversely, in countries where standards of living are very much lower, it has been found that demand is not always a function of price as the economists would suggest. Often a disproportionate amount of income is spent on goods which have prestige or have been effectively advertised (Harper, 1975).

The marketing infrastructure

In most developing countries the marketing infrastructure is underdeveloped. Commercial media, banking and other financial facilities, research agencies, postal and other communications and physical distribution are generally under-represented, creating additional constraints on the organisation. Furthermore, because education may be lacking or may stress history, law, economics or other non-business disciplines, the supply of managers and entrepreneurs who might otherwise develop and improve facilities is less than optimal. Finally, governments adopt differing stances on their role in developing the infrastructure.

Both communications and physical distribution in developing countries tend to be poor, leading to waste and impeding development generally. The transportation facilities can often determine the extent of the market area. Even where demand exists it may not be supplied since there is no incentive to a producer to expand production if there is no decent transport to transfer his merchandise to the potential market. Where agricultural products are involved storage facilities are often limited whilst lack of capital prevents much needed refrigeration in many parts.

Marketing channels are consequently long, complex, highly fragmented and labour-intensive, with products passing through multiple channel intermediaries. Because only small amounts of capital are required to enter retailing, many do, adding to the proliferation of channel members. Financial constraints cause retailers to buy in small quantities from wholesalers (often referred to as hand-to-mouth trading). Because of the sellers' market which usually exists, the wholesalers' initiative in purchasing supplies comes from the retailer. Together with the fact that there are many small producers and manufacturers with small-quantity production schedules and no uniform quality standards, all requiring more middlemen, it is not surprising that there is overall inefficiency in the system.

Again some dualism can be witnessed, especially in relation to retailing. Only in the rich urban areas is there any degree of specialisation of retail outlets catering for the middle and upper classes. Elsewhere all retailing may be through one general store, or in the form of small traders and rotating markets catering for little more than a subsistence economy. The modern commercial sector is likely to have supermarkets. Many belong to multinational corporations, as seen, for example, in Sears Roebuck's developments in Mexico, Brazil, Cuba, Venezuela, Colombia and Peru. Such outlets offer a wide selection of goods and include many of the characteristics typical of Western developed countries. They are well stocked and include attractive displays and standardised packaged foodstuffs. Goods are sold for cash at fixed prices and whilst profit margins are low, high sales volumes are achieved. Advertising and modern expansionist policies are employed. The small trader, on the other hand, offers poor choice, chaotic presentation, minute quantities and poorer quality goods. He relies on bargaining or haggling and works on higher profit margins as well as relying on word of mouth advertising.

In Latin America where modern supermarkets have been established, competing retailers have reacted and improved their services. Consequently such developments have had a beneficial impact on the infrastructure generally. In some countries the multinationals have been largely responsible for whole distribution systems as, for example, United Africa Company (UAC) has been in West Africa. However such developments do not reduce petty trading. Indeed, because an expatriate minority has established a system in a country, this may lend weight to the perception of distribution as a parasitic function. Distribution therefore remains neglected and continues to constrain the organisation. To counteract this, many governments have taken initiatives, setting up organisational structures to improve food distribution and reduce market prices. More attention is being paid to improving the physical infrastructure by providing warehouses, railway sidings, parking areas, packing plants and road and canal facilities, training retailers and standardising weights and measures. Other governments, as in Southeast Asian newly industrialising countries, have gone much further, taking it upon themselves to be responsible for providing infrastructure to the extent of creating industrial zones and installations suitable for incoming manufacturing plants.

The lack of other types of communications, however, is harder to resolve. Given that there is a difference in availability and quality of communications both between and within developing countries, media availability is likely to be poor, sporadic in nature and reaching only a relatively small audience. There are few advertising agencies in developing countries and the problem is often exacerbated by the lack of one common language in the nation as well as high illiteracy levels, throwing more emphasis onto packaging and labelling. Thus barriers to communications are likely to be a function of distance and culture.

At the same time the inadequacies in the communications infrastructure must be closely examined, for it may be that, despite less than maximum coverage, greater impact than anticipated is achieved. For example, readership levels may be low but the coverage greater than expected because of the literate reading to the illiterate. Similarly, despite few people owning televisions in some countries, many people may crowd round each one. Finally, simply because the communication infrastructure is underdeveloped and little used, the marketer, through advertising, can create an almost unassailable position of strength in the market place: a position which would be unobtainable in a more sophisticated marketing environment. The impact of any communication may, consequently, be greater and last longer.

Again it is often the multinational marketer who is able to develop and use advertising and the other elements of the marketing infrastructure the most. If the marketing infrastructure is left to develop spontaneously it is unlikely to do so, since the financial resources are lacking. Low productivity means little surplus for investment and any agricultural surplus which does occur may be nullified by fewer deaths and a consequent increase in population. The structure of society may also have a bearing: if there is any surplus finance, it may be siphoned off into imported luxury goods, or wasted. The financial infrastructure therefore is not improved.

Elsewhere, however, the situation may be very different. In some developing countries (notably the most successful), capital is put to work. This is typical of many Southeast Asian newly industrialising countries. Indigenous economies here always had lively commercial trading (in tea, vegetable oils, wood, and so on) and an informal credit structure with banks and pawn shops. On top of this have been added modern commercial long-term credit and trust banks. The government has further sponsored development banks whilst organisations such as the World Bank have also been put to good use.

In this part of the world governments have been most active in promoting the most favourable marketing infrastructure. Although banks and financial institutions are not regulated, cost, market share and profitability parameters for businessmen are made more certain by the government's overseeing the allocation of resources. The government may also direct investment to strategic sectors. For example, Singapore at present has a controversial ten-year plan for the 1980s which sees Singapore as becoming the regional capital for 'brain industries' such as computer programming, consultancy, financial services and medicine. Often plans are supplemented by forecasts for specific sectors indicating to industrialists which sectors the government is willing to support.

The way in which governments can reallocate resources is well demonstrated by Singapore's Central Provident Fund (CPF). This is a compulsory saving scheme whose objective is to ensure that workers are provided for in old age or disablement. Unlike other systems, such as the United Kingdom's, which redistribute money to the unemployed or to the poor, the CPF ensures that the worker gets back what he and his employer put into the fund, with interest. At the same time, and more important in this context, the government can use this fund for demand management – by manipulating the percentage of money withheld, and thereby influencing the savings rate of the economy. Thus the CPF can reduce pressure on prices and provide the government with a (non-inflationary) source of funds for development. And whilst Singapore's wages rose 20 per cent in 1979, consumer price inflation fell from 4.8 to 4.3 per cent.

Governments also have the facility of making the multinational marketing environment more favourable for commercial organisations. This can be done by the government taking the risks in developing key industries before they are transferred to private hands, and by adopting protectionist measures in the early stages of development, inflating domestic prices and offering tax incentives and advice through bodies like the Korean Organisation for Trade Advancement.

However such initiatives are at present the exception rather than the rule. Elsewhere the marketing infrastructure is more likely to be a handicap both to the organisation and to economic development as a whole. This can be witnessed at all stages. Initially market research bodies and researchers are few. The result is that there is no response to demand where it exists, since this cannot be identified. Physical waste, resulting for example from growing the wrong crop, is the consequence. Next, even where demand is realised, the inadequate physical infrastructure causes further waste and inefficiency. Finally other aspects of the marketing infrastructure: communications, financial frameworks and so on, prevent the stimulation of demand and the essential improvement in response to this is again stifled.

The relevance of historical factors

Many developing countries claim that they have warped economies and difficult marketing environments because of their legacies of international trade and colonisation. All the problems associated with 'dualism' began here, they suggest.

Traditionally raw materials from developing countries were exchanged for manufactured goods so that it became the norm for industrialised powers to have numerous colonies. For example, Britain had colonies ranging from North America to Africa south of the Sahara, India, parts of China, India, Australia, New Zealand and South America. Colonialism introduced some form of administration and a money economy but in terms of the present day marketing environment, its impact on the infrastructure is perhaps most noteworthy. Harbours, railways and roads were built for exporting raw materials. Cities such as Bombay, Madras, Colombo, Singapore and Hong Kong developed, epitomising the 'enclave-system'. There was no corresponding investment in the local economy, for land and trade were the major ways of becoming rich. Any agricultural surplus which remained after the foreign companies had exported their requirements was therefore invested in urban estate, rural land, trade and money-lending.

Thus two separate commercial systems developed: the export-import system, and the local supply system of share-cropping and periodic markets. The traditional marketing system which had previously existed, and which had involved more balanced agricultural and industrial development, was destroyed. In India, for example, before colonialism, there were two types of industry – in the cities catering for the nobility and producing luxury goods such as embroidery, jewellery and carpets, and in the rural areas catering for the masses and producing such items as pottery and household implements. But once imports started, many traditional village crafts decayed. Entrepreneurial development as a whole was reduced. Both the redundant craftsmen and better public health led to population growth, and, consequently, increased pressure on the land. Thus the imbalance was initiated and was fuelled by a new social structure emerging. Initially supporting the Europeans, the merchant class took over the distribution of foreign goods, the collection of exports and money-lending activities as the need for money grew. Landowning and the profit motive became all important.

After independence, in many countries, this dualistic social structure was enforced. For example, in Zambia, Africans moved into the positions vacated by the Europeans, inheriting their salaries, houses, cars and servants. In this way a colonial system may survive political independence and continue with a momentum of its own, having individual flags, anthems, laws, administration, schools, curricula and so on.

The dualism between the impoverished hinterlands and the affluent (often coastal) areas remain, with different demand characteristics and marketing environments. Many countries are still caught in a web of economic relationships which make them vulnerable and subordinate. To a lesser or greater extent the marketing environment is characterised by much multinational activity, foreign skilled manpower, neglect of rural development and the importation of basic products.

However, from the point of view of the multinational marketer, such historical factors may result in greater political uncertainty in the marketing environment. Government may be more hostile, as a result of the past, towards multinational activity, and insist on indigenisation or a certain percentage local participation in the multinational's operation. In extreme cases they may nationalise foreign investment. For the indigenous marketer, too, historical factors have frequently complicated the marketing environment. In addition to impeding the development of a more uniform national market, the marketing infrastructure is likely to be adversely affected. In many countries middlemen minorities or foreign trading corporations dominate the retail/wholesale trade and other services. Such groups may be resented by the indigenous population since they are enriching themselves at their expense. Thus the immigrants' efforts in taking risks in building up trading enterprises go unnoticed whilst aspiring nationals wishing to enter such small businesses may be put off by their 'foreignness'.

Colonialism therefore brought some advantages, for example the introduction of a money economy, administrative and legal systems, new technology and more 'modern' values, but at the same time has resulted in many problems in today's marketing environment in many developing countries. As well as furthering their dependence on the advanced world, it has led to imbalance in economies. This exists not only in relation to the idealistic demand structure, but also in the two-tier infrastructural developments.

Again it would be unfair to dismiss as negative the impact of all historical factors on the marketing environment. Firstly, it may be argued that many developing countries' marketing environments, albeit warped, would have been even less favourable had there been no outside interference. Secondly, history may have a very positive impact. A common sense of history and the belief that East Asian nations are a modern extension of empires which claim universal loyalty have been seen to be an underlying driving force in East Asian synergy today (Hofheinz and Calder, 1982). East Asians assume that their own culture (deriving directly or indirectly from ancient China) deserves to be the centre of the world. This commitment to the survival of a larger culture permits a motivation, a sense of direction and an ability to meet external threats. It also may explain the willingness to sacrifice individual interests to those of the group. Thus this sense of historical destiny may help account for the success of many newly industrialising countries in this part of the world.

The relevance of cultural factors

Culture is perhaps one of the most fundamental and far-reaching influences on the marketing environment. It affects all areas of an organisation's operations, both internally and externally. Within the organisation culture shapes work practices, marketing objectives, strategies and tactics. Externally its effect on the market and demand, distribution channels, competition, governmental, financial, consumer and other pressures is profound. And because many developing countries have more than one culture within their national boundaries, the relevance of cultural factors is even greater.

An early definition of culture was 'that complex whole which includes knowledge, belief, art, morals, law, customs and any other capabilities and habits acquired by man as a member of society' (Tyylor, 1871). Culture is basically a body of economic, political and ethical beliefs which have historically evolved in a society. It is a distinctive way of life involving language, religion, architecture, music, preferences and taboos, and is expressed by the way people communicate, perceive and exploit resources and organise their region. It provides a framework for society and is learned rather than inherited.

Culture may be subdivided into the economic system (the way in which people exploit their environment), the social system (how people live and

relate to each other), the political system (how people organise themselves into units and choose leaders), and the belief system (comprised of
knowledge which people have of the world about them), (Beals, 1967). It
may also be broken down into constituent parts such as language, values
and attitudes, education, religion, law, politics, social organisation and
technical material culture (Terpstra, 1978). Religion may be regarded as
the mainspring of culture, providing an ordering principle in life, and the
major influence on attitudes. It organises the individual's experience in
terms of ultimate meanings, provides a rationale and coerces individuals
externally and internally into observance of society's norms. The social
organisation of a culture is perhaps the next most significant influence,
dictating such aspects as the obligation to kinsfolk, and the means of
gaining prestige through socially-approved symbols.

(a) Culture's effect on demand

Demand is clearly affected by culture. All people have basic needs, but
their drive to satisfy these is influenced by compulsions, checks and
guidance systems which are a function of their culture. People's behaviour as buyers, therefore, cannot be artificially separated from such
socio-psychological influences as family systems, the willingness and
ability to accept new and perhaps more technologically-complex products, attitudes as to what constitutes 'the good life' and so on. Such
factors will temper, mould and dictate the manner in which people
consume, the priority of their needs, the wants they attempt to satisfy and
the way in which they satisfy them.

(b) Culture's effect on the organisation's task environment

MARKETING STRATEGY AND TACTICS

As well as influencing what is needed, culture will also influence *how* it is
bought, *who* buys and who decides to buy. An organisation's *marketing
strategy and tactics* must be adopted accordingly. For example, advertising
must be directed at the men where women are regarded as junior rather
than equal partners in a marriage and where the man not only makes the
decision but also buys the product. Where personal interaction and

bargaining is regarded as normal in a buying situation personal selling should receive greater emphasis in the marketing mix. Where education is well below standard, greater stress must be placed on packaging and visual advertising. Because culture varies spatially both between and within national boundaries, further alterations are likely. If many languages are spoken, some translation (and therefore extra expense) becomes necessary. Different quantities or methods of distribution may be required.

Thus the greater the complexity of culture in an organisation's marketing environment, the more likely the costly consequences for the organisation and the greater the need for the correct use of marketing skills. However good, qualified people are often lacking, again due to culture's negative impact on the organisation's task environment. This is because in the first place, marketing/business may be regarded as being at the bottom of the professional scale, possibly more associated with the merchant–trader group, and may in turn be undertaken by non-nationals. The type and quality of education will affect the extent of vocational training. Other disciplines than business which permit entry into more prestigious but less useful professions may be stressed. The result is that not only is the calibre of personnel reduced, but, worse, marketing may be undervalued and not made full use of by the indigenous marketer. Social systems often reinforce such attitudes.

For example, in Latin America, until recently, it was not considered appropriate for any upper-class family to have a career in business with a large company. This meant that an organisation could not develop beyond a small-family sized one without having to recruit from less educated middle- or lower-class families. Elsewhere the distinction between blue- and white-collar workers may be so pronounced that the educated prefer to go for 'status' but dead-end clerical jobs, rather than work their way up to management by starting on the shop-floor. In Thailand men prefer to enter the Civil Service or legal profession and women are left to play the major role in all segments of business. Elsewhere the importance given to personal life rather than profit will result in individuals seeking lower-status jobs for fear of alienation from their social class.

PERSONNEL

Secondly, in addition to reducing the quality of human resources available, culture may further hamper management efficiency and prevent the best use of marketing techniques. For since all people are captives of their cultural heritage and cannot escape such influences as religious background or social and family ties, culture will dictate employers' and employees' attitudes and objectives. Managerial attitudes to innovation, new products, authority, achievement, wealth, materialism, risk-taking, change, inter-organisational co-operation, doing business with foreigners and the mode of doing business will all be influenced. In relation to lower-level employees, culture is likely to affect employment continuity, type of personal involvement with management, extent of identification with the company and so on.

Religion, by providing a rationale in life, is the obvious starting-point in any attempt to understand people's orientation towards work. Max Weber's Protestant ethic teaches that work is not only a means of getting ahead but is of positive moral value. Profit is accepted as the evidence of rational action by the all-important individual. However, many religions in developing countries incorporate vastly different rationales, Islam and Hinduism, for example, stressing the irrelevance of temporal life and promoting fatalistic attitudes. Because materialism and wealth are regarded as less important than spiritual satisfaction, attitudes to achievement will differ and innovation may be seen as less important than a respect for tradition. Furthermore, time may be envisaged as a circle – so that if it is lost today it will return tomorrow. This is in great contrast to the Western concept of mechanical time when the focus is the future and where schedules, split-second decisions and rigid deadlines are paramount. But because emphasis is more on leisure, contemplation and an unhurried way of going about things 'efficiency' as measured in Western societies may be impaired.

Social systems generally reinforce religious influences, whilst the extent of family ties, obligations to chiefs and elders and respect for clan tradition can help explain such aspects as authoritarian, paternalistic and nepotistic styles of management. Taken together social and religious systems give meaning to such aspects as (i) the acceptance of bribery, which may be so common as to be an institutionalised form of direct taxation, (ii) truth being a relative matter, (iii) weight being given to politeness rather than directness and decisions being delayed to avoid unpleasantness, (iv) the extent of mutual confidence and (v) significance being attached to enjoying the pleasures of the moment. Equally they will determine what is defined as security, goals and achievement and status-giving.

Finally education, besides determining the type and quality of human resources available and influencing such attitudes as risk-taking and willingness to accept charge, also plays an important part in perpetuating cultural attitudes. The child may be taught to base reciprocity and expectations for performance on who is involved rather than what is accomplished.

SPATIAL VARIATIONS OF CULTURAL INFLUENCES

As well as affecting the 'efficiency' and 'quality' of management within the organisation, the same cultural factors will have a bearing on the successful operation of the organisation in different cultural contexts. Obviously the tempo, formality, ethical standards, contact level and communication emphasis in doing business will be affected and will consequently vary spatially. For example, in Arab countries management is often reluctant to relinquish authority, with the result that business is carried out at a high level. In Central and South America, on the other hand, employees often seek to aggrandise their position by attempting to participate in decision-making, for which there is no justification. Personal involvement is just as diverse. In the Far East letters are sent out under a file number in contrast to the Middle East where the individual *per se* rather than the office is important.

In order to try and categorise spatial variations Hall (1960) identified different 'languages' in business practice. Attitudes to time, space, things, friendship and agreement are compared in different parts of the world. Time in Latin America is regarded casually. In Ethiopia the time taken to make a decision is directly proportional to its importance. In the Middle East time is less important than family and other close relationships. The distance between people when talking and the location and size of management offices will vary similarly. Some cultures are more materialistic than others, some more casual towards friendship, and whilst agreement is not binding until in the form of a written document in some parts, Moslem sensitivities elsewhere may be offended by the written word.

The ability to understand such factors affecting the task environment of the organisation operating in different cultures and to adapt marketing planning, organisation, control, staffing, procurement and production accordingly, will largely determine success or failure. And whilst the indigenous and governmental marketers must take cultural factors into account, it is the multinational marketer who is likely to be most affected.

Five dimensions in which culture may vary have been identified. These are cultural variability, cultural complexity, cultural hostility, cultural heterogeneity and cultural interdependence (Terpstra, 1978). *Cultural variability* – that is, the extent to which conditions within a culture are changing – determines the level of uncertainty for the multinational marketer. Where there is a low and gradual rate of change, prediction is easier than where the rate of change is high and unstable. *Cultural complexity* determines the extent of the learning problem faced by the multinational marketer. In low context cultures, behaviour is overt, information is transmitted in explicit messages, bonds between people are fragile and change is easy and rapid. As one progresses along the continuum to the higher context cultures, where information is internalised within people, where bonds are strong and there is a greater distinction between insiders and outsiders and where cultural patterns are slow to change, the learning problem for the multinational marketer is magnified. The extent of *cultural hostility* determines the threat to goal achievement and ability to survive. Severe hostility can prevent an organisation from acquiring inputs such as capital, personnel and information. Equally it may not be able to dispose of its goods and services easily. *Cultural heterogeneity* determines the extent to which decisions and operations can be centralised. Finally, *cultural interdependence* – that is, the degree to which conditions in one culture are sensitive to developments in other cultures – determines the multinational's vulnerability to intergroup conflict. Because of increasing cultural interdependence, the actions of the multinational in one culture are likely to be exposed to the scrutiny of governments and interest groups in other cultures.

As cultural environments become more variable, complex, hostile, heterogeneous and interdependent, the greater the likely problems for the multinational marketer.

(c) Culture's effect on the organisation's public environment

The government is often the most significant aspect of the organisation's public environment in developing countries. Culture's influence on attitudes to administration in general, and bribery in particular, is likely to be of special significance. Administrative ability is often poor, especially where culture dictates that personal connections are more important. In order that decisions are taken at all on the organisation's behalf, a 'tip', 'bribe' or 'facilitating payment' may be essential. Such a system generally erodes moral fibre and leads to cynicism, frustrating the growth of a spirit of idealism and enthusiasm often considered essential for expansion. In relation to the organisation, it is an extra cost to be borne and dictates that a certain amount of energy be spent on bribing officials where this could be put to more creative endeavours leading to greater efficiency.

Often the situation may be aggravated by the overblown status of the Civil Service, which results in indifference, arbitrary decisions or even arrogance towards the organisation. The total impact is likely to be restricting influence. Alternatively, cultural factors may result in a government working closely with industry, removing barriers, and promoting a more favourable public environment.

(d) Culture's effect on the macro-economic environment

Many aspects of the macro-economic environment have been dealt with elsewhere. However, in general, culture's impact on the macro-economic environment will set the scene for the organisation's operation. Culture will influence the rate of population growth. This in turn will influence demand levels, but whether this is actual or potential will depend on levels of disposable income, which in turn are likely to be influenced by attitudes to technology, savings and achievement. Where fatalistic attitudes prevail change, innovation, risk taking and productive use of capital are less likely. Where more progressive attitudes exist a more favourable marketing environment will result.

Thus in some parts of the world culture has imposed certain impediments to advance and this helps explain a more negative marketing environment. In other parts culture has helped to provide a more favourable marketing environment and has removed the blocks found elsewhere. Some of the southeast Asian newly industrialising countries again provide good examples of the more positive impact of culture – notably the Chinese culture.

Here education lays stress on technical competence. For example, in Taiwan even the top administrators tend to be engineers. Equally government and bureaucracy are held in high esteem, being regarded as high arts in comparison with law (seen as a prestigious profession in other countries). Lawyers in southeast Asia are fewer on the ground because tradition distrusts formal rules and regulations, disdains written contracts and emphasises ethical rather than legal forms of conduct. Society relies on tolerance, mutual adjustment and mediation to solve disputes and accomplish tasks. Thus there is less waste of time on niceties of law and more time spent on preserving human relationships. Many southeast Asians have a strong cultural pride in their nation and whilst they have copied Western technology, they believe it can be separated from Western politics and religious institutions. In many ways this has allowed them greater flexibility than other less selective cultures who have borrowed Western technology and also adopted Western institutions alongside.

Team work, group consciousness and loyalty, derived from social influences, permit a most favourable task environment for the organisation which does not have to confront divisive trade unions. Compromise rather than confrontation is inherent in the culture whilst the paternalism of management is expected.

Other favourable aspects stemming from culture include the attitude to savings. This has allowed capital to be used for growth. East Asia peoples have always had the highest savings ratios in the world. Psychologically this is because of a feeling of uncertainty which has promoted a continual striving for security. Therefore prudence, frugality and sacrifice for the future are bred in these people.

Culture in southeast Asia has provided values which reinforce respect for authority, promote education and reward diligence. These factors together with a more organically-organised society and a favourable political system have made for culture creating a marketing environment which is envied elsewhere.

Conclusion

This chapter has considered the interrelationship between the organisation and its ever-changing environment. The marketing environment provides inputs, opportunities and threats for the organisation. The organisation in turn shapes the marketing environment positively and negatively. The marketing environment can be subdivided into component parts, and the differences between developed and developing countries analysed.

Whilst developing countries collectively possess great riches of inputs into the system, their characteristics usually make for an unfavourable marketing environment. Rapid population growth, warped economies, a high percentage of the work-force employed in subsistence agriculture, fragmented markets, poor infrastructure and many cultural constraints do not provide the most favourable conditions. Greater government involvement allied with poor administration and perhaps nepotism, lack of management education, greater political instability and dynamism generally are other negative aspects, especially for the multinational marketer.

All the above conditions largely constrain the organisation. The supply and demand situation is very different from that encountered in the developed world. Together with fragmented markets and poor distribution systems there may be little incentive to produce efficiently for mass markets. Only in the urban centres will demand for consumer goods be high. Culture will affect all areas of an organisation both internally and externally since it influences the organisation's task, competitive, public and macro-economic environments.

As always it is difficult to generalise. Each developing country's marketing environment will differ. The country's size (in terms of population) and wealth (in terms of natural resources) will strongly influence the type of industrialisation policy followed. This in turn will influence the demand for, and supply, industrial and consumer goods.

The country's level of economic development and culture, together with quality of government and priority of spending, will be other significant factors in the determination of the favourability of the marketing environment.

Whatever the resultant marketing environment, all areas of marketing must respond accordingly. Since marketing focuses on the consumer as the beginning and end of the problem, the way in which the conditions existing in developing countries affect consumer behaviour provides the subject of the next chapter.

Consumer behaviour in developing countries

Contents

Introduction

This chapter considers the behaviour of the individual and ultimate
consumer (as does the chapter on Consumer Behaviour in Baker's
Marketing – An Introductory Text). The basic concepts and principles
concerning consumer behaviour remain valid. The consumer is still at the
head of the marketing process, and in order that marketing should be
carried out more effectively by an indigenous, state or multinational
marketer, it is equally essential to know who he is, what he is buying,
when, why and how he buys as well as who is involved in the buying
process.

However the developing country context may diverge enormously
from the developed world situation upon which the traditional writings
on consumer behaviour are based. And because of differences in such

aspects as (i) income levels and the nature of demand, (ii) the supply situation, (iii) cultural factors and (iv) less sophisticated use of marketing generally, there are also significant differences in consumer behaviour. Some areas become more important whilst others do not necessitate the same emphasis.

Chapter 3 begins by considering how the developing country context affects needs and the wants which result. The decision-making framework is then considered, after which attention focuses on the type of goods purchased. In most parts of the world today traditional necessities have been supplemented by goods imported from other parts and other cultures. The extent to which these are accepted, modified or rejected is analysed. Often advertising can have a big impact, promoting convergence in consumer tastes. Advertising's effect is therefore the theme of the next section, whilst the penultimate part of the chapter discusses the buying process, which is dominated by bargaining in large areas of many developing countries. Finally the implications for the indigenous multinational and governmental marketer are highlighted.

Again generalisation, although inevitable in a book of this nature, must be treated with caution. For despite the fourfold classification of large rich, large poor, small rich and small poor countries being to some extent useful, and therefore referred to, its relevance is reduced because of the numerous influences on consumer behaviour which vary enormously both between and even within countries. Thus, once individual developing countries are considered in isolation, some modifications of any broad picture drawn are necessary.

Basic needs and basic differences

All people throughout the world have certain needs – spiritual, physical, sexual and reproductive, needs of the ego, the intellect and the belly – and the wants which result will always be influenced by the same factors: psychology, learning, motivation, personality, attitudes and the rest. Maslow (1943) has suggested a theory of motivation based on needs. People's needs may be ranked in importance. According to Kotler (1984, p. 138), these are,
1. Physiological needs (the fundamentals of survival, including hunger and thirst),
2. Safety needs (concern over physical survival which might be overlooked to satisfy hunger and thirst).
3. Belongingness and love needs (striving to be accepted by intimate members of one's family or others to whom one feels close).

4. Esteem and status needs (striving to achieve a high standing relative to others).
5. Self-actualisation needs (a desire to develop a personal system of values leading to self-realisation).

Each person seeks to satisfy the most important need first; once satisfied, this will cease to be a motivator so that the next need higher in the hierarchy can receive attention. In many developing countries where low income prevails, notably the large poor countries, the less successful small countries and also the rural areas of large rich countries, the lower levels of Maslow's hierarchy of food, shelter and clothing may well assume greater importance, whilst non-Western culture, history and stage of economic development have significant ramifications of influence over the way in which needs are satisfied. Basic differences in consumer behaviour therefore result.

The conditions surrounding the basic needs are all important in determining how they are satisfied. On the supply side factors such as the scarcity of goods, less price competition, monopoly, tied distribution systems, low rates of product change and less differentiation of products will have a big impact. Because the majority of people in developing countries outside the most successful newly industrialised countries of Southeast Asia or the small or rich nations have lower disposable incomes than those in the advanced world, and because conditions of supply and demand are very different, it is assumed that biogenic needs are predominant and resultant wants are simpler. This may be the case in some instances, but not always.

For example, the need for transportation may be met by using one's feet, beasts of burden, bicycles, public transport, private cars, planes, and so on. In many developing countries where disposable incomes are low, distances involved short, the most sophisticated technology not available and existing infrastructure generally poor, the need for transportation may have to be satisfied by walking or using a beast of burden. But in other areas of consumer behaviour, where greater choice has been introduced, the situation may be very different. Harper (1975), discovered that all Kenyans, whatever their status and wealth, sought self-improvement and were often prepared to spend a disproportionate amount of money to achieve it. Although at the time he had discovered no homogeneous pattern of material aspirations developed by the Kenyan population – the small high-income minority having adopted colonial ways and the rest feeling their way towards a socially-acceptable pattern of expenditure – higher psychogenic needs were assuming a greater importance than one might expect.

An even more alarming picture has been painted by Walter (1974), who discovered that the poorer the economic outlook the more important the small luxury of a flavoured soft dring or perfumed soap. And to the dismay of the would-be benefactor, the poorer the malnourished are, the more likely they are to spend a disproportionate amount of whatever they have on some luxury, rather than on what they really need.

The influence of culture

Culture is one of the most significant aspects which may be used to explain differences in consumer behaviour. For whilst basic needs are the same the world over, the drives to satisfy them are affected by the compulsion, checks and guidance systems which originate in culture. The cultural overlay therefore forms the foundation for all motivational differences between groups.

It is not difficult to see how culture affects the influences on consumer behaviour discussed in Chapter 4 of Baker's *Marketing: An Introductory Text*. In relation to *perception*, the process by which the individual selects, organises and interprets information inputs to create a meaningful picture of the world, culture explains how products perceived in one way in one country or region may be perceived in a very different way elsewhere. *Beliefs and attitudes*, learned initially from family and then from groups to which one belongs or wishes to belong, similarly have cultural underpinnings. These will affect the way in which all levels of Maslow's hierarchy are satisfied. For example, love needs include the feeling of belonging to a group, but primary, secondary and aspirational *reference groups* are likely to differ from culture to culture. So too will the way in which one achieves recognition, status, prestige and reputation, affecting the way esteem needs are satisfied. *Opinion leaders* will vary in type and number, as will roles and stature attached to each one. And since personality, perception and motivation are socialised in cultural traits, norms and values, life-styles will vary enormously.

The way in which culture directly affects needs and wants may best be discussed with reference to the major aspects of culture. Religion, being the mainspring of culture, will affect the degree of materialism which exists. It will therefore help explain what goods will be bought in any one culture. Because many major religions in developing countries emphasise spiritual rather than materialistic gains, and tend to be fatalistic, they might, if taken to their logical conclusions promote negative attitudes to a wide range of goods and services, or at least a lesser emphasis on attaining higher levels of Maslow's hierarchy through conspicuous consumption. For example, Hinduism is a way of life in which intellect is subordinate to intuition, dogma to experience and outer expression to inner realisation. This, together with the caste system in India, promotes fatalism, resistance to change and spiritual ideals rather than wordly possessions. Similarly Islam encourages fatalism and even Catholicism stresses spiritual rather than material needs to a greater extent than does Protestantism.

In reality, rarely are religious ideals taken to their ultimate conclusion. Furthermore there has been much 'watering down' of traditional values through the introduction of new values and products from other cultures. Nevertheless religion still affects tradition, superstitions and taboos and may help explain otherwise inexplicable consumer attitudes which determine how needs are fulfilled. For example, typical religious taboos include alcohol and insurance in Moslem areas, beef in Hindu regions. Tradition and superstition may be exemplified by the Thai insistence that all the wood for a new building must come from the same forest and homes have an odd number of doors. The significance of colour may account for other basic differences, whilst belief in ghosts, spirit worship, fortune-telling, palmistry and phrenology may sometimes help explain strange consumer attitudes in parts of Asia. Finally the impact on consumption of religious festivals should always be noted.

Religion always serves as a rationale, legitimising social structures and coercing individuals externally and internally. Its impact on attitudes towards change, achievement, wealth and material goods is likely to be particularly significant in large areas of many developing countries, and must therefore be examined closely before the way in which consumer needs are fulfilled can be fully understood. Although it is always dangerous to generalise one can say that, where aspirations are low, it is likely that there will be less desire for products other than bare essentials and no thought for the higher levels of Maslow's hierarchy. Where change is resisted, consumer behaviour is likely to be significantly different from that in societies which attach more positive innovative value to the acquisition of goods.

Often change is resisted more where strict social stratification is present and where social mobility is impossible. Indeed social class and family influences on consumer behaviour are particularly significant in many developing countries. For, whereas social class in the United Kingdom or United States is dominated by the middle or lower-middle classes (Figure 3.1), class structures reveal a markedly different picture in developing countries.

Generally the middle class is small or completely absent, with a small elite and masses of poor people. In very low income, large poor countries like Afghanistan or Ethiopia, there is a very small, well-educated elite, a minute middle class and a vast mass of illiterate peasant farmers or nomads. The resulting structure has been likened to a knitting needle stuck in a pancake (Farmer, 1966) and is shown in Figure 3.2.

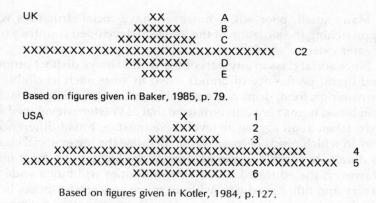

```
UK                        XX        A
                        XXXXXX      B
                      XXXXXXXXX     C
          XXXXXXXXXXXXXXXXXXXXXXXXXXXXXXX    C2
                      XXXXXXXX      D
                        XXXX       E
```

Based on figures given in Baker, 1985, p. 79.

```
USA                      X         1
                        XXX        2
                    XXXXXXXXX       3
        XXXXXXXXXXXXXXXXXXXXXXXXXXXXXXXX        4
     XXXXXXXXXXXXXXXXXXXXXXXXXXXXXXXXXXXXXXX    5
                  XXXXXXXXXXXX      6
```

Based on figures given in Kotler, 1984, p. 127.

Figure 3.1   Social class structure in the UK and the USA

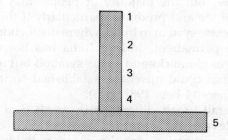

Figure 3.2   Social class structure in many low-income countries

The large, rich newly industrialised countries like Brazil, Mexico and Argentina are characterised by a small elite, a relatively large well-educated college-trained upper status group, and masses of poorly educated peasants, nomads and unskilled urban dwellers. Their class structure is represented in Figure 3.3.

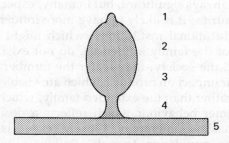

Figure 3.3   Social class structure in many large rich newly industrialised countries

Many small, poor NICs, however, have social structures which are approaching the situation of the Western developed countries to a much greater extent.

Since social class in any part of the world shows distinct product-form and brand preference (if brands exist) in areas such as clothing, home furnishings, food, drink and entertainment, and since the social structure is in broad terms very different from that of Western developed societies, then taken at an aggregate level there must be broad differences in the way in which needs become wants. Because the lower social classes tend to dominate basic biogenic necessities are likely to be most important. However, the educated urban elite minorities will buy a wide range of luxury and other products, without much concern for price, in order to satisfy higher psychogenic needs. Usually representing not more than 20 per cent of the population, this group tends to demand the same food, clothes, housing, cars, and the rest as are demanded in Western developed societies. But the majority of people may still stick to the traditional ways of life and products, particularly if there is little social mobility, as in the caste system in India, where distinctions are likely to be greater and more permanent. Indeed India has been described as a country 'which loves gimmicks and status symbols but resists inventions and innovations that could upset the established social and economic order' (*Financial Times* 14 Feb. 1987, p. 3).

Within this overall broad difference in needs and wants between developed and developing countries and between different groups within developing countries, on the more individual level, family systems are equally significant. How any individual feels, thinks and acts is influenced by the groups to which he belongs. The family is always the most powerful group, since it nurtures children and passes on the values of society. It determines how one gains prestige through socially-approved symbols. It dictates the rules of courtship and marriage, the degree of freedom allowed in the choice of partners, the age at which children become adults, the role of women, and so on, all of which ultimately affect consumer purchases. The role of the family as a primary reference group is always significant, but in many, especially rural, areas of developing countries, it is likely to have more influence where other peer groups or educational institutions, which might otherwise have taken over many of the family influences, do not exist. Generally, the more sophisticated the society, the greater the number of peer groups, and the bigger their impact on products which are visible. Also, the more likely the nuclear rather than the extended family, which again will tend to promote consumer behaviour which reflects a desire to attain the higher levels of Maslow's hierarchy. Closely related is what has been referred to as 'the population triangle' (Jefkins, 1982). Whereas in Western developed societies and some small poor newly industrialised societies such as Singapore ageing populations are typical, in many developing countries 50 per cent of the population are under fifteen years of age, which means that half the people have no income and are outside the market for most advertised goods.

Family structure also has an important influence on roles and status. For example, women are important as both workers and consumers. Where women work primarily in the home they contribute only indirectly to family buying power and the satisfaction of needs by making items such as clothing. Where they work for payment, the disposable income of the family is likely to be higher but the woman's role in buying decisions may remain insignificant. However, since life-styles are likely to be much more complex in developing countries, generalisations about wants which result are difficult to make. Nevertheless the family as a primary reference group remains the most enduring influence on attitudes.

Education, a third major cultural component, is also likely to be highly influential in either promoting traditional attitudes or introducing new attitudes towards needs and wants. Whether provided by schools, elders or oral historians, education often promotes negative attitudes towards materialism by perpetuating traditional values and feelings, and by being of a sufficiently low level to prevent a cultural group from using or understanding a new product. Where schools are the responsibility of the Church, values are likely to reflect this. Conversely, the greater the amount of education and the more widely available it is, together with higher disposable incomes, the more likely it is to be an agent of change in the definition of needs and wants. In many societies, particularly in the urban area, the traditional extended family has been rejected in favour of the conjugal family and with this change have come new buying habits.

In addition cultural borrowings are always occurring as society seeks better solutions to its problems. Once found, regardless of their origins they are adopted and passed on. Clearly, then, consumer life-styles change as economic development progresses, and this process has been promoted by the multinational introducing new products. People's habits, styles, tastes and behaviour therefore are not constant but ever-changing. It has been argued that consumer products characterising the 'good life', for example, cars and consumer durables, are wanted and needed throughout the world. Indeed many multinational marketers have based their global policies on this assumption that consumer tastes throughout the world are converging.

However attitudes do not change at a uniform rate. And whilst it is generally the case that as people become conscious that a better standard of living is possible, new needs develop as old ones become satisfied, the innovations which are most readily accepted are those which are the least disruptive. Thus new patterns of buying are occurring, helped by the acceptance of such factors as mass merchandising and the use of credit cards in many urban areas. And whilst some new products, satisfying new needs for prestige, status and a desire to be like the West, are being introduced and immediately accepted, others are first modified before they are assimilated. For example, a soup advertised as an evening meal in the Far East was found to be unsuccessful. But once promoted as a breakfast food, it was seen to satisfy a genuine need and was accepted.

The way in which basic needs are satisfied therefore remains strongly dependent upon culture. All people need food but what they want to eat, where they want to eat it and how they want to eat it, and so on, will reflect their culture. Equally, rituals will differ since all societies have a rich repertoire of natural and socially-invented symbols. What is regarded as clean, dirty, desirable, undesirable, the significance of left, right, front, back, inside, outside, and so on, all aspects of social significance, will account for many of the differences shown in the way in which needs are satisfied.

Classification

Unfortunately there is no simple method which can be used to classify the way in which basic needs become basic differences in developing countries. Instead complexity is evident both within and between developing countries. Certainly culture is largely responsible. In India there are six religions, with fifteen major and many more minor languages and dialects. Whilst the urban consumers are more predictable the rural consumers are extremely heterogeneous and 'probably much more complex than the whole market in Europe in terms of cultural, religious, linguistic and other diversities' (Kumar, 1973, p. 218). In order to understand how needs are translated into purchasing habits, rural attitudes, social standards, important festivals, the significance of astrology and local institutions must all be understood.

In Africa, too, there are hundreds of ethnic groups, languages and religions. Distinct tribes like the Yoruba of Western Nigeria and the Hausa of the North, give rise to general characteristics – the Yoruba said to be more outgoing and friendly, the Hausa being quieter and more reserved (Baker, 1969). Such factors may provide some basis for distinguishing differences in consumer wants. But the picture has been further complicated by internal migrations and infusions of European and Asian minorities. The result is that there is no such person as a typical African (Hodder, 1978). Some have been quicker to accept European ideas and techniques than others. Ibadan, an indigenous Yoruba town of over one million in Nigeria is a good case in point. The Moslem Hausa and the

Western Ibo (two non-indigenous tribes) were each allocated specific residential areas in the 1920s. Both have been subjected to the same pressures, forces and opportunities. Both have had to fulfil the same basic needs, but they have developed differently. The Hausa have deepened their cultural distinctiveness with the appropriate dress, symbols, language and religion, developing their own Tijaniya brotherhood sect. The Western Ibo have adapted and lost their cultural distinctiveness.

The attempts which have been made to devise categories into which cultures can be put are largely unsatisfactory and oversimplified. They ignore much of the sort of complexity just discussed. In 1950 Reisman et al. (1950) suggested a division of societies into three categories: traditional societies, inner-directed and other-directed societies. Traditional societies are characterised by strong family influence dominated by a paternal figure. Religion is significant, and old ways and opinions of elders very important. Wants, not surprisingly, do not change easily or quickly, since the *status quo* must be preserved. Inner-directed societies are defined as those present in nations which are experiencing rapid economic development. Rugged individuals, usually owning new industrial and financial institutions, dominate the society and individualistic patterns of consumption develop as traditional values and relationships are broken down. Other-directed societies are only to be found in the highly developed affluent societies where reference groups other than the traditional ones have begun to dominate, and buying motives are now difficult to identify.

Dichter, some years later, in 1962, based his classification on levels of economic development. His categories are (i) almost classless societies, (ii) affluent societies, (iii) revolutionary societies, (iv) primitive societies and (v) new class societies. Other researchers have concentrated on values held, for example attitudes to materialistic gain, wealth, change and the future. Sommers and Kernan (1967) examined to what extent societies were (i) egalitarian or elitist, (ii) prone to stress accomplishment, (iii) expectant of material or non-material reward, (iv) subjective or objective in evaluating products, (v) orientated to personal or group rewards and (vi) used to focusing on the whole or distinctive parts. Using such criteria, it is possible to interpret a society's priority of needs, the way in which needs will be satisfied and the extent to which new products will be accepted in order to satisfy new wants.

However the fact remains that no one set of criteria can be universally applied to produce a meaningful classification of the way basic needs become basic differences in all developing countries all over the world. The best generalisation which can be made is to suggest that as economic development progresses the way in which needs are satisfied becomes more standardised. In the most successful small, poor newly industrialised countries life-styles are rapidly approaching, and in some cases overtaking, those of the Western developed nations in many ways. In the urban areas of all categories of developing countries, there is a certain amount of convergence of consumer tastes among the elite minority who are better educated and have higher disposable incomes. But in the more rural areas of large rich and large poor countries, where traditional culture is more intact, the way in which basic needs are satisfied is likely to show great variations. And Islamic societies in small rich countries, although conforming in many ways to Western materialism, still display significant variation in others due to the strong religious underpinning.

Consumer decision-making

Throughout the world, the principles involved in consumer decision-making are the same. These are linked to the same five roles that people may play – initiator, influencer, decider, buyer and user. Equally, in any buying situation there will be the same influences, these being (i) buyer characteristics, (ii) product characteristics, (iii) seller characteristics and (iv) situational characteristics.

However the roles involved in, and the influences on decision-making are significantly different in developing countries. Buyer characteristics, which involve culture, sub-culture, social class, reference groups, family and personal characteristics (for example, age and place in the life cycle, occupation, economic circumstances, life-style and personality) along with psychological factors (attitude and perception, motivation and so on, as discussed above) go a long way towards explaining the differences in the roles that people play.

In the Western developed countries the nuclear family with a goal-orientated husband who 'gets things done' and the supporting wife playing a social emotive role of keeping the family together may be typical (Baker, 1985). In such a situation the husband is likely to be responsible for decisions which are concerned with the interface between the household and the external world, the wife taking responsibility for activities within the family. Notwithstanding this distinction, the wife is likely to have a certain amount of autonomy and be at least almost an equal partner in decision-making.

However, in many traditional societies in developing countries, culture (especially one with a dominant Hindu or Moslem religion) dictates that the family system, usually an extended one, is more authoritarian and patriarchal. Thus the elders and menfolk are the major decision-makers, the women being subordinate and at best junior partners. As well as the balance of power in the marriage being altered, the child's role is likely to be different, as is the age at which he is considered to be an adult. All these factors make for a different emphasis in terms of the roles that people play. Generally, in the traditional extended family, the menfolk are likely to be the initiators, deciders and buyers. Even where the woman is the main user of the product she is likely to have less influence on the decision, and possibly less power as an initiator too.

Nevertheless, as noted above, in many developing countries, particularly in the urban areas, change is under way. The extended family is giving way to the nuclear family and new reference groups are gaining in importance. The new life-style which reflects the influence of other cultures, products and better economic circumstances means that new decision-making patterns are emerging. These are more like those found in Western developed societies.

Between these two extremes, however, there is the typical lack of homogeneity. Buyer characteristics vary greatly both within and between developing countries. Consequently, decision-making is likely to follow many different patterns.

Complexity is also evident in the other influences on the buying decision. In terms of product characteristics, considering all developing countries together, the choice is less than in the developed world, whilst availability will also differ markedly. Furthermore there is likely to be less standardisation and quality control in many parts. Scarcity, resulting in a sellers' market, may well alter the emphasis of the decision-making process while seller characteristics too will assume a greater importance. Under such conditions the seller may become more of an influencer or decision-maker. Firstly he will be important in making the products available. Secondly he will act as an important source of information about the reliability of weights, measures, contents of packages, and so on. If there is mutual trust established between buyer and seller, the seller's influence will undoubtedly be very great, whilst if he offers some form of credit to buyers this too is likely to be an important factor in influencing the buying decision. This is likely to be typical of many rural areas, for example in India, where the local store owner may allow consumers to purchase goods on credit, taking his payment in the form of crops at harvest times. To a very large extent therefore, under these circumstances, the seller is the major person in deciding what can or cannot be bought.

Finally, situational characteristics, such as time available to make a decision, type of weather, time of year, and so on will always affect decision-making. Although just as relevant anywhere in the world, the emphasis in importance of these factors will again be different in developing countries. Weather may well be more extreme, distribution channels less developed and time taken to make a decision more dependent upon traditional cultural values. Generally, as with all influences on decision-making, complexity is likely to be greater.

Range of products purchased

In February, 1985 United Biscuits announced that it was considering starting an operation to manufacture biscuits in India if its first venture – a Wimpy Bar in the capital – proved successful. After being open one week in New Delhi's fashionable Connaught Circus shopping centre, the Wimpy Bar – selling hamburgers made of lamb – was proving extremely successful. It had attracted 1000 customers per day (*Financial Times*, 12 Jan. 1985).

This development epitomises many trends typical in the Third World today. Firstly, the fact that hamburgers (although made of lamb) are acceptable to a Hindu shows how cultural constraints can be accommodated. More importantly, the venture demonstrates that the range of products available is being increasingly extended and accepted. This would seem to confirm the view which the multinationals have assumed since the 1960s – that consumer tastes throughout the world are converging.

Because few countries since the 1950s have been content with the *status quo*, but instead have sought the perceived 'material paradise' achieved in advanced nations, the majority have willingly accepted a larger range of 'Western' products. Better international communications and the operations of the multinationals have furthered the process. Foreign products are usually considered superior since they incorporate more sophisticated technology and internationally-renowned band names and trade marks.

Often a multinational can set up in a developing country, introduce new products, create and, to some extent, manage new tastes. On the one hand it can introduce new products built for world markets which may be highly beneficial. On the other, whilst introducing new values reflecting the Western way of life, it may also introduce products which are inferior to traditional ones but are seen to be superior. This is often the case in convenience foods. The situation is made worse when the product is not used correctly. For example, in Jamaica infant cereal is produced by Mead-Johnson, a subsidiary of Bristol Myers. Used as a substitute for breast-feeding it is purchased not only by the bourgeois classes who can afford it, but by the poorer peasants who imitate the consumption habits of the higher social classes. And because the poorer purchasers cannot afford it in sufficient quantities, they dilute it too much, aggravating the malnutrition problem (Girling, 1976).

Such an example would tend to confirm the cynic's view that the Third World is obsessed with the Western way of life and the range of products that this involves. Harrison has argued that it is all due to the West's intention to enforce 'cultural imperialism' on the developing countries.

Achieved initially through the indoctrination of the elite local collaborators, it has been continued by the promotion of the Western life-style as the most important aspirational reference group. By adopting a wide range of international products, blacks can prove to the advanced nations that 'they can be civilised', whilst at the same time impressing their neighbour the only way everyone recognises – the Western way (Harrison, 1979).

This is undoubtedly an individualistic, contentious viewpoint, and is by no means typical of all developing countries or all parts of developing countries. There are many newly industrialised countries which have managed to keep their culture intact and still adopt a wider range of products. There are many parts which have not been exposed to innovations. Again it is important to consider individual cases and note the varying levels of economic development.

On the whole convergence of consumer tastes, and the corresponding broadening of a uniform range of products available, is associated with higher levels of economic development. Undoubtedly, increased spending power means an increased demand for a wider range of products. In the Middle East, for example, the consumer is no longer an illiterate person with limited purchasing power, but an educated, travelled individual with considerable purchasing power, and aware of all the industrial world has to offer him. Equally, in South Korea, despite government controls to hold back pent-up demand, domestic car sales rose by 100 000 in 1983 to 400 000 in 1984. Today more than three million of the country's eight million homes have colour television, despite colour transmissions only being introduced in 1982. Department stores have grown rapidly in number, from 14 in 1960 to 100 in 1984. Supermarkets began operating in this country in 1971. By 1984 there were 4300. Credit cards (introduced in 1974) are now widely accepted and the average household consumption increased sixfold in the ten years between 1974 and 1984.

In the urban areas of most developing countries, similar trends are evident to varying degrees. Affluent upper classes in all societies are likely to be more similar to each other than to the rest of their societies. Better-educated consumers in such a category, demanding a wide range of goods with often little regard for price, are developing new spending patterns. Traditional values tend to get discarded in the process. For example, the extended family has been discarded in the urban areas of Nigeria in favour of the conjugal family of Western industrialised societies. The relationship between husband and wife has become more egalitarian and more money is spent on the home, hygiene, instant food and labour-saving devices in place of the traditional cheaper foodstuffs and basic necessities. Greater individual profits for all members of the family reinforce the different emphasis in spending patterns.

Not surprisingly, the urban consumer is more predictable and homogeneous than formerly, and the range of products has expanded accordingly.

However this broad theme of converging consumer tastes and a corresponding rise in the range of products available and consumed is not typical for *all* products, nor for all areas within developing countries. In the rural areas, along with lower disposable incomes, culture often remains a powerful force in hampering the diffusion of a wider range of products. Here religion, low levels of education and the strict stratification of societies reduce the diffusion rate of new products. If lack of materialism and fatalism is inherent in the system, it is likely that new products and processes will be regarded as undesirable, disruptive or even evil. Low levels of education and material culture may prevent the adoption of more sophisticated products. Unless society holds materialistic aspirations, many innovations will be rejected.

Thus culture will help dictate how *quickly* new products are accepted and incorporated. Generally the new products which are accepted correspond closely with traditional values. But even where there is no conflict, a society never receives all new products passively. Modification may still be essential, since aesthetic values will determine the acceptability of such aspects as shape and colour. What is regarded as a socially-approved symbol will dictate which products are prestigious. There will always be certain taboos, such as pairs in the Guinea Coast, feet in Thailand, beef in Hindu countries. And where there are a number of cultures within a country the range of goods will vary accordingly. For example, as noted above, Africa has many hundreds of indigenous ethnic groups, supplemented by European, Asian, American, Australian and Canadian minorities. Each group is likely to react differently to changes, pressures, forces and opportunities. Each will select an appropriate range of goods, as is well demonstrated by the development of the Western Ibo and Hausa communities in Ibadan.

This is not to say that change is not possible. Quite the reverse. People's habits, styles, tastes and behaviour are constantly changing and new values are introduced. This process therefore complicates the assumed simple relationship between culture and the acceptance of new products. Naturally in the urban areas and more developed parts of developing countries change is likely to be more rapid, with traditional cultural objections being more easily overruled as new values are introduced along with products and services which are not culture-based. But even in the rural areas, where products and services are more likely to be rejected if they do not conform to traditional values, change is possible. For example, despite birth control products being at odds with the Hindu's belief in having sons for security in old age, if village elders, the opinion leaders, accept a break with tradition, so will the rest of their communities. Rogers, (1962) demonstrated how this applied in relation to the acceptance of vasectomies by village elders.

Nevertheless change will often be restricted by other non-cultural factors. Where levels of economic development are low and there is less spending power, the impoverished masses will tend to devote a higher percentage of income to food and other essentials. Together with conditions of scarcity, a production orientation, fewer distribution outlets, poor infrastructure and a lower ability to absorb more technically-advanced products, this means there will be little incentive to introduce a wide range of new products. Peasant markets concentrating on selling basic necessities or small shops with scrambled merchandise will result.

The impact of colonialism or other historical and political factors in the past may also have an impact on the range of goods. In some circumstances openness to change may have been promoted among certain groups. For example, public officials in some African countries have developed into a new elite, filling the gap left by the Europeans and adopting their symbols and homes. Through this new market segment convergence of consumer tastes has been promoted. Conversely the impact of the colonial past may lead to the rejection of certain products. An African will tend to dismiss products which he feels have been created specially for him. However he may well be interested in products which appeal to strength and vitality, due to his desire for power. This situation may still be consistent with the convergence of consumer tastes. But where the acceptance of innovations from the Western World is regarded as neo-imperialism, products will automatically be rejected.

A variation on this theme is the xenophobic attitude of some Islamic nations towards the non-Arab world. For example, in some oil rich states such as Libya there is a great fear that Western products and techniques will destroy the ancient faith. This intense identification with the known and familiar results in great resistance towards new ideas, products and techniques from another culture. The need to modernise traditional ways – which no longer work to Libya's satisfaction – is acknowledged, but the society has rejected both Western capitalism and Eastern communism, and all that these regimes involve. This is not to say that materialistic products are rejected out of hand but the intense need to secure cultural continuity with the past has led to extra strong religious and nationalistic feelings which ultimately have a strong impact on the range of products available.

The above example questions the convergence of consumer tastes argument. Other examples support it. In an up-market department store of Manila's financial centre designer fashions are sold, whilst a nearby delicatessen stocks snails, truffles and fine wine. All this is possible because of smuggling, coupled with good political connections, despite the severely contracting economy of the Philippines (*Financial Times* 19

Sep. 1984). The demand for international products is there and is being met, even if illegally.

The impact of advertising

It has frequently been suggested that advertising, especially that by the multinational company, has contributed significantly to the convergence of consumer tastes throught the world. Certainly multinational enterprises producing consumer durables, or convenience products in some cases, stand to benefit enormously if they can convert the market to the product rather than modifying the product to suit the market. Not only do economies of scale become possible through the global sourcing and production of a standardised product for one world market, but costs may also be saved through having one international advertising campaign, which reinforces the 'internationally-acceptable' image.

However advertising by both government and indigenous marketers is also likely to have a big impact on consumer behaviour in developing countries. This is largely because, in general, the amount of money spent on advertising per capita is insignificant besides that spent in the United States or United Kingdom. Advertising expenditures in developing countries do vary (Table 3.1) but this is all relative and still small in relation to developed countries. Consequently any advertising which does occur is noted and remembered to a much greater extent than in advanced societies where the sheer volume has tended to result in more apathy by the consumer. Although there may well be certain limitations in media availability and the types of advertising which are possible, considering lower literacy rates and the limitations associated with verbal and non-verbal forms of communication, the marketer can often create an almost unassailable position of strength in the market place which would be unattainable in a more sophisticated environment (Harper, 1975).

For example, Guinness is associated with health, strength and vitality by most Nigerians. This demonstrates that not only has advertising's impact been powerful but it has also had a much more lasting effect than that achieved in the West. So that, whilst the expenditure is likely to be small by Western standards, the number of people affected and the durability of new spending habits mean that advertising often unwittingly plays a significant role in the formation of new ways of life.

Advertising, therefore, offers an enormous opportunity for the marketer. But because its impact is likely to be profound, it must also be used with responsibility. If used correctly, it can be valuable in introducing beneficial new products. Much research has demonstrated that, since

Table 3.1 **Advertising expenditures in a selection of developing countries in 1977 and 1982**

	Total population millions	Advertising expenditure (total) $ million	(per capita) $
Argentina	26.1	459.1	17.59
Bahrain	0.3	2.1	7.0
Bangladesh	82.7	8.3	0.1
Bermuda	0.06	7.1	118.33
Brazil	113.2	1 679.8*(3,386.3)	14.84(28.2)
Egypt	39.2	74.1*	1.89
Ethiopia	29.4	1.2	0.04
Hong Kong	4.5	106.7*(123.0)	23.71(24.6)
India	631.7	163.7	0.26
Indonesia	133.5	78.8	0.59
Kenya	14.4	14.4	1.0
Libya	2.6	16.6	6.38
Malaysia	13.0	45.6*(110.0)	3.51(7.9)
Mauritius	0.9	1.8	2.0
Mexico	64.2	310.7*(436.7)	4.84(6.15)
Nepal	0.7	1.5	2.14
Nigeria	79.0	55.0	0.7
Pakistan	73.4	18.2	0.25
Peru	16.5	72.3	4.38
Saudi Arabia	9.3	48.7	5.24
Singapore	2.3	54.3*(112)	23.61(44.9)
South Korea	36.5	217.6	5.96
Sudan	16.5	4.7	0.28
Taiwan	16.6	197.3	11.89
Venezuela	12.7	280.2*(594)	22.06(39.6)
Zimbabwe	6.8	21.3*	31.3

* Some items, e.g. sales promotion, omitted.
() 1982 figures where these exist.
    Sources: World Advertising Expenditures 1979; World Development Report 1984;
        International Monetary Fund: International Financial Statistics 1982.

advertising is regarded as an important source of information, known brands are considered more trustworthy (Bates 1981, Harper 1975). Advertising can be used to change value systems, which may result in positive social and economic consequences (assuming that it is accepted as morally correct to change traditional cultural values). If government marketers use it to promote the purchase of better seeds and more fertilisers, undoubtedly the chances of economic development improve.

However, where advertising is used to promote a product designed for one type of market, and not suited to another, but accepted because of the prestige value associated with the words 'Western' or 'international', the consequences may be disastrous. The much quoted example is Nestle's promotion of dried milk for babies in South America. This was immediately accepted as a prestigious product but, because of poor literacy rates and poverty, it was not mixed to the correct strength. In such a case malnutrition is exacerbated. Worse occurs when water with which the dried milk is mixed is contaminated. Death may then be the result.

So advertising's impact is generally profound. As economies develop some of its power is likely to be lost, but in the meantime it is playing a large part in increasing the range of products available in developing countries by influencing people's needs and wants. Depending upon who is using it and how it is used, its impact may be positive or negative.

Buying and bargaining

Again all basic buying behaviour principles apply to developing countries as to developed ones. Buying can always be subdivided into routinised response behaviour, limited problem-solving and extensive problem-solving. Equally the stages of need arousal, information search, evaluation behaviour and post-purchase feelings are still relevant. However the emphasis is likely to be different in developing countries, due to cultural and other environmental conditions.

At first sight, it might appear that routinised response behaviour is of greater significance, since most buying in developing countries (taken as a whole) concentrates on low-cost, frequently-purchased items. But this may not be the case, as choice is likely to be less. There are usually fewer products to satisfy any need class, fewer if indeed any, brands, fewer vendors to choose from, and more restrictions on timing, quantity and payment decisions. Consequently, limited problem-solving and extensive problem-solving may become relatively more important. However this tends to manifest itself in a different way. If there is just one product and no competition, the emphasis will be on haggling over price. Basic necessities will need to be assessed by discovering how fresh and what quality is the product, how reliable is the seller, and so on. The information search for new products is likely to be even greater. Thus more attention needs to be given to finding out about the seller, examining and handling his goods in order to collect the information required to make a decision.

Once more culture cannot be ignored, and again there will be enormous differences in buying behaviour both within and between developing countries. As always, the rural and least economically advanced areas are likely to contain the most extreme deviations from buying behaviour typical of the Western developed nations.

In addition to culture determining who buys, how people buy, what they buy, who makes the decisions, who holds the money and so on, in the rural and least economically developed areas there is much greater risk involved. Lack of quality control by local manufacturers, under-developed storage facilities to preserve fresh foods, cheating by sellers (adulterating packaged goods, giving approximate, but generally short measure with unpackaged goods, and getting away with it as a result of lack of official product standards), a seller's market, perhaps involving monopoly or cartel conditions with scarcity of goods and little or no price competition, tied distribution systems, low rates of product change and low income and therefore low consumer purchasing power, all result in an intensive search effort for information on the seller and his products. Bargaining is the natural outgrowth of such uncertainty and is often regarded as an enjoyable social experience (Thorelli and Sentell, 1982). Indeed in many parts shopping is an important part of life's routine, satisfying psychological needs by bringing people into contact with the outside world. The market, in this context, is a social gathering, a natural meeting place for news and gossip.

In peasant markets characterised by market rings, many of the above conditions are demonstrated most clearly. These markets, generally located between five and fifteen miles apart, on average drawing on a radius of seven miles, are often dominated by female traders. Their merchandise lacks uniformity, there being no standard weights or measures. Quantities tend to be tiny – for example, individual matches, drops of perfume, dishfuls of grain. 'Piles', 'arm's lengths', slices, handfuls or even individual nuts and sweets are common, since lower purchasing power dictates that consumers shop frequently, intensively and in small quantities. The consumer must be careful in appraising not only the quality and value of the goods, but also the trustworthiness of the seller. Equally the seller will be interested to discover how eager the buyer is, how aware he is of the alternatives (if these exist) and so on.

The consumer has two main strategies – to collect information from numerous sources, or to trust the seller. Often a combination of the two is used. Information is highly valued but tends to be poor, maldistributed or badly communicated. Bargaining provides an alternative method which is more laborious, uncertain, complex and irregular, but often essential. Haggling is also the method of establishing price. A great ritual often accompanies the whole process. There will be threats, counter-threats, meaningful shrugs of the shoulders, grimaces, and shows of disdain. High and low estimates of price by seller and buyer are not established haphazardly. They tend to represent the amount of variation in the price of a particular product on any given day in any given market.

As always there are likely to be wide variations in local conditions which may cause deviations from what is described above. For example, there may be little price-cutting if a network of social and family relationships bind together members of a trading community. Here it would be considered bad manners to undercut one's relative or to be greedy in receiving payments. Alternatively village traders may charge less to a friend or member of the family and more to a debtor. Where a village shop with a monopoly dominates, such deviations in price are even more likely.

As trade spreads, and as economic development levels rise, buyers are likely to gain greater confidence in sellers. Because of more standardisation of product, the need to differentiate and therefore develop brands, the search switches from inter-product to inter-brand. But certain cultural factors may still intervene to prevent buying behaviour from paralleling exactly that typical of developed nations. For example, in Thailand there still exists general disdain for businessmen, middlemen and merchants. In Singapore, one of the leading newly industrialised countries, service remains generally disappointing, and a tedious bargaining session must still often be held before price is established.

However it is in the poorer areas of developing countries that inefficiency of distribution, together with dishonest activities on the part of merchants, have given governments most cause for concern. Many have intervened to supply basic foodstuffs at low prices through their own more efficient distribution systems. This, to some extent, has changed buying behaviour. For example, in Mexico, as part of the government's social welfare programme, the Compania Nacional de Subsistencias Populares (CONASUPO) has been established as a non-profit-making, government-owned, vertically integrated distribution channel for distributing staple food products at low cost. In addition to purchasing from, and providing warehousing facilities for, low-income farmers, it offers consumers additional retail outlets in competition with private sector ones. Although it accounts for less than one per cent of all retail sales of food products in the country, it is intended to regulate commodity prices, reduce overall intermediary margins and break up monopolistic speculation in the food channels. Targeted at the low-income groups, whose share of national income has steadily declined in the last 25 years, Conasupo stores today attract middle-income in addition to low-income groups. In research undertaken in Monterey (Hilger 1980), it was established that buyers' perception of Conasupo stores is different from that of private stores. Higher accountability by CONASUPO, which is perceived to be 'contributing to the economic development of Mexico' was expected. CONASUPO was not seen to offer better value, however. This largely reflected a belief that it had a comparative advantage. Nevertheless buyer behaviour is still likely ultimately to be affected by the better buying environment created.

Indeed, CONASUPO, price controls, the enforcement of specified standards and regulation of food and drugs through such bodies as the Nigerian Standards Organisation all constitute attempts by governments to protect the consumer. Whilst there is little consumerism in developing countries, there is a great need for it – to counteract the many unscrupulous business practices which thrive in conditions of scarcity of supply. But, until this is achieved, buying in most developing countries will largely remain different from that experienced in Western developed societies, and bargaining will persist as a necessary alternative to standardised products, prices and distribution outlets.

The implications for indigenous, multinational and governmental marketers

The three different types of marketers are considered in their own right in Part II. Suffice it to say here that although indigenous, governmental and multinational marketers should all be considering the consumer first and foremost before formulating their strategies, the way in which each perceives consumer behaviour and seeks to respond to it varies markedly.

Certainly all three types of marketer should consider the influences on consumer behaviour more carefully than they might in a developed world context, since the complexity is likely to be much greater. Equally they may all find useful the generalisation that the higher the level of economic development, the greater the standardisation in which needs are satisfied. The fact that a basic distinction can be made between (i) the urban areas and the most successful small, poor newly industrialised countries and (ii) the rural areas, particularly in large poor, large rich and small poor countries outside Southseat Asia, may also be helpful. But whereas the indigenous marketer will need to understand influences on consumer behaviour on a more limited scale, the multinational marketer is likely to consider these of even less significance. For while modifications may need to be made in terms of packaging, method of selling or advertising, this category of marketer will largely be more interested in promoting the use of a range of standardised goods through advertising. He is therefore most concerned with the extent to which consumers will resist or will be unable to use new products he seeks to introduce. And because he is most interested in more advanced levels of economic development, whether in the urban centres or in countries where standards of living are generally higher, the difficulties are likely to be perceived as fewer and the complexity less.

The governmental marketer on the other hand has the most difficult task. Not only must he attempt to understand all aspects of consumer behaviour and all groups of consumers within his nation in order that he can control what products are introduced and what advertising should be allowed, but he must also reduce any consumer resistance to change he considers necessary. Again India provides an excellent example. Rajiv Gandhi is often mocked for trying to move his country from what is characterised as the age of the bullock to the new world of the computer. High technology's latest attempt to invade and reform many deeply resistant Indian villages – which number 600 000 – is a computer-designed aluminium bullock cart. At present there are 15 million bullock carts made from wood, with over 300 regional design variations, and these form the basis of India's rural transport system. And although the aluminium cart weighs less than half the traditional version, has a 30 per cent greater payload and reduces the drain on India's vanishing forests, it is not being welcomed by rural consumers with open arms (*Financial Times* 14 Feb. 1987).

The government marketer's task is made even more difficult if he seeks to stamp out malpractices which distort consumer behaviour. Although the improvement of the marketing environment and the promotion of consumer emancipation (discussed in the final chapter) are laudible objectives, to eliminate black markets, other forms of competition and haggling in the market place is tantamount to changing culture, which introduces all manner of moral arguments. Finally where he chooses to act as entrepreneur and develop new distribution systems and retail outlets in order to protect the consumer's interests, he may find himself subject to matters such as public accountability which not only constrain him as a marketer but also introduce an additional complication into consumer behaviour. And since consumer behaviour is generally not well researched or understood by government marketers, the efficiency of their intervention remains somewhat doubtful.

Conclusion

Chapter 3 discussed how, despite basic concepts and principles of consumer behaviour being the same the world over, the conditions existing in developing countries resulted in many differences in consumer behaviour.

Basic needs become basic differences because of such factors as the conditions of supply and demand, low income, culture, advertising and the influence of the multinational. However, because people do not respond in a uniform manner throughout the world, classifications of the way basic needs become basic differences in various developing countries remain impossible. The best generalisation which can be made is that basic differences become fewer as economies develop. Consequently wants in small, poor newly industrialised countries and urban areas of small developing countries are fast becoming more standardised, but in the rural areas much complexity remains.

Decision-making is similarly affected by external conditions. But, as in any area of consumer behaviour, change is occurring in many parts of the world as attitudes alter and the range of products grows. The multinational, with its global policy based on the assumption that consumer tastes throughout the world are converging, has been held largely responsible. Certainly the impact of advertising has been enormous.

But whilst many of these generalisations hold good in the urban areas, traditional values and methods of buying and bargaining continue alongside. Culture may be one very significant factor – affecting attitudes to needs and wants, buyer's behaviour, decision-making and people's flexibility in accepting new products. Low levels of economic development, conditions of scarcity, poor infrastructure are others. In many instances governments have attempted to overcome these by setting up their own vertically integrated distribution systems.

The implications for the indigenous, governmental and multinational marketers are considerable. But each of these types of marketer tends to regard consumer behaviour from a different perspective. The fact remains that until more uniform conditions throughout each developing country are achieved, great care must be taken in order to understand the complexity. Only then can the right marketing mix be formulated. These aspects are considered next in Chapters 4 and 5.

CHAPTER 4

Marketing research in developing countries

Contents

Introduction

Marketing research is particularly important in a developing country context in order to understand the consumer who is operating within an extremely complex and versatile marketing environment. At the same time, the successful undertaking of marketing research in developing countries is usually particularly hazardous too, so that whilst there is an obvious need for more good research, there are also enormous barriers to achieving it.

This chapter considers in detail the scope, organisation, process and methods of marketing research in a developing country context. As in *Marketing: An Introductory Text* (Baker, 1985), a broad definition of marketing research is adopted. This may be summarised as 'the systematic gathering, recording and analysing of data to provide information useful in marketing decision making' (Cateora and Hess, 1979). Equally, many of the fundamental issues discussed are still relevant. The objective of marketing research is always the same – to provide information to help make better decisions in a world of uncertainty. The scope of the questions which must be answered – who, what, when, where, how and why – remains valid. The areas for research – sales research, product research, advertising research, business economics, export marketing and motivational research – are just the same. However the emphasis given to each of these areas may well be different, whilst the organisation and methods of marketing research in developing countries are likely to be wildly at variance. Although it was noted in *Marketing: An Introductory Text* that few British companies have actual marketing research departments, it is likely that these are even more rare in developing countries. And whilst the process of marketing research is the same there, the techniques of marketing research usually need significant modification to make allowance for the vastly different marketing environment. Each of these aspects is addressed individually.

Marketing research: objectives, scope and perception of its value

The objective of marketing research (to help reduce uncertainty in order to make better decisions), whilst just the same, is perhaps even more critical in a developing country context, since the decisions which have to be made can influence more profoundly the lives of so many. In Chapter 1 the way in which marketing can promote economic development was explored. But it is marketing research which, first and foremost, provides the means to determine how best to use scarce resources through discovering latent demand, indicating ways to convert it to effective demand, directing producers to develop marketable goods and suggesting more effective distribution channels and so on. Once effective marketing mixes have been established, marketing research then provides the means for continually monitoring changes in the environment.

This is particularly important in developing countries since the environment is both complex and dynamic. As noted in Chapter 2, it is usually characterised by greater instability, a different competitive situation, more fragmented markets, poorer communications and more cultural diversity than those experienced in the developed countries. But, in addition to this, it is highly probable that the developing country needs to export in order to increase market size, fend off competition and earn foreign exchange. And, although the domestic situation may be difficult enough, there will be a certain amount of familiarity with it which may be completely lacking in the greater uncertainty associated with overseas markets. The scope for marketing research is consequently much broader, for it permits countries to look outside and make the most of their exportable product(s) or potential for export. This is increasingly necessary as the internationalisation of business progresses and as international space continues to shrink with better communications.

Growth in international markets is likely to become more and more significant for developing countries and therefore an increase in export marketing research will be essential. Risks and opportunities of overseas markets must be carefully assessed so that the right selection is made. Initially, research must discover the political, financial and legal situations so that such factors as stability, rate of inflation, foreign exchange risk, import restrictions, and so on can be established. Climate, topographical details, accessibility and stage of economic development must also be examined. Opportunities in terms of the macro-market potential – GNP per capita, growth of GNP, population size and density, urbanisation, type of industrialisation policy, education levels and, more specifically, market size, stage of development, growth trends for similar products and cultural acceptability of established products – must be determined, so that market potential and company sales potential can be estimated. On the more micro level an examination of the existing and potential competition, business philosophy, the physical and communications infrastructure, the ease of market entry and details on market segments will ensure that the right target market is attacked and the correct strategy adopted.

Yet despite marketing research having the ability to allow the optimum co-ordination of activities within any parameters and on any level, and despite the increased need for marketing research both to understand the developing country's complex environment and to assess international markets, paradoxically, the value attributed to this function is often underestimated. Where a production- rather than a marketing-orientation exists, sales research, product research and motivational research are likely to be regarded as unimportant. The nature of competition too invariably offers no incentive to increasing efficiency.

This is particularly the case with the indigenous marketer who, dealing with a situation of excess demand, little competition, concern solely with local markets and personalised feedback, see no value in marketing research. This view is likely to be even stronger where a country suffers from constant inflation and devaluation of currency. Under such conditions speculation is all important, and the type of advice sought is how to protect oneself against losses from such monetary movements. Alternatively, the concept of profit-maximisation may mean little. In its place is the preservation of the *status quo*. Lack of management training is undoubtedly a contributing factor but even the manager of large local indigenous concerns tends to pay little attention to marketing research. Nor is he prepared to allocate people or funds to this function. This is perhaps to be expected in economies where efficient production systems to meet demand are the major priority. Under such circumstances there is no need for concern with profits through consumer satisfaction and the assumption is generally that, in any case, consumer satisfaction will be achieved through simply making products similar to those produced in developed countries. And even where marketing research is beginning to be recognised as important, there may still be greater emphasis given to judgement and indirect informalised feedback from consumers rather than formal market research.

If formal research is undertaken it is often done primarily to estimate sales. This was found to be the case in an examination of the 36 largest consumer goods manufacturers (of detergents, foods, beverages and domestic appliances) in Mexico (Loudon, 1976). Over half the companies used marketing research on a regular basis but mainly for the purpose of sales analysis, the setting of sales quotas, estimating and revising sales territories. Advertising and product research were much less widely undertaken.

The government administrator too is often unlikely to give marketing research its due. This may be because he perceives marketing as a mechanistic process involving simply transport, storage and exchange. It may also be due to fear – that his own inadequacies will be uncovered and status will be lost. This bureaucratic attitude has frequently been singled out as a major obstacle in the collection of more reliable, meaningful statistics (Lauter, 1969). Yet, if used correctly, marketing research can help the governmental marketer enormously in his decision-making, so that more efficient production and distribution systems are promoted.

The multinational marketer, on the other hand, is likely to appreciate the value of marketing research and is the most likely to have a marketing research department within the organisation. However, due to the nature of many multinational activities, it is probable that marketing research will not be used to uncover basic needs and wants and develop a product accordingly. This is largely because many multinational companies tend to be more product-orientated in outlook, especially in such fields as cars and consumer durables (an issue discussed later, in Chapter 7). Under such conditions, marketing research will be used more for determining the acceptance of an established product, for assessing the political risk situation, and for devising the appropriate advertising strategy to ensure that the market fits the product.

Thus, whilst the objectives of marketing research remain valid, and the scope of marketing research is increasingly broad in developing countries, its value is frequently underestimated by the indigenous marketer and the public sector marketer, and it is used with a different specific emphasis by the multinational marketer. Yet its potential in a difficult, dynamic environment internally and in assessing marketing opportunities externally is enormous. Clearly, greater education is necessary so that this function is appreciated. If this can be achieved many of the other inhibiting problems discussed below will have a better chance of being eliminated.

Organising for marketing research

The small number of firms with formal marketing research departments in the United Kingdom was noted by Baker (1985). However it was also suggested that many companies still perform the function even if it is given another name, such as economic intelligence. The situation in developing countries is much worse. Generally the smaller the firm, the less the marketing research undertaken. And in addition to marketing research departments within indigenous firms or the public sector being extremely rare, there are severe difficulties in setting up such departments because of the lack of appreciation of the utility of marketing research and the absence of qualified people to undertake it.

For the same reasons outside marketing research agencies are often few and far between in developing countries. It may well be that a well-established international agency has a branch in a country, but J Walter Thompson (Ghana) will not be the same as J Walter Thompson (London). Often such branches are established through acquisition and the standards of research are likely to vary markedly. Local indigenous agencies which do exist should know local conditions in relation to attitudes, consumer behaviour and trading practices. But, as well as having to contend with the general problem of lack of qualified staff, they may well be less experienced or specialised than those found in developed countries. This is largely because overall demand is much smaller whilst their scope is much broader – some firms requiring specific studies, others looking for basic reliable statistics in an environment where secondary sources may be highly dubious.

Other commercial services are not numerous and whilst they are much needed there are severe difficulties in starting such services. For example, in Mexico there are particular difficulties in conducting store audits. The co-operation necessary from stores is not there and the resulting lack of accurate data makes projections very difficult. Equally, broadcasting ratings constitute another problematic area since lack of widespread telephone ownership prevents coincidental interviewing, and literacy levels may not be high enough to allow the diary method of recording. Finally mechanical measurement systems are usually out of the question. Trade associations and local research analysts are not readily available, and where they do not exist may well provide only poor unreliable data.

Yet, increasingly, marketing research's value will be noted as competition grows and as economies develop. Many idigenous firms will therefore begin to establish marketing research departments, at which point the same problem of responsibility and positioning of the department within the company, as discussed by Baker (1985) will apply. In addition to these, however, there may be further difficulties associated with the various cultural contexts. For example, personal integrity may be less important than personal connections in some countries, while male staff as opposed to female staff may be necessary in others.

In export markets the situation may be different. When dealing with a developed nation, a number of good international and domestic marketing research agencies will usually be available which, although expensive relative to those in developing countries, will provide good, reliable information about potentially rich markets. In export markets within developing countries, the same problem as those described above are likely. In such a case an agency should be chosen according to its integrity and ability. Directors, recommendations, local consultants, trade associations and other businessmen may be useful in selecting which agency to use. However, where an exporter attempts to compare different export markets, there is the extra difficulty of establishing equivalence across boundaries and co-ordinating the design and execution of the research. Definitions may vary and concepts and analytical techniques may not be understood on an international basis. This is all in addition to the varying quality of available marketing research agencies.

Often companies use their overseas salesforces to try to overcome these problems. However, whilst a salesman may be valuable for marketing intelligence, it is incorrect to assume he can undertake objective marketing research, since the two functions are so different. A salesman is trained to never say 'no' and is committed completely to his product. If he were asked to undertake marketing research to define promising markets, he might assume his number of sales was being questioned. If asked to establish future sales potential, he would be tempted to try and sell the respondents the number they anticipated buying. Since marketing research must ensure confidentiality, a salesman is useful only to the extent of giving his impressions of the market, warning of new products and changes in the prices of competing products and so on. Agents and distributors may also be used for such market intelligence factors but it is unlikely that they will be able to give any less dispassionate views than the salesman.

Thus the organisation of marketing research in developing countries is not easy. Indeed the enormous organisational and administrative problem in some countries may even determine what can actually be done.

The process and methods of marketing research

(a) The process

The process of marketing research described in *Marketing: An Introductory Text* (Baker, 1985) remain the same. The basic procedure involves determining (i) what kind of data would be useful to aid specific decision-making situations, (ii) how to collect it and (iii) how to use it. There should always be continuous marketing research being undertaken through secondary source data (both internal and external), whilst the planning and execution of *ad hoc* research follows the normal stages:

1. recognising and defining the problem in statable terms
2. setting the parameters
3. specifying the objectives
4. formulating the research design
5. collecting the data
6. analysing and presenting results
7. evaluating the results within the constraints used

There will always be a discrepancy between the ideal information required and the information which can be collected and/or used. But marketing research seeks to provide a compromise between the ideal and the most accurate, reliable data possible within the limits imposed by time, cost and other constraints.

Unfortunately in a developing country context these 'other constraints' are usually numerous and may vary widely even within a single country. All aspects of marketing research are affected. Secondary data may be scarce and that which is available of questionable accuracy and reliability. Primary data is usually costly to collect and hampered by sampling difficulties, poor physical and communications infrastructure and numerous cultural problems which are likely to affect such aspects as response rate and the quality and quantity of market researchers. Since good meaningful research depends upon such factors as well as a well-designed survey, a carefully chosen representative sample, organised and well-trained researchers and interviewers familiar with all local conditions, there are sizeable problems.

Although the techniques developed in the developed countries can still be applicable, extra caution and severe modifications may need to be incorporated too so that marketing research is tailored to existing conditions. Secondary data needs to be evaluated much more thoroughly, and it may be necessary to make decisions on more limited data. Indeed, secondary data may have to be relied upon more since primary data will undoubtedly be more costly to collect. A substantial investment may first be necessary to develop the basic information which will provide a sampling frame or to train interviewers. Next the problem to be investigated needs defining more clearly. A careful research design, taking into account local difficulties, is essential, as is the adaptation of research instruments. Throughout the research more supervision is likely to be necessary whilst the results must be interpreted with much more caution so that any bias by researchers and respondents is taken into account.

Thus throughout the process of marketing research – from the organisation through to the fieldwork and interpretation of results, the additional constraints typical of most developing countries call for extra care and attention.

(b) Data and methods

Despite the necessary modifications, research methods can still yield objective, reliable, sensitive, valid and inexpensive results. The following discussion highlights the problems involved with both secondary and primary data and suggests appropriate courses of action to ensure maximum benefit.

Desk research

The main objective of desk research is to save time and money. It is the logical starting point to provide broad background information against which primary data (if needed) can be put into perspective. Some secondary data will provide the actual information needed whilst other data acts as a guide – to pinpoint specific factors to be investigated further and to identify sources of information to be collected in field research. In practice both objectives are often achieved at the same time. For example, a survey in an industrial journal may provide specific data on a market and mention the companies which are the major suppliers or buyers in that market.

Secondary sources tend to receive greater emphasis in developing countries because they are quicker and cheaper in comparison with difficult primary sources. Also, since developing countries are generally likely to be interested in export markets, secondary data is useful in the first instance to identify the most promising overseas markets before further research is undertaken.

As always, secondary sources may be subdivided into internal and external. *Internal sources*, whilst the logical, most accessible, least expensive starting point, are likely to be less complete than those maintained in developed countries. This is because, firstly, indigenous companies in developing countries are likely to have been established more recently. Secondly, the six areas of purchasing, production, personnel, marketing, sales and finance mentioned by Baker (1985) may well be less complete because, due to the nature of the marketing environment, their perceived need is less. For example, an indigenous company is unlikely to have a large salesforce. Nor is it likely to monitor or evaluate it. Salesforce reports therefore will not exist. And unless it is an industrial company which has a significant amount of dialogue with its customers, data relating to customers and consumers will generally be limited.

External sources of data may be subdivided in the first instance into information acquired from personal contact and that collected from documentary sources. In developing countries personal contacts, such as competitors, colleagues, embassy and bank personnel may assume a role of greater importance since the pitfalls associated with documentary sources originating from that country may be more considerable (as detailed below). Documentary sources can be grouped under the five headings found in Baker (1985):

(i)   Government
(ii) Universities and non-profit researh organisations
(iii) Trade associations
(iv) Academic and professional journals and trade press
(v)   Commercial research organisations

However, since information will often be sought on export markets, the classification needs to be somewhat more flexible and simple to allow for different organisational/governmental regimes in different nations. The structure used here is one suggested by J. M. Livingstone (1977):

(i)   Commercial
(ii) Institutional
(iii) Competing firms
(iv) Official

After each category has been considered briefly, the types of information available and likely to be of use to a developing country are discussed. Some sources found in developed countries are also included since they will in many cases be relevant to developing countries. This is firstly because the developed countries may be export markets. Secondly, data produced here for exporters to other developed and developing countries is equally useful for exporters in developing countries exporting to these same markets.

Commercial sources

The standard marketing research agency services normally available in most developed countries are not widely available in developing countries. Certainly some agencies do exist, and more are developing. For example, the Middle East Market Research Bureau, established in 1962, is the largest research organisation in the Middle East and Africa, with offices in Nicosia, Athens, Kuwait, Beirut, Jeddah, Riyadh, Tehran and Dubai. However, whether such organisations are indigenous or international, they need to be scrutinised carefully for their expertise and ability.

In addition, standard guides, catalogues and journals may be bought, which, although largely printed in the developed world, provide information and surveys on specific developing countries too. Examples in this category include:

Quarterly reports from the Economic Intelligence Unit
Newspaper surveys, e.g. the *Financial Times* market surveys
Periodical journals, e.g. *Trade and Industry Journal, Business Week, Advertising Age*
Trade Directories of the world
Dun and Bradstreet Publications, e.g. *International Market Guide, Latin America Exporters' Encyclopaedia*
Price Waterhouse's information guides on many countries

Broad economic trends and indicators for a selection of countries may be found in such documents as *Business International, Euromonitor* and

Worldcasts. Business International provides most frequently updated indicators both economic – for example, national income, GDP, imports and exports, and so on – and selected production and consumption data, such as number of passenger cars, steel consumption and energy consumption. One hundred and thirty-one countries are covered, historical records are kept and forecasts made. *Business International* has correspondents in all major cities of the world and publishes six weekly newsletters, which detail political and economic developments affecting international business and companies' experiences. These letters concern Europe, Asia, Latin America and Eastern Europe.

Euromonitor provides a broader range of economic indicators. One of its volumes focuses on the European market, the other on the world. Data is taken from official sources such as the United Nations and thus a wealth of information is contained in a breadth of coverage. However it is not updated until revised statistics become available. Finally *Worldcasts* publishes annual statistics on general economic indicators for the world, and for individual countries.

Institutional sources

Institutional sources cover a range of organisations – Chambers of Commerce, trade associations, business and service organisations such as banks and advertising agencies, universities and polytechnics. Chambers of Commerce exist in most countries and provide a useful fund of information and experience. Often they have a library and offer advice to exporters on tariffs and other conditions. There is also an International Chamber of Commerce with headquarters in Paris.

Trade associations, on the other hand, tend not to exist in many developing countries and where they do, their usefulness varies. Many are simply pressure groups on governments but some may also have export advisory staff. They may also commission surveys and have qualified people to deal with promotional aspects. Advertising agencies are equally rare. Banks, however, are usually a good potential source of information. They often publish periodic reports or special newsletters relating to the local community. For exporters this is highly valuable background material. For example, the Banco National Commercio Exterior in Mexico publishes *Mexico Facts, Figures and Trends*. Naturally the aim of such material is to encourage further client business. A spin-off is that appropriate agents and customers (and their credit-worthiness) may be suggested, which again is very relevant.

Universities and polytechnics are usually very important sources of information for the local businessman in developing countries. They should not be overlooked and yet frequently are because there is often a clear distinction made between academics and businessmen. Local companies are reluctant to go to the universities and polytechnics even if the skills and relevant information are available, simply because they are not seen as a source of expert advice. Equally the academics tend to see themselves as educators, not industrialists, and do not want to be involved either (Kracmar, 1971).

Competing firms

Public limited companies (or the appropriate form of legal incorporation) in many countries publish annual accounts and reports. Mail order catalogues, advertisements and other material put out by companies should always be collected, for they are cheap to collect and provide background information about one's competitors. Although the amount of such data is likely to be lower in developing countries, it should, nevertheless, always be sought. In developed country markets it can be invaluable in assessing competitors' strategies and performance.

Official sources

This category is likely to be the most useful for many developing countries in terms of overall availability. Official sources may be subdivided into (i) government-produced, on a national basis and (ii) international organisations.

Government-produced data – emitted through ministries and state organisations – are often free and also often undervalued. Although the wealth of government-produced statistics available in the developed countries is unlikely to be matched in developing countries, there is usually some form of data available from ministries which are concerned with planning and industrialisation.

Censuses and economic development plans will always give some indication of future purchasing. Sometimes studies are undertaken on particular sectors and, together with other statistical information from government, may provide some indications of sales opportunities, import requirements, local marketing techniques and importers, wholesalers and buyers, all of which are useful for both the domestic and export marketer. Examples of such government-produced data include:

The Korea Statistical Yearbook
Monthly Statistics of Foreign Trade in India (1975)
Sudan Yearbook of Agricultural Statistics

Government sources produced in the developed countries may also be useful for the export marketer from developing countries. Not only will they produce background data about the conditions existing in the country itself but may also provide data on other export markets elsewhere in the world. For example, the British Overseas Trade Board (BOTB), which is responsible to the Department of Trade, publishes hints to businessmen which are designed for British exporters but which are also relevant to any exporter, irrespective of his country of origin. The BOTB also has weekly and monthly publications, whilst the Department of Trade controls the Statistics and Market Intelligence Library in London, which is open to all and provides much valuable information on many parts of the world. Again designed for the British exporter, it may be visited by exporters from developing countries who may be meeting a business contact in the United Kingdom market but who would like to learn more about another export market. Equally, in America the United States Department of Commerce publishes international marketing handbooks covering 138 countries.

International organisations

Many international organisations provide broad socio-economic indicators such as population figures, population growth, areas of countries, GNP, inflation rates, structure of production and demand, energy production and consumption. This data, unlike the earlier commercial source data, is free in most cases. For example, the United Nations and its agencies provide a wealth of information. The United Nations statistical yearbooks give social and economic data for over 250 countries. The United Nations Economic Commission conducts and publishes individual surveys, such as *An Economic Survey of Latin America*. UNCTAD publishes conference papers and special studies. In addition, other United Nations agencies such as the World Health Organisation (WHO), the International Labour Organisation (ILO) and the Food and Agricultural Organisation (FAO) provide figures in specialist fields.

Another source of general indication is the World Bank which, as shown in Chapter 1, divides countries into low income, a middle income, industrialised, capital-surplus oil exporters and planned economies. The Organisation for Economic Co-operation and Development (OECD) also provides bimonthly general economic indicators and special studies of member countries. Whilst these tend to be developed countries, nevertheless they constitute an important market for exporters from developing countries. The International Monetary Fund (IMF) produces international financial statistics monthly, and information on currency and tariffs. The General Agreement on Tariffs and Trade (GATT) supplies world trade data and the International Trade Centre (ITC) in Geneva provides useful market reports. The Council for Mutual Economic Assistance (CMEA) publishes a statistical yearbook. All these sources are particularly relevant for the export marketer.

A method for locating appropriate secondary sources

Besides consulting standard international marketing research books such as *International Marketing Research* (Douglas and Craig 1983) which might list and discuss how to use relevant secondary sources, it is also necessary to check what sources are available. A local library may be the first step in the search. Libraries generally tend to be undervalued, but inside it is likely that directories, abstracts and indices will be kept. The first directory which should be consulted is called *The World Guide to Libraries*. This lists all libraries – public, university, those attached to government and so on. Other reference books which may then be consulted include the *International Bibliography of Directories* and *Trade Directories of the World* which will indicate which directory should be sought. The *World Guide to Trade Associations* and the *Yearbook of International Organisations* are likely to be other useful guides in indicating what additional sources may be available and where.

Reference books aimed at the Western developed country exporter may still be useful for the export marketer from developing countries. For example the *European Yearbook* lists such aspects as commercial and investment banks and research institutes. Equally, abstracts and indexes should be consulted, even when these are produced for specific groups. The Department of Trade in the United Kingdom, for example, publishes through its Statistics and Market Intelligence Library handbooks listing such aspects as statistical offices in overseas countries and directories throughout the world, as well as individual booklets on specific areas. Although again aimed at the British exporter, such publications may also be invaluable to developing country exporters serving the same markets.

Once major directories, guides, abstracts and indexes have been identified, other, more specific government and commercial sources should be useful in supplementing the broader background picture.

Country handbooks, reports, economic surveys or national plan sum-
maries by government departments should always be considered, after
which journals, periodicals and institutional publications such as bank
and trade association reports can be scrutinised. Although there is no
standard procedure which will ensure that all relevant sources are
discovered, by working from the broad (directory of directories) source to
the specific, a better chance of locating sufficient sources to provide
meaningful data will result.

However, even when relevant material has been found, difficulties still
exist in its use.

Problems in the use of secondary data

There are always problems in the use of secondary data but these are
likely to be magnified in developing countries. In any context, one should
always ask who collected the data, for what purpose, how it was collected
and whether the data is internally consistent and logical in the light of
other known sources. However in developing countries sources tend to
be fewer and those which are available suffer more from problems of
accessibility, accuracy and comparability. Generally there are fewer
secondary sources and their reliability is less the lower the level of a
nation's economic development. But even amongst the newly industrialised countries, there is still not the wealth of data or the historical records
found in developed nations. And it is unlikely there will be much on
retailers, wholesalers and other facilitating services in any developing
country. The accuracy of whatever is available, at whatever level, must be
questioned. Censuses and other official statistics will vary widely in
quality and usefulness and data and this must be borne in mind even with
data published by international organisations which use raw data
supplied by governments.

The reasons are many and often interrelated. Governments may be
under-resourced. Statisticians may be unskilled and/or uncaring. There
are always the problems associated with the collection of data. Sampling
frames are usually poor or non-existent so that interviewers, using
convenience samples, may introduce significant bias into the results.
Often, too, figures are collected on an infrequent or unpredictable
schedule basis and where they are regularly collected may not be
comparable from one year (or collection date) to the next. Besides out-of-
date figures or non-comparability of figures collected on a different basis,
there is always the additional uncontrollable element of economic
development. Where this is progressing at a rapid rate, there will be

greater socio-economic change, which makes any attempt at comparability with past figures even more hazardous. Finally the reliability of data may be further questioned where lack of objectivity exists. In many developing countries national pride may be at stake when producing official figures. Consequently they are inflated or deflated or otherwise distorted to present a rosier picture. Tax evasion is another reason for businessmen to provide inaccurate figures.

Where cross-country, or even cross-regional (within the same country) comparisons are desired, problems are compounded. For example, the year of collection of census data is likely to differ internationally, as is the time interval of collection. Definitions may differ. In India a population of over 5000 constitutes an urban one. But in Kenya the corresponding figure is 2000, whilst elsewhere it may be 50 000. Similarly what constitutes a commercial vehicle, school or dwelling unit in one country may not be defined as such in the next. And sometimes the relevant 'unit' definition may be more dependent upon culture than administrative boundaries.

As a result of all these deficiencies there is an enormous need to evaluate secondary data sources much more carefully, to establish their quality, relevance and cost. Much can be discarded, for it is likely there will be duplication between sources, but no one source should be relied upon until it has been cross-checked with others. In order to establish the data's validity, reliability and homogeneity, it is always necessary to ask about the following areas:

1. *Coverage*: Does the data cover the subject comprehensively, and if it is to be compared with previous records, does it follow a similar format?
2. *Level*: Is the level right? For example, is it sufficiently technical, or too technical?
3. *Emphasis*: What is the bias? Depending upon why the information has been collected, there will be an obvious bias. For example, a bank report will have a financial bias.
4. *Timeliness*: Is the right period covered? Is the information out-of-date, or have subsequent events caused it to become outdated?
5. *Accessibility*: Can the data be used quickly, conveniently and cheaply?
6. *Accuracy*: How close is the source to primary material? Is the data internally consistent and logical in the light of other known data sources and market factors? Here one should ask who collected the data and how.
7. *Relevance*: Does the data source specifically help the area of decision-making under examination?
8. *Cost*: How much does the information cost and what benefit will it yield? No information is free since any information at least takes time to collect. Selectivity is all important. It may be more beneficial to pay

dearly for specific data than collect wider, broader figures more cheaply.

Field research

Despite the need to evaluate secondary sources of data extremely carefully, users will, in many cases, rely upon such data rather than investigate further through field research. This is because the difficulties of field research in many developing countries are formidable. There are social, psychological, economic, technical and political problems to be overcome.

Nevertheless, as economies develop, as the value of marketing is noted and as exporting actively increases, the need for field research also increases. Indeed, in some cases, it may be the only way to answer such questions as how people buy, how much, where and when they buy, how much profit is possible and what is the best way to market one's product. Secondary sources are unlikely to yield answers to questions on colour, taste, size preference, performance expectations and general attitudes and behaviour, and although the five areas of research (advertising, consumer behaviour, distribution, packaging and product) may not receive the emphasis they currently do in developed countries, increasingly they will.

The basic aspects of sampling, establishing contact, questionnaire design and attitude scales, as described by Baker (1985) remain relevant. However the different environment has to be taken into account. Once the major factors which create problems have been considered, the likely sampling and non-sampling errors which arise, and the modifications which are required to permit the most objective, reliable, sensitive, valid and inexpensive results are discussed.

Collection of primary data

As usual there are three main methods used to collect primary data – observation, experimentation and sample survey. The same limitations as mentioned in Baker (1985) still apply. However, observation in developing countries may be of greater significance, since often it is the only way to draw up a sampling frame. The use of experimentation, on the other hand, is less likely while the sample survey is, not surprisingly, the technique used the most.

A sample survey may be undertaken in three ways – by mail, by telephone and by personal interview. In addition to the problems mentioned by Baker (1985, p. 191), there are additional difficulties – particularly on the technical and social side – in developing countries, which cause an even greater emphasis to be given to personal interviews. Where a poor postal service coupled with low literacy levels exists, a mail survey becomes impossible. But even where conditions allow a postal survey the generally low response rate associated with this technique is normally even lower in developing countries, due to cultural constraints such as unwillingness to respond to an unknown individual. If follow-up efforts are used only an 8–15 per cent return can be expected in towns and cities (Kracmar 1971).

Mass telephone surveys, too, are often impossible where the communications infrastructure is poor and where telephone ownership is low. If this method is used, it may still be a fast, inexpensive way of attempting to interview the rich minority whose buying power is likely to be different from that of the average person. Nevertheless the response rate is still likely to be low, due to cultural constraints.

In many situations personal interviews are the only alternative. More expensive and time-consuming, this technique is likely to face many extra social, cultural and technical constraints which do not figure in developed countries. For example, poor physical communications – lack of roads, cars and regular public transport – may limit such a survey to urban areas. Access to political interviewers may then be further hindered by social or cultural constraints. For example, individual opinions may be shifted by group norms, especially in rural areas where a formal spokesman or village elder may exist. It may not be feasible to interview women who are unwilling to talk to strangers, as occurs in Moslem countries and businessmen may be unco-operative for fear of giving information to competitors, or to the government who would use it for tax purposes. On top of the social constraints, where different languages and dialects exist within a country, there is the extra complication and cost of translation and back-translation. And even where there is no language barrier, there may be 'technical' illiteracy, so that respondents give a negative or wrong answer unless new concepts are adequately explained. Finally, where there is a lack of education, the availability of well-trained interviewers is a further obstacle.

And even if all these difficulties are overcome, results may still be useless, due to the way in which the sample was drawn up. Thus the mathematical aspect associated with sampling must go hand in hand with the collection of data. A perfect sample is useless if the data collected is incorrect, fragmentary or misleading. Conversely the information gathered from the best conducted interviews would be likely to lead to serious errors of interpretation if it were unduly extended to whole groups through no more than individual cases. Therefore both sampling and non-sampling errors must be considered and relevant modifications to technique made in order to account for the conditions existing in developing countries. These are considered next.

Sampling problems, errors and modifications needed in developing countries

Sampling is likely to be more difficult in developing countries because of non-existent or poor sampling frames. Coupled with, in many cases, questionable competence and honesty of the sampling field staff, sampling error and bias results.

In developed and some newly industrialised countries, such as Singapore, it is possible to get a good idea of the total population to be studied: its composition, location and the rest. From this a probability-based sample can be drawn up, with predictable error and deviation from the universal. But if there are no registers, no age/sex breakdowns, no telephone directories, no maps or out-dated maps, no numbering of dwelling units, it is very difficult to get details of universal characteristics from which meaningful samples can be drawn. This is the case for many areas within developing countries. Even where sampling frames exist, as they do in most municipalities where election registers and household lists are usually kept, they may be inaccurate or incorrectly used.

Thus, because of poor sampling resources, the low competence of management and staff doing the sampling, and poor, often mobile, groups of people, large segments of the population may be missed. Even between two cities there may be discrepancies. For example, Rio de Janeiro and Sao Paulo have different sampling frames because sampling resources tend to be distributed differentially throughout the nation. A 'national urban sample', combining these different sampling frames in different cities, is likely to yield less than perfectly accurate results. An additional problem is that of *maintaining* adequate sampling frames in rapidly expanding cities. The expense of keeping them up-to-date is often prohibitive. And even where some historical records exist, and past samples have been used, it is important to establish sampling bias as regards, for example, what is considered a 'dwelling unit' in different areas. Consequently the coverage and comparability of existing sampling frames in developing countries often leave much to be desired and modifications in the sampling procedure are necessary.

Firstly, because of the lack of comprehensive information on the target population and the costs of establishing such details, convenience, judgement, quotas and snowball sampling may have to be relied upon rather than probability random sampling. Such methods are usually more cost effective, especially since personal interviews have to be relied on to a greater extent. *Convenience samples* are undoubtedly the lowest cost method of sampling. However, they are not likely to yield the most accurate results.

Judgement sampling is based on the assumption that some people in a developing country are better informed about a certain field and can therefore provide a realistic sample. Questioning of a village elder, priest or other local authority figure, for example, may provide enough information on number of inhabitants, current purchase behaviour, and so on.

Quota sampling again requires some form of informed advice to be able to set quotas for given categories whilst *snowball sampling* involves choosing initial respondents randomly and subsequent respondents are found from initial interviewees. Limitations involved with using all these methods must be borne in mind.

Secondly more samples (and more discriminating samples) are likely to be required, due to fragmented, different markets within developing countries. Each sample should be representative of the population that represents a potential market. Two extremes might be affluent consumers in the cities and the poorer, more self-sufficient consumers of rural areas. Under such circumstances, inadequate clustering procedures are often employed. Rural areas just outside cities are often chosen, in order to reduce the cost of transport and supervision of interviewers. This usually results in an increase in the margin of error. A better method, which is possible if time and financial resources permit, is for researchers first to devise their own sampling frame through observation. This is particularly useful where there is a poor, mobile population under study or where rapid economic development makes sampling frames rapidly out-of-date or where no sampling frame data at all exists. If there are no maps of urban houses or blocks, researchers can prepare these themselves and number the dwelling units in a logical fashion. Then a number of houses can be randomly sampled. For rural areas a random walk procedure, sampling at the same time, can be employed.

Thus obstacles can be overcome and as countries advance and their data bases improve, probability sampling will become increasingly possible. In the meantime sampling errors must be minimised through using the best technique within the given constraints and ensuring the competence of sampling staff.

Non-sampling problems, errors and modifications needed in developing countries

Much has been written on sampling error but this is likely to be small in relation to non-sampling error which is more likely where many cultural groups are concerned (Davis et al., 1981). Indeed, cultural factors explain most non-sampling errors. In the formulation of survey design topic errors may occur. In the implementation of the survey there is the danger of both interviewer and respondent bias, often because of such factors as social acquiescence, courtesy, social desirability or specific cultural traits. In the analysis the evaluation of data interpretation bias is possible. This may be due to lack of perfect familiarity with the respondents' environment or incomplete training.

Although the different types of error are often interrelated topic bias, interviewer bias, respondent bias and interpretation bias will each be considered separately, after which methods of reducing bias are discussed.

Topic bias

Language is always likely to be a problem, especially where several languages or dialects are common. There will always be lexical, idiomatic, grammatical, syntactical and conceptual difficulties. But these are aggravated if there are low levels of literacy making written questions useless. Furthermore there may be different conceptions of such factors as time, income, debt, employment and distance and these may also have different meanings at different times of the year. Thus even 'factual' topics are problematic.

In order to avoid these errors as far as possible, a high degree of cultural understanding is essential so that familiarity with customer, viewpoints, semantics, attitudes and business customs is achieved. Where numerous languages are concerned translations and translations back into the original language must be rigorously undertaken.

Interviewer bias

In many developing countries research staff with specific skills, such as ability to conduct in-depth interviews, may not be available. For example, in India interviewers tend to be 'jack of all trades' and are not regarded highly since the status of marketing research is poor. Women may be difficult to recruit if the culture places less emphasis on education for girls. If skills and integrity are lacking, errors in recording responses will result. If imported researchers with the appropriate skills are used they may not be able to establish contact, let alone rapport with respondents because of language and other cultural barriers.

Interviewers should be of the same racial group as the people being interviewed. Even the social class of interviewers in many places should be as near as possible to that of respondents. But usually such trained interviewers with the correct social background are difficult to find, while local people with the right cultural and social characteristics will not have the necessary interviewing skills.

The only answer in many instances is to recruit and train new staff. If possible such candidates should be of above average intelligence, pleasing in personality, able to mix with others well, inquiring, observant, reliable, honest and knowledgeable about the commercial world. However the ideal and the reality are usually very different and a compromise is often necessary. For social and political surveys village headmen, teachers and county prefects have been found to be good interviewers (Frey, 1970). But until a body of competent research staff is built up, interviewer bias is likely to remain a problem in the near future.

Respondent bias

There are many reasons why there is frequently response error. Firstly *non-response* is one problem which results from social and cultural inaccessibility in certain groups. Within a country there will be distinct population groups differing in their accessibility, but between countries the problem is likely to be worse. Men may be inaccessible in some countries, women in others. For example, Thai and Indonesian women are unlikely to talk to strangers, while Indian women require some known acquaintance to accompany the interviewer. Businessmen in some cultures will regard the objective of interviewing as industrial espionage, and will therefore be reluctant to give figures on such aspects as profits or technical collaboration. Telephone interviews in such circumstances are undoubtedly out of the question. It may even be preferable – under such circumstances as are typical of India – to knock on doors, hoping to obtain an interview, rather than to try and make an appointment by telephone first.

Another instance where non-response may be a problem is where minorities within countries are held in low esteem, as is the case with the Chinese in Malaysia. This group is likely to show a marked reluctance to answer political questions. Yet because they constitute an important, large minority, they cannot be ignored. Finally, non-response through the individual not being at home may be common. This is normal if women work alongside their husbands in the fields as in some parts of Malawi and Mozambique.

A second source of bias which results in errors being introduced is *social acquiescence* or *courtesy bias* by the respondent. This is particularly common in Southeast Asia. Under such circumstances the respondent seeks to please the interviewer, because norms governing interpersonal relations suggest he must do so when dealing with higher social class strangers. The rules of courtesy are strict and demand self-control. They do not permit opinions which are felt to be contrary to what is expected.

In order to reduce courtesy bias, a number of techniques are possible. Firstly the sponsorship of the study should be concealed. Secondly interviewers should be trained effectively. Thirdly the wording of questions should be chosen carefully so as to minimise courtesy bias. No pleasing coded answers should be used. Pictures rather than coded responses is another solution, as is the use of phrases like 'people tell me that . . .' which help to make the respondent feel he is not alone in an embarrassing position. Using a middleman may be useful if the interviewer and interviewee are a long way apart socially.

Closely related to courtesy bias is *social desirability* bias. Here the respondent seeks both to please the interviewer and to be seen to be doing the done thing. It is necessary under such circumstances to understand what is socially desirable in the culture or social group under examination and try and ensure that allowance is made.

A fourth, overlapping aspect is *cultural trait* bias. Sophistication, loquacity and articulateness vary from culture to culture. Yea- or nay-saying may be evident. The Chinese in Malaysia have been found to be more reluctant to answer questions than the Malaysians or Indians, who are noted for being yea-sayers. The Chinese consequently give more 'no' and 'don't know' answers and shorter responses to open-ended questions. Willingness to respond has also been correlated with income and/or age (Douglas and Shoemaker, 1981). However, when several different groups are being studied, it is possible to overcome cultural trait discrepancies by using correlation techniques. For assessing the correlation of responses of groups to similar items, data may be normalised.

In other circumstances cultural traits produce other effects. For example, in the Middle East respondents are prone to exaggeration, particularly in relation to achievements, class positions and knowledge. Elsewhere they may result in difficulty in getting any responses, particularly in relation to certain topics. For example, in India individuals may feel they have no right to answer. This is also true in other tradition-directed societies where the lower classes have no opinions.

To overcome such situations it is first necessary to identify topics which are culturally sensitive. Secondly it may be necessary to gain permission from a village elder or headman or someone else in authority so that respondents feel the local leader is sponsoring or supporting the survey. But even their responses are likely to reflect a general, collective rather than individual, opinion. An alternative is to have resident interviewers who can check on the information provided and recognise inconsistencies.

The perception of the interviewer, however, is a much broader problem. In many countries the interviewer is regarded with suspicion. If he is considered to be a government employee or, worse, an inspector of taxes, respondents will be reluctant to provide information. Sometimes such difficulties can be overcome by arranging interviews through a trade association, chamber of commerce or friends, so that confidence is gained. On other occasions it may help to stress the authority of the interviewer by emphasising his institute or organisation. Another possibility is to appeal to the respondent's self-interest by offering him a copy of the results.

However under some circumstances more needs to be done. Agencies in developing countries often use college students – from middle and upper-class backgrounds. Because of the way they are perceived, communication problems may result. Alternatively interviews are sometimes conducted in the presence of a third party 'clinical witness'. The implications for the data being collected will vary according to (i) the content of the questionnaire, (ii) the status of the third party and (iii) general culture rules. Where sharp status and authority cleavages are most marked the effect of the third party is greatest. In order to overcome the probable bias ballots, teams of interviewers or resident interviewers can be used.

Other situations are more difficult to remedy. Male interviewers may be essential, for example where women refuse to travel alone or enter poor areas with inadequate lighting or a high crime rate. The response rate under such circumstances will be low and errors may be large.

Interpretation bias

All previous types of errors should be considered when interpreting the results of the survey. Thus bias resulting from the assumed meaning of words, from attitudes of respondents and interviewers, from willingness to respond and all other sources of error must be carefully assessed. If not, more errors will occur. And, if the competence of the person interpreting the figures is not high, even more of a danger exists. This is especially true in a culturally complex environment where more than one person may need to interpret results. Extra care and attention by competent staff is therefore the only way to attain the best evaluation.

Overcoming problems in field research

Bias arises from many areas, but throughout the process of field research many aspects can be carefully examined to eliminate as much as possible. In the design stage it is necessary to be careful in defining the problem and anticipating difficulties. Equally, in drafting the questionnaire, a knowledge of the social, psychological and ethnic aspects of a society is essential. This will indicate how people are likely to respond to specific topics and questions, whether their personal details are regarded as extremely private, whether they are willing or not to spend time being interviewed and what likely biases are likely in the way in which they respond. People's verbosity, sophistication, credibility, conformity and extremism of response should always be examined. Such information will give guidelines for types of scales possible, the necessary wording or other form of presentation, the length of questionnaire and the best type of question to use.

When scales are used it is first necessary to establish that the respondents will understand them. Next it must be established whether they will go for extreme points, as is typical in many parts of Latin America, or the mid points as is common elsewhere. Wording, too, must be clear, and where different languages and cultures are involved conceptual equivalence must be checked to ensure that the same thing is being measured. Linguistic resources may need to be large. For example, a national study of the Philippines will involve nine languages, of Indonesia thirty languages. In such instances pre-coded questions should be avoided as they lead to most errors. It is often preferable to attach a rationale for each question so that it can be constructed correctly for each environment. And whilst verbal rating scales are desirable in some areas where literacy levels are low, non-verbal stimuli may be essential. Symbols, pictures, steps or even samples – where consumers have not been exposed to products being tested – are alternatives.

The length of questionnaire is another consideration where respondents have a short attention-span, many sessions of interviews may be necessary. More time and money spent pretesting may be essential. The type of question can also be changed. Open-ended questions, as noted above, are likely to result in less cultural bias where many different cultures are being interviewed and where the interviewer knows less about a respondent's culture and life-style. However analysis and coding afterwards may prove problematic. Direct questions may in some instances avoid ambiguity but where respondents are unwilling to answer certain types of questions or where socially acceptable answers are given, indirect questions may need to be used.

If such modifications are made research may still be objective, (that is, classified in the same way by different people or different modes of research), reliable, sensitive (measuring something under the control of the decision maker), valid (measuring what the research is supposed to measure) and inexpensive (yielding the most information per unit cost of production).

Conclusion

To argue that it is impossible to bring modern marketing research techniques developed in developed countries into developing countries hitherto untouched by them is fallacious. As has been demonstrated, the need for marketing research is strong and strengthening. The objectives and scope of marketing research will always be the same in any environment since the basic aim is to try to reduce uncertainty in order to make better decisions.

Undoubtedly there are extra difficulties involved in undertaking marketing research in developing countries. The rapid rate of change occurring in many economies makes for problems in maintaining adequate data bases. But at the same time, as economies develop, there is an increased need for both secondary sources and primary research method skills. Unfortunately the lack of research skills and a poor appreciation of the value of marketing research generally hamper the situation. The indigenous marketer may not see the need for any marketing research at all, while the government official, at worst, may well fear that results from it will expose his inadequacies. Finally the multinational marketer, although well versed in marketing research, has a tendency to use it, to determine the acceptability of an established product and the political risks, in a product-orientated fashion.

Consequently few indigenous firms have marketing research departments, commercial marketing research services are often limited and government departments do not use marketing research sufficiently. Yet the need to upgrade official statistical information, to use more research in private companies and to develop independent research organisations is obvious and is accepted by many nations. Initially problems will remain until the adequate documentary detail and infrastructure are established.

However the overall process of marketing research remains valid, and with extra caution and modifications to take account of the difficult cultural, economic and physical conditions found in developing countries, research methods can yield useful results. Desk research, despite the care needed in interpreting data, still provides valuable material. Sources exist for most customers on the local, national and international levels and provide the marketer with useful broad indicators. Indeed secondary sources tend to be relied upon fairly heavily. Field research is often most hazardous and reliance on certain methods and techniques may be greater in order to eliminate the likely sampling and non-sampling errors.

But, despite the limitations and modifications necessary, the undertaking of marketing research is essential for all aspects of marketing. It is particularly relevant if the marketing mix, considered in the next chapter, is to be optimally formulated.

CHAPTER 5

The marketing mix in developing countries

Contents

Introduction

The marketing mix, like marketing research, needs more careful consideration in a developing country context. Not only is the external environment more difficult, but also the internal constraints which affect the formulation of the marketing mix are likely to be more numerous and harder to overcome.

In the broader marketing environment the complexity of cultural, legal, political, economic and financial frameworks results in a need for more marketing mixes to be formulated to suit individual segments of the population. In broad terms the rich urban sub-culture will normally require one mix (more akin to that used in developed countries) while the rural segment will require another completely different one. Here processed, instant foods, labour saving devices and retail outlets in the form of supermarkets will be replaced by traditional foodstuffs, greater resistance to new products and more emphasis on personal selling by market traders. On top of this dualism, there will usually be a need to formulate many more mixes to correspond to different ethnic groups, languages, religions, non-indigenous minorities or even certain professional groups. For example, as mentioned in Chapter 3, in some parts of Africa public officials of newly-independent states have taken over the symbols and houses of their previous European imperialist masters.

In any context the external marketing environment will influence the way in which each marketing mix variable is used. But because many more factors have to be taken into consideration in developing countries, extra complications are evident. For example, colonial and historical effects may have resulted in attitudes and values which require certain (sometimes unexpected) adjustments to promotional themes and strategies. Themes involving health, strength and vitality are usually successful for promoting a wide range of products in newly independent African states. Conversely, the product itself may not need to be changed, even if it appears inappropriate at first sight. Nivea cream, for example, is acceptable especially if promotion stresses the whiteness of skin, since an African is more likely to reject a product he/she feels has been created specially for him/her.

Finally external factors also often determine how certain marketing mix elements can be used. The distribution system and its organisation, the availability of media, the extent of competition and the level and structure of disposable income and education, as discussed in Chapter 2, will put certain constraints on the scope of each marketing mix element. Generally less sophistication will be possible and many modifications will have to be made. Some questions which need to be asked are summarised in Table 5.1. Further, on-going complications resulting from perpetual change and an increasingly active role by Government – especially in the distribution and pricing areas – need constant monitoring and call for additional responses.

Although marketing research, if effectively carried out, can indicate the right marketing mix to mitigate successfully the limitations which result from the external, uncontrollable factors, the internal organisational constraints are often more difficult to overcome and result in self-imposed sub-optimal marketing mixes. This is particularly true of the indigenous and governmental marketer.

In terms of the indigenous marketer, the very conditions which characterise the typical external environment, such as strained communications, a sellers' market, no price competition, a monopoly or cartel situation and tied distribution systems, breed certain attitudes and practices. Complacency and an inability and/or an unwillingness to

Table 5.1 External factors to be considered in the formulation of the marketing mix

	Product and design	Branding and Packaging	Communications	Distribution	Pricing
Social and Physical Environment	Attitudes to colour, shape? Climatic problems? PLC situation and expectations?	Suitable, pronounceable names?	Language? Literacy levels? Attitudes to advertising, promotion, salesforce?	Buying habits? Physical transport possibilities?	Attitudes to price? Disposable income levels?
Competition	Competing products' strengths and weaknesses?	Effectiveness of competing brand names & images? Quality of competitors' packaging?	Advertising practices used? Successful messages?	Channels used and costs?	Price used and scope for change?
Institutions	Bodies controlling standards? Issuing advice?	Institutions to help choose brand names?	PR facilities? Media research? Code of advertising?	Level of infrastructure? Government-controlled channels? Cartels?	Government controlled prices?
Legal systems	Laws affecting the use of a product – safety, pollution? Constraints on shapes, sizes? Legislation on weights, measures?	Trademark protection? Legislation on packaging?	Use of languages? Trade description legislation? Laws governing selling practices?	Laws related to transport? Channel members?	Resale price maintenance? Price regulation?

Source: Adapted from S. Majaro, *International Marketing* (London: George Allen & Unwin, 1977).

measure the success or failure of a brand or product on its own merit become typical. High pricing and low quality being the norm in many cases, there is no incentive to understand the market or develop new products. Promotion is unlikely to be used adequately, while distribution is usually inadequate to cope with market demand. Consequently the formulation of the most satisfactory marketing mix tends to be elusive. And whilst domestically, in the short term, this may not be of fundamental significance, in international markets the consequences are usually severely negative. Nowhere is this more obvious than in the production and sale of agricultural products. Because the market is little understood and no attention is given to the correct corresponding marketing mix, the right production, handling, packaging, processing and grading of products are seldom achieved. Much physical waste and loss of revenue results.

The governmental marketer is usually largely responsible for waste and inefficiency in agricultural production and marketing. Not only is he unlikely to be adequately trained in the use of marketing generally, but, as more of a 'planner', he may well perceive marketing mix elements in a very different light than that which would be most fruitful. He may well be used to controlling areas such as production, pricing and distribution, usually in isolation from each other and in response to some ill-thought-out forecast. Consequently the formulation of the most successful marketing mix is unlikely to occur.

The multinational marketer, however, tends to have fewer problems, especially where product policy and advertising are standardised internationally. A successful marketing mix for the home market having been created, this is often 'imposed', with as few modifications as possible, on new markets. And where obstacles are very great, the initiative is taken to overcome them, as shown by many multinationals setting up their own distribution channels. Already understanding and using the marketing mix optimally in more sophisticated markets, the multinational benefits from the 'prestige' and 'image' associated with being an international enterprise, which considerably widens the scope for using the marketing mix to best effect in developing countries.

This chapter examines each marketing mix element, the problems, possibilities and modifications which must be made and the way in which each tends to be used by the indigenous, multinational and governmental marketer. Although reference where relevant will be made to *Marketing: An Introductory Text* (Baker, 1985), the emphasis will be on building upon this basic foundation, for one cannot assume that the function and impact of a marketing mix element as used in the developed world will be the same in developing countries. After each element has been examined some examples of the use of the marketing mix in selected countries will be discussed.

Product policy, planning and development

In Baker (1985) product policy is emphasised as perhaps the major factor
which determines the success of a company. Yet even in developed
countries where there is intense competition, product policy tends to be
poorly planned and often too narrow a perspective is taken. For
successful operation a company must continually appraise the wider
business situation and devise new and better ways of satisfying basic
needs. New product development, especially where shortening product
life cycles are evident, becomes imperative. Finally it is important
continually to monitor the performance of all products, and product
portfolio analysis has been found useful to this end.

In developing countries, although the basic principles of product policy
and product development remain valid, even less attention is paid to
them by indigenous and governmental marketers, while multinational
marketers have other (often more product-orientated) goals. Much can be
attributed to the different internal and external marketing environments
which dictate generally longer product life cycles, a much reduced need
for new product development and a greater emphasis on adapting
products developed for other markets.

In most cases the manufactured products sold in developing countries
have already been established in developed countries. The multinational
enterprise is largely responsible for introducing them. Product policy of
the multinational will consequently influence to a significant extent the
product policies of the indigenous marketer. Generally the core product
manufactured by the multinational in a developing country remains the
same (unless impossible to produce and/or use because of the productive
or technical infrastructure). However the additional aspects, such as
quality, life expectancy, packaging and labelling, which make up the
augmented product may well be changed to match local circumstances.
Levels of education and consumers' disposable income, cultural values,
the technical infrastructure and industrial structure are likely to have a
profound effect. For example, attitudes to colour, shape and general
appearance may necessitate some changes to design and colour. Culture
is also likely to affect branding and labelling, for it must be ascertained
whether the name is suitable, pronounceable, easily recalled and conveys
the correct message and so on. Packaging, too, will need to be re-assessed
in the light of physical factors such as climate and availability of materials.
Despite safety and pollution legislation being generally less, legal
constraints may still affect both functional and design aspects of the
product. There may be trade description rules and regulations concerning
shape, weight, measures and prohibited materials.

Likely modifications include (i) generally higher durability, since
developing countries, not unnaturally in conditions of scarcity, have

embraced planned obsolescence and a throw-away attitude to a much lesser extent; (ii) fewer numbers and versions of products to match lower income levels and, often, poor storage facilities; (iii) more robust products requiring less maintenance, to take account of lower skills and the desire for durability; (iv) simplification of markings to match literacy levels and (v) more manual versions if the technical infrastructure is poor or if convenience products and labour-saving devices are not relevant in a cheap labour situation. These changes are summarised in Table 5.2.

Table 5.2 Typical modifications necessary when products designed for developed country markets are introduced to developing country markets

Limiting factor	Modification necessary
Low technical skills	Simplification of product
Low labour cost plus poorer technical infrastructure	More manual versions
Low literacy	Simplification of product and markings
Low income levels	Different price/quality ratio
	Longer life-expectancy of product
Different maintenance expectations and/or isolation	More robust product

Naturally, as always, there will be variations between developing countries and within any developing country. For example, in a rural area with no electricity a robust sewing machine operated by a treadle will be more appropriate than the most up-to-date sewing machine which may be acceptable in the urban areas. Equally, reusable containers may be a major selling point in poorer areas, whilst throwaway containers may be the norm in the more sophisticated urban market.

Notwithstanding these slight modifications, which may be essential, multinational companies to a very large extent prefer, and have the power in most developing countries, to adopt a product standardisation policy. This is particularly the case with numerous consumer durable goods and cars. Basing their approach on the assumption that consumer tastes throughout the world are converging, which may well be true in certain fields, as shown in Chapter 3 (pp. 70–4), there are many benefits which result. Firstly economies of scale are possible through long production runs. Next there are also economies to be gained in research and development expenditure, since less effort is required for individual markets and all resources can be channelled towards new product development, essential in competitive developed world markets. Thirdly economies are also possible in marketing. For, despite the need to translate such documents as sales literature, training manuals and so on, very often the beneficial carry-over effect of a standardised promotional campaign can provide an extra return on advertising. Fourthly, in relation to consumer goods, it is a fact that consumer mobility is increasing. Naturally if the same product is available throughout the world more acceptance and recognition results and sales increase. Finally the multi-national can use its Western 'prestige' image of sophisticated technology as a major selling point, thus to a large extent adapting the market to the product rather than the product to the market.

The different usage conditions caused by climate, skills and national habits, the different market factors resulting from income levels, the size and nature of demand and consumer tastes, and the legislative environment may necessitate the multinational's building a product to higher or lower standards, or even building a different generation of products now obsolete in developed countries, such as the VW Beetle which is still constructed in Brazil. But basically the policy of product standardisation is still evident. For industrial products buyers are normally more uniform. Product performance specifications, delivery dates and price are usually the most important factors, the product itself being fairly standard. However the level of economic development will determine the sophistication of the industrial infrastructure and there may be differences in operating and maintenance specifications.

Equally the export marketer, whether from a developed or a developing country, whether a multinational enterprise or not, will have similar product-orientated considerations. The idea of finding needs and filling them will be less important than making the minimum modifications to existing products sold in the domestic market. Selecting which products to export from an existing line may be the biggest problem. Ideally products which are selected should meet the company's goals as well as offer the greatest potential for growth and profits. By examining the domestic product line (which tends to be a function of tradition, inertia, lack of good cost-profit analysis, vested interest and, more defensibly, common raw material inputs, excess capacity, acquisition and merger, and response to the competitive situation) strengths can be identified and matched with opportunities in the export market. The competitive situation both at home and overseas, the market situation and the method and cost of entry will all be major influences. The resulting product line will tend to be shorter, but should nevertheless result from a cost-benefit analysis to determine what existing products should be sold in the developing country.

Culture is a factor which should be analysed very closely in this context. If correctly understood, big profits for the export company result. However, incomplete understanding has led to many costly mistakes.

• For example, Kuwait provides the largest export market for Philips' video recorders, reflecting the cultural importance given to entertainment in the home. After-sales service, or emphasis on prestige, style and brand-name can win a competitive advantage in the whole of the Arabian Gulf and the Japanese have been particularly successful in offering service, maintenance and repair of products which also symbolise status, prestige and prosperity. Alternatively, automatic dishwashers were unsuccessful, despite the Arab's high disposable income and liking for western, technologically-advanced goods. This was because firstly the product was not sufficiently adapted to accommodate the large communal dishes and extremely small cups used, and secondly such labour-saving devices are seen as unnecessary where people are sufficiently rich to employ servants. Equally western clothes and products which violate religious values are unacceptable. Generally, however, these products are in the minority, and once sensitivity to local circumstance has been developed, the appropriate products from an existing line can be selected for export.

The above product policies of the multinational and export marketer have a profound impact on the indigenous marketer in the developing country. They largely determine what products he will manufacture. However the industrialisation policy of the country must also be considered. The large rich developing country has the negotiating power to insist on local ownership and production specifically for the domestic market. Under such circumstances a global policy of product standardisation by the multinational is much more difficult and, on first sight, it would appear that a greater marketing-orientation would be adopted. This would be particularly beneficial since in such countries an indigenisation policy tends to exist alongside and good indigenous marketers would be 'grown'. Sadly governmental goals are often questionable and the resulting product and production process may be inappropriate. These issues will be discussed in greater detail in Chapter 7. Suffice it here to say that if the government's goal either of employment or foreign exchange or sophisticated technology (if the government is sure of its goals!) calls for one product or production process, this may not be the most beneficial for the economy as a whole. Worse, often several objectives are desired and whilst a certain production process meets one, for example employment, it fails to meet another, for example foreign exchange. Equally a product should be useful and affordable for the user. But often this type of country protects its domestic production and since labour costs may be high and there is no effective competition, the consumer suffers. Further, if labour-intensive technology suitable to local conditions is insisted upon (and this may be the most appropriate), what is made locally may be obsolete and therefore uncompetitive on world markets. In the long run problems are inevitable.

Consequently the indigenous marketer who is born out of this process has no incentive to be efficient and any local competition which develops follows suit. In other newly industrialised countries which have adopted export-earning, outward-looking policies, the multinational marketer remains dominant and more free to carry out a global standardisation policy. This may cause a reduction in local competition in certain fields but has also tended to stimulate more competitiveness domestically and internationally in indigenous marketers in other fields.

However, outside the most successful newly industrialised countries (particularly the small, poor ones), indigenous marketers tend to cater solely for small domestic markets and the resultant situation is very different. Generally perspectives are limited. The type of product manufactured is a substitute for that produced by the multinational or foreign export firms. There is little concern with quality which tends to be low, or with finding needs and satisfying them. Instead there is a preoccupation with the actual production process. Because there is a big demand, machines work to full capacity and often break down. The whole effort is devoted to keeping them working. Packaging is infrequently changed, since the major difficulty is trying to meet demand. Indeed, sales volume is likely to be restricted only by productive capacity.

Since most products are in the growth or early maturity phase of the product life cycle, and product life cycles are likely to be longer overall, the indigenous marketer has no incentive to be heavily involved in product planning or development. Any new products are first introduced by the multinational and the local entrepreneur will follow. Furthermore he is unlikely to have the finance (or marketing advantages possessed by the multinational) to introduce completely new products himself, and since his horizons tend to be limited is unlikely to be involved in any exporting. Yet, unless he manages to enter a wider, richer market, there is always the danger that he will remain at a disadvantage, and his product policy, although viable in the short term, will fail once needs become satiated. This factor is well demonstrated by the governmental marketer in the field of agriculture. Products are frequently at a disadvantage on world markets, yet with greater appreciation of product policy great advances could be made.

Although it would appear that the multinational holds all the trump cards in the form of a global perspective, tangible and non-tangible (for example, prestige) marketing advantages, many indigenous and governmental marketers can (and must) improve their situation by developing better product policy and a wider marketing perspective. Although this may be extremely difficult, given the situation in which some indigenous marketers are operating, only by monitoring product performance, developing new, more competitive products and supplying wider markets can they hope to survive and prosper in the long term.

Promotion

The promotional activities dealt with under this section include advertising, sales promotion, personal selling and public relations. Branding, packaging and labelling, already mentioned above under product policy, are again considered briefly. The relevant chapters (13, 16, 17, 18, 19) of Baker (1985) remain fundamental but as always certain differences are apparent and some modifications are necessary. Promotion is always the most visible marketing mix element and the overall objective of all communications – to communicate a message to a firm's audience so as to achieve certain goals in any context – is the same. However the possibilities for using it may be more restricted, whilst its impact is often greater, in a developing country context. This is because firstly promotion is the most culture-bound element of the marketing mix and secondly the necessary infrastructure which allows promotion to function in a developed country context is often lacking. Conversely, simply because of the lack of its widespread use, greater notice is taken of that which does exist.

All marketers, whether indigenous, multinational or governmental, are constrained by external and internal factors when using promotion. Culture, with its impact on education, norms of religion, social values and tradition, is the first major stumbling-block. Culture will determine the who, where and how of buying, indicating which promotional mix element should be used and how it should be used to make it meaningful, verifiable and acceptable. Equally, language and literacy levels, the hostility and receptivity of consumers to advertising, and the consumer's relationship with and attitude towards the seller must all be taken into account.

However the influence of the level of economic development is closely related. Generally the lower the level of economic development and the lower the disposable income, the less the scope the marketer has in his promotional mix. In low-income economies, where a sellers' market is typical, promotion if often perceived (particularly by the indigenous marketer) as unnecessary, and there is usually a strong correlation between level of economic development and advertising expenditure. Furthermore the supporting infrastructure is likely to be much poorer, so that advertising agencies and media are extremely limited, branding non-existent, packaging largely irrelevant and personal selling may be the only promotional mix element which has any real value. However it must always be remembered that in any developing country there may be remarkable variety within the nation of availability, cost and output of the communications infrastructure. Consequently, communications in any one developing country can range from the primitive to the most sophisticated, from brute force and coercion in the traditional or collective market to soft persuasive selling in the richer urban areas.

The legal framework is more constant. Governments may have a restrictive or a permissive approach towards promotion. Generally governmental interference tends to be less, but since communications are growing in most developing countries and competition is increasing, this may become more important in the future.

Finally the internal constraints of any organisation cannot be ignored. Again culture is important. To compound the indigenous marketer's problem of limited financial resources resulting in a reduced scope for promotional activities, his ability to use promotion may well be in doubt. This is because, in addition to his apathy created by his strong position in a sellers' market, his educational background tends to be non-business. Consequently, his appreciation of marketing as a whole is poor. The governmental marketer also may well suffer from a passive attitude or complete lack of understanding, while the multinational marketer may be influenced by other corporate goals.

In addition to these environmental, competitive, institutional and legal constraints, the choice of which promotional mix element is given emphasis will also be influenced by the market, the industry and the product, while individual cases need to be considered against these differing conditions. Nevertheless some generalisations can be made about each promotional mix element.

Advertising

Advertising may be defined as any paid form of non-personal presentation of products, services or ideas placed in one or more of the commercially-available media by an identified sponsor. The objective is increased awareness but, whilst there is an abundance of advertising and an associated high expenditure in the developed countries, generally there is much less in the developing countries. Indeed the lower the level of economic development, the lower the level of advertising expenditure (Table 5.3). This is especially so when volume of advertising expenditure is set against GNP or per capita income.

This may be explained by several factors. Firstly, outside the rich urban areas there are fewer processed or branded goods, as one might expect in conditions of scarcity and where many products are too expensive. Next, as always, culture will create difficulties. Many languages within a developing country mean that many translations are necessary – adding to the costs as well as to the problem of communicating the actual

**Table 5.3   Advertising expenditure as a % of
GNP in 1982 in a selection of
developing countries**

Brazil	1.16
Chile	0.16
Philippines	negligible
Puerto Rico	1.86
Greece	0.38
Hong Kong	0.67
India	0.21
Malaysia	0.5
Mexico	0.38
Peru	0.16
Singapore	1.0
Thailand	0.84
Venezuela	0.94
UK	1.36
USA	1.4

Source: Advertising Association, 1985.

message intended. Technical accuracy and perfect translation may not be available, while a lingua franca may not be acceptable because of its colonialist overtones and conflicting nationalistic attitudes. Even where these obstacles are overcome, literacy levels may limit the actual audience receiving the message, while the target audience may change drastically according to who is the decider or who is the buyer controlling the purse strings. This is a particular problem in the field of consumer durables, where the wife is the user yet has little or no influence on the product purchase.

The next constraint is media availability. Taking all developing countries as a whole, this is likely to be poor, sporadic and applicable only to a limited number of people. The possibilities vary from country to country but again the less developed the country, the smaller the range of media available. Furthermore it is always more difficult to assess the effectiveness of various types of media. The auditing figures by socio-economic groupings which exist in developed countries for newspapers, radio, television, journals, magazines and cinemas are unlikely to exist in many developing countries. The impact of posters, leaflets, point of sale advertising and direct mail is equally difficult to judge. Literacy levels may be low, but someone may read one newspaper to many others, thus increasing the audience while numerous people may gather round one television. Alternatively word of mouth advertising may be the most important in gossip-prone Arab cities. Consequently the amount of information on which one has to make decisions will tend to be less in developing countries, and whilst industrial advertising will be more straightforward with technical journals being the most relevant media, consumer goods advertising needs great care in the choice of media. The character, atmosphere coverage and cost of each medium will vary not only between but also within nations. Furthermore it is likely to change through time. For example, in the Middle East the growth in ownership of television sets has been phenomenal over the last few years. However the owners may still be illiterate and television as a medium may still be inaccessible to advertisers, as in Saudi Arabia.

Certain guidelines are, however, possible. Despite the difficulty of acquiring an accurate description of the circulation or of the social groupings of readers, newspapers and journals are often very useful in reaching the wealthy opinion leaders. Even with television and cinema copy will not be wasted since, although the richer groups will be the initial audience, the effect will filter out. Most countries today have transistor radios and anyone with any disposable income will possess one. Therefore this is usually a very effective medium for reaching a large audience. The only difficulty which may occur here is that an illiterate person may not be able to recognise visually the product advertised. Provided that the comprehension of the audience is achieved – perhaps through an appropriate symbol which can be linked to the relevant package – posters, leaflets and point of sale advertising can be very effective too. And whilst lists of the target market cannot be bought from a specialist direct mail house, as is common now in the United Kingdom or United States, nevertheless the relatively fewer opinion leaders can still be identified through correct training or through the appropriate personal contacts, so that this medium should not be ruled out either.

However an even bigger obstacle often exists. This is the actual organisation for advertising within the firm. Before an assessment of what sort of message, medium and so on is required can be made, a thorough understanding of the market, the product, the distribution channels and the available media is necessary. But the indigenous marketer in his production-orientation is likely to perceive advertising as a waste of money and superfluous in the typical marketing environment of scarcity, little competition and limited stocks. If more enlightened indigenous marketers exist they are unlikely to have either the expertise or finance for the in-house organisational option. Equally the multinational marketer, despite a possible standardised advertising approach which may overcome translation problems or consumer education levels, will usually seek the services of an advertising agency to check that cultural and legal conditions have been accommodated. Sadly advertising agencies tend to be less common than in developed countries. There may even be none – as in Saudi Arabia. Furthermore, where they do exist, they must be scrutinised carefully.

An advertising agency may be international, but this does not guarantee a common standard from one country to the next. A single domestic agency may well understand local circumstances better and be more eager to build up business despite not always having the most up-to-date techniques. Thus there is a need to assess carefully an agency's market coverage, quality of coverage, market research, public relations and other marketing services, and image. Where no advertising agency exists an alternative may be to leave all promotion in the hands of a local representative such as an agent or distributor. But sgain his competence needs to be carefully assessed, as does the danger of his using allocated funds to promote solely his own image.

Thus the problems involved in developing and executing an advertising campaign can be enormous in numerous developing countries. But, notwithstanding the cultural problem and frequent lack of appropriate infrastructure, it has been demonstrated that, with a small amount of advertising expenditure, a marketer can create a powerful position in the market place which would not be possible in a more sophisticated environment (Harper, 1975 p. 222). The impact tends to be significant socially in terms of the number of people affected and the durability of their spending habits, provided that the message is right. For example, in Nigeria advertisements tend to be associated with energy and power. Washing powder with the power to wipe out dirt, peppermints as a symbol of power, and beer advertisements showing people with strong muscular physiques have all been very successful. Legal restrictions tend to be fewer, and together with the fact that it has been shown that people in developing countries, despite limited income, are not prepared to satisfy solely simpler needs but require products which will allow them a sense of self-improvement and a socially-acceptable pattern of expenditure (Harper, 1975), it is not surprising that advertising expenditures in many developing countries are increasingly rapidly. Growth in radio advertising of 100 per cent was recorded in Nigeria between 1972 and 1975. Often it is the multinational marketer who reaps the greatest reward from advertising – especially if an international advertising campaign is adapted. If buying motives are similar, languages the same and some international market segment can be identified, enormous benefits follow in terms of cost and impact/acceptability of the campaign. Governmental marketers, however, have been slow to see that, through the use of advertising the right type of seed or fertiliser can be promoted and economic development speeded. And, until the indigenous marketer's operating conditions change, he is unlikely to see the full worth of advertising. Nevertheless its potential remains enormous.

Sales promotion

Sales promotion may be defined as 'below the line' short-term efforts directed at the consumer and/or retailer to achieve the objective of an increase in sales. As well as being useful in highly competitive markets, sales promotion is often very valuable in markets where the consumer is hard to reach because of media limitations, such as in the rural, less accessible parts of developing countries.

As in the developed world, the estimation of cost and effectiveness of sales promotion is a much easier matter than estimating the cost and effectiveness of an advertising campaign. However the type of promotion possible is likely to be more limited. Whilst all those listed by Baker (1985, pp. 354–6) will be appropriate for the rich urban markets and in the most successful newly industrialised countries such as Singapore and Hong Kong, in the poorer rural areas the choice will be much less. Often the major objective of the promotion will be to get the consumer to try what to him or her is a new product. To this end carnival trucks have been found useful by Coca-Cola in Latin America. The carnival trucks show a film, the price of admission being an unopened bottle of Coca-Cola bought from the local retailer. This bottle is then exchanged on entry for a cold one and another coupon towards the next purchase. Such a promotion not only stimulates sales but also encourages the local retailer, who is given advance warning. Elsewhere village stores are in the habit of giving free samples to promote sales.

In richer markets such as the Middle East promotion in the form of free air tickets, cash for introducing new buyers and lottery-type promotions with a free car for the winner have proved most effective. But whether used in the poorer rural markets or the competitive urban ones the regulations and legal restrictions on promotion in developing countries are likely to be insignificant besides those encountered in the developed countries (see Baker, 1985, pp. 359–62). Consequently the scope for sales promotion is much greater.

Personal selling

Personal selling may be defined as an oral presentation to one or more prospects. Whereas personal selling is usually regarded as complementary to advertising, as well as more suited to high-priced technically-complex products in the developed world, in developing countries personal selling often receives the greatest emphasis in the promotional mix for all products. Indeed it is the most common form of communication. This is largely because of the emphasis on bargaining by the majority of consumers in developing countries and the fact that many products are still being introduced.

In relation to consumer behaviour, outside the urban areas personal selling remains the major form of merchandising, with haggling being the order of the day. In relation to salesmen pushing new products through the distribution system, the salesforce is naturally more important than in developed countries, since initially the salesman must carry the product itself – to show it. Only after some time can selling be done by sample or description, and until better confidence is generated salesmen will continue to be essential. Only once this is achieved can routinised sales by initiated based on earlier agreed specification, and selling which revolves round negotiations based on delivery, packaging and payment criteria would seem to be a long way off in many parts of numerous developing countries. Until standardisation, grading, inspection and supervision of production is improved, personal selling is likely to remain very significant in the promotional mix outside the urban areas.

However salesmen are often mistrusted and poorly paid, and in a sellers' market the need for an active, professional salesforce is reduced. Whilst the salesman remains indispensible, selection, motivation and evaluation procedures are likely to be extremely different to those described in Baker (1985). Because the calibre of the salesforce is likely to be low where selling is held in low esteem and motivation may well depend upon other non-monetary rewards, malpractices are common. At the retail level there is frequent cheating by sellers. Adulteration of packaged goods is common, while the absence of official production standards makes for everything being approximate where measured goods are being sold. Where salesmen are involved with consumer durables or industrial goods appropriate back-up material may well be in short supply. Newsletters, audio-visual material, data sheets and bulletins are not always up-to-date or of the right quality. And to add to the difficulties different cultural contexts will affect all aspects of personal selling – from the criteria used to select salesmen to their actual method of undertaking their duties.

Again, not all developing countries will suffer to the same extent. The outward-looking export-orientated economies such as South Korea, Hong Kong and Singapore are much more likely to have well-educated, well-trained highly motivated salesforces representing their companies. However, taking all developing countries as a whole, despite the relatively greater importance of the salesforce in the communications mix, problems are likely to be greater and more complex than those experienced in developed countries.

Public relations

Public relations which can be defined as publicity through a mention in the media can be extremely important in developing countries. Often they rank second in importance after personal selling in the promotional mix since they can be used very effectively to reach the most influential people. The impact of reaching opinion leaders such as politicians, radio, television or press commentators, through appropriate editors and journalists working for publications and broadcasting programmes, is likely to be much greater than it would be in a developed country. However there are also limitations associated with this form of communication. Once the press release is given to an appropriate medium the marketer loses control over it.

Next the best media and editors must be identified and for this a public relations firm may be essential. Unfortunately organisations offering expertise in public relations tend to be thin on the ground in developing countries and personal contacts tend to be relied upon to a much greater extent to ensure publicity in a medium which may not be the most appropriate. Nevertheless the potential for this means of communication remains enormous and is likely to grow in the future.

Branding, packaging and labelling

Finally, branding, packaging and labelling offer scope for improved communications. Although branding by multinational companies is common, and multinational brands do well, indigenous brands tend not to be regarded in the same prestigious light, since they are considered to be of inferior quality. Consequently theft of brand names and counterfeiting of packaging is common. Furthermore legislation is often poor and does not give sufficient attention to protecting consumers. This does not make for the most effective use or development of branding. However, as communication improves, demand will increase for details on weight, volume, origin, content and producer. As commercial codes are established power will shift to the manufacturer rather than the retailer or wholesaler and at this point branding, packaging and labelling will be of paramount importance.

As with product policy, in the short term many marketers using poor promotion will be able to continue operating successfully in developing countries. However careful and effective promotion is essential for long-term survival. If developing country marketers can now begin to use promotion well they will create for themselves a head start in what will ultimately become very competitive domestic markets.

Distribution

Distribution is typically under-emphasised as a marketing mix element. The objective of distribution anywhere in the world is to provide a strategy which minimises cost and provides an acceptable level of customer service. But it is only recently, perhaps due to better analytical tools, in the form of computers, and increased competition (Baker, 1985 p. 265), that distribution as an element of competitive strategy is receiving more attention in the developed countries. In the developing countries, however, poor distribution in terms of both physical transport and channel structure remains a major stumbling-block and has often been quoted as the major impediment to faster economic development. Its impact on all other marketing mix variables and marketing strategy generally is profound. Although later chapters examine specific aspects of distribution such as retailing and wholesaling, the movement of agricultural products and government initiatives, by presenting an overview of the typical characteristics and inadequacies of the distribution system in developing countries taken as a whole, it is easy to understand why this marketing mix element is so difficult and yet so critical, and why it has such an impact on all other mix elements.

In contrast to the typical situation found in developed nations – highly sophisticated distribution systems with good transport, high technology warehousing, skilled labour and a variety of distributional support systems – distribution channels in developing countries tend to be long, fragmented and inefficient. There is a large number of intermediaries supplying an ever larger number of small retailers. Quantities offered for sale tend to be small and inaccurate measures, high wastage, and unsaleable stocks in foodstuffs are common. Channels as a whole tend to be labour- rather than capital-intensive, with numerous stages incorporated. They are supplied by a large number of widely scattered manufacturers and producers, each providing a limited output. Poor storage (often publicly owned) and inadequate transport with an absence of other physical distributional support systems are factors which are largely responsible for this. For poor transport, as well as resulting in higher costs for the producer and manufacturer, can determine the extent of the market, since it limits both demand and the producer's or manufacturer's incentive to expand and change. This has frequently prompted the multinational to develop its own distribution system. Finally it is often the case that distribution is regarded as an undesirable parasitic function, a perception strengthened by the large number of different ethnic minorities working in it (particularly on the retailing side) in many countries. Alternatively control is concentrated into a few hands. In Iran, although a number of consumer co-operatives have been organised, most wholesale (99 per cent) and retail (99.9 per cent) outlets are privately owned and, until recently, by one or two families. 'A "clutch" of families has established a grip over government contracts and virtually all channels of distribution', wrote Kaikati (1976, p. 18). Since Ayatollah Khomeni took over from the Shah many of these families have left the country. But in Saudi Arabia the concentration of control is still typical, particularly in relation to importing. For example, the Juffali family, as well as having interests in carpets, electrical utilities, imported appliances, telecommunications and cement manufacture, represent 30 western companies such as Daimler–Benz, IBM and Babcock and Wilcox. Such aspects again reduce the incentive for change. The total effect may be seen as waste and an obstacle to optimum economic development (Figure 5.1).

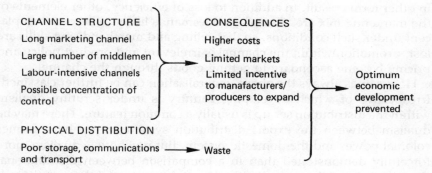

Figure 5.1 Typical channel structure and physical distribution in developing countries

As always there is no generalisation which can be applied to all developing countries. A progression in the development of distribution can usually be seen which is closely related to the stage of economic development. In the very remote areas barter may still exist. Under such circumstances there is no infrastructure or cash. But where consumer needs are more developed and exchange markets are established a few itinerant traders and country storekeepers selling to consumers in the immediate neighbourhood are the norm. Gradually more storekeepers take over and the channel lengthens. In the more prosperous areas there may be two or three general stores with a wider variety of goods offered for sale. Ultimately, in the rich urban areas, the distribution system is more akin to that encountered in developed nations. All types of retail outlets, including department stores, are represented. But it is still possible to make distinctions within the urban areas. The majority of lower-income consumers tend to divide food purchases between several stores – grocers for groceries, butchers for fresh meat and so on – and tend to shop more frequently in their immediate neighbourhood, buying small amounts. This is because they lack finance for travelling, storage, freezing and so on. The minority of high-income consumers patronise the more modern multi-line food outlets and have necessary finance to travel greater distances, buy greater volumes and store their purchases. Consequently they can shop much less frequently.

However in most developing countries distribution systems are under strain. Often ports are congested while many parts of the interior are inaccessible. Much discontentment and malpractice result. Distributors and wholesalers are likely to become dioscontented if they have invested in vehicles and staff but cannot respond to high demand because of lack of stock to sell. Price inflation, hoarding, conditional selling and corruption in other forms result. In addition to loss of efficiency, other elements of the marketing mix are affected. A salesman is likely to become complacent under such conditions, so that selling and merchandising skills are lost, promotion within the channel is irrelevant and product policy and pricing become secondary to getting goods through the channel.

However as always the above generalisation can be further classified. Irrespective of which developing country is under scrutiny dualism within the distribution set-up is usually a common feature. There may be dualism between the export distribution system set up by a former colonial power and the domestic system. But nowhere is dualism more forcefully demonstrated than in a comparison between distributional characteristics of the agricultural self-supply sector and those of the rich urban centres. Although it is fair to say that in the retailing and wholesaling sectors as a whole in developing countries margins tend to be lower than in the developed countries, with most intermediaries living hand-to-mouth, and control being in the hands of large wholesalers who tend to have something of a monopoly, nevertheless the characteristics of retailing in the traditional store or open market in the predominantly rural areas are distinctive. Each merchant and storekeeper tends to regard the market as unchanging and unchangeable. Little attention is paid to price elasticity of a market or a lower price resulting in higher turnover and profits. Rather a 'live and let live' approach is adopted and each transaction is seen as non-recurring, the whole objective being to achieve the highest possible price (often through bargaining) with no thought given to repeat sales and building reputation.

Unwillingness to experiment and improve may be reinforced by the fact that small retailers are often held in low esteem – despite the fact that they offer advice and credit in many societies. (As usual, there are always exceptions. In Puerto Rico the retailer enjoys considerable prestige, his store being a clearing house for news, a centre of advice and credit, which reinforces his leadership status). And because retailers tend to be drawn

from particular social classes or ethnic groups negative status is compounded. The isolation of such ethnic groups as the Chinese in Asia, or
the Pakistanis, Syrians and Lebanese in parts of Africa, results in less
competition or collaboration from indigenous people, and means family
ownership is the norm, limiting the size and development of retailing and
reinforcing ineffectiveness in retailing generally. Often a poor assortment
of products of uncertain quality is offered for sale in insanitary conditions.
Understocking is common while services offered may be very poor. Yet
because only a small amount of capital is required to set up such a
business many do, resulting in a large number of small retail outlets
characterised by poor management practices:

By contrast in the high-class shopping districts of urban areas the
supermarkets which cater for the upper-income groups are multi-line
operations and more competitive. They offer better efficiency, lower
prices, greater variety and a higher quality of service. But these
establishments must achieve a certain volume of business to overcome
their low margins and high fixed costs. A high outreach (that is,
consumers prepared to travel outside their immediate area) and a larger
consumer base are essential.

Supermarkets are seen by many developing country governments as
among the most effective means of promoting economic development
since, by replacing the traditional system of small family-operated outlets
with large efficient retailing which reduces the cost of food and increases
'real' income, a multiplier effect will be set in motion. Furthermore local
competition is believed to be stimulated. Indeed, in Central and South
America (Mexico, Brazil, Cuba, Venezuela, Colombia and Peru), the
establishment of supermarkets by Sears Roebuck has been quoted as
extremely successful in causing existing retailers to react and improve,
new businessmen to start up manufacturing to Sears' standards and
management techniques as a whole to advance. However in total terms
there are only a few large supermarkets in developing countries, and they
account for only a very small percentage of food retailing sales. And as a
means of providing low-cost food to low-income areas their success and
even relevance has been questioned (Goldman, 1981). This is discussed in
the next chapter.

Nevertheless the government has intervened in other ways to improve
physical distribution, in the expectation that, through more efficient and
less costly distribution, 'real' income will rise. Government initiatives
take two main forms: organisational structures and improved infrastructure. Typical organisational structures which have been developed
include agricultural co-operatives, government shops and marketing
boards, since most developing countries are concerned with improving
food distribution. *Agricultural co-operatives* have been established in order
to reduce the influence of the wholesaler, who can conceal interest of over

60 per cent by offering loans to farmers and taking payment in crops at harvest time. Often agricultural co-operatives are linked to a government bank. Unfortunately some of these banks found problems in getting farmers to repay the loan. *Government shops* are an attempt to reduce the market price of basic necessities. Again their success has been mixed. Often what has occurred is that few customers have benefited since produce tends to be bought and then resold at higher prices. Sales can be controlled through coupons but this system is difficult to administer fairly. *Marketing boards* have been set up so that prices to farmers and consumers can be controlled. However, while some of these boards have been successful with export crops, their success domestically is less since, unless a socialist state exists, it is difficult to enforce all sales being made to the board.

Improved infrastructure may be subdivided into provision of buildings, supervision and training. Warehouses for storage of agricultural produce and protection from pest damage, which can account for up to 50 per cent of wastage, provision of railway sidings, parking areas, packaging plants, refrigeration plants, municipal slaughterhouses, road and rail facilities have been given attention by many governments. Furthermore there have been attempts to standardise and supervise weights, measures and quality. The licensing of wholesalers and traders, market charges and levies are other means adopted. Finally training for retailers through simple courses on running a store and keeping accounts have been implemented in some countries. However these are often difficult to get under way since retailers suspect such courses as a means of investigating taxation paid. There is an obvious need to provide more information about the need for better quality, weight cleanliness and so on, and to demonstrate the true objective of training.

But, until this is done, the marketer (particularly the indigenous marketer) concerned in some way with distribution in a developing country must carefully examine and respond to numerous external uncontrollable constraints whose effect is usually profound. The political and legal environment, socio-economic forces, the market structure, competition and the level of technology used in the distribution system will affect any company's distributional strategy. For example, where a sellers' market prevails, the interface between wholesaler (whether private, co-operative or state) and retailer is very different from that experienced in a buyers' market. In a shortage situation the initiative in purchasing supplies is likely to come from the retailer, who is forced to seek out the wholesaler. Consequently 'push' promotional strategies through the channel are less relevant. The infrastructure available may well limit the choice of distribution channel whilst transport services availability and costs will affect what mode of carriage is used.

Nevertheless, given the constraints, some choice is usually possible and certain responses made. Wherever distribution occurs there will always be the same three flows of information, ownership and physical transport. In export markets the information flow is likely to be more important in order that the marketer can learn more about the less familiar export market whilst the physical flow is usually more complex. But whether for domestic or overseas markets, the procedure for selecting distribution channels is the same. Once the nature of the market, the producer, the competition and the resources available to the organisation have been considered, questions can be asked about the availability of middlemen, the cost of their services and the functions performed by them (and their effectiveness). Performance specifications for the channel may then be set. These will be determined by what is thought necessary in relation to (i) market coverage, (ii) selling and promotional efforts of channel members and (iii) logistical performance in terms of stocks and delivery systems. Then the channel type can be determined and channel members selected. Naturally consumer goods are likely to prompt a different distribution strategy from industrial goods, but with either distribution should be considered before other marketing mix elements.

Appropriate adaptations can then be made elsewhere. Production scheduling can often be improved so that ineffciencies in physical handling are minimised. The right design and packaging of products can help in overcoming such physical problems as climate, transport and handling and pilfering. Accurate grading, standards and measures which save inspection of each consignment by channel members can be useful in building a good reputation and competitive advantage. More communication with intermediaries in some instances regarding future plans and forecasts can also be extremely useful.

Finally more attention should be paid to the extent of change under way in developing countries. For in many countries rural distribution is improving as governments increase investment in infrastructure and as urban distribution systems become more sophisticated, thus offering a greater number of alternatives for the marketer. For example, in Tehran and other provincial capitals in Iran the traditional bazaar – a labyrinth of winding lanes covered with a vaulted roof where merchants rent booths or alcoves as their shops – although still the centre of wholesaling and retail trading, is gradually facing increasing competition from modern department stores, specialised stores, chain stores and supermarkets. A similar development is under way in India and is having desirable effects on attitudes towards retailing. Kacker (1976) maintains that retailing in parts of India is no longer associated with 'petty peddling', but is now acknowledged as a prestigious vocation as a result of the development of department stores like Super Bazaar. Further, because of more investment, by manufacturers, traders and the government, large scale trading institutions are developing and transferring power towards the market place. Wholesalers, forwarding and clearing agents, transporters and retailers are beginning to establish an identity of their own – developing private brands and creating more physical distribution facilities. And through their increased competitiveness and a reduced emphasis of family owned distribution channels, a more objective breed of intermediaries is emerging.

Kacker (1976) suggests that many specialised distribution houses will be unlikely to survive as sole regional distributors for manufacturers but will have to enter manufacturing themselves, whilst the near-saturation of some urban markets means that more attention must be paid to rural market segments and the development of appropriate infrastructure. Another initiative is franchised retail outlets. Delhi Cloth Mills have pioneered direct distribution channels and by 1979 had over 500 retail outlets with plans for 200–250 more. Similarly, Guest Keen Williams have entered retailing but high investment costs may prohibit large-scale developments. The result is that 'parasitic' middlemen in India are begining to be slowly squeezed out of the system and efficiency in distribution is improving.

Such developments offer the marketer greater scope (if potentially more legal restrictions) in his distributional strategies. But the overall difficulties involved with less adequate, less sophisticated distribution than that experienced in developed countries mean that extra care must be taken with this fundamental marketing mix element. At the same time the potential reward of overcoming obstacles is likely to be much greater.

Pricing

Within developing countries price tends not to be used as a major competitive tool. This is because demand is usually greater than supply and the typical considerations of such aspects as the availability of substitutes are largely irrelevant. Consequently, whilst still valuable for international markets, within the domestic market the material on pricing objectives and strategy as quoted in *Marketing: An Introductory Text* needs some modification. However, as always, generalisations are difficult since not only will the perspective of the marketer (indigenous, multi-national or governmental) affect pricing strategy but also the size (in terms of population) and wealth (in terms of natural resources) of countries will have a significant bearing, since it will influence the industrialisation policy followed, which in turn will affect the extent of protectionism domestically and competitiveness internationally.

As noted earlier, the indigenous marketer in developing countries normally seeks short-term high profits. This is more obvious as one progresses further along the distribution channel. Using a cost-plus approach, he tends to use a market skimming strategy and gives insufficient consideration to lower prices in order to promote higher volumes. This is, to a large extent, understandable in many instances where demand tends to be inelastic, competition is minimal and where countries (particualarly large rich ones) tend to reinforce this domestically through high protective tariffs. Money from oil in many countries has also added inflationary pressures. The indigenous manufacturer usually loses control of prices early, since he is often dependent on large wholesalers who determine the margins for distribution. Athough prices may change, this is usually in response to uncontrollable factors such as cost of raw materials, inflation, changes in the exchange rate and government interference. Only in the successful outward-looking small poor countries such as Hong Kong and Singapore do the market forces and efficient distribution systems allow replication of developed countries' pricing strategies.

In most developing countries the government plays many roles with significant consequences. Firstly it often attempts to control prices, particularly of basic foodstuffs. Secondly it may be the major purchaser, creating something of a monopoly. Thirdly, through its policy on foreign exchange restrictions and barter, it may cause further distortion in domestic markets. As a marketer in its own right it tends to see pricing as distinct from other marketing mix elements and therefore not to use it to best effect. Nor does it always accurately estimate demand correctly. This is particularly true when selling agricultural produce in international markets, but is also typical within countries where high-protein, low-cost basic foods have been distributed through government channels in order to aid the poorest people but where the middle-income groups has benefited the most.

The multinational marketer has greater scope for using pricing competitively than the indigenous marketer, since some distribution channels may well be owned and controlled by the multinational. However, through its intangible marketing advantages such as the 'prestige' associated with being foreign and using sophisticated technology, it also has the opportunity to inflate prices on many products, knowing that there is a captive market for them. Indeed multinationals are often the price leaders with their brand dominating the market, the local competitors (if existent) producing inferior products at lower prices.

The imperfections in developing countries' markets, promoted by supply and demand conditions, the dominant position of multinational companies, typical trading practices and by many government attempts to redress the balance in favour of consumers, have resulted in many malpractices. Black markets, hoarding and smuggling are characteristic manifestations. One of the best examples of a country with a thriving black market is Nigeria, where smuggling has been estimated by one senior government official (*Financial Times*, 30 Nov. 1985) to account for 25 per cent of all goods sold. Local industry is constantly unable to meet demand. The result is smuggling of (most commonly) foreign-label prestigious goods. And even when a foreign label has been indigenised manufacturers find it difficult to compete with the smugglers price-wise. One of the few exceptions is Max Factor, who struck back – level pegging their prices with the smugglers – and eventually drove them out of the market.

In other areas where smuggling is less possible a black market flourishes just as successfully. Despite the recent recession and sharp cutback in government construction projects, every day Elephant House, headquarters of West Africa Portland Cement Co. (WAPCO), Nigeria's largest cement manufacturer, is besieged. Despite efforts to increase direct sales to users and reputable distributors, there is an active black market, a 50kg bag of Portland cement selling at twice the official delivery price. On a smaller scale speculative hoarding by intermediaries of foodstuffs and other basic products contributes to an unstable price structure.

Many governments, such as Saudi Arabia, have introduced measures (dating back to 1975 in Saudi Arabia's case) to control prices – limiting businessmen to a mark up of 15 per cent on imported goods, and imposing stiff penalties for hoarding. Nevertheless these imperfections remain in most developing countries and result in a very different framework within which to set price than that typical of developed countries. Apart from the multinational marketer who continues to hold most of the high cards, the indigenous and governmental marketers still give insufficient thought or emphasis to pricing, seeing it as distinct from other marketing mix elements and thus failing to relate it to brand image, advertising or stage of the product in the life cycle. Whilst this may not matter in the domestic market, especially when protected and an import substitution policy adopted, internationally it is likely to be fatal. Thus whilst pricing considerations detailed in Baker (1985) may become more important domestically once supply and demand are more in balance and governmental influences are reduced, they are relevant immediately for the developing country marketer exporting to the developed world or to rich urban markets of other developing countries. Here he must decide whether a skimming price policy is relevant or whether to price slightly above or below the competition. A stable pricing policy (that is, one unaffected by outside conditions) or a pricing policy to achieve the highest profit contribution over the entire range are other possibilities. Although there are likely to be more costs to take into account in the form of tariff barriers, physical and commercial risk, longer payment periods, countertrade deals and the unexpected, the acceptance of a local price and thus the need for marginal costing is often more important than the typical cost-plus approach which might be suitable at home.

For the moment, however, it would appear that pricing will generally remain under-utilised as a competitive tool and until the imperfections in domestic developing country markets change the incentive to do otherwise will be absent. For the possibilities for being more innovative with pricing depend largely upon eliminating production and distribution problems.

Another significant aspect which is a feature of many developing country's markets is bribery and corruption. Although having a significant effect on pricing – particularly for the multinational marketer who must add bribes to the cost of production and distribution – bribery and corruption is likely to alter the balance of power of all other mix elements. Indeed it should be considered perhaps as an additional marketing mix element in its own right, so great may its significance be. For example, in India, where some experts estimate that the black market economy totals one half of the official GNP, it is difficult to have a telephone installed or mended, obtain a bottle of gas for cooking or book a sleeper on a train without a bribe or tip. In the international arena it may be impossible to win a contract without some payment of 'black money'. It has been estimated by one Indian representative of a foreign company in Delhi that 0.5–2 per cent of a project's cost can be paid in small tips to junior officials in order to get paperwork moving and acquire information while 5 per cent is needed to 'buy' the decision-maker (*Financial Times*, 22 Jan. 1985).

Various attempts have been made to categorise bribes in such government departments. At the lowest level (according to the *Financial Times*, 22 Jan. 1985) are small payments such as a couple of bottles of whisky to junior officials in order that a company's file is noticed by more senior officials and moves more quickly through the bureaucracy. Next, larger payments may be made to junior officials who then make copies of Cabinet committee documents concerning rival bids. This may involve 0.5–2 per cent of the cost of the contract. Finally 'buying the decision-maker' is likely to involve substantial sums, perhaps in the order of £1m (which may be worthwhile if a defence contract of several million pounds is involved). In Mrs Gandhi's government money was generated by adding mark-ups on international deals and was paid into banks abroad. French, Italian, British, Korean and Japanese companies were most willing to pay (in this order). Although Rajiv Gandhi is now attempting to stamp out corruption, civil servants still take black money payments for favours large and small, 'a tradition of baksheesh being expected for virtually every service' (*Financial Times*, 3 June 1985).

On the more mundane level agents may need an extra allowance for tips in order to win orders, prices may need to be inflated to account for these and other extra mark-ups in the distribution channel, salesmen may have to be appointed on the basis of who they are and how important their personal contracts rather than how competent they are, whilst promotion through normal media may need to be secured by tipping the appropriate editor. Such 'business customs' add a new dimension to the external environment which affects the marketing mix – a dimension not usually considered in the developed world.

Thus the external environment in developing countries is usually far more complex and changeable than in developed countries, while the internal operating situation may be much more constraining (especially for the indigenous marketer). Not surprisingly the ideal marketing mix is likely to be more elusive and yet at the same time more essential in areas of rapid development. This is well demonstrated by using two specific cases as examples. The first – electronics in India – demonstrates many typical problems encountered by indigenous marketers and their response: usually a sub-optimal use of the marketing mix. Although certain modifications in their strategy are desirable, they are perhaps not as immediately obvious as the modifications which must be made in the Middle East, where consumer behaviour is changing much more rapidly.

Use of the marketing mix by electronics firms in India

Electronics accounts for 1 per cent of India's net National Product. It is a rapidly developing field with unique marketing problems. There are three types of firm – government-owned, multinational and private indigenous ones which manufacture and/or assemble imported components. Because of the fast-moving nature of this sector of activity, India needs constantly to import technology so that the gap between this nation and the developed world does not become even wider.

Consequently the government has authorised the setting up of a large number of electronics firms which are attempting to cope with the high demand (increased by the withdrawal of IBM). A rush of entrepreneurs into this less capital-intensive but high-profit industry has begun and there is intense competition to introduce new and improved (either indigenous or imitated) products. However for the indigenous manufacturer there are several external and internal problems which, because not adequately identified and countered, result in a sub-optimal marketing mix.

In terms of *product policy*, it is difficult for the indigenous manufacturer to introduce *new* products since a crucial component – large-scale integrated chips – is available and used by all competitors. Furthermore skills and expertise are normally lacking. Therefore, once a new product is introduced, piracy is the normal response. More careful forecasting of demand and more skilful monitoring of the competition might help, however.

Next the *communication* element of the marketing mix as used by these indigenous manufacturers requires some improvement. What often occurs is a misunderstanding by consumers of the product's use, usually because they are insufficiently educated and trained. If messages in the communications mix element can be improved through simpler instructions demand and utilisation of individual products generally is likely to rise.

Pricing too needs greater consideration. Since the government has encouraged this sector of activity many small and medium-sized companies have developed and are all competing with each other. None benefits from economies of scale but to make matters worse most use a random pricing strategy (that is, starting with a high price for a new product and reducing it once consumer dissatisfaction becomes evident). If, however, pricing strategies were changed to reflect a medium-rather than a short-term focus, ultimately demand would increase and the whole industry would benefit.

Finally *product servicing* is usually underestimated. Again this may reflect the desire to develop new products. But whilst R & D expenditure is often high, too little attention is given to the back-up aspects such as service personnel. Although in the short term this will not put firms out of business, in the longer term, when supply and demand are more equal, it will be the companies which provide relevant maintenance and warranty and the rest which will attract repeat business and service.

Thus the present operating conditions allow firms to continue to operate despite their poor marketing mixes. But lack of an integrated marketing approach, starting with the consumer and formulating the optimal marketing mix, will undoubtedly ensure the failure of many of these firms in the longer term.

The marketing mix in the Middle East

Much of the Middle East provides an area where, because of rapid change in the form of a stabilisation of supply and demand, high disposable incomes and intense competition, good use of the marketing mix is already essential. Furthermore marketing mixes are assessed and modified regularly to respond to more recent social change within the distinctive cultural setting.

Nowhere is this better demonstrated than in Kuwait. Here women have discarded their Islamic cover and are the most liberated of all Gulf women, driving cars and being employed in important positions in government. Such professional women are spending even more on luxury items. Men, too, are having to spend more in order to keep up with rising female expectations which may result in more clothes, holidays in Europe, a villa, new furniture and jewellery and so on. However, although women's societies have existed in Kuwait for over 20 years and are today attempting to raise the consciousness of women, there is still tradition which inhibits the woman's movement and prevents social codes being broken or the family name risked. Thus there is unlikely to be any storming by women of the stock exchange and men will continue to advise women what to do with their money. Nevertheless the pace of change is significant when one considers that 20–50 years ago in Kuwait a woman only left home twice – once to go to her husband's house and the second time to go to her grave.

The marketer who can accommodate such developments whilst at the same time understanding and catering for Arabian culture is likely to be most successful in the formulation of the marketing mix. For whilst values can be modified they cannot be changed abruptly and the marketer must still incorporate basic Arab values. For example, in Kuwait as well as many other Arab markets the motive for buying is not always definite. 'Newness' and sophisticated 'Western technology' may be sufficient and these aspects should therefore be used in the advertising strategy. Brand consciousness too is high since Arabs tend to personalise things. A product with a name therefore has a stronger identity and marketers who arrived in the 1960s with brand names have been able to establish fierce loyalty.

Advertising, whether on posters, in newspapers or on the television, is much less effective than in the developed countries, since people tend not to notice advertisements, have difficulty relating them to actual products and because the quality of advertising in the Middle East tends to be poor. Sales promotion is usually a much more effective weapon in gossip-prone cities and many extravagant promotions have proved extremely success-ful. For example, in car sales 'buy and fly ticket' promotions have been used: the bigger the car bought, the further the purchaser is flown for a holiday. Cash promotions involving coupons which could be exchanged for cash if further buyers were introduced were also tried. However perhaps the most successful promotion of cars was to give each buyer a number. At the end of each week six numbers were drawn and the people who had the corresponding tickets received their cars free. Within a matter of hours of the announcement of this campaign 81 Chevrolets were sold. Subsequently each Thursday the company would assemble the week's buyers for the draw and television and newspaper coverage resulted in extra free publicity. (*Financial Times*, 12 Jul 1984).

In industrial marketing, or when dealing with intermediaries in distribution channels, personal contact has been identified as the key to success. Individuals rather than institutions are all-important, reflecting the Arab's interlinkage of personal and business life. For example, in Saudi Arabia, where all sales and distribution companies have been wholly-owned companies since 1980 and where all contracts with government must go through servicing agents, the only way for the export marketer to break into this market is likely to be through a good working relationship with the right indigenous person. It is also likely that who he is and what his connections are going to be more important than his competence.

Thus an understanding of the Arab culture when formulating the marketing mix in the Middle East is essential. At the same time the marketer who can respond to further developments in this changing environment and the differences in buying habits between the Arabs and the non-indigenous groups (which may necessitate various marketing mixes) is at an advantage.

Conclusion

Although it is true that there are extra difficulties to take into consideration when formulating the marketing mix in developing countries, the optimum marketing mix should still be attempted. Certainly external uncontrollable factors, such as scarcity, culture, poor infrastructure and so on will affect the way in which each marketing mix element is used and may well alter the balance of power between each mix element. Equally internal factors such as finance or ability are likely to restrict marketers (particularly the indigenous and governmental marketer) even more. Product policy is likely to be less sophisticated and dynamic than in the developed world and promotion is likely to be more restricted, but its impact may be greater. Distribution is usually more important in the mix and affects other mix elements to a greater degree but offers little room for manoeuvre, while pricing is largely ignored as a strategic weapon. Bribery and corruption is an additional dimension, which should perhaps be considered as an additional mix element.

Also who is formulating the marketing mix and the type of country in which it is being used will have a bearing. Generally the indigenous marketer will be more complacent and less successful than the multinational marketer, while the governmental marketer may well assume mix elements can be successfully controlled independently of each other.

The multinational marketer is the one with the best international perspective and consequently the most competitive marketing mix in export markets. However the type of country (whether rich or poor in natural resources, large or small in population) will also be significant. Small, poor newly industrialised countries with their outward looking export-orientated policies are the most likely to generate the most successful marketers with internationally-competitive marketing mixes. The large developing countries, particularly the rich ones with their inward-looking policies and high protective trade barriers, may well promote complacency and poor marketing mixes by all marketers (although the present hostile world economic climate is now beginning to have a counter-balancing effect).

But, whoever the marketer (whether indigenous, multinational or governmental) and whatever the nature of the country (rich or poor, large or small), in the long run effective marketing mixes are essential. In the shorter term, domestically, imperfections in the market place may allow companies to survive with less than perfect marketing mixes (especially if they are protected). But in the longer term domestically and immediately in international markets optimal marketing mixes are essential.

However the operating picture of the indigenous, multinational and governmental marketer involves many extremely complex issues. These are addressed next in Part II.

PART II

MARKETING IN PRACTICE IN DEVELOPING COUNTRIES

Having considered the issues involved in marketing in developing countries and the way in which difficulties may be accommodated, the second part of the book focuses on the way in which marketing is actually used. Three perspectives are examined – that of the state official, that of the multinational marketer and that of the individual indigenous entrepreneur.

In many instances marketing is hardly used at all and where it is there are many imperfections in the way in which it is applied. Nevertheless it is possible to set down the state of marketing's use by the various 'marketers', the reasons for its non-use or poor use; the problems which may result from the introduction of Western marketing techniques and management, and the way in which marketing could be used to better effect.

Many difficulties remain, but when the present and potential use of marketing are examined one may hope that its value will be appreciated and its application improved.

CHAPTER 6

Marketing by the state: I

Contents

Introduction

Marketing by the state is generally poor or even non-existent in many economies. At the same time it has a fundamental role to play, for, as noted earlier, the state intervenes in the economy to a much greater extent than in developed countries. In order that a country's resources can be used optimally, marketing must be effectively understood and applied.

It is accepted that state planning is necessary in most developing countries in order that the pace of economic development can be increased and population growth controlled. But examples of planning failures abound. Industrialisation policies in many countries have been regarded as costly, ineffective and promoters of unemployment, inequality and stagnation. Equally agricultural planning in many nations has been a disaster. Cynics have argued that shifts in emphasis from 'agricultural co-operation' to 'community development', 'basic democracy', 'the green revolution', 'anti-poverty campaigns' and 'integrated rural development' are nothing more than 'fads' to keep international developers busy.

This may be a somewhat extreme view. Nevertheless a basic weakness of all planning has been to assume that individuals are homogeneous in the way they respond to the market and in their economic behaviour. This may well reflect the influence in the planning process of the economists, who have tended to believe that social welfare is increased if the welfare of an individual is increased without causing a decline in the welfare of other individuals. Unfortunately this breaks down if individuals in a society do not belong to the same community or do not have the same value system. Nowhere is this better demonstrated than in many Asian societies where economic and political stability is achieved through people dividing themselves into rigid groups and sub-groups, all in a hierarchical relationship with each other. But often planning has either failed to recognise this symbiotic relationship and the absence of competitive instinct, social mobility and responsiveness to economic stimuli, or adopted the wrong method of dealing with it. For example, in India the government offered several scholarships and jobs to depressed castes in the hope that the rigid social system, recognised as an impediment to economic development, would be broken down. This frontal attack on the caste system did not work. And failure to achieve broader objectives was the logical conclusion. Furthermore, because of the typical power structure, any resources which are injected tend to be siphoned off by the top ranks of the hierarchy and spent on imported luxuries, or worse, deposited in foreign banks.

If marketing had been incorporated within the planning process many of the above deficiencies might have been at least anticipated and reduced, if not eliminated. For not only is the chance of the right industrialisation policy and/or agricultural plan greater given the countries' resources but also institutional factors, often a major stumbling-block, can be identified and accommodated. To return to the above example, Asian societies have a long history with over 3000 years of institutions, values, and beliefs being clearly rooted in social tradition. The policies imposed which are not consistent, or based on the experience of other cultures, are likely to be harmful. Although there are many barriers, theoretically, marketing, with its central focus on people, can, through market research, investigate cultures and adapt planning policies so that they are consistent. Alternatively where breaking down a traditional hierarchical structure so that society conforms more to egalitarian democratic principles is necessary, marketing, through social marketing, has the ability to accomplish this.

These issues will be discussed in more depth in this chapter. First the need for, and relevance of, marketing by the governmental marketer is addressed. Next the actual obstacles encountered in using marketing more efficiently are considered. Specific areas of planning, notably population, distribution and agriculture, are then examined. Present weaknesses in the system are identified and marketing's relevance and use is considered.

The relevance and role of marketing in government planning

Because the government intervenes in the economy to a large extent in most developing countries and because marketing has an important role to play in the economic development of any developing country (as demonstrated in Chapter 1), the relevance of marketing in government planning should not be in doubt. Marketing provides both the means to assess what favourable resources a country possesses and a method of ensuring they are used to best effect. If values and attitudes need to be changed social marketing can be used, while perhaps the major basic strength of marketing is its holistic approach. For marketing requires that the whole system within which it operates is examined. Unfortunately this lack of a broader perspective has been a major failing of many countries' government planning in the past. For example, population growth has not been satisfactorily dealt with in most developing countries, whilst agricultural planning is usually seen as separate from industrial planning. Indeed two distinct points of view can often be identified as a basis of economic development. These are:

1. Agriculture – as a sure foundation for successful industrialisation.
2. Industrialisation – as a rapid way to break out of underdevelopment.

The first approach is attractive to developing countries heavily dependent upon agriculture and possessing few natural resources. It has been argued this is the most pragmatic approach, since the advantages of technology can be applied to agriculture first, social change will be promoted gradually and industry can be built upon increased demand.

The second approach – that is, development based on industry (often modern, capital-intensive) has tended to be emphasised more in the literature and to have received more attention by governments. The developed world, where industrialisation has led to a higher standard of living, is used as a model and it is also argued that industrialisation is the best way to achieve economic diversification and stability as well as specialisation and the reduction of under-employment in the rural sector. Other advantages include flexibility – industrial supply being easy to control in relation to costs, prices and demand, whereas the demand for agricultural products is less elastic – and the possibility of reducing population increase through more urbanisation. But perhaps the biggest attraction for the government official is the psychological one – civilisation and power usually being equated with industrialisation.

Because there has often been too much emphasis on one approach, weaknesses have become increasingly apparent, especially in a difficult world economic climate. Although it had been postulated as early as the 1950s that there is interdependence between agriculture and industry (Lewis, 1955; Nurske, 1953), only recently is this view becoming more acceptable. For, if rural income is not increased and distribution improved, effective demand is reduced. Furthermore concentration on industrial development leads to overcrowding in cities and without the corresponding increase of channels to get produce to the urban centres, food needs to be imported. On the other hand industry and agriculture are complementary; industry providing fertilisers and cheaper machinery for inputs into agriculture, and surplus rural population being siphoned off into industry. However before such theory can be put into practice a marketing perspective – to assess in total what resources a country has and the best means to develop them – is essential.

Within individual sectors of planning a similar approach is required. Consequences of initiatives are usually not anticipated, whilst rarely is the whole process from consumer, working back to producer, considered. When the roles that government plays and the way in which marketing is relevant are examined, indications of the importance of marketing become evident.

The government's first function is that of *planner*, deciding how the economy should be developed and where it is going in terms of the world trade picture. Market research should be undertaken to identify opportunities and match countries' strengths with them. The whole domestic and international marketing system must be envisaged so that the most foreign exchange can be earned by both ensuring the highest revenue on exports and reducing dependency on basic commodities and raw materials. Although lack of data, maps, statistics, and the rest make integrated planning more difficult, nevertheless a marketing approach offers some basis for choosing strategies and lists priorities such as (i) greater emphasis on agriculture, or industry in national development, (ii) private or public investment and (iii) where, in the main the greatest spending in agricultural development should be – irrigation, land reform or price stabilisation, and so on. It also allows a matching of the phasing of planning to achievement of objectives and makes sure human resources are developed to fulfil a specific need. Finally it forces a focussing on the *consumer* and thus on the demand, rather than the supply side of the equation which has been so typical of so many planning failures.

This aspect is likely to be the key to more successful planning in the future. For, whereas in the past resources were used to increase production without any consideration of the consumer, today the characteristics of internal and external markets are being noted more. It has been realised that export markets, although large, may be inaccessible because of distribution systems within developing countries, while internal markets are narrow due to low purchasing power, low capital formation and inadequate and costly transport. Under such conditions, an increase in production (for example of agricultural produce) is unlikely to have any effect, since there is no accessible demand. Instead the government's first task must be to increase demand, which means improving infrastructure and transport in order to widen markets. This is possible through the government's second major role – that of *facilitator*.

In this guise the government aims at kindling the entrepreneurial spirit, developing export promotion programmes, modernising wholesaling and retailing and providing the necessary infrastructure such as education, health, transport and communications. Having identified the priority areas to develop, marketing is also useful in promoting understanding of local customs and culture so that modernisation can be undertaken with the least disruption. Social marketing may have to be used to promote certain changes of attitude. For example, explosive population growth is a major problem and threat to development in many countries. In sub-Saharan Africa the present population of 470m may become 700m by the year 2000 and 2000m by the mid-twenty-first century if the 3 per cent per annum growth rate is allowed to continue. Although the potential for family planning services has barely been tapped, unless values concerning sons as security for old age are first changed, any implementation of such programmes, particularly in the rural areas, is likely to meet with failure. Equally, before an efficient internal system of transport is planned, some identification of food surplus areas and food-deficient areas is required, while sophisticated supervision and technical management is often essential for the logistical support of export crops. Centralised marketing boards may be another solution, but none of these initiatives will be successful without an understanding and proper utilisation of marketing.

The third role a government plays is that of *regulator* in the economy, ensuring fair dealings between business firms and their customers and between individual firms, as well as attempting to control the multinational's operations. Again it is essential that market forces are understood as well as the multinational's marketing strategy, which if global, calls for some reappraisal of textbook marketing principles and concepts. Many attempts at regulating prices and distribution in an economy have failed because of poor understanding of marketing.

Closely associated with its regulatory role, the government may be regarded as *entrepreneur* in its own right, since it often chooses to operate certain business and industries. A good example is the Compania Nacional de Subsistencias Populares (CONASUPO) in Mexico. This parastatal[1] government mechanism, which aims at improving distributional efficiency and providing high protein foods at low cost, involves government shops and a government-run distribution channel, is perhaps one of the few, more successful examples of the government playing an entrepreneurial role. Elsewhere a marketing perspective has not been incorporated and many costly mistakes have been made. The relevance of marketing by the state is clear. So unfortunately is its lack of use.

Barriers to the adoption of marketing by the state

The reasons why marketing is not more widely embraced are many and complex. Some are more difficult than others to overcome but most stem from the typical conditions which exist in most developing countries, notably the culture.

Barriers to the adoption of marketing by the state may be listed as:

(i)   lack of marketing qualifications and ability of government officials to use marketing
(ii)   'official omnipotence' and centralised power structures often characterised by corruption
(iii) resistance by government officials to marketing being used for fear that their inadequacies are revealed
(iv)   an extremely complex marketing environment within developing countries and conditions which intervene in the easy implementation of marketing.

The first three factors listed are closely interrelated. There are few government officials in developing countries with marketing qualific-

---

[1] A parastatal is a state-sponsored organisation which takes over existing private enterprise or creates new enterprises resembling in legal form the type of company which is normal in the private sector of that country. The majority or all shares are held by the agency on behalf of the state.

ations. In many states, often because of historical circumstances, degrees in politics, economics, or other arts subjects are regarded highly, with marketing and business generally being held in low esteem. Consequently government officials' competence is in doubt. There is a low ability to understand or use marketing and poor decisions result. Not only does this affect domestic initiatives, but it may well deter foreign investment. In Indonesia, for example, many ill-thought-out conditions have been imposed on foreign investment. Downstream petrochemical projects have been prohibited, the multinational is required to sell a majority of equity locally within ten years or float shares on a somnolent Jakarta stock exchange. Alternatively multinationals are required to set up a joint venture – despite the shortage of reliable, acceptable local partners. Elsewhere, through lack of understanding of the multinational's global marketing perspectives, governments have failed to secure foreign investment on the most advantageous terms. Furthermore, if the government marketer is not effective in soliciting inward investment, it is unlikely that he will be able to promote marketing effectiveness in the indigenous private sector in his facilitating role.

Clearly there is a need to develop a body of experts who are aware of current marketing knowledge and thinking. However, because of the importance accredited to the Civil Service and the centralised power and influence structures and associated corruption in many developing countries, this is unlikely to occur very easily. Under mandarin as well as colonial tradition administration was regarded as a supreme and ultimate authority in all worldly matters. After independence in many countries the authority of the administrator increased and the empire of the administrative service spread a long way to heads of universities, research institutes, bank and import-export houses, and the like. This has led to something of an attitude of 'official omnipotence' made worse by the abuse of power by the highest ranking politicians. For example, in Kenya where a 4 per cent per annum population growth is outstripping the economy's capacity, whether measured in land, job creation or agriculture, the President's men have ensured that his tribe – the Kalenjin people – have not suffered. For if one has access to the President's office decisions are made fairly quickly. If not, it may be necessary to wait weeks or months. Similarly, in Indonesia, the key power groups are said to be the military, religious and political groups. In reality a small group – the army – holds the levers of power, 'but patronage and compromise create the illusion of consensus' (*Financial Times*, 10 Mar. 1986). The transition from Sukarno's nation-building government style to Suharto's government was not peaceful, with up to one million killed, several thousands imprisoned and a whole generation of vital people either wiped out or cowed into submission. Although the Suharto government has managed through its policies to boast some success such as self-sufficiency in rice production, power and the ability to make decisions rest in the hands of a few – Mr Suharto and his wife and a dozen or so *trusted* advisers. This 'inner circle', who are almost all military men who have proved their loyalty, together with the president, supervise appointments down to relatively minor officials. Under such a system ability and marketing expertise is unlikely to be considered a major requirement for a post.

To make matters worse, corruption is normal at all levels. At a high level there is a well-entrenched system of patronage and nepotism. The Javanese regard high office as a grace and its spoils as a natural prerogative (*Financial Times*, 10 Mar. 1986). Suharto rewards those loyal to him with lucrative business licences, directorships and other official positions. Retiring generals are often given a coal-mine or timber concession and they have first priority in government tenders and contracts. The Indonesian Armed Forces (ABRI) control one of the biggest commercial–industrial enterprises of the nation. Its interests are wide, ranging from shipping and timber to entertainment and cars, but because the sort of people in high official positions of government and industry are unlikely to have any marketing expertise inefficiency is the result. Problems in the world economy have recently led the Javanese-dominated military elite to take the unprecedented step of turning to the Chinese in Indonesia to advise them on how they may streamline their business empires.

Corruption is also typical in the economy at lower levels: the customs man who waves through taxable packages, the telephone engineer who insists on ten times the official price and the legions of expediting agents who grease the palms of the cumbersome bureaucracy for import and export licences. Naturally there are no statistics which show the entire picture but even those which do exist show how it is getting worse. 2000 were found to be guilty in Indonesia between 1983 and 1985 of various corrupt practices (a 100 per cent increase on the previous two years). A large percentage of aid is always misappropriated. The present Vice Principal and former Chairman of the National Audit Board estimated that waste and corruption accounted for 30–40 per cent of the state budget (*Financial Times*, 10 Mar. 1986).

In India international contractors are approached by 'collectors' of political bribes running into millions of pounds. In New Delhi civil servants take black money payments for favours large and small, whilst in the rural villages local government and bank officials illegally cream off aid and benefits from the poor. Tax evasion, widespread smuggling of gold and a tradition of baksheesh for practically every service make up a large part of India's massive and deeply ingrained black economy, which has been estimated to be half the size of the official GNP (*Financial Times*, 3 June 1985).

Paraguay provides a third excellent example. Here there is 'a military government sustained by corruption that is fed by Brazil', suggests A. Zuccolilo. (*Financial Times*, 6 Sep. 1986). The President, General Alfredo Stroessner, has been running the country as his personal fiefdom for 32 years. Although his supporters argue that he has totally transformed their isolated country and brought it into the modern world by removing its dependence on rivers, cynics suggest it was because of the self-interest of Brazil which, in return for capital, acquired a convenient backyard for contraband and access to vital hydro-electric power. Zuccolilo maintains that it is the military who have benefited the most by controlling the contraband business in perfect security, since a law made in 1980 governing the status of the military personnel allows them to conduct their own personal affairs and be answerable only to Stroessner, who is Commander-in-Chief of the armed forces.

The regime's motto is 'peace, justice, democracy'. In effect it is a benign military dictatorship only for people who do not demand their rights and question the corruption which is endemic. Recently an investigation revealed a foreign exchange scandal in the form of a $34m loss from the bank's exchange rate system. Losses might be as high as $100m. Together with an unfavourable economic climate, drought affecting agriculture and a tougher attitude by the United States, it is debatable how long this state of siege can continue, but it does and the corruption remains.

Naturally under such a system there is great resistance by government officials to marketing being adopted. For market research would un-doubtedly uncover malpractices and inadequacies of officials, as well as being quite unacceptable to the traditional attitude of official omnipotence. Furthermore, where rigid cultures are involved, the perceived threat is even greater, because change is required. It has been suggested for example, that the Hindu economic ethic is 'high savings, low risk, low return and slow progress', which leads to the Hindu rate of growth. Change is feared because it upsets the established course dictated by the Hindu religion and bounded by tradition such as the caste system. It can put jobs at risk and endanger power and prestige in a country where status matters enormously. Thus even top civil servants avoid decisions which expose them to personal accountability. Deferring a decision involves less risk of being criticised than making a wrong one. The adoption of marketing principles would overthrow this system and therefore is unacceptable.

But even if a country is willing to try to change the administrative mechanism and eliminate crude, inefficient, corrupt methods, there is the question of whether it is able to do so. For most developing countries are characterised by an extremely complex environment, as detailed in Chapter 2, which hampers further the implementation of efficient marketing by the government sector.

Firstly the corruption endemic in many developing countries is a major handicap. Nigeria provides many classic examples which have thwarted attempts to introduce more honesty to the trading system. Outside the entrance to the quays of Port Apapa (Lagos) there is always a throng of men and women with black plastic bags. This group constitutes a black market, since they are the intermediaries who sell the rice, sugar, salt and other commodities which dropped off a fork-lift truck, accidentally! Despite increased checking by army, navy and a national security organisation in addition to customs, the police and the Nigerian Port Authority, there is still much pilfering, even by uniformed men. All is made easier by the lack of co-ordination between checking bodies. Large-scale smuggling has been stamped out but it still exists on a smaller scale. Goods in short supply domestically continue to be smuggled in whilst others capable of earning foreign exchange, such as several thousand Peugeot cars assembled in Nigeria, are smuggled out (*Financial Times*, 3 Mar. 1986). Furthermore disputes over tariff classification still leave much room for 'financial compromise'. For example, the definition of 'manufacturing plant and equipment' has been used for a container of bicycles said to be needed to get workers round a large factory floor. Other techniques involve relabelling Eastern European drugs with well-known brand names and reselling them at the full and brand price or supplying products in knock-down form in two batches, each with a set of documents.

In India, where similar conditions exist, Rajiv Gandhi has launched a campaign to try to remove as much corruption as possible. He has dismissed some corrupt officials and politicians frosm key posts, reduced industrial and other controls and cut some taxes, hoping this will remove the incentive to bribe. There have been major attacks on smuggling and civil servants and politicians now know they are not supposed to accept bribes. However there is much cynicism about tax cuts and people (from poor villagers to multinational directors) asked to pay up often do, unsure of whether the person asking for money has really lost his power of influencing the decision.

The truth is that corruption is usually an adjunct to any market-place bargaining-oriented economy, where the price of everything from a bag of oranges to a death certificate is open to negotiation. In over-controlled societies such as India's, it has even been claimed that the black economy serves a very necessary purpose. For black money is the oil lubricating the wheels of the economy, buying decisions and favour from the lethargic, corrupt officials at the controls. Even low-paid bureaucrats see 'tips' as an essential means of increasing their pay and as a right for supporting an extended family. But such 'indirect taxation' togerther with corruption at higher levels means that the domestic economy has to subsidise these activities. Monopolistic control of certain sectors of activity by individuals or groups has been an additional burden. For example, a subsidy to promote the growing of crops for export may be intercepted by commercial intermediaries and never reach the actual producers. As a result prices have been driven upwards, and goods have been made uncompetitive on world markets. For those trying to promote more normal market prices, these factors are serious impediments.

Another difficulty may be the racial structure of a nation. In many Southeast Asian nations, for example, the business community consists of non-nationals such as the Chinese or Indians. Not only would it be seen as politically unacceptable to support and encourage the efficient, marketing-oriented enterprises of such groups, but the mere fact that another racial group, held in low esteem, runs a particular sector of business means that indigenous people, whatever the incentives, are discouraged from doing likewise.

In addition to the potential institutional factors and monopolistic control which are usually part of the culture and therefore extremely difficult to eradicate, the government often has to live with problems created by poor decisions taken in the past, such as inappropriate technology, or excessive emphasis on industrialisation, or lack of attention to agriculture, especially where petroleum has been discovered. Such constraints have been particularly difficult to overcome in the present unfavourable economic climate.

However perhaps the most problematic uncontrollable element which makes marketing more difficult to implement is the very complexity of many developing countries. This has been dealt with to a large extent in Chapter 2 where the general characteristics of richness of natural resources but also warped, highly vulnerable, dualistic economies, with imbalanced market structures, poor infrastructure, and so on, were detailed. By simply considering two large extremely complex countries, Nigeria and India, it is easy to see how the implementation of effective marketing is made more difficult.

Nigeria is considered as the 'big brother' of Africa, having the largest population and being one of the wealthiest nations. But there is within its boundaries a striking change of environment as one progresses from the hot, wet rain forest to the dry, open woodland, the grass savannah and lastly the sandy scrublands. Equally the 80–90m people show a variety of ethnic groups, each with different languages, religion and cultures, such as the Muslim Hausa and Fulani in the North and the Christian Yoruba and Ibo in the South and an under-developed empty middle belt, which hampers social, economic and political integration. The influence of the European is clear in the rubber plantation system limited to the South and South-east, and the associated more developed transport networks, urban areas and centres of industrial growth such as Lagos and Port Harcourt. Generally, however, physical communications are poor and bottlenecks in telephone and postal systems are normal. Political problems are aggravated by the composition of the population, the regional disequilibrium in its distribution and the conflict of interests between state and national governments. A greater sense of national unity and integration and a more inward-looking orientation is required, but the influence of history and unequal economic development make this particularly difficult to achieve. And with such problematical attitudes, physical and economic conditions it is extremely difficult to implement effective marketing throughout the nation.

India, with a population of over 700m in a country four times the size of Nigeria, has even more constraints. With many climatic regions, vegetation types and an abundance of ethnic groups complicated by class, caste and other social constraints, uneven road and rail development largely resulting from the British influence, to mention but a few factors, it would seem very ambitious in the first instance to attempt to develop a plan for such a large, complex country. To set up effective marketing institutions on such a scale is likely to be even more difficult.

Nevertheless, despite all the obstacles to the adoption of marketing by the state, economic necessity is, in many countries, forcing some change. The actions of state mechanisms are being scrutinised, privatisation is being encouraged and the need for marketing is, one hopes, being realised. Unfortunately this is only a recent trend. Consequently the record of marketing by the state has not been very impressive, as shown by the next section, which considers the state of the art in population control, distribution and agricultural planning.

State involvement in population control and the use of social marketing

Apart from one or two of the most successful newly industrialised countries such as Singapore, explosive population growth is a major problem for state governments. Growth rates of 3 and 4 per cent are not uncommon and the consequent poverty, unemployment and overcrowding, especially in cities, defeat other planning initiatives.

Yet the problem is not sufficiently dealt with and there have been many planning failures. For example, in India, where population was 717m in 1982 (according to the World Bank) and will rise to over 900m by 2000, problems in the late 1970s occurred when Mr Rajiv Gandhi ran an aggressive population control programme which included coerced male sterilisations. It has been estimated that this unsuccessful programme has set the country back five years.

More recently a government helicopter hovered over the slums of

Madras where 1985 had been declared a 'No Child Year'. Leaflets were scattered asking 'Why bear unnecessary children?' The result was that 4500 slum-dwelling women marched through the city demanding the 'right to decide' and 'freedom from conception'. This major expression of feminine independence in India's male-dominated society shows how the governmental planner involved with population control is learning how to use marketing more effectively. The relevance of social marketing, that is, 'the design, implementation and control of programmes calculated to influence the acceptability of social ideas involving considerations of product planning, pricing, communication, distribution and marketing research', (Kotler and Zaltman, 1971) has been noted.

But there are still many barriers to overcome. Besides the ever-present problem of government officials regarding any form of marketing with suspicion, those who have used it have tended to concenrate on advertising. Furthermore there has tended in the past to be too much of a product-orientation centred around birth control services and devices and distributed through clinics. The distribution system obviously may need changing. Medical knowledge is not always necessary and clinics are too widely dispersed. It may be more appropriate to use the country's present distribution channels such as retailing outlets or posters where possible. Equally the product, packaging and other elements of the marketing mix need to be carefully determined. Finally marketing research must be effectively carried out first, in order to establish existing values and attitudes so that a gradual, rather than drastic way of changing them can be worked out.

Fortunately the Indian government, at least, have come to realise this. They have seen that, until social perceptions change, there will be no acceptance of contraception, and the change will only be brought about through social engineering, with the emphasis on education and communication of information. Today a new approach is being developed to try and bring down the birth rate from 2.3 per cent to 1.2 per cent. It involves *private sector* advertising agencies who are helping to prepare the publicity, and local committees which are being set up. A budget of £1.9b has been put aside for a five-year period (*Financial Times*, 12 May 1986).

Also of interest is the fact that multinationals are being given some credit. A motor components subsidiary of Lucas Industries won the 1985 award for family planning. In this factory none of the top management has more than two children and out of 2716 employees (mostly male) 1604 have no more than three children. This has been achieved basically through word of mouth, principally by the chairman advising employees on an individual basis.

These developments, it is hoped, show some reduction in the negative stance by government officials towards the use of marketing, particularly in the area of social values. Certainly there are always ethical problems and the danger of being able to manipulate cultural change. An undesirable element of society with sufficient resources could well use this technique for its own ends. However, the use of propaganda has been with us for some time and any group well represented in a social system has the leverage to abuse power. The reduction of population seems a beneficial objective and to break down such traditional values in India as the one which suggests that more sons means security in old age seems a low price to pay. Social marketing, if therefore used responsibly, has an enormous role to play in the reduction of population growth and the speeding of economic development. It is hoped that more governments will follow India's lead in the near future.

State involvement in distribution

Distribution is one area which has seen much state involvement in developing countries. It often accounts for more than 40 per cent of the total public outlay in development planning. This is because distribution is generally inefficient and waste and loss is common. As noted earlier distribution problems constitute possibly one of the biggest barriers to economic development. Individuals using their head, shoulders or back, supplemented by wagons, carts and bicycles, are the mainstays of many poorer economies. Whilst these may be appropriate to certain economic and social conditions they restrict development. Water is a cheap form of transport, but is often underestimated and insufficiently developed, although rivers remain a focus of economic life in many areas, such as North Brazil. Rail transport tends to be underdeveloped and usually associated with the export of commercial crops, as, for example, with the Nigerian railway system or the Accra–Kumani railway, which made large scale cocoa production in Ghana possible. Roads are becoming more important and despite controversy as to whether road or rail development stimulates the economy more, it is likely that roads will take on an increasing share of internal traffic in most developing countries.

Nevertheless problems are enormous. Cultural constraints and inadequacies in distribution channels add to the physical transport problems. Intermittent shortages and surpluses for many consumer and industrial goods are typical. Even in the most sophisticated urban areas existing retailing and wholesaling structures leave much to be desired.

Governments are aware that physical transport and efficient distribution are important in all areas. If left underdeveloped the diffusion of knowledge of, for example, better fertiliser, seeds, and so on, in subsistence agriculture is likely to be prevented, and the number of people who can be supported is limited. Conversely, if improvements are made, markets are opened up and interchange between rural and urban areas is promoted. Specialisation of labour is likely to follow. Finally, with the right logistical support framework, better transportation systems can permit greater earnings at home and overseas from local production.

Consequently, as noted in the last chapter, governments have been active in attempting to develop better storage and transport facilities to reduce losses of agricultural produce and expand markets. Measuring and grading systems have come under scrutiny so that each transaction is faster, since smaller traders do not have to inspect each lot. Better production, processing, preserving and packaging have been stimulated in several countries to help reduce waste. Other nations, such as India, have taken measures to regulate resale prices on basic necessities such as foodstuffs including grain and sugar, cloth, kerosene and edible oils. Others have established their own distribution channels and many have been active in encouraging more modern forms of retailing, such as supermarkets in urban areas, to act as stimulators of further development. (Often the required managers/entrepreneurs are absent and the government has to take over the function of entrepreneur in distribution channels).

Some success has been achieved. Kacker (1976) suggests how in India channel control is now moving towards the market place and there are closer ties within the channel, for example between retailer and wholesaler, and consequently greater integration. Furthermore new forms of retailing such as super bazaars, fair price shops and more government and semi-government agencies in the distribution of essential consumer and industrial goods have led to more of a consumer orientation. Eventually this may lead to a similar situation to what occurred in the West – better distribution, shorter channels and manufacturer-owned or franchised retailing.

However, taking the picture as a whole, many inadequacies remain and much may be attributed to the failure by governments to adopt and utilise more of a marketing perspective. Impressive storage facilities are often built without considering the final demand. The whole picture, from consumer working back to producer, is usually not sufficiently considered. Logistical support frameworks are ignored and new types of retailing outlets are developed without sufficient market research. Indeed, if the consumer were identified and analysed a little more, state involvement in distribution, already important, could result in even more of an impact.

The following two examples of (i) supermarkets in Developing Countries and (ii) The Compania Nacional de Subsistencias Populares (CONASUPO) demonstrate two different attempts at governments' involvement in distribution. Certain weaknesses and areas for improvement are identified in the supermarket example, while CONASUPO shows how governments can be fairly successful but also constrained as marketers.

Supermarkets are seen by governments as a means of stimulating development, modernising retailing and providing low-priced food to low-income areas as well as being highly acceptable politically. Their development is therefore encouraged, for it is assumed that high volumes and low margins will reduce retail prices, which will in turn have an impact on real incomes, pushing up demand. It is also thought that greater local competition among other retailers and wholesalers will result.

But many of these assumptions are based on the market conditions and infrastructural support systems which exist in advanced countries but do not replicate themselves in developing countries. With more research into the situation the governmental marketer might find (as Goldman did in 1981) that low income urban consumers tend to divide food purchases between several specialist stores: grocers, bakers and so on. They also tend to shop frequently, buying small amounts in their immediate neighbourhoods, where the dominant institutional retailing system consists of specialist 'traditional' stores with personal service. And although the majority of high income urban consumers do patronise more modern, multi-line food outlets and regard supermarkets as a welcome, successful development, it may be that multiple product assortment and a mass merchandising strategy based on low profit margins and high turnover are irrelevant for the majority of lower income consumers. For it is incorrect to assume that this latter group will be willing, or able, to change shopping habits and travel greater distances at higher costs, which would have to be compensated for by reduced frequency of shopping. It is impractical for such consumers to buy large quantities of perishable food, since they have no storage facilities at home. Furthermore, they cannot afford to do so! In addition to which this type of consumer is unlikely to feel comfortable in the social environment of a supermarket which lacks the credit facilities and personal relationships offered by the traditional store.

Next there is always operational dependency involved with supermarkets. Poor infrastructure typical of most developing countries may not allow such a retail outlet to function as it does in the developed world. In addition to basic necessities such as electricity, banking, finance, transport, storage and the rest not being universally available, the effective implementation of self-service requires pre-packaging, product standardisation and grading, which are not generally established. Conversely most items of food are sold in bulk, and since only the well-to-do can afford to buy packaged goods, the producers are unlikely to take on this function. It therefore falls to the supermarket to package. Grading is another problem. The nature of agricultural produce and perishables' high level of deterioration make it difficult for the supermarket to standardise goods. In contrast to the advanced world where this is done by farmers, in developing countries the supermarkets often have to offer mixed quality assortments – the first customers buying the best, the later ones having to purchase poorer quality, which results in a poor image for the supermarket. (Even the traditional retailers can grade goods on the spot and price accordingly.) Finally mass merchandising depends on a good existing communications infrastructure and adequate branding. But in most developing countries branding, pre-selling and communication mechanisms are in their infancy.

In terms of direct inputs into the supermarket system there are further difficulties. For successful supermarket operation low labour costs, store equipment and economies of scale are essential. But it may be difficult to reduce the cost of labour sufficiently. For, although numbers employed are likely to be fewer relative to the traditional store, the cost may still be higher because it is not possible to use the unpaid family labour which is typical in the traditional outlet. Store equipment has to be imported and is likely to be taxed on entry to the country, all this adding to the cost. Also economies of scale are more difficult because mass purchasing and purchasing well in advance are not so relevant where there are only a few small suppliers charging all customers the same, and to shorten the distribution channel would be very difficult, given the complexity existing in developing countries.

Furthermore, where governments have attempted to promote the use of new retailing technology, the traditional retailers have put pressure on the government to allow them preferential treatment in importing the equipment. The result has been the development of small 'intermediate' supermarket-type stores carrying fewer lines of both staple and non-perishable goods, with self-service in some areas, personal service in others.

It may be that this is a welcome development. However the fact remains that basically there are often two distinct market segments in the urban area – the low-income majority and the high-income minority. And whilst supermarkets may be successful for the high-income minority who are prepared to travel outside their immediate area, they are unlikely to provide the lower-income group with low-cost food. If government planners paid more attention to such dual market systems, the needs of each and the operational constraints of different types of retail outlets, the planning record of the state in relation to the use of supermarkets serving the whole community might be better.

A more direct integrated approach has been taken in Mexico but, though much more successful, even here there are inadequacies, due to both the constraints on the government marketer and lack of marketing expertise. Distribution is undoubtedly a big problem in a country which has a population growth rate of 3.5 per cent per annum and insufficient capacity to feed its people or provide sufficient jobs, and where the low-income group has received a declining share of national income over the last 25 years. As a result a parastatal organisation – Compania Nacional de Subsistencias Populares (CONASUPO) was established with a view to mitigating the negative effects of development on the poor. By providing a vertically integrated distribution channel for staple foods, it has had an enormous impact, even though it accounts for less than one per cent of all retail sales of food products in the country. CONASUPO also regulates the import and export trade of commodities and is the sixth largest single contributor to GNP in Mexico.

The Government sees CONASUPO as central to many aspects of economic development, complementing and aiding other policies. For example, CONASUPO's commodity purchasing and warehousing functions provide low-income farmers with access to regional and national markets, thus acting as an incentive for the farmers to break out of their subsistence level sub-economy. The vertical integration of food distribution is seen as helping to regulate commodity prices, as well as a mechanism to break up monopolies and excessive margins by intermediaries who are major competitors. Furthermore it aims at increasing consumer welfare via low-income purchasing power.

But besides playing a facilitating and regulatory role the government has acted as entrepreneur by setting up 4000 retail shops which are indistinguishable from privately-owned food retailers. Most are small and their product policy is to sell a variety of grocery products which are indispensable to the health and physical well-being of low-income consumers. On average 1500 items are stocked. Prices are generally 10–20 per cent less than private sector outlets and these shops are located in working-class suburbs or on major arterial routeways.

However, although the government marketer targeted CONASUPO at the low-income group, Hilger (1980) found that the economic appeal of CONASUPO's low prices and product range was also attractive to middle-income shoppers. Furthermore, and more constraining for the planners, there was the fact that CONASUPO was perceived as having a developmental role and public accountability was expected (shoppers assuming that lower prices meant profits had been, and should be, sacrificed). This means that attempts to develop new market segments may be out of the question since social needs rather than market opportunities must be satisfied. It is also likely to strengthen the desire to demonstrate short-term highly visible results through a low-risk marketing strategy rather than develop long-term objectives. Finally there is likely to be less room for manoeuvre in the formulation of the marketing mix. Prices must be low and therefore so, too, must profit. Cost and revenue cannot be optimised because it is confused by other non-monetary goals. Product, promotion and distribution strategies may well be determined by law.

Although CONASUPO has generally been very beneficial in Mexico, there is always the danger that such a body can be used to gain political profit. The governmental marketer in such a framework could operate unscrupulously as a monopoly, or exert unfair pressure upon suppliers and develop an unfair competitive advantage over others. this has occurred in some countries.

Thus the government marketer has much power in the area of distribution. Used ethically and with the right marketing perspective, notwithstanding such constraints as public accountability, he can help improve the distributional situation enormously. Used incorrectly for personal motives many malpractices can be promoted.

Agricultural planning and the role of marketing

Agriculture is one of the major sectors of economic activity in most developing countries, often employing up to 80 per cent of the workforce and being a major earner of foreign exchange. But, as noted in Chapter 2, there are many problems and retarding factors associated with agriculture in developing countries. In addition to a hostile physical environment of poor leached soils and monsoons in many tropical environments, there are numerous cultural and institutional obstacles. Corruption is usually common. Where money-lending systems prevail profits are not so high, thus reducing future investment and the spending power of peasant farmers. Scarcity of capital and monopolies by money-lenders mean that interest rates remain high whilst monopsony in various forms (often government-buying) keeps prices low.

Peasant farming itself has many limitations. It is small scale, inefficient and basically for home consumption rather than being market-orientated. In some countries, such as parts of Asia, population growth together with the destruction of rural industries has resulted in pressure on the land, higher ground rents and lower wages. Elsewhere there has been a movement of younger people to towns and a consequent shortage of rural labour. But whatever the development taking place in the urban areas, it is unlikely that technology will be introduced into agriculture where semi-feudal landowners can earn more from existing systems (which often involve usury). On top of this, infrastructure is generally poor.

Not surprisingly, marketing by the individual farmer is not usually carried out effectively. In addition to having to cope with bulky perishable seasonal products, land tenure systems are often a handicap while transport and communications are generally poor, preventing the growth of specialised marketing agencies. Most agricultural producers are still confined to local markets, while the need for roads, railways, storage handling, packaging and refrigeration plants is obvious. Official weights, grading, information on markets and credit all need to be developed and co-ordinated. Instead wholesaler monopolies and price speculation abound.

Obviously, under such conditions, market forces do not operate normally but are replaced by bribery, corruption and price unrelated to costs. Some form of intervention is essential. Consequently, despite the majority of governments focussing their attention in industrial development, in national plans the field of agriculture is given a significant amount of weight. Unfortunately the marketing of agricultural products and marketing as a whole in agricultural planning is practically non-existent by comparison. For example, in the last Indian Plan (over 400 pages) four and a half pages are devoted to marketing. And, where it is mentioned, this may amount to little more than window-dressing. For example, Ecuador has a government department of marketing services which aims at price stabilisation. Other countries have developed milk marketing and export boards. But generally there is no information on their mode of operation, or their funding. Indeed, the amount of finance allocated to marketing in the field of agricultural planning is extremely low.

Instead finance tends to go to fixed plant and facilities. Undoubtedly it is easier for an economist to work out the cost–benefit ratio and the internal rate of return on a fertiliser plant, warehouse or storage depot. It is much more difficult to work out the effect of a training programme on the promotion of better farming methods, although this is more likely to improve efficiency. But only if a marketing perspective is employed will this become evident. For a major role of marketing is to help devise the most satisfactory overall plan. If there is little understanding of markets and the marketing environment, it is unlikely that available resources will be correctly assessed. Nor will the best objectives and strategies be formulated.

Unfortunately the need for marketing is not seen, and consequently there are many failings in agricultural plans. By examining specific weaknesses (Table 6.1) and marketing's relevance in overcoming these, it is easy to see how very important marketing is.

The first and most fundamental failing in many plans is poor estimation of demand. Both domestically and internationally there is a tendency to underestimate. Furthermore targets, often based on wild estimates of population growth and income per head, are set and it is assumed that they will be miraculously met. There is little attempt to look at consumer tastes, preferences and habits, an examination which is particularly

Table 6.1   Basic failings in agricultural planning and the relevance of marketing

Basic failing	Relevance of marketing
1. Poor estimation of demand Little attempt to consider consumer tastes, preferences. Low range of variables, e.g. population growth, per capita income used to estimate demand.	Marketing's role = the matching of supply and demand Appropriate techniques first to *measure* demand both domestically and internationally. Ability to include tastes, preferences of consumers and other dynamic variables.
2. Poor assessment of opportunities and threats	Threats/opportunities always being considered Marketing research.
3. Poor estimation of the competition Domestically and internationally. Underestimation of alternatives.	Marketing asks 'what business are we in?' Identifies and considers *all* the competition.
4. Poor estimation of competitors' marketing strategies	Ability to assess competitors' marketing mix strategies and their position within the market
5. Aspects of agriculture considered in isolation No integrated marketing strategy. Consequences of specific initiatives not foreseen.	Marketing has a holistic approach Assessing the situation via marketing research, formulating marketing strategy and integrating strategy and integrating the whole process – from consumer to supplier – with distribution between.

important where less familiar and more specialised crops are concerned. For example, a nationwide campaign to increase potato production in Colombia turned out to be a disaster because of a serious miscalculation of demand. Once the mistake was realised another was made by attempting to sell more potatoes in the maritime provinces where sweet potatoes, yams and cassava were preferred. Similar miscalculations have been made where consumers have not accepted innovations such as frozen products, which often negate high investments in refrigeration and processing facilities.

However, if marketing were incorporated more into planning, the estimation of demand, both domestically and internationally, would improve. For dynamic variables such as economics, technological, social forces and consumers' tastes and preferences can be assessed and taken into account. And where it is deemed necessary to introduce or emphasise nutritionally valuable foods such as oilseed or fish, consumer resistance can be identified and reduced. For marketing has at its disposal the tools and techniques to work out people's attitudes and, if necessary, modify these through social marketing.

The next great failing in agricultural planning tends to be lack of attention to competition. Again underestimation is common. Domestically competition from alternatives tends to be overlooked. For example, in Nigeria and Dahomey targets for the poultry industry were not met despite protection from imports for the industry. This was because the availability of relatively lower priced beef and fish was not taken into account sufficiently. Alternatively, distribution costs are not adequately assessed. Thus a fruit tree development in the Kassala area of Sudan had to be abandoned because the cost of transport made the product uncompetitive with other suppliers on the Khartoum wholesale market.

On international markets problems are compounded. As well as lack of attention to alternatives and consumer needs not being adequately researched, competitors' marketing strategies are not sufficiently examined. Consequently product offerings fare badly with similar ones from elsewhere. For example, pest and disease control may be poor and consumers naturally prefer to buy other producers' better quality products. Distribution strategies may be badly formulated, so that arrival times of shipments compare unfavourably with the competition's, while packaging may also be inferior.

Again the correct use of marketing can rectify many of these weaknesses. Firstly marketing demands an answer to the question 'What business are we in?' The answer should help identify the competition both domestically and internationally. It can then be assessed further for its marketing strategies and its position in the market. Together with a good understanding of what is actually required by the consumer in terms of quality, packaging, availability and so on, a successful competitive advantage can be developed.

However instead there is usually a piecemeal approach adopted by planners. There have been many examples of offering incentives to producers without foreseeing the consequences on the logistical support framework. As a result there have been sizeable omissions in terms of developing transport, storage, processing. This helps explain why losses (up to 50 per cent) through waste and deterioration are common in developing countries. Alternatively huge amounts are spent on physical infrastructure without considering the demand or production.

Marketing, correctly used, provides an overall framework for the assessment of needs, logistics and the consequences of any individual initiatives. Since the process of marketing is to start with demand, then match up the supply and distribute accordingly, it has the ability to weld together the different areas which are used in planning. The logistics of distribution, storage requirements and the rest can be worked out, feasibility studies undertaken and a matching of what is possible with what is required is then possible. Market research can discover how much people are willing and able to pay for products, how to motivate farmers to produce the appropriate crop under the right conditions and how to estimate future requirements through a consideration of the opportunities and threats in the broader environment.

Many of the problems above can thus be modified or improved, if not eradicated. Land tenure and ownership which results in excessive fragmentation of holdings can be researched since all too often they are insufficiently understood. Potential for change can be assessed, as well as the best method of achieving it. Through social marketing uniform high-yielding disease-resistant crops (commercial or staple) can be promoted, as can the use of manure and the control of pests and weeds. The relevance of large-schemes and increased mechanisation can be investigated. The necessary infrastructure, water supply, irrigation and human resources can be determined. Intensification of agriculture and higher productivity should result.

But the sad fact remains that there are many conditions in developing countries which mitigate against effective marketing by the agricultural planner. First and foremost, as noted earlier, there is usually a lack of people qualified in marketing and management. Thus, even if the physical infrastructure and capital investment is correctly developed, accompanying management is lacking. As a result many schemes have come to grief. For example, in Sudan a large-scale tannery and a fruit-canning plant were built with bilateral aid. But operating costs proved excessive because of incompetence. The government officials who authorised the scheme had no experience in the field of agriculture. They did not foresee the problems and, once operating, there was no incentive to change the situation, since it was a monopoly. At the same time bribery was rife.

Yet this is the typical isolated development, often carrying great 'prestige', which continues to be given emphasis. Not only are such government-controlled schemes useful political platforms, and a method of swelling politicians' private bank accounts, but they are also encouraged by a general attitude of hostility towards private enterprise. Whereas farming is regarded as productive the crop's subsequent processing, storage and distribution are not. Private traders are seen as manipulators of profit and their contribution is not appreciated. Yet private enterprise with the right, efficient management, such as West Asians setting up local purchasing and packaging stations or Africans building up a trading and transport business from Nigeria to Khartoum, can have significant ramifications. A whole region can be lifted from subsistence level and a multiplier effect set in motion.

This official negative attitude is worse in relation to multinationals' proposed developments, which may not be granted the necessary support in the form of market protection or security against expropriation. Consequently private enterprise is often deterred. Yet the multinationals are filling gaps the state marketers should be identifying and where multinationals have invested and brought in effective management farmers have often become more commercially-minded as a result: there is the example of Libby's Pineapple Plant in Kenya. Unfortunately in many nations state involvement is increasing and distribution networks set up by multinationals in the production and export of sugar, coffee, rubber and so on are now controlled by African and Asian governments who lack the necessary management and awareness of consumer needs.

Typical organisational structures favoured by government planners in an attempt to introduce more successful operations include co-operatives, marketing boards and state-trading organisations. Rarely, however, do parastatals encourage efficiency, one of the few exceptions being the Kenya Tea Development Authority which is discussed below. Co-operatives are often official policy, based on a desire to overcome inadequacies in existing marketing channels. In theory democractic management, profit-sharing and perhaps the elimination of some alien group's stranglehold sound advantageous. It may work, too, if lower costs and better service are achieved. There has been some success in the Ivory Coast where coffee and cocoa farmers have been encouraged to grow better cash crops with high yields, such as palm oil. An efficient distribution system has also been promoted – the crops being collected on a daily basis and taken to the factory (Harrison, 1980). But elsewhere monopolies have resulted and the farmers have suffered.

There are many reasons for this. Culture may not be sufficiently researched or understood. Where traditional loyalty is to the family or clan, it may not carry over to the co-operative, promoted by the government. Next the co-operative employees may exploit their monopoly position to achieve better pay to the detriment of farmers. And finally the creation of co-operatives by administrative regions or by government, may result in dependence and apathy, not democratic participation. Consequently co-operatives have not always been the most successful. Some have even become obstacles to agricultural development. Goals are not met and integrated programmes built round them fail. Inexperienced, poor management is usually a major problem.

Marketing boards take many forms. They may be advisory bodies or regulatory boards applying uniform standards of quality and packaging procedures through licensing and inspection. They may negotiate prices with large scale processors, wholesalers and so on or guarantee prices for a given volume. Some own storage and marketing facilities and have the means to buy and hold in store. They may also be monopoly boards – either for export, the board in this case being the sole buyer and seller of produce for export, or for domestic consumption, where the objective is a uniform and stable price for some basic necessity such as bread. Farmers have 'controlled' status on the board, not being members as in the co-operatives. They may benefit if marketing boards are successful at raising prices and equalising differences between markets. This is more likely to occur where marketing channels are few and concentrated. In some instances the bargaining power of farmers has been raised. However, often there are high costs, wastage and inefficiency associated with this organisational structure for, to a large extent, price stabilising in the short term depends on good forecasting and, again management may be of dubious quality. Overstaffing too is common and the misuse of power and money for group or individual profit is often difficult to eradicate.

Finally the consumer's attitude may mitigate against local produce which figures prominently in the agricultural plan. There have been many instances of competitive, foreign (usually multinational) products such as Weetabix being considered superior and status-giving. They are consequently bought at the expense of domestic production which may be plentiful, more nutritious and cheaper.

None of these problems is insurmountable. Management can be trained and marketing can be applied so that agriculture is more efficient, contributes optimally to economic development and earnes the max-imum revenue possible. And where attitudes are a stumbling block, they can be modified through social marketing. For example, marketing extension workers can help in moderninsing plans. Through their explanation and demonstration of more efficient methods and provision of a basis for understanding marketing channels and credit sources, several farming communities have changed their attitude towards the profitability of agriculture.

However, to date, evidence of the successful implementation of marketing in agricultural planning has been disappointing. While there have been one or two outstanding successes, many problems remain, as shown in the following examples.

The situation in Africa and the Kenya Tea Development Authority

In Africa as a whole many governments are attempting to reverse the dramatic decline in agriculture since their countries' independence. Three-quarters of Africa's people depend upon agriculture but the record of the 1960s and 70s has been disastrous as export crop production stagnated, food output fell (6 per cent in the 1960s, 15 per cent in the 1970s and likely to be more in the 80s) and population soared. In the famine of 1985 more than two million Africans perished and on present trends of population growth and food production the continent will have 650 million more people and an annual deficit of 100m tonnes in cereal supplies by 2010, according to an estimate by the Food and Agriculture Organisation (FAO). Whilst war, drought, adverse international economic conditions and the heritage of colonial times which has encouraged the neglect of cash crops are all partly to blame, much of the fault must lie at the feet of post-independence governments. For generally they have paid insufficient attention to agriculture – pricing too low, taxing too high and relying on swollen bureaucracies which have both acted as a drain on the economy and proved unresponsive to peasants' needs. Consequently Africa's peasants today pay some of the world's higher confiscatory taxes; for example, cocoa farmers in Ghana paying 70 per cent of their net proceeds, peanut growers paying 80 per cent. At the same time the concentration on industrialisation has led to a labour shortage in the countryside and unemployment in the cities.

Not surprisingly most African countries have a disaster story, such as cashew-nut growers in Tanzania, tobacco farmers in Zambia, coffee producers in Angola and cocoa producers in Ghana. Huge sums have gone into state farms, grandiose schemes and shiny machinery, but agricultural complexes in Zaire are still not working ten years after completion, and in Ghana there are more than 70 makes of tractors in various stages of disrepair on state farms (*The Times*, 27 May 1986).

Africa's agricultural revolution failed because the strategy ignored marketing, but emphasised prestige, modernism and mechanisation and paid little or no attention to individual farmers who produce the bulk of its food. Indeed it has been argued that the peasants have been exploited ruling elites using their authority to extract wealth from them and spend it on short term projects and conspicuous consumption (*The Times*, 27 May 1986). For many African leaders run their countries as if they were their personal property. And with such oppressive, misguided, kleptocratic policies, it is unlikely that financial donations from elsewhere will help. Already large quantities of aid have been misappropriated. For example, of the $7.5b which went to the eight countries of the Sahel (Chad, Mali, Upper Volta, Senegal, Mauritania, Niger, Cape Verde and Gambia) between 1975 and 1980, it is estimated that only one-quarter was spent on agriculture. Massive sums were allocated to capital-intensive schemes such as irrigation, which yielded disappointing results. For every new hectare of land brought under cultivation at cost of $20,000, a roughly equivalent amount of previously irrigated land became barren because of poor drainage which led to waterlogging. Money was also spent on easy options such as road construction, administrative training of the Civil Service and urban construction. Worse, money was used to set up new government departments to oversee the aid! And money that did get to agriculture went into cash crop production, such as ground-nuts for export. All this reflects poor management, an inability to assess the situation and foresee consequences and an urban bias. Even food prices have been depressed by price control in order to placate restive urban consumers. No attempt was made to motivate or involve the farmers in planning, or to try to control population growth which is rapidly outstripping agricultural growth. The result is an even greater discrepancy between the pioneer subsistence farmer, usually situated on the poorer marginal lands, and the wealthier commercial farmer and civil servant.

Worse, perhaps, is the bribery and corruption which has been evidenced. In Senegal it has been claimed that state monopoly peanut-buying agencies will not distribute seeds unless bribed. They also underweigh crops and cream off farmers' profits. Elsewhere violence and brutality have accompanied attempts at price control. In Ghana markets were dynamited, burned and destroyed by air-force personnel and police when peasants refused to sell at government-dictated prices. The result was a 600 per cent rise in locally-produced food prices between January, 1982 and April, 1983. The government responded by setting up a price control tribunal to hand out even more stringent penalties. Traders selling above government-recommended prices were thrown into jail, where many died because of the lack of food!

Nigeria provides an excellent example of a large rich country which has not only concentrated most efforts on industrialisation (believing it could buy its way out of underdevelopment) and failed to adopt a broader marketing perspective towards the whole economy, but also made matters worse through disastrous management. The result is that 'more than a decade after the first of a succession of Nigerian governments all declared a commitment to reviving agriculture as a top priority, the country is still awaiting its Green Revolution' (*Financial Times*, 3 Mar. 1986, p. 8 Nigerian Supplement). The 'Operation Feed the Nation' programme of the 1970s became Shagari's 'Green Revolution' drive of the early 1980s.

Until now all incentives have failed and the decline in per capita agricultural output continues. Nigeria, once the world's largest producer of ground-nuts, now needs to import this commodity. Cocoa has seen a similar decline through a combination of bad luck and appalling planning. The 1986 forecast is disastrous. In 1985 170 000 tonnes of cocoa is believed to have been produced by traders. (It is difficult to know exactly, since an estimate of 20 000 tonnes per annum is smuggled to neighbouring countries). Gill and Dufus (the London Cocoa traders) estimate that the 1986 figure will be nearer 110 000 tonnes, despite Nigeria's cocoa industry once being the world's second largest. Around independence in 1960 agricultural commodities, led by cocoa, generated 70 per cent of Nigeria's export earnings. Today they account for less than 3 per cent.

In order to try to improve the agricultural base which has been eroded by years of neglect and mismanagement of massive sums of money committed to agricultural development, Babangida's 1986 budget is based on the principle of agricultural-led development. It involves less state intervention and a more realistic exchange rate to boost exports and stave off competition, as well as a shift in emphasis to lower-cost, smaller-scale (less prestigious) initiatives. The Accelerated Development Area Programmes (ADPs) which are funded by the World Bank and Nigerian federal and state governments have consequently received more attention. The three-year-old Imo State Accelerated Development Area Programme (ISADAP), is one of ten set up since 1971 and covering four million farming families (mainly small-holders) and is today the flagship of this programme. With the objective of improving small farmers' access to physical inputs, credit, technical advice and focussing on 'core' food crops like cassava, maize, rice and yams, it has been fairly successful in lowering costs of production (unlike some of the other ADPs which have been criticised for spending too much on housing and administration). However it is difficult to say whether ISADAP's success has been solely because of good management or fair weather and a movement of people back from the towns. Indeed, ironically, the impact of Babangida's present policy may be insignificant too. It has been argued that it is the state of the economy which is sending people back to the land. Lack of jobs in the towns and a shortage of imported raw materials (as a result of difficult import licences) may be the main factors which are causing agriculture to emerge from the doldrums of the past decade. The policy shift away from excessive dependence on oil and import-fed industry is therefore unlikely to be because of any new marketing perspective, but simply the result of economic necessity.

Obviously there is a need in Africa for free market forces to be allowed to operate naturally. It has been well demonstrated that price control does not work either in the developed or developing country. If prices are set higher than the producer can obtain on the free market, over-production is the logical conclusion – as shown by the butter, milk and other mountains in the EEC. If price is set too low under-production results. In Africa similar examples abound. In Malawi, Somalia and Zambia price controls were lifted in 1981. The result was a rise in food production. Within two years Malawi's maize crop doubled, creating a surplus for export. In Somalia the output of sorghum rose by about 50 per cent. However it is significant that price controls were lifted because of pressure from the IMF and the United States' Agency for International

Development, not because of a good understanding of marketing by the governmental marketer. Indeed it has been argued that raising food prices is an extremely emotive issue in countries ruled by urban elites, who prefer to rely on free food aid and cheap grain imports rather than take the more unpopular, tough decision to boost agriculture at home (*Financial Times*, 4 Sep. 1986). But, unless farmers (big or small) in Africa are given a reasonable incentive, they are unlikely to move from a subsistence style of agriculture to one in which they produce for a market.

In the whole of Africa, however, there is one notable exception. This is the Kenya Tea Development Authority (KTDA), a state-controlled agricultural institute which has successfully applied marketing principles and encouraged the smallholder to think along commercial lines. Today many of the 145 000 tea farmers in the foothills of the Aberdere Mountains of Kenya are shareholders in what the *Financial Times* referred to as 'one of the largest and most successful small-holder schemes in the world, competing with privcate estates dominated by household names like Brooke Bond' (*Financial Times*, 20 Jan. 1984). For whilst in the early 1960s these farmers produced a negligible contribution, today the smallholder produces over 35 per cent of Kenya's tea crop (and some of the world's finest quality teas). Tea is Kenya's fourth foreign exchange earner (after coffee, tourism and refined petroleum) and the KTDA's 39 factories now constitute the largest single exporter of black tea in the world. The growers and their families (one million out of a Kenyan population of 19.5 million) earn cash incomes well above the rural average.

This has been achieved through accountability and participation. The KTDA, which has its origins in the Special Crops Development Authority (SCDA) set up in 1960 to encourage African growers of tea and other crops, was formed in 1964 after Kenya's independence. With the sole responsibility for tea – from provision of the bushes to marketing the crops – and backed financially by the Commonwealth Development Corporation and the World Bank, the KTDA was established with the right management expertise and with the right commercial principles on which it is run.

The KTDA services farmers, collects their crops, pays them on time and is accountable to them. There are no delays in any part of the operation. Quality control is good and an additional payment is usually made to farmers, dependent upon the quality of the tea and world prices. This is highly desirable but unusual, for normally the relationship between government and growers is distant and the relationship between the world price and the return to the producer very tenuous.

More direct involvement by farmers is witnessed elsewhere. Grower representation is from local to board level and each of the 39 factories processing the tea is semi-autonomous. Smallholders are encouraged to become shareholders, and 15 000 of the 145 000 growers hold some 1.6

million shares in the 16 factories so far incorporated as public companies.

The scheme demonstrates how small farmers and a state controlled agricultural institute can collaborate and flourish if marketing principles are applied. However there are two critical features which have much bearing on KTDA's remarkable results. Firstly the Kenyan government has been willing for the authority to act as an autonomous institution. Secondly KTDA's management is good. It has watched its overheads carefully and been strict in running on commercial principles. This is most uncommon and perhaps even more exceptional in Kenya, where the government has admitted that parastatal mismanagement is a major factor in the country's current economic difficulties.

Apart from the KTDA there is a complicated bureaucracy of 4 government ministries, 40 statutory boards, 5 national co-operatives and 70 commercial concerns. Little has been done to rationalise this situation, nor has much advance been made on the question of land tenure. And numerous other policy reforms remain on the drawing board, despite agriculture producing 65 per cent of foreign exchange earning and employing 75 per cent of Kenya's population.

The KTDA is not completely without problems. Traditionally children worked on the land, but as living and educational standards rise more jobs are being sought in the city, causing some labour problems. Also, now that KTDA's main planning programme is completed, the challenge is how to maintain growth in crop output. Essential improvement in bush yield and husbandry may be more difficult, since there is little new land to cultivate. Next there are some question marks hanging over whether the government can meet its spending objectives with regard to the KTDA. And, to make the situation more complicated, KTDA's autonomy may be under threat, since the government is seeking to exercise tighter controls over managerial appointments and salary levels in all parastatals. Finally there remains the complication that some percentage of output (usually around 15–20 per cent) is sold on the domestic market at well below world prices. This effective subsidy is borne by the peasant growers.

Nevertheless the Kenya Tea Development Authority's success has been impressive and the concept has been exported to Malawi, whilst Zimbabwe, India and Sri Lanka have sent experts to study its methods. It remains one of the few examples in developing countries of the effective utilisation of a marketing perspective.

The situation elsewhere

Outside Africa the picture is mixed. There has been some success. There have also been the typical disasters, even in the most successful NICs; for

example, South Korea has been very successful in industrial development, but agriculture has been pointed to as a bottleneck against more
rapid growth. For the growth impulses from industry have not been
transmitted to the agricultural sector as was anticipated. The South
Korean planners fell into the typical trap of believing their society to be
more homogeneous and having fewer internal tensions than was the
actual case.

Despite the inadequacies, generally of government officials not using
marketing sufficiently, there has been some success in Indonesia, which
is now self-sufficient in rice and even exporting a little. Much can be
attributed to the use of social marketing. For, through its guidance
programme BIMAS it has educated farmers in new production techniques. New 'green revolution' rice strains have been introduced and
'intensification' and 'extensificiation' have become buzz-words among
government officials. Reclamation, rehabilitation and irrigation were the
main weapons of the extensification programme and smallholders have
been organised into co-operative units. 4000 village banks have been set
up to provide cheap credit. Furthermore there has been some integration
of industry and agriculture. For, through sensible and prudent economic
policies, oil income has been ploughed into key sectors such as the
fertiliser industry. This has undoubtedly played a major role in turning
the country from the world's biggest importer of rice in 1980 into self-
sufficiency with a small surplus for export.

At the same time there remain problems, mainly as a result of poor
management, corruption and a distorted perception of the situation
because of cultural or historical considerations. For example, price levels
and supplies to the market are maintained via the government's state-
procurement agency BULONG. This organisation is at present on the
verge of bankruptcy because of its large stocks. The government is
seeking to redress the balance by reducing credit and imposing more
stringent quality control. The policy of price control may be one difficulty.
Inability to perceive the whole marketing system and anticipate the
consequences of a policy is undoubtedly another.

In the plantation sectors, which are mostly state-run, everything has
gone wrong. Targets have been too optimistic and losses are typical. The
Nucleus Estates programme planned that 80 per cent of a plantation
should belong to smallholders, the other 20 per cent to the developer (the
government) who would finance the land clearance and assist in
planting. But attitudes and cultural factors were not sufficiently examined. For investing in a plantation requires a long-term business horizon,
but Indonesian investors traditionally seek quick profits. Furthermore the
Chinese were wary in case the land acquired would later be seized from
them under a new regime more hostile towards this cultural group.

Obviously more foreign investment might help. But although there is still some foreign ownership such as the Harrisons & Crosfield (UK) group which runs palm oil, rubber, tea and cocoa plantations mainly in North Sumatra, this is unlikely to increase as a result of the government's paranoia towards foreign investment.

Finally India, an agricultural economy *par excellence* with so many people's future bound up with the land, demonstrates a typical lack of co-ordination in agricultural planning and bad management. In 1985 there were surplus grain stocks – largely because of a 4 per cent growth rate in production that year. But much was wasted because of inadequate storage space. This is all the more scandalous since 30 per cent of the Indian population are living in dire poverty (in terms of life expectancy, infant mortality, malnutrition and GNP per head) and India remains one of the most blighted countries in the world.

It would appear that schemes to alleviate malnutrition are going slowly because of faulty co-ordination between central government and state authorities (*Financial Times*, 12 May 1986). In addition to the cumbersome, ineffective bureaucracy there seems to be a lack of planning as to what should be produced. Whilst India has surpluses of grain, it continues to buy heavy imports of edible oil, even though domestic oilseed reached a record level of 13.1m tonnes in the year 1984–5.

Co-operatives have been established with a view to increasing receipts of farmers for the sale of their produce and giving them more bargaining power was part of a team in direct contact with the final buyer. But unless more adequate infrastructure such as warehousing, grading and processing arrangements and credit are developed, their success may be hindered.

India, because of its sheer size and dependence on agriculture, may provide dramatic examples of the consequences of weaknesses in agricultural planning. However, all developing countries need to develop a co-ordinated, well-thought-out strategy. The need for marketing is clear – not only on the broadest level to assess agriculture's objectives and emphasis in the country's corporate plan but also at the more specific level to work out what infrastructure is necessary, what capital is required and what the consequences will be of specific initiatives in the field of marketing.

The way ahead

Clearly it is not possible to offer a set formula which will elimiate all the inadequacies of the state marketing described above. But it is possible to state briefly what should be done and what process may be carried out and what process may be allowed in order that government officials understand and use marketing more.

First and foremost marketing training must be stimulated and negative attitudes towards marketing changed as far as possible, given the cultural constraints. Next an appropriate marketing planning approach must be adopted and used for all areas and on all levels. Chapter 21 of *Marketing: An Introductory Text* should be consulted. Suffice it to say here that some formal procedure, such as the APACS (Adoptive Planning and Control Sequence) model, spelled out on p. 410 should be used.

The process remains the same for developing countries or developed ones and may be used by the state marketer just as it would be by a private company. But it is also likely that the emphasis will differ. More emphasis should be given to appraising the overall situation and estimating expected results of various strategies. More market research will be required initially. For not only is the complexity within developing countries likely to be worse and less understood but the costs involved in making a mistake are likely to be much greater, especially where large schemes are involved. Demand must be adequately established while society must be closely examined so that the strategy adopted fits in with local culture and attitudes. The forecasting and anticipating of results is therefore of paramount importance while the initial audit of internal strengths and weaknesses and the external appraisal of opportunities and threats must not be dealt with lightly. Finally the concept of a broader holistic perspective must be used to the full.

The procedure is not in doubt. But the will to use it must be there. To reduce heavy state bureaucracies and promote free market forces and a more favourable marketing environment through efficient management may be difficult to achieve in some countries.

Conclusion

Although there are massive barriers to the integration of marketing into state planning, its relevance cannot be doubted. It can be used to assess a country's resources, devise an overall plan on how best to use them, and identify and overcome social barriers to development. The government official in his role as planner, facilitator and entrepreneur should have a good knowledge of marketing so that a broad perspective is used, all relevant factors considered and the most appropriate strategies adopted and monitored.

Unfortunately there are many complex reasons why marketing is not sufficiently embraced. Most, such as lack of emphasis on marketing and business education, corrupt and centralised power structures and rigid social systems, have their origins in culture, but there are also the environmental conditions which pose further handicaps. Consequently the record of marketing by the State is not very impressive. Population growth, distribution and agriculture have all received attention from most governments but many inadequacies remain. Despite the fact that some advances in the area of social marketing and controlling population growth are being made, the marketing mix generally needs to be considered more. In the field of distribution the development of super-markets as a means of increasing efficiency is hotly debated while direct state intervention has led to new problems. Many of the weaknesses of agricultural planning stem from a basic lack of attention to demand, competition and logistical support systems within an overall uninte-grated approach made worse by poor, publicly-controlled organisational structures. A holistic approach needs to be adopted to a much greater extent.

But although the record in agricultural planning has been poor generally, there are success stories such as the Kenya Tea Development Authority. And it is noteworthy that such positive developments have been based on commercial principles and the use of a marketing perspective. If a similar approach is used more, not only in agriculture but also in such fundamental areas as population control and distribution, great advances are likely to be made. The procedure for efficient marketing planning exists but the will to use it remains a major stumbling block in many countries.

CHAPTER 7

Marketing by the state: II

Contents

Introduction

Industrial planning has generally received more emphasis than agricultural planning in most developing countries, since the assumption has been that the Western world's model of economic development based on industrial revolution must be followed. Obviously there is a need to switch from dependence on agricultural commodities where prices have tended to decrease dramatically on world markets in relation to those of manufactured goods.

Furthermore, as with agriculture, the need for industrial planning and state involvement is not in doubt. After independence in most developing countries, the drive to secure industrialisation was strong but the barriers to achieving it were many. Few have disappeared. Often the national bourgeoisie (especially in ports of Asia) was weak, with little capital stock or risk-taking ability, especially since higher profits were to be earned in lending money. Furthermore the domestic market was small because of low purchasing power, and market opportunities were further reduced by inadequate and costly transport. Overseas markets were dominated by the multinationals. This dual economy situation killed local competition and hampered further the development of an indigenous industrial base, while corruption, monopoly and unacceptable racial groups in existing business were additional problems. Entrepreneurial shortages were therefore another difficulty. Worse, the potential industrial labour force was of poor quality. Social, psychological and economic problems have some bearing but lack of training, experience, organisation and, above all, management was, and still is, the biggest brake on industrial development in many nations.

State involvement was therefore essential, as was some relationship with multinational companies in order to secure the necessary technology, along with managerial and industrial training. Governments' attitudes towards foreign investment differed, and tended to be dependent upon the degree of economic development, the size and wealth of the nation, the international strength of the national bourgeoisie and the level of opposition towards former colonial powers. Indonesia and Burma drove out their imperialist masters after a bitter fight, and foreign enterprises were nationalised. Other nations, such as the Philippines, Thailand, Malaysia, Pakistan and India, limited further investment, some countries imposing more severe restrictions than others. At the other end of the scale many smaller, poorer (in terms of natural resources) countries, which had less bargaining power, have actively encouraged close collaboration with the multinational. Programmes of industrial development have therefore varied enormously.

But the complexities involved with industrial planning are enormous. For not only must an overall industrial strategy be formulated, but technology assessed, multinationals controlled and indigenous entrepreneurs encouraged. And all this must be done within the typical broader framework of lack of expertise by government officials, corruption, bribery, malpractices by multinationals and other cultural and environmental constraints.

Not surprisingly there have been many costly mistakes which have become all the more apparent in the present increasingly competitive climate. This chapter considers the broad failings of industrial planning, the role for marketing (which to date has largely been ignored) and the barriers which prevent its more rapid adoption. The extent to which marketing has been used and the corresponding rate of success is then shown by comparing industrial planning in India with that of Singapore. Finally the future of marketing by the state is considered.

Major failings in industrial planning and the role of marketing

Many weaknesses in Industrial Planning can be identified. These are listed in Table 7.1, with the role of marketing in order to eliminate such deficiencies considered alongside.

Table 7.1 Basic failings in industrial planning and the relevance of marketing

Major Failings in Industrial Planning	The Role of Marketing
1. Objectives stated in terms of output with insufficient attention to social objectives. Thus often incorrect technology, emphasis on supply.	Marketing provides the means of creating more balanced objectives, having made an assessment of resources and conditions within the country.
2. Lack of attention given to social structures which may handicap strategies being fulfiled and/or promote inequalities within the nation.	Marketing can research these and change them, if necessary, through social marketing.
3. Poor consideration of the consequences of strategies adopted (whether import-substitution of export-earning policies).	Marketing encourages planners to anticipate consequences.
4. Lack of understanding of multinational operations and lack of clear objectives as to what the government requires from the multinational. This leads to (a) poor negotiation (b) wrong production processes (c) inability to assess benefits of multinational operations (d) lack of transfer of technology (e) less tax revenue (f) poor control over the multinational	Marketing can provide an understanding of the multinational's operations and its perspective which can lead to (a) the best deal (b) the right production process (c) better ability to assess benefits of multinational operations (d) improved technology transfer (e) higher tax revenue (f) better control over the multinational
5. Lack of attention to small firms and controversy as to whether government should interfere in small firms' development.	Marketing with its broad perspective considers small firms as well as large-scale developments. It also suggests how governments should facilitate small firm development.
6. Lack of a holistic approach to industrial planning.	Marketing encourages a holistic perspective.

(a) Objectives stated in terms of output

The first and foremost failing in industrial planning has been that objectives still tend to be stated in *output*. And because all emphasis has been on the *supply* side of the equation, there has been too much emphasis on capital-intensive technology and too little attention on final demand. It has also led to the situation where social justice, equality and employment are not sufficiently considered. Consequently urban-rural disparities have in many cases been promoted.

Although output as a measure is consistent with early definitions of economic growth (as discussed in Chapter 1) and is seen as important in the economists' models, which use a capital-intensive project such as an iron and steel mill as the productive initiator of a multiplier effect, the weaknesses of this approach are becoming more and more apparent. But, despite the fact that it is increasingly realised that a labour-intensive strategy is more suitable if labour is abundant, Governments may still reject the relevant intermediate technology as being static, negative and an obstacle to economic advance in the long run. Furthermore, and perhaps more pertinently, they are likely to gain little prestige for themselves or their country. Indeed the official attitude has tended to be 'small is stupid'!

If marketing had been incorporated more into the planning process, it is likely that objectives would have been broader, incorporating social goals as well as simply output. For marketing has the ability to select the industrial strategy according to the country's resources and final demand. The social implications too will be taken into account and because an assessment has been made of the country's existing conditions and resources, the decision regarding the type of technology is likely to be better. Although capital-intensive technology may be more prestigious and more effective in reducing the technological gap between developed and developing countries, it may be the most appropriate in all countries – particularly populous ones experiencing rapid growth rates or where existing technical know-how is extremely limited. These issues are discussed, in relation to the multinational, below. Suffice it to say here that there are many arguments for using intermediate technology, especially in the indigenous small firms field.

Firstly intermediate technology usually uses local and therefore accessible raw materials, which reduces dependence on imports (in addition to the large savings on the initial capital equipment). Foreign exchange is therefore saved. Secondly intermediate technology employs more labour per unit, thus providing more much-needed jobs. Thirdly, because it builds on existing technology, new processes are more easily absorbed. Local skills can be used and imported foreign exports are unnecessary, for machines can be serviced and spare parts built locally, while training is often unnecessary. Fourthly intermediate technology usually fits in more with existing social structures than does advanced technology, which is often socially disruptive. Finally intermediate technology, is more likely to be used at full capacity. Conversely it is often the case that where the necessary infrastructure is inadequate and the company has to cope with intermittent electricity supply, lack of maintenance expertise and the like, advanced technology can only operate well below capacity.

There are potential dangers involved with intermediate technology. For example, care must be taken to assess the market availability, particularly at the international level, of products manufactured by an intermediate technology process. Nevertheless marketing, with its ability to assess both the conditions within the country and the consequences of intermediate technology, should be sufficient to predict and overcome such problems.

In the small firms' area, where the value of intermediate technology has been stressed, marketing can be used to smooth its introduction. Harper and Soon (1979) have suggested a set of guidelines for the government planner:

1. Foreign machinery should only be introduced after a consideration of alternatives.
2. There should be a gradual substitution of imported equipment and components.
3. Care should be taken not to import oversized, or highly sophisticated, plant which might have the capacity but cannot be used.
4. Second-hand equipment should be encouraged.
5. A reward system should be devised for innovators and inventors.
6. Incentives are necessary to encourage appropriate technology.

Marketing's role in the first three directives is to provide, through marketing research, an assessment of the situation. It can be used to devise the necessary promotion in the fourth, whilst research into culture and social marketing may be appropriate for the last two guidelines.

(b) Lack of attention given to social structures

The next major inadequacy of industrial planning is often the reverse side of the emphasis given to output and capital-intensive technology. This is the lack of attention given to assessing the existing social environment, and changing it, if necessary.

The social structure, property-ownership, power alignment and any monopolies by a small number of families must all be closely examined. Yet usually they are not, since either there is unwillingness to do so, or it is assumed that social obstacles to change will melt as industrialisation progresses. But frequently they do not. For example, in parts of Asia the concentration of power into the hands of a few favours oligopoly and makes it particularly difficult to stimulate new small- and medium-sized industries. In India the business class with their enormous economic and political power have golden opportunities to earn enormous profits, which may not be to the good of national development. Their planning horizons are usually shorter, their profit incentives stronger so that their investment may lie in the field of luxury goods rather than basic necessities. And whilst a few people may gain employment as a result, distortion in market demand is promoted, the wants of the rich being catered for, but the needs of others remaining in short supply.

If marketing is incorporated into planning, a greater understanding of the social system is likely. Industrial planning can then be modified to incorporate these structures. Alternatively, where change is considered essential in order that economic progress occurs, attitudes can be modified gradually through social marketing.

(c) Poor consideration of the consequences of strategies adopted

In addition to the above failings, a third area where the government planner falls down is his lack of attention to the possible consequences to broad strategies adopted. As noted earlier, the size and wealth conditions of countries often determine the industrialisation strategy adopted. A large, rich country, for example, is likely to follow an inward-looking, import-substitution policy to save foreign exchange, whilst others, notably the small, poor countries, often need to adopt outward-looking, export-orientated strategies to earn foreign exchange. There are difficulties associated with both extremes.

Because the import-substitution strategy is often used in large, rich countries where market demand is already well established, it is easier to estimate possible costs and profitability of industries internally. Other advantages include the fact that typical import-substitution industries tend to be those producing simple consumer goods which do not require highly skilled know-how, and tariff protection is quite possible. But there are also problems: (i) there is a requirement to import machinery and materials as industries develop; (ii) the net gain in foreign exchange savings is consequently not always so significant; (iii) tariff protection often breeds inefficiency and tariff barriers have to be reduced to encourage industry which is more competitive on world markets; (iv) over-concentration on industry as opposed to agriculture.

Equally the outward-looking, export-orientated strategy, although allowing developing countries to make the most of their comparative advantage, promoting free trade, eliminating inefficient industries, and proving extremely effective as a route to development for many of the newly industrialised countries, is not without its problems. Firstly comparative advantage may lie with raw and partly-processed materials, and if a strong government, controlled population and inflation growth do not exist, there is the danger that such a strategy could lead to perpetual reliance on labour-intensive industries which would always be behind technologically. Next it is difficult, if this strategy is adopted, for local entrepreneurs to assess and enter export markets, since they are unlikely to develop an essential strong home market unless there is some protection for them initially.

If marketing is incorporated into the planning process, the government official is more likely to foresee such consequences of a chosen strategy. He can extrapolate from past experience and devise measures to prevent typical problems which have occurred elsewhere before.

(d) Lack of understanding of multinational operations and lack of clear objectives as to what the government requires from multinational corporations

Many of the above weaknesses are closely related with the fourth fault listed in Table 7.1. This is concerned with the multinational enterprise, usually an essential element in the transfer of technology and industrial development. The basic failing is an insufficient understanding of the multinational's operations and the lack of a clear statement regarding what the multinational is expected to deliver. This leads to (i) poor negotiation, (ii) wrong production processes, (iii) an inability to assess the benefits of proposed foreign investment, (iv) lack of transfer of technology, (v) loss of tax revenue and (vi) poor control over the multinational. Many of these consequences overlap and the multinational's marketing perspective, well documented in Chapter 8, should be borne in mind. Nevertheless some attempt is made here to highlight the weaknesses of planning and the way marketing can help in accelerating improvement.

In relation to production methods, there have been many mistakes. The multinational will, if possible, choose a production method which is to its own advantage rather than that of the host country. It may be that in certain fields a global product policy (discussed in Chapter 8) can be used, which is enormously beneficial in terms of cost. Under such circumstances the multinational often seeks to specialise production in order to build one standardised product suitable for a global market. This involves the most up-to-date standardised technology worldwide. Conversely it may wish to build different generations of a standardised product. Here it will use technology which is considered obsolete in the developed world. The Volkswagen Beetle car built in Brazil provides a good example. Sometimes the plants built and the technology used are completely unsuitable to the host country, and the multinational is entirely to blame. But the fault often lies with host governments. There have been many cases of governments insisting on the most up-to-date technology, often for prestige reasons, without considering whether it is the most suitable for the conditions in the country.

Obviously the government official is in a stronger position when negotiating with the multinational if he understands something about production methods and product policy. The incorporation of marketing will encourage him to consider the factors which determine production methods and the state of these in his country. These may be listed as:

(i)   Size of market
(ii)   Level of technology which can be absorbed
(iii)   Distribution of factors of production
(iv)   Cultural attitude to change

(i) SIZE OF MARKET

It is easy to see how size of market affects methods of production for, basically, a large market is required if mass production and specialisation of labour are involved in production. Consequently, if the government decides that a certain technology is required to build a specific product for the domestic market, its chances of acquiring this are better if it is a large, rich country. For, with a population of over 30 million and wealth of resources resulting in some disposable income, there is a potential domestic market. But, as noted earlier, there are surprisingly few large, rich countries like Nigeria, Indonesia, Brazil or Mexico, and most others fall into other categories with less negotiating power. For example, small, rich countries tend to be unattractive, since it would not be worth the multinational setting up a production process for a small domestic market where labour costs are high and where, consequently, goods produced would be uncompetitive on world markets. Small, poor countries have little negotiating strength and may have to accept a multinational producing on its own terms for export.

Certainly the international enterprise usually has all the advantages over local industry. Not only does it have superior technology, but it also possesses brand names and trade marks which can be used to conceal the source of production. Furthermore it brings jobs and foreign exchange (resulting either from saving on imports or earning on exports). The bargaining power is consequently with the multinational and the developing country, especially the small one, can do little to reverse this situation. The only action a country can take is to group together with neighbouring countries to form a larger market, more attractive to the multinational. Peru provides a good example. In the 1970s it was wishing to encourage one of its multinational car assembly operations to set up local production. But a domestic market for 30 000 vehicles a year did not justify this. Peru joined the Andean Pact and, immediately, an enhanced domestic market with a demand for 150 000 cars per annum was formed.

Subsequently, several regional groupings like the Andean Pact, such as the Association of South-East Asian Nations (ASEAN) and the Economic Community of West African States (ECOWAS) have emerged. Modelled on the European Economic Community (EEC), few have been very successful. Most are composed of countries with extremely different economic, political and sometimes cultural backgrounds. The long planning process which went into the formulation of the EEC is absent and, although countries regard a regional grouping as advantageous in that they can export more to their neighbours, few countries are willing to accept their neighbours' imports! Historical linkages between members tend to be lacking and often one larger or more successful country dominates the group, causing jealousy elsewhere. Indeed many groupings have doubts hanging over their chances of survival. Nevertheless they provide one bargaining counter which should be considered when negotiating with a multinational, especially if agreements on constraints and concessions to multinationals can be reached and adhered to by all members.

(ii) Level of Technology Which Can Be Absorbed

The next factor which must be considered by the government official is the level of technology available within the nation and the level of technology which can be absorbed. Often the gap between the technology brought in and that which is available is too great – frequently because of an assumption by officials that technology transfer is easier to achieve than it is in reality. Although it is easy for the multinational to incorporate all the most up-to-date features when designing new production facilities, so that the subsidiary may be more sophisticated than the parent plant in a more technically advanced nation, very often this leads to disaster. For often the new plant cannot be operated efficiently because the experience of maintaining machinery is lacking, and this may well be an argument for more intermediate technology. However this tends to be less acceptable to many government officials seeking prestige for their nation through modern, sophisticated technology.

(iii) DISTRIBUTION OF FACTORS OF PRODUCTION

Perhaps even more important is for the government official to consider factors of production (that is, capital, land, labour, raw materials and so on) within his country. The issue of appropriate technology is closely related. For a multinational moving into a less developed country where labour is relatively cheaper than capital, it may make more sense, particularly if the country is large with a rapidly-rising population – as in the case of Mexico, to bring in more labour-intensive methods to provide more jobs. In reality there are few nations which are in the position to insist on capital-intensive, sophisticated rather than labour-intensive technology. Only in some very successful countries like Singapore where both inflation and population growth have been kept down is this trading-up strategy possible. Elsewhere, raw materials may be an important consideration. For example, in the Middle East where there is free heat (obtained by burning off natural gas) it may well be advantageous to use methods of production not normally contemplated in the West.

(iv) CULTURAL ATTITUDE TO CHANGE

Lastly the cultural attitude to change must be assessed. For technolgy transfer involves more than just patents and general know-how. It relies upon an attitude which favours innovation, and accepts change as inevitable and desirable. But in some cultures there is an in-built stability, a resistance to change and the maintenance of values is more important than monetary rewards. Consequently non-economic obstacles have been found not to melt in the face of economic change. A technology gap may therefore exist, not because of the unavoidability of a certain production process, but because of the lack of willingness to use it. Again some thorough market research helps before such factors can be adequately determined.

In assessing both product methods and product policy the government marketer should already have a clear indication of what the government wants from the multinational. Although the multinational brings a package deal of benefits – as discussed in Chapter 1 – there are three major ones which stand out. These are jobs, foreign exchange and technology. Although it is difficult to separate one from another completely, nevertheless the industrialisation policy (dependent to a large degree on the size and wealth of a country) tends to focus on one more than the others. Thus the large, rich country should place the greatest emphasis on jobs while the small, poor country will seek foreign exchange first and foremost through exporting.

Unfortunately many Third World governments have no clear idea of what they want. And even if their objectives are clear because of their poor knowledge of production methods, product policy and the multinational's functioning generally, they cannot be sure that they are getting what they want. Not surprisingly attempts to ensure that benefits are transferred and to control certain elements of the multinational's operations enjoy scant success.

One of the major problems for any developing country is to ensure that *technology transfer* does in fact take place. Often it does not and there is much bitterness towards the multinational, which is seen as monopolising vital patents, and placing indigenous enterprise at a permanent disadvantage. Even where legislation requires the international enterprise to lease out its technology, patents can be replaced by a new generation of technology, causing the benefits of existing know-how to evaporate. Furthermore the multinational usually insists on trade marks which ensure brand loyalty and outlast patents.

Much of the advantage the multinational possesses arises from not only the tangible assets like technology, patents and trade marks, but also the intangible assets of prestige and superiority which are associated with a multinational being 'Western' and 'foreign'. This bundle of tangible and intangible assets has been referred to as 'intellectual property' by some developing countries who have questioned whether the multinational should possess all rights to it.

There have been various lines of attack upon intellectual property rights by developing countries, eager to ensure the transfer of technology. Some verge on the immoral, for today counterfeiting of goods, from handbags to pharmaceuticals and car parts, is big business worth $60b per annum. (*Financial Times*, 1 Sep. 1986) and many Third World countries, particularly in the Far East, regard counterfeiters as providing jobs and income for the local population. But, while piracy may have been very effective for certain consumer durable products, in industrial processes, the balance of power still lies with the multinational. Legislation has emerged in certain developing countries with the objective of limiting intellectual property rights and enabling them to be transferred at

minimum cost. Together with other methods the lines of attack include (i) establishing technology boards, (ii) excluding certain areas from patent production, (iii) shortening patents protection, (iv) compulsorily licensing patents, (v) nationalising trade marks, and (vi) using association of trade marks.

The aim of the technology transfer board (typical in Latin America or the Philippines) is to monitor the quality of technology being imported and to regulate royalty payments. Excluding areas from patent protection embodies the concept of the international patent, which is based on the assumption that certain technological processes should become common knowledge and that there should be an automatic public right to any domestic enterprise wishing to use them. Shortening the length of patent protection may mean that the patent passes into the public domain in a developing country long before the patent rights have expired in the country of origin. Alternatively many developing countries require patents to be licensed out at a royalty determined by the host government (maybe through a technology transfer board). Under these circumstances a patent is no longer restricted to the multinational's subsidiary and local industry acquires technology at very favourable royalty rates. Nationalisation of trade marks gives a local company the right to use a trade mark internally without the consent of the multinational or the payment of further royalties. Finally a less drastic method which has been attempted is 'association' of trade marks. This means the foreign trade mark is used in conjunction with a locally-owned trade mark. The government usuallly then only has to pay half the royalties to the multinational whilst the major advantage (it is hoped) is that, once the foreign trade mark is discarded, the prestige associated with it is also associated with the local trade mark.

In reality all methods are open to question. For technology in its broadest sense is difficult to define, and even harder to quantify. And if such intangible aspects as 'prestige' cannot be defined, how can the relevant legislation be formulated? Furthermore the multinational, whilst it is always subject to host country legislation, can still maintain its lead through its ability to innovate as fast as technology can be absorbed.

Nevertheless, once more, a better understanding of marketing allows insights into the tangible and intangible marketing advantages possessed by the multinational. The government planner is then in a slightly better position to use appropriate measures to ensure that technology is transferred at minimal cost to the host nation.

A similar burning issue is that of *tax revenues* from multinationals. Again, because of their enormous power of manoeuvrability, it is possible to shift capital to countries where taxation may be more favourable. This is usually achieved through transfer pricing and results in a loss of revenue to the host nation. Even in advanced countries it is difficult to eradicate – as shown by several states in the U.S.A., where California, for example, attempted to impose unitary taxation. In developing countries, where the administrative machinery is less sophisticated, the problem is even greater.

Certainly some knowledge of marketing by the multinational should help assess pricing, and may therefore be a first step to setting up the necessary administrative machinery. However both the technology and taxation issues are related to the wider problem of methods of controlling the multinational. These are limited, and often ineffective. Five main measures can be identified:

(i)   Nationalisation/expropriation
(ii)   Some ownership of the multinational's operation
(iii) Insistence by the host government that local management is employed in the multinational's operation
(iv)   Regional groupings
(v)   International agreements

Nationalisation is common, and generally accepted by the multinational when extrative-type operations are involved and there is an agreed time-scale. Although there have been some unpleasant instances of sudden nationalisation by governments where products, such as oil, are considered to be of vital importance and where governments know they have support in the United Nations, it seems only fair that countries should own their natural resources. Therefore, unless the multinational is offering some complex technology which the host government does not have and cannot easily absorb (an unlikely event in the extraction of all but the most specialised minerals, such as uranium), the days of the multinational's operations in extractive industries in host nations are numbered.

However nationalisation has also been used for manufacturing operations. Usually it is the result of governments who, having agreed on a time-scale after which ownership will fall to the host nation, then break such contracts, often for discreditable reasons. For example, an opposition politician with an anti-foreign stance can use it to win votes. Alternatively governments fearful that the multinational will run down its operations before the take-over date have brought in nationalisation, and under such circumstances the multinational may be in an impossible situation. For if profits before nationalisation were low, the recompense given will be small. If high profits were being achieved, this is regarded as exploitation. However nationalisation should be treated as a last resort by a host government, since future foreign investment is likely to be deterred.

Some form of *ownership* in the multinational's operation is favoured much more, for ownership, to a large extent, means control. Often a sliding scale of taxation – the locally-owned part being exempt – is used to promote this. Alternatively it can be encouraged to sell off its holdings and repatriate its capital, or allow the original investment to run down and be replaced by local industry. If this is the strategy chosen, the company has to sell its holdings to local nationals and is prevented from investing further in the economy. If taken to an extreme this means the company has to sell at any price, and if foreign capital reserves are not available within the host country to permit capital repatriation, this borders on expropriation.

A less extreme and more common method is for developing countries to prevent further wholly-owned subsidiaries from being established, but instead insisting on a joint venture or indigenisation programme. Both joint ventures and indigenisation are attempts to ensure that the local interests of the country are being taken into account. Although it is sometimes difficult to differentiate between the two, a joint venture has two, three or four *active* partners (either private individual(s), the public sector in the form of a parastatal or a financial holding company such as a bank), whereas indigenisation means that there are *many less active* owners. For in the latter case the government requires that the multinational sells off shares to local buyers – often laying down prices and conditions too. The government may also restrict the multinational's holding to 40 per cent or less. India and Nigeria have been the most restrictive in their indigenisation programmes, which both began in the 1970s.

In India's 1973 Foreign Exchange Regulation Act, the objective was to reduce foreign ownership to 40 per cent in all industries, apart from those in key sectors bringing sophisticated technology or earning large amounts of foreign exchange. In 1976 amendments were made so that there was three categories of foreign enterprise:

(i)   Key sector activities, capital goods and petrochemicals, which, because of their sophisticated technology and foreign exchange earnings, were allowed a higher percentage ownership.

(ii)   Industries not so widely committed to key sectors but still involved and with significant exports. Here foreign ownership of 51 per cent was allowed.

(iii) Industries not contributing to either of the conditions above. In this case the 40 per cent rule applied and this was subject to further dilution through time.

Many companies refused to operate under this regime. IBM, Coca-Cola and others pulled out of India. However, recently, regulations have been relaxed and IBM has returned.

Nigeria operates a similar scheme, with three categories of industry. At one extreme are the enterprises contributing neither sophisticated technology nor export earnings, for example distribution companies. Here the objective is to completely 'Nigerianise' the company within a given time period. This has been accomplished in several companies (although, with bribery rife in Nigeria, evasion too has been possible). At the other extreme are enterprises bringing sophisticated technology or earning large amounts of foreign exchange. Here 60 per cent foreign ownership or even more may be possible. Between these two categories is a third which is determined by the contribution of the industry to the Nigerian economy.

However the intention to accelerate local ownership and thereby achieve more control does not always work. Sometimes the joint venture partner is a parastatal (there being no able or politically-acceptable private partners). This means that because of the parastatal's lack of business ability in the particular field, the multinational retains control. In other cases where indigenisation is insisted upon shares may miraculously fall into the right hands, for example of politicians, top civil servants and their relatives. Perhaps worse is when the multinational finds and pays individuals to lend their names as shareholders. This is a situation which borders on the illegal but still ensures that the multinational maintains control.

Insistence on Local Personnel as management is a third method, often used in association with greater ownership. The idea is to build up local managerial ability, and if locally-born executives are used the multinational is more acceptable, since it is assumed that the interests of the host nation (rather than of the shareholders in the multinational's home country) will be taken into account. However this strategy may be difficult if local managerial ability does not exist.

To become part of a *regional grouping* is a fourth way of reducing the power of the multinational. It provides a useful method of increasing a country's market and therefore becoming immediately more attractive to the multinational, while at the same time giving more negotiating power to the grouping. This is especially true if maximum concessions to, and minimum constraints on, the multinational can be agreed by all members, for a united front is then presented and the multinational is no longer free to play one government off against the next for the best deal.

The Andean Pact (established in 1969) represents an extra-ordinarily bold effort on the part of five (later six) countries in Latin America to pool their economic power in a joint policy towards the multinational. It broke new ground in the developing world because it laid down new rules. Firstly it denied foreign-owned enterprises the advantages of free trade among Andean Pact countries, unless the enterprise committed itself to a divestment programme that would place majority ownership and control in local hands. Secondly foreign participation in public utilities, communications, banking and raw materials was to be limited. Thirdly contractual ties, such as loans or licensing agreements between foreign plants and local subsidiaries were to be restricted in order to prevent profits being drawn out of the country.

But the actual application of these controls was limited. Chile disregarded the provisions during most of its membership of the Pact, and then withdrew. Others, like Colombia, found loopholes. Although the Andean Pact remains the most successful regional grouping in the developing world, its problems are typical and more exaggerated elsewhere. Members of other regional groupings have broken ranks, and are likely to continue to do so. Together with jealousy within the regional grouping, with, for example, Nigeria being regarded as 'big brother', taking advantage of other members of ECOWAS, and the present increasingly competitive climate world-wide which means multinational investments overseas are curtailed, regional groupings in the developing world are playing a relatively minor part in the attempt to control the multinational.

International agreements have been equally unsuccessful, despite the growing realisation of the need to control the multinational and the logical assumption that control on the international level (to match the international enterprise) might be easier. For whilst developing countries have with one voice accused the multinational of exploiting them and promoting bribery, they have not been so unified in their implementation of international codes of conduct.

The Organisation for Economic Co-operation and Development (OECD), the United Nations and its associated bodies and the International Chamber of Commerce (ICC) have all attempted to provide guidelines on such aspects as (i) the behaviour of multinationals in host countries, especially in relation to ethical practices; (ii) how multinationals should be treated by host governments, and (iii) the sort of incentives which should be offered to multinationals and the constraints which should be imposed. The non-aligned group of developing countries have also attempted to present a united front to the multinational by setting out a list of demands, among them that (i) capital, technology and access to markets should be provided by industrialised countries on easier terms than those which currently exist, and (ii) each developing country must be free to take any measure against the multinational in order to promote national interests.

But because these codes of conduct are both voluntary and unenforceable, they are ineffective. And the list of demands set down by the non-aligned group are extreme to say the least. Countries do, and always will, break ranks. Furthermore the only real remedy against transfer pricing, tax evasion and the rest is a local civil service sophisticated enough to be able to keep an eye on multinational activities within its territory. And to eliminate bribery in most instances would involve changing countries' cultures.

The need for marketing here is clear, in order to develop expertise, understand transfer pricing and try to differentiate between facilitating payments and bribery by understanding market conditions. The international codes of conduct provide the basis from which to build up skills and make possible the implementation of guidelines suggested, at least on a national level.

In relation to the various methods of controlling the multinational the role for marketing is to provide some basis for choosing an appropriate strategy, given the resources of the country. Furthermore marketing is useful in monitoring the strategy chosen, and changing it if the international environment changes. It has already been noted that an unfavourable economic climate has reduced new multinational investment world-wide. Countries with stringent controls have fared badly and many have had to relax their constraints. But frequently this is too late. If marketing had been adopted earlier proactive rather than reactive action might have been possible and the loss of investment less.

Finally, through an overall better understanding of the multinational's marketing perspective, not only will control be more effective but it is likely that the other related inadequacies mentioned above – such as poor negotiation, poor choice of production processes, inability to assess benefits brought by the multinationals, lack of technology transfer and loss of tax revenue – will be reduced.

(e) Lack of attention given to small firms and controversy over whether the governments should interfere in their development

Perhaps as a result of the above weaknesses in industrial planning, compounded by an increasingly competitive economic climate, more Third World governments are turning their attention to the role of small firms in their economies. For, although it is often easier to allocate resources to start up an iron and steel mill than deploy efforts to encourage small enterprise, there is an appreciable shift in this direction.

In the developed world the small-firm sector, however defined, employs between one-fifth and one-third of the working population. In developing countries it is likely to employ many more, as well as providing a bigger opportunity for employment in the future. For small firms have many functions which are summarised in Table 7.2.

Table 7.2   Possible roles for small firms in industrial planning

1. Restorer of the balance between agriculture and industry.
2. An agent of development in backward regions, thus preventing further over-concentration and urbanisation elsewhere.
3. A means of expanding the domestic economy.
4. A method of modernising attitudes and allowing for diffusion of scientific knowledge.
5. A generator of income, employment and more equitable distribution of wealth, without reducing the pace of economic growth.

Firstly small firms can help restore the balance between agriculture and industry. In the past rural craftsmen were eliminated once imports of manufactured goods started and the number employed in agriculture rose. More recent strategies focusing on capital-intensive industry have not helped the unemployment in rural areas. But the development of small village industry would.

Secondly small firms can help promote some decentralisation and thus help develop backward regions whilst alleviating the over-urbanisation and over-concentration of industry elsewhere. Towns, often developed initially as part of an export economy with appropriate lines of communication, have continued to draw skilled and unskilled labour from the rural areas, and although there may now be the beginning of a reversal of this trend in some countries, the majority of large cities still serve as nerve centres to which further development is attracted. The rural areas on the other hand have remained backward and are suffering from serious decay. Once such areas become depressed, it is difficult to halt the decline and opportunities continue to decrease, since most skills and capital have already left. Loss of identity and national disintegration can result, especialliy if religious or other minorities occupy such regions, as has occurred with separatist movements in Thailand and the Philippines. Small-scale industry, however, may be able to reverse such trends, uplifting income, creating links with urban areas and helping to integrate a country politically and culturally.

The third function of small firms may be to encourage domestic market expansion. Since many domestic markets are small, the economies of scale associated with modern technology are not possible (as seen above) unless an overseas market is being supplied. Small scale industry can therefore fill this gap. At the same time, it can help bring a new way of life to society, introducing new attitudes more akin to those referred to by Myrdal (1968) as modernising and essential before economic development can take place. Where traditional societies with hierarchical social structures are involved, small-scale industry has a better chance of providing change than large-scale developments such as those which have been found not to work in some parts of India. Finally more income and employment is likely to be generated by small firms since labour-intensity is higher.

Unfortunately weaknesses in planning also abound in the small firms area. A consequence of capital-intensive developments being given priority is that small firms have generally received little attention. Although this situation is now changing, there remains the closely associated controversy as to what government involvement in small firms should be. It has been argued that it may be better for the government to concern itself directly with larger scale developments and only help small firms increase their chances of success through integrated systems of assistance, rather than directing them in certain sectors. For in many instances government assistance has been found to be ineffective and may even cause damage through regulation, enforcement or corruption.

But although there are significant barriers to the achievement of more effective planning of small firm development (discussed later), areas which have been identified as needing help are (i) credit, (ii) training (iii) acquisition of the correct technology.

Small firms often need funds for machinery, equipment and working capital but cannot acquire loans from banks because of lack of collateral. Suggested solutions to this include (i) the establishment of institutions specialising in small business finance, (ii) small business divisions within industrial (development) banks and (iii) small business development funds within certain banks or agencies. Other ways in which small firms could be helped is by subsidising consultancy, providing advisory services and setting up promotions and trade fairs (Harper and Soon, 1979).

Training is a second area where help is generally required, while some help with the acquisition of the correct type of technology is a third problematical area. Intermediate technology was mentioned above as being particularly suitable for small firms. However this may not always be the case and in order to identify precisely what technology should be adopted, Harper and Soon (1979) have suggested that technology development centres should be established. These would match up what is available with the needs of the small firm under consideration. It may involve upgrading basic production processes, or scaling down high technology developments. For example, in some parts palm oil processing has been upgraded by the introduction of a simple mechanical digester taking over from the old pestle and mortar pounding process. Conversely scaling-down and redesigning of such developments as brick plants is possible, so that the plant's capacity may be lower but more labour is also employed. Emphasis can also be given to developing new product design which bridges the gap between the most sophisticated available technology and that which exists in the developing country. At the same time there may be a case for using sophisticated technology, if appropriate for example, for subcontracting activities.

Finally there are all sorts of problems faced by small firms in relation to the infrastructure. Often the situation has been made worse by the majority of available capital being invested in the large-scale developments, and leaving little to be put to good use in making the small firm's marketing environment more favourable. Instead small firms often have to cope with poor physical transport networks, erratic and high-cost supplies related to protective restrictions and inadequate information about assistance from the government on all aspects of small firm operation.

Obviously the need for marketing in the planning process related to small firms cannot be denied. Firstly, as a result of the broad perspective that marketing encourages, the government planner should incorporate small firms into his strategy, deciding what role they have to play and how much money should be allocated to their development, given the resources of the country and the overall industrial strategy selected. Secondly, through encouraging the government official to examine the existing culture, attitudes, financial set-up and other background conditions, marketing suggests the best organisational frameworks to be developed. For example, in relation to the need for more credit for small firms, the use of marketing can help to ascertain whether institutions specialising in small business finance are superior to small business divisions within industrial development banks, or small business development funds within central banks or agencies.

Next, if government officials themselves understand and use marketing, the training which they offer to small firms should improve dramatically. Similarly technology will be better understood and advice about what technology a small firm should use ought to be much improved.

Finally, through good marketing research into the problem faced by small firms, and by understanding the whole marketing process from consumer to producer, the marketing environment within which small firms operate can be made much more favourable. For governments can then ensure that:

(i)   the infrastructure developments in terms of road, rail, industrial estates and so on are adequate;

(ii) raw materials are available at a reasonable price – often an enormous problem where supplies are erratic and the small firm has to lock up capital in stock;

(iii) the entrepreneur knows of government assistance available;

(iv) help with particularly difficult areas such as importing, exporting and marketing generally is provided;

(v)   incentives and protective tariff restrictions do not benefit solely the multinational and, where extra concessions have been made to the multinational, small firms are in some way helped or subsidised;

(vi) the most favourable overall marketing environment is provided.

(f) Lack of a holistic approach to industrial planning

Not only can the marketing environment of small firms be improved, but also the environment for any type of industrial activity within the economy. For the sixth and final weakness of industrial planning has been the lack of a holistic approach towards planning, and this is clearly evident from the distortions which have occurred in many countries through unintegrated emphasis in one area without consideration of the whole.

By incorporating marketing into the industrial planning process, it is likely that the full picture, including small firms, multinationals and state-owned industry, could be better considered and planned. Thus the typical consequences of local small-scale industry being forced to close in the face of a new development, which often involves sophisticated technology and foreign investment, would be anticipated and prevented, or contingency plans made. Furthermore, if the existing conditions and strengths of the country were matched with the opportunities in the wider context, whilst at the same time bearing in mind weaknesses and threats, it is likely that a better corporate plan for the country with the appropriate industrial strategy would be achieved. And many of the failings of industrial planning would be reduced, if not eliminated.

Barriers to the adoption marketing into industrial planning

As with introducing marketing into agricultural planning, distribution or any other area of government planning, there are barriers preventing the easy incorporation of marketing into industrial planning. As always, it is most frequently the cultural conditions, particularly social structures, which, together with the lack of training, cause the biggest obstacles, and they are perhaps even more significant in industrial planning, since frequently so much personal gain is at stake. At the other extreme is the government official who suffers most from lack of marketing education or training. Table 7.3 highlights this by adding a third column to Table 7.1

Table 7.3 Barriers to the incorporation of marketing into industrial planning

Major failings in industrial planning	The role of marketing	Barriers to the assimilation of more marketing into industrial planning
1. Objectives stated in terms of output with insufficient attention to social objectives. Thus often incorrect technology and emphasis on supply.	Marketing provides the means of creating more balanced objectives, having made an assessment of resources and conditions within the country.	Lack of marketing training. 'Prestige decisions'. Corrupt decisions. Political decisions and political relationships.
2. Lack of attention given to social structures which may handicap strategies being fulfilled and/or promote inequalities within the nation.	Marketing can research these and change them, if necessary, through social marketing.	Lack of marketing training. Unwilliness to change social structures if personal gain is at stake.
3. Poor consideration of the consequences of strategies adopted (whether import-substitution or export-earning policies.	Marketing encourages planners to anticipate consequences.	Lack of marketing training. Unwillingness to consider long-term consequences. Short-term personal gains are all important.

4. Lack of understanding of multinational operations and lack of clear objectives as to what the government requires from the multinational. This leads to (a) poor negotiation (b) wrong production processes (c) inability to assess benefits of multinational operations (d) lack of transfer of technology (e) less tax revenue (f) poor control over the multinational	Marketing can provide an understanding of the multinational's operations and its perspective which can lead to (a) the best deal (b) the right production process (c) better ability to assess benefits of multinational operations (d) improved technology transfer (e) higher tax revenue (f) better control over the multinational	Lack of marketing training. Lack of status associated with engineering and business qualifications. Lack of willingness to consider the nation's interest and to control the multinational if this interes with personal gain. + Manoeuvrability and power of the multinational.
5. Lack of attention to small firms and controversy as to whether government should interfere in small firms' development.	Marketing with its broad perspective considers small firms as well as large-scale developments. It also suggests how governments should facilitate small firm development.	Lack of marketing training and ability to instruct others. No perceived need or willingness to consider small firms.
6. Lack of a holistic approach to industrial planning.	Marketing encourages a holistic perspective.	Lack of marketing training. Holistic perspective considered unnecessary.

and, against each major failing identified, showing the corrupt government official at one end of the spectrum, his more honest but ill-trained counterpart at the other. In addition there are barriers which, to some extent, are independent. These generally result from the multinational's strength and maneouvrability.

It seems likely that in many countries objectives stated in terms of industrial output will continue. For, notwithstanding the lack of marketing training, it is often to the benefit of those in power. Output is usually viewed as a measure of economic progress on the international level, and thus 'political' decisions, 'prestige' decisions, associated with capital-intensive technology, or even corrupt decisions, associated with bribes from multinationals, are likely to favour this type of objective.

Equally there is little incentive to research and change social structures if the decision-makers with the political connections are the ones who are going to lose as a result. Indeed, simply because of power alignments in many nations, social structures have been ignored and inequalities promoted. The multinational's power has often been strengthened through politicians and their close friends and relatives becoming major shareholders, even though on the surface it appears that the indigenisation programme is beneficial to the country as a whole. Under such circumstances projects involving luxury goods to cater for the rich are unlikely to come under attack. Thus the call for marketing to be used to uncover such inequalities and change the attitudes of certain groups is unlikely to be heeded.

It is not surprising that in countries where the above conditions exist the consequences of industrial strategies are not sufficiently anticipated. For there is likely to be a general unwillingness to consider long-term consquences. Where political instability is common short-term personal and political gains are more important. In other more stable and less corrupt countries a basic lack of marketing training is largely responsible.

In relation to the multinational a more complex picture emerges. As usual there are the corrupt politicians who seek individual gain above all else but here we are also dealing with lack of understanding of the multinational's marketing perspective, poor technical knowledge and the terrific power and manoeuvrability of the multinational. Under these circumstances it is extremely difficult to have clear-cut objectives or to control the multinational. And these barriers affect most countries to varying extents.

Generally those who make the decision to permit a multinational to operate locally are politicians. Several key posts may be filled by their nominees or family and close friends. Consequently qualifications will not be an important consideration, but the decision-makers appointed will still have the power to make important decisions (often based on what is the personal interest of their superior rather than the national interest). In more honest regimes decision-makers will still tend to be insufficiently qualified in marketing, engineering or business generally. Consequently their objectives are hazy and they have no experience or know-how of they way things are produced. What often does sway their judgement instead is national pride, and because of their ignorance in technical matters they are often wildly optimistic about overcoming the practical difficulties involved in moving towards the position of a first-rank industrial power. Under such circumstances governments have often requested the most up-to-date technology, regardless of its relevance. Intermediate technology may be more suitable to the country's factors of production, but under these conditions, with prestige being all important, it will be discarded.

Even if intermediate technology is requested, lack of technical knowledge may lead to other problems. There is the question of how much should be paid for technology which is considered obsolete in developed countries. Since the multinational is the one with the better knowledge it is not surprising that there have been cases of governments paying more for a production process than its scrap value.

Indeed the difficulties of controlling the multinational in all areas are enormous – largely because of its manoeuvrability and power. Even when objectives are clearly stated by governments, it is often difficult to work out what incentives should be offered and whether objectives have been achieved. For example, if foreign exchange is the major goal, a government offering tax incentives to produce this may be giving a multinational more advantages than necessary. International enterprises tend to be more successful at earning foreign exchange in any case, simply because of their global perspectives and operations. In relation to technology transfer, one may pose the question: is it possible for any government to facilitate this and how can one measure whether it is being achieved when technology transfer involves knowledge transfer and cultural attitudes which are all quite unquantifiable.

There is the equally thorny question of whether governments have any totally satisfactory means of controlling the multinational's profits. If the host government insists that they are ploughed back into the local economy the result is that more of the nation's industry becomes foreign-owned, especially since the multinational will tend to buy over local industry. Alternatively, if the host allows a percentage of profits to be repatriated, it runs the risk, if it has no real ownership in the company, of losing tax revenue through transfer pricing, for few developing countries have administrative machinery sophisticated enough to check what is happening.

Indeed many of the problems involved with the multinational stem from the fact that no one government has any day-to-day control over it, because of the nature of its operations and its legal incorporation in more than one nation. This is a very severe barrier to the achievement of more effective planning where multinationals are concerned, irrespective of any improvements in officials' marketing knowledge.

In the small firms area, however, it is mainly cultural aspects which preclude more marketing being used in planning. At one extreme is the government official who specifically ignores small firms in his strategy, since there is no personal gain to be had. At the other extreme is the usual lack of marketing training, which is particularly disastrous in this area, for the need for training within small firms is great. But if the government planners and their staff themselves are not trained in a practical way, it is difficult for them to train others!

There are also additional culture-related problems within organisational structures and small firms themselves. Corruption at lower levels may be endemic. Thus the official whose job it is to aid small firms, may only help selected ones who have offered him bribes. There is also the attitude of the small firm owner to be taken into account. He may not be willing to use any information centre or organisation set up by the government to help him, since he regards the whole exercise as a method of extracting more tax. Where co-operation among small firms has been encouraged by government to counterbalance the power of larger companies, some have come to grief through poor management, mistrust by members and dishonesty on both sides (government and small firms). Other initiatives are beaten by the nepotistic structure of many small firms. Many others are organised in such a way that there is a sole proprietor with good informal relationships with customers and workers. But when he dies, so too does the business.

Finally, the lack of a holistic approach to industrial planning may be difficult to change where there is little desire to improve marketing knowledge and incorporate it into the planning process.

Therefore, according to the individual country, the manner of breaking down these barriers will vary. Where willingness at the top exists, there is much that can be done to provide marketing training and to make greater marketing in industrial planning. As can be seen from the following examples (of Singapore and India) countries with an outward-looking marketing philosophy and well-qualified government officials have been more successful than those with heavy bureaucracies where corruption is rife.

Industrial planning in Singapore and India

Singapore provides the perfect example of a newly industrialised country which, through an export-oriented outward-looking policy, has incorporated marketing to good effect and avoided many typical weaknesses of industrial planning. Not only has it had an overall industrial strategy which it has modified to take account of changing conditions internally and externally, but it has also considered (perhaps too rigorously, some would argue) social structures. The consequences of strategies attempted have been anticipated and responded to whilst clear objectives and good control when dealing with the multinational have been evident, and small firms have not been neglected.

Furthermore marketing, engineering and business are held in high esteem and the government has done all in its power to promote a very favourable marketing environment for any industrial activity within the state by providing excellent infrastructure. It has also helped reduce energy prices, encouraged 'target' industries through subsidiaries, developed basic industries and then handed them over to private industry, discouraged firms which were not export-orientated and encouraged multinationals to take advantage of cheap labour for their subcontracting assembly operations.

However, having matched its initial strength of cheap labour with the opportunity of foreign investment, it has closely monitored the situation so that the potential danger of Singapore becoming a permanent low-cost centre of production for labour-intensive industries using intermediate technology did not occur. By keeping down population growth and inflation levels it has actively encouraged wage levels to rise. This has resulted in not only greater purchasing power and changes in demand from luxury goods for the rich to wage-goods for the majority, but has also made it necessary for multinationals to bring in more sophisticated technology with higher productivity to reduce unit costs. Robotics, genetic engineering, artificial intelligence, informatics and biotechnology are being encouraged and educational programmes are being developed to match. The objective of Singapore's ten year plan for the 1980s is to make Singapore a 'brain centre' for Southeast Asia. Cenral to this strategy of upgrading computer expertise from mainly parts assembly to the design of 'thinking machines' at the very forefront of computer technology is Singapore's new £7m Information Technology Institute which serves as a centre for applied research and development in all aspects of information technology. It is hoped that Singapore, already a first rate computer software design centre, can win a share of the lucrative market in computer programs (*Financial Times*, 23 Apr. 1986).

Until recently Singapore's success has been staggering. Carved out of the jungle and clawed back from the sea Singapore has pulled itself up from nothing with no resource but its people. Today it is a clean, green, modern and efficient cosmopolitan city state. With high-rise living, safe streets and super-efficient communications, from the airport to the telephone system, disposable income is high and anything, apart from drugs and pornography, can be bought with an abundance of choice.

Singapore, not surprisingly, has been regarded as an example to the world and especially the Third World.

There remain some hints still of a developing country. For example, the power structure is such that Lee Kuan Yew, having ruled for 27 years, is now being accused by some of wanting to create a dynasty. Over-regulation has become an irritant for many of the inhabitants. Although the death sentence for drug pushing, heavy penalties for outlawed habits such as littering or spitting, and censorship of sex can be accepted, there is some disquiet expressed when Lee starts voicing worries about the growing tendency of graduate women not to marry or have children, or introducing measures to reverse the trend (as he did in 1984). It has been noted *Financial Times*, 23 Aug. 1986) that Lee may be having difficulties coming to terms with Singapore's more mature phase, which does not need so much direction.

But despite this and the shattering blow in 1985, when Singapore for the first time in 20 years showed a contraction in output of 1.8 per cent in real terms – compared with an 8.2 per cent expansion in 1984 and similar levels in previous years – the success of Singapore cannot be denied. Even if, as has been suggested, the improbable island is nothing more than a confidence trick in which people are willingly persuaded of its stability and prospects, credit must be given to the industrial policy which has made this possible.

At the other extreme lies India, which epitomises many of the typical failures of industrial planning. Output has been considered all-important, social issues have suffered, the multinational in many cases has been driven out, small firms ignored and a few (often politically-connected) individuals have gained.

India provides one of the best examples of maximum intervention in industrial development by the state, associated with an inward-looking import-substitution policy at the other end of the spectrum to Singapore's. Since 1956 the government has been exclusively responsible for certain basic industries such as mining of coal and iron ore, petroleum, non-ferrous ores, heavy engineering, machine tools and nuclear power. Other industries such as aluminium, chemicals, fertilisers, pharmaceuticals, are owned publicly and privately while other sectors such as textiles and food processing are all in private hands.

Controls on foreign investment are strict. Licensing is insisted upon to prevent over-concentration of multinational power, but this has often meant that the government needed to take the initiative, since indigenous entrepreneurs do not have the desire or capacity to invest in projects of national interest.

In all development plans heavy (often capital-intensive) industry has been stressed, with a lower growth in consumer goods industries. This required a large government involvement and the suppression of market forces. Although some basic industrial structure was quickly established, there has been much criticism of industrial planning which has (wittingly or unwittingly) failed to consider social issues sufficiently. It was stated initially that the policy would ensure that (i) citizens had a right to an adequate means of livelihood, (ii) ownership and control of material resources of the community should be distributed to serve the common good, and (iii) the operation of the economic system would not result in concentration of wealth and the means of production to the common detriment.

In the event, the reverse occurred. Unemployment increased and over 40 per cent of India's rapidly growing population are below the poverty line. The increase in national income (an objective stated in output terms) has gone to a limited number of individuals. Thus today there are many doubts about the sincerity and dedication of the political and administrative authorities, the paramount value of heavy industry and the conceptual basis of Socialism (Sarkar, 1978). In classic terms the government assumed Indian society to be more homogeneous than it was and that growth via heavy industry would overcome social obstacles, transmit growth to other sectors, stimulate new investment and generate demand. This did not happen, largely due to the hierarchical social structures. Surpluses were syphoned off and the lower strata paid the price.

Today India is changing its industrial policy. The government hopes to transform a closed economy making high-cost, low-quality products inefficiently into one which is in step with international productivity and technology. As a result private sector industry is being allowed to diversify, to compete in areas formerly closed to it and to increase its output. Government restrictions on the multinationals, which in the 1970s caused many to pull out of India, have been relaxed. The closed-door policy which resulted in the stifling of industries such as computers because of restrictions on imports began to change in 1981, when the government decided to make components, with foreign collaboration if necessary. A strong export orientation is being encouraged whilst other sectors such as television production and telecommunications have opened up. If a foreign project is really seen as desirable even the usual 40 per cent ownership rule on non-essential industries may be waived. Licences to manufacture foreign designed equipment such as television sets are being given out freely and tariffs are gradually being lifted, making international competitiveness essential, particularly in relation to electronics.

In conclusion it has been decided that market forces *are* important and that more factors, including savings, employment and foreign exchange, must be carefully examined *together* before an integrated holistic plan is possible. With Gandhi's present (however ambitious) attempt at stamping out corruption it would appear that India is at least recognising (even if only subconsciously) the need for more marketing in industrial planning.

Marketing by the state in the future

Not only, it would seem, is it in industrial planning, that governments are realising their mistakes. Many are now convinced that there is a need for less state involvement, more private sector activity and more response to market forces. From Communist China through state-orientated India to nations professing 'Confucian Capitalism' off the eastern shore of the continent, Asia is going private. Governments (of various colours) are actively decollectivising agriculture, pulling out of state-owned industries and services, restoring private enterprise to its previous role and finding new ways to encourage individual businesses, which they hope will step in to take the risks, provide the finance and the skills.

Whereas in the 1950s and 1960s state control was all-important in the eyes of socialism, today privatisation is, in many parts of Asia at least, the key both to reduction of state spending and promotion of efficiency. Today men like Yousuf Haroon, motor car magnate of Karachi, who saw his father's business expropriated in the name of socialism, are reviving their prospects for the future. Businessmen are now regarded as necessary – to keep the economy going, organise funds, supply managerial skills and meet the demands of the market without being a big drain on the public purse.

Perhaps this situation has come about because of the success of those nations such as Hong Kong, South Korea, Singapore and Taiwan that did not go along the state-run path; or it could be that the contraction of international funding has forced governments to choose between giving up new development projects or offering them to the private sector. But what is not in doubt is that it is increasingly accepted that governments are not properly equipped, with their stifling bureaucracies, to promote successful economic development on their own. Even in Malaysia and Indonesia, both previously concerned to increase the public sector in order to protect the Bumiputras' interests and restrict the Chinese, the tide is turning. In Malyasia it is realised that the public sector is too large. Government projects are being carefully examined, the rural service is to be held to its present size and the privatisation of key state enterprises is being speeded up (*Financial Times*, 13 Aug 1986). Furthermore foreign investors are no longer bound by the rule which requires all projects to have a minimum 30 per cent Malay shareholding. This has removed one of the central pillars of the New Economic Policy which was introduced in

1969 after the Malay–Chinese racial tensions erupted to the surface with rioting. The objective was to transfer one-third of the country's wealth to the poorer indigenous Bumiputras (or 'sons of the soil') by 1990 and a host of parastatal organisations were created, some of them holding shares on behalf of the Bumputras, who are not as entrepreneurial as other groups, particularly the Chinese, who under the New Economic Policy were allowed a 40 per cent holding. This also shows how cultural factors, which can impede the formulation of commercially-bound economic policies, are seen as less important in the light of economic necessity. For the New Economic Policy was initially considered necessary to dampen Malay resentment against foreign and Chinese supremacy which increased racial tension. But now it has been realised that its arbitrary nature frightened away investors who were otherwise keen to capitalise on Malaysia's strategic location, low wages and relatively highly-skilled labour force.

Private sector activity is seen as the key to future economic growth. Despite the fact that the Malaysian government now owns (through 60 parastatal organisations) hotels, office blocks, plantations, factories and banks, the privatisation of ports, railways and hospitals is now being discussed. Protective tariffs, cheap productive labour and fewer foreign controls are being stressed in an effort to attract foreign investment both to provide import-substitution of basic consumer goods industries for the domestic market and to earn foreign exchange through export-orientated industry.

Indonesia's stance is perhaps even more surprising. Here there is much outspoken debate continuing about the harm protectionism and state intervention is causing. Leading the attack Professor Sumitro Djojohadi-Kusumo, a former minister and the country's most respected economic thinker, has suggested that protectionism is growing and inefficient and well-connected companies are 'feather-bedded' by a widespread system of licensing arrangements (*Financial Times*, 13 Nov. 1985). There is also a maze of tariffs, quotas and other import restrictions affecting over 1000 commodities whilst entrenched industries, after acting in collusion with various government departments, continue to press for, and win, more protection. A distorted, high-cost economy encouraging corruption and discouraging private investment and initiative is the result. The evidence supports Kusomo's arguments. There are at present more than 220 state companies operating in the manufacturing and service sectors in Indonesia. Most have a reputation for inefficiency. Protectionism and high costs threaten international competitiveness of non-oil and gas exports and whilst total investment is falling, many private investors, foreign and domestic, have complained that they are shut out from areas of potential profit by government regulations or well-connected monopolies controlled by politicians or their relatives. Indeed the sceptics have argued that in most sectors, especially manufacturing, state intervention and protectionism is so well entrenched that it will be impossible to dismantle.

Nevertheless discussion is at least under way and the fourth plan has been revised so that half of the new investment is now actually expected to come from private sources. Indeed in May 1986 the Indonesian government announced a major package of liberalisation of rules covering foreign investment, which waters down the previous blanket requirement of at least 51 per cent Indonesian ownership in joint ventures after ten years of commercial operation. Measures have been taken to ensure foreign investment is not frightened away because of lack of interest by Indonesian nationals. Possible extensions to the disinvestment rule after 30 years are also likely and rules requiring a minimum 20 per cent Indonesia investment in joint ventures for high-risk operations have also been relaxed. Elsewhere even more hopeful signs are evident. Pakistan is reviving the private sector, while Bangladesh is returning its nationalised jute and textile mills to their owners. The Thai government has decided to privatise ten ports, while 50 state-owned enterprises, employing 250 000 and making no profits, are to be sold off to the private sector. Some initial recognition of the market, even if it is not a wide embracing of marketing practices and principles, is obvious. State involvement is likely to be very different in the future from what it has been in the past, and there is likely to be much more marketing by the state.

Conclusion

Industry has received much attention and expenditure from government planners but there have been many inadequacies in planning programmes. Typically objectives have been stated in terms of output with insufficient attention given to social structure or the consequences of strategies adopted. Worse, multinational operations, usually essential for developing countries' development are insuffiently understood and controlled, while small firms are only now beginning to receive the attention they deserve.

The incorporation of marketing into the planning process is highly desirable, for as well as providing a method of assessing resources and conditions within a country so that objectives may be realistic, given existing social structures, consequences of strategies may be foreseen and the negative implications of multinational activity minimised. Furthermore a holistic perspective is more likely to emerge with all aspects of industrialisation – from the smallest to the largest scale – optimally integrated.

Despite the typical cultural and educational barriers preventing the easy incorporation of marketing into industrial planning it is clearly demonstrated that, where commercial principles and a marketing perspective have been used, as in the case of Singapore, success has resulted. It is also interesting to note that in the present increasingly competitive economic climate, and with the reduction of aid to developing countries, more and more nations are turning to the private sector as a route to salvation and to the reduction of crippling state spending.

It would seem that the writing is on the wall. Market forces cannot, and must not, be ignored. In an increasingly interdependent world the state official will have to become very much more of a marketer in the years ahead. The planning procedure – noted at the end of the previous chapter – already exists; it only remains for the state marketers to come to terms with it and use it.

CHAPTER 8

Marketing by the multinational enterprise

Contents

Introduction

The growth of multinational activity in developing countries in the last 30 years has been unprecedented. Seen by host governments as an indispensable means of speeding economic development, multinationals have been encouraged to locate in developing countries, rather than simply exporting manufactured goods to them or extracting their raw materials. At the same time there has been a rationalisation of economic activities on a world scale. The enterprise, which once simply produced for domestic and export markets has been replaced, since the 1950s, by diversified corporations or conglomerates which buy, produce and sell in many countries world-wide. And such companies no longer emanate solely from the Western developed world.

Japanese multinationals are rivalling and even questioning some operational aspects of the longer established multinationals, whilst developing countries themselves are beginning to become a source of multinational corporations. South Korea provides a good example. A few years ago this country had no multinationals. Today it has several. Daewoo is one of the fastest growing conglomerates. Founded in 1968, its sales topped $4b by 1985. Its interests include: (i) textiles, from which it is now withdrawing investment, while still having the world's largest shirt factory at Pusan, where 8000 are employed and 3.6m shirts per month are produced, (ii) shipbuilding, into which it was directed by the government, (iii) light engineering and (iv) heavy engineering. Its strategy is undergoing some modification. Having proved that South Korea can build the biggest, it is following the Japanese route, and now hopes to show that South Korea can produce the best. It has already established a joint venture with General Motors who will market Daewoo cars under the GM badge for 1987. Hyundai, another major South Korean multinational, now has a permanent presence in the USA with its sales and marketing headquarters recently set up there.

Such multinational enterprises, whatever their country of origin, are characterised by extremely effective marketing strategies. At the same time multinational marketing is likely to be significantly different from that described in the general marketing textbooks. This is largely because of a more global emphasis in production, sourcing and markets. The marketing concept as a result is not always the starting point. Indeed it could be argued that in many fields multinationals are more product-orientated, assuming that, because of international convergence of tastes, there is only one market segment – the world.

Consequently products manufactured for the original market are considered suitable for new markets elsewhere, notably in developing countries and, helped by very effective advertising, this often proves to be the case. However it is often argued that through this strategy local culture is destroyed, inappropriate technology and management techniques imposed and bribery and corruption increased.

Perhaps not surprisingly something of a love–hate relationship exists between host developing countries and multinationals. Whilst loved for the benefits they bring (notably technology, jobs and foreign exchange and the general multiplier effect they can set in motion) they are at the same time hated for the power and manoeuvrability they possess. And despite the argument that developing countries today have a more confident relationship with multinational firms (Hill, 1981) there is little chance of a multinational changing its method of operation or its marketing approach. The best a developing country can do is to understand it and monitor it accordingly.

To this end this chapter seeks to examine the most important issues, first by considering what exactly a multinational is, what it stands for and how its operations have developed, so that some of the issues in the love-hate relationship are uncovered, and subsequently by putting marketing by multinationals under the microscope. The issue of global markets, the convergence of consumer tastes and multinational manoeuvrability is described so that the multinational's perspective becomes clear. Thirdly the impact of the multinational on the host country is discussed, with the claims and counterclaims being listed and evaluated. Next the question of transferability of Western management techniques is addressed. Finally the significance of some of the broader issues of the cultural environment of developing countries with regard to the operation of the multinational is examined.

The definition of a multinational enterprise and its development

There are many definitions of multinational enterprises. Some authorities have suggested that turnover and number of operations are the most important distinguishing characteristics. Vernon (1971) defines a multinational as an organisation with a turnover of over $100m and manufacturing operations in more than six countries. This has been accepted by the United Nations as the formal definition of a transnational corporation.[1] Other authorities have considered functions of enterprises (Dunning, 1971), or management styles (Perlmutter, 1969).

The definition used here is Livingstone's: 'An international enterprise is one which, by choice, has a permanent personality in more than one country, the personality being of such a nature that the enterprise is no longer under the complete control of a single national government on a day to day basis. In most instances this personality will have a legal status with the appropriate form of incorporation' (Livingstone, 1975, p. 9). It is a significant definition because it conveys the idea of the manoeuvrability and power that multinationals possess. This is due to the fact that they can evade control by not being under the day to day control of any one single government. Instead, through their personalities in numerous countries, they may use the different legal, fiscal and other systems to their advantage, and it is unlikely that the administration machinery of most developing countries is sufficiently sophisticated to uncover any malpractices.

---

[1] Multinational, transnational and international enterprise are used synonymously.

Thus the multinational in one sense brings with it the idea of foreign dominance, neo-colonialism and power. But at the same time, because multinationals are responsible for transferring not only products across international boundaries but also know-how, finance, patents, trade marks and marketing advantages, there is a movement of tangible and less tangible assets which have been referred to as a package of benefits, the three principal ones, as noted earlier, being jobs, technology and foreign exchange. To this extent the multinational is welcomed.

To what extent the multinational is seen as a saviour, or regarded as a manipulator which must be rigidly controlled, is considered later. Suffice it here to say that the multinational's growth and importance cannot be denied, especially since there have been significant changes in location and type of operations through time.

Just after the Second World War the spread of multinational activity was mainly into similar cultural, economic and technical environments of the developed world. Since the 1950s, however, multinational investment has spread increasingly to non-western societies with different cultures, ideologies and levels of technology. The type of operation too is very different. The extractive type of multinational activity which existed in developing countries dating from the nineteenth century is in decline. Host countries now (rightly) wish to own their raw materials, and unless the multinational has an integrated operation which involves more than simply processing, or has an extremely sophisticated technology which cannot be absorbed by the host nation, or controls the final market, it is unlikely that there will be any of this type of multinational activity by the end of the century. In its place the multinational has brought two very different types of operation which have been referred to by Livingstone (1975) as: (i) horizontally integrated manufacturing, and (ii) reverse vertically integrated manufacturing.

The pressures on the multinational to do this have been both external and internal. Host countries have increasingly insisted on some form of permanent presence, rather than simply buying the multinational's exports. In return inducements such as protective tariffs have been offered. Internally the multinational has been subjected to many forces. Greater knowledge of export markets, a desire for more control of the overseas market and the need to avoid hostility from developing country governments have been significant factors. Surplus capacity – either technical, managerial or financial – or surplus equipment which may be obsolete at home but tailored to developing countries' needs have been other motivators. At the same time spreading the risk politically, reducing pressure from customers who prefer face to face contact and being established in a strong competitive position in a future growth market have been other powerful reasons. At the end of the day, however, much of this movement of manufacturing to developing countries has been unplanned, more the result of difficulties in the market place (notably restrictions on imports by developing countries) than a reasoned strategic decision.

Horizontally integrated manufacturing means producing the same product, or product range, in many different markets. A wide variety of activities, from computers to soft drinks, fall into this category and IBM and Coca-Cola provide good examples of multinationals operating in this way. Sales are built on knowledge (both technical and marketing, often in the form of brand names) together with an ability to deploy them internationally. Frequently industries producing luxury goods develop. This may be what the rich minority want but it is unlikely to benefit the developing country's national interest.

Reverse vertically integrated manufacturing involves the multinational transferring technology from the developed country where the goods are produced (or 'sourced') and then exported back to the developed nation. The end result is a reversal of the export/import situation which was developed by multinationals extracting raw materials from developing countries, producing the manufactured goods in the developed nation and exporting them back to the developing country. This type of operation is unusally established in order to take advantage of cheap labour in developing countries. It can be subdivided into three types.

The first is where dynamic technology is used. In this situation rapid, or even explosive technological developments call for hand assembly which is cheaper than investing in expensive equipment which would become obsolete almost immediately. Furthermore cheap (often female) labour is highly adaptable and dispensable. The computer industry has, in the past, provided such an example, although this is now in a more technologically mature phase. Transistors and televisions are other examples. The fact that the whole product is made in Hong Kong, South Korea or Taiwan is easily camouflaged by the multinational's brand name or trade mark.

The second category of products are those dependent upon technology which is slowing down. Indeed it may be verging on obsolescence. Cars, ships, steel and textiles are good examples. Exemplifying the concept of the international product life cycle, developing countries with cheaper labour are increasingly becoming the major manufacturers of these items.

Finally there is the category of contract manufacture. Here the multinational sources some of its components in developing countries, but since these products are made to the multinational's design and specification they cannot be sold anywhere else on international markets, since the multinational controls the distribution channels. Thus the producers of such products (often local businessmen with their own companies) are captive producers. The multinational, however, can conceal the source of production by again using its brand name.

To a large extent both these latter, more recent types of multinational operation assume that there is a homogeneous world market with high mass consumption. An appropriate marketing strategy is necessary. This is discussed next.

Marketing strategies of multinational enterprises

Conventional marketing theory suggests that needs and wants should be determined before an appropriate product can be produced and sold. To a large extent multinational marketing turns this theory on its head. For the multinational prefers wherever possible to adapt a market to an existing product. Economies of scale can be developed and profits increased.

This approach, which reflects more of a production than a marketing orientation, has been promoted by the belief that consumer tastes around around the world are converging. This began in the 1950s and 1960s when there was a general assumption that the American model of cultural development was the one to which all non-Communist countries aspired.

It was promoted further by the appearance of large-scale, relatively free-trade areas in the form of North America, the EEC. in Western Europe and, to a lesser extent, Japan. As consumer tastes and industrial requirements within these three markets converged in a consumer-orientated, high mass-consumption framework the possibilities of product standardisation appeared. They have been reinforced by the revolutionary shrinkage of international space which has subsequently occurred with the introduction of new forms of transport and better communications and the multinationals themselves speeding the inevitable flow of technical services and capital across frontiers.

Not surprisingly in the 1970s and 1980s more and more multinationals have standardised their products wherever possible and adopted a global market perspective. Today many consumer durable goods are very similar irrespective of where in the world they are used, while the world car and world truck have taken over from 'European' or 'British' models. The latest development may be to attempt to tailor products to individual regional markets within an overall global standardisation strategy (*Financial Times*, 11 Feb. 1987).

However, whilst these generalisations are true in the broadest sense, the multinational may not be able to follow such a strategy once individual host countries are considered. There are several issues which are likely to constrain the multinational's choice. Indeed they may even determine the market strategy which must be adopted. To oversimplify, there are two major extremes of market strategy which the multinational may choose to follow. These are the global market strategy and the individual market strategy.

The global strategy involves a global market, global sourcing and global production. As discussed above, the multinational has every incentive to standardise products and perhaps also to specialise on an international basis. It is not likely to confine production of a product to any single national source, but at the same time will not be eager to allow each national plant to produce a complete range of products. For in this way maximum flexibility as well as profit is possible. This strategy implies both ability and willingness to switch production facilities market and sourcing on a global basis.

An individual market strategy, on the other hand, means local production and local sourcing for local markets (each one of which is assumed to be different). Although more acceptable to host nations, it is more advantageous to the multinational in terms of control and profit.

Whichever strategy is adopted the multinational's corporate goals are usually different from those of the host government. The multinational's objectives include profit maximisation, maintaining foreign market positions, overall world-wide growth in sales and earnings, with the shareholders in the home country being the major preoccupation. The host government's goals, however, may include job creation, export stimulation, maximisation of tax revenue and other broad social and economic objectives, most of which are likely to clash with the multinational's. If a host government can attract a multinational on its own terms and insist on certain production methods and products being manufactured for the domestic market, its chances of achieving its objectives are higher. But, as noted in the last chapter, it is only a few countries which have the power to insist that the multinational follows an individual market strategy. Thus the category of the developing country (large or small, rich or poor) and the closely related *ownership structure* which it permits will have a profound effect on the strategy the multinational is allowed to follow.

As noted earlier developing countries are extremely heterogeneous. They range in attitude towards the multinational from those which permit investment on a 100 per cent ownership basis to those which allow no foreign investment, only dealing on a licensing or turnkey basis.

(a) Marketing strategy in relation to type of country

However, having considered these attitudes, one can see that it is predominantly the type of country which is the most important factor

(Table 8.1). A large population and wealth of resources generally mean negotiating power for the government, which is likely to call for an individual market strategy to achieve its inward-looking import-substitution industrialisation policy. Small, poor countries, on the other hand, which must rely on foreign exchange and have little bargaining power, usually have little choice but to allow the multinational to pursue its global market policy. The ownership pattern will be closely related, the large, rich country being in a stronger position to insist on some form of ownership which often necessitates an individual market strategy to avoid clash of interest between the multinational and the host nation, the small, poor country often allowing up to 100 per cent foreign ownership.

Table 8.1 summarises how attractive the various categories of developing countries are to the multinational. Large, rich countries such as Indonesia, Nigeria and Mexico are especially attractive since they provide potentially large, rich markets as well as relatively cheap labour. These countries can, therefore, safely impose tariff barriers and other import restrictions in the knowledge that the multinational which formerly exported to them will be induced to set up production facilities. However, since these countries also are likely to insist on some form of host country ownership either through indigenisation or joint venture the multinational which locates may be facing risks in the longer term.

Table 8.1   The attractiveness of developing countries (by type) to multinational companies

Category of developing country	Attractive to multinational activity?	Reasons
Large rich	Yes	Potentially rich protected market. Relatively cheap labour.
Large poor	Not very	Political instability. Lack of disposable income. Only suitable for assembly, licensing or in some cases an exporting operation, since labour is cheap.
Small rich	No	Small domestic market. High cost production site – products manufactured here uncompetitive on world market.
Small poor	In some cases – e.g. NICs of Far East	Cheap labour. Exporting encouraged. Reverse vertical integration and global market strategy possible.

Large poor countries are not so attractive to the multinational. Although possessing a population of over 30 million most people are likely to be at subsistence level which means that a market may not exist. Furthermore they do not possess earnings from natural resources to pay for industrialisation whilst the political instability of such countries makes the multinational unwilling to risk large amounts of finance. If it decides to locate here it will restrict its involvement to licensing or an assembly operation. However, governments are sometimes willing to offer financial concessions to encourage exporting, and under such conditions the multinational may be tempted to locate some more permanent form of operation (albeit often using a no-ownership structure) to take advantage of cheap labour for exporting on a global market basis. A rapid return on investment will be sought since this high political instability is an enormous risk.

Small, rich countries such as the Middle Eastern states possess an extremely high per capita income and are relatively stable politically (trouble-makers being 'bought off'!). However they are not attractive as a location for multinational activcity simply because of their degree of wealth, rapid inflation and the expectation of the citizens (which is not to work manually). Migrant labour must be used and the cost of this is high and rising. Even though governments are very eager to industrialise, and are willing to offer tariff protection, a multinational setting up here would need to supply a wider market, and the costs of production in small, rich countries tend to be high, making goods uncompetitive on world markets. Furthermore, the culture may mitigate against the multinational's operation. Consequently multinational activity is likely to remain limited to advice, contract manufacture and exporting to their countries.

Small, poor nations can be extremely attractive to multinationals. Because they are small and not considered a threat by other nations they can offer incentives to the multinational to locate and export. Attractive initially because of cheap labour, they allow the multinational to pursue a global market strategy, often on a no-ownership basis. Indeed many of the small NICs of the Far East provide excellent examples of the multinational using reverse vertical integration where components are manufactured, foreign exchange earned for the host country and trade marks and brand names used to conceal the source of production. If labour costs become more expensive and more sophisticated technology is sought, these small, poor countries may remain relatively attractive – as in Singapore's case, where other benefits such as good infrastructure and government inducements are now available.

(b) Marketing strategy in relation to organisational structure

In theory structure should follow strategy. In reality structure often determines whether the multinational will pursue a global or individual market strategy. There are four ownership structures possible for the multinational. These are: (i) no-ownership, (ii) joint venture, (iii) indigenisation and (iv) a wholly-owned subsidiary. All may be adopted by choice, but increasingly joint ventures and indigenisation are set up by necessity.

A *no-ownership* structure, which may take the form of a turnkey operation, subcontracting of components or licensing, is often preferred where (i) there is fear of confiscation of more direct investment, (ii) there is a desire to have no employees – in a country where, for example, local work practices would be unacceptable, or (iii) where multinational companies are treated less advantageously than local companies.

Turnkey operations, that is, the building of factories or production processes, are well exemplified in the Middle East. Here South Korean multinationals have been actively involved in construction and petrochemical projects. Subcontracting is typical in the reverse vertically integrated manufacturing operation where the multinational transfers its production facilities from a high-cost plant in the West to a lower cost one in a developing country. However, rather than risk bad publicity at home through substituting imports for local jobs or employing people under poor working conditions, the multinational permits a local entrepreneur to produce the goods under contract. Provided that this local entrepreneur does not have access to the multinational's lucrative markets himself, he will remain a captive supplier; a most satisfactory arrangement for the multinational. Licensing is often insisted upon by a developing country which is hostile to foreign investment. However the multinational may also prefer this arrangement if the political environment is unstable and if there is little danger of a long-term competitor being created. In all cases, a global or individual market strategy may be pursued, for there are no restrictions offered by a no-ownership structure.

A *joint venture* is defined as a situation where a multinational has one or more local partners in a subsidiary company. The multinational usually supplies the technology and know-how, the local partner(s) the market knowledge and perhaps political contacts. The local partner(s) may be from the private sector, the public sector, in the form of parastatal organisation, or may even be a holding organisation such as a bank.

Although joint ventures are usually welcomed by host governments, are cheaper than wholly-owned subsidiaries and provide a means of both spreading risk and giving immediate access to a market, a multinational's freedom of action is curtailed because of the likely clash of interest between the multinaional with its more global perspective and the local partner with the host nation's interests at heart. An individual market strategy must generally be followed. Despite the fact that joint ventures tend to be unstable, one side usually wanting to buy the other out once the initial advantages brought by the other are understood or acquired, this method of operation is likely to become more common as many developing countries are now more insistent upon some form of ownerhip. Increasingly, too, the partner will be a parastatal organisation, since many governments in developing countries are either socialist or directly intervene in planning their economies and wish to actively control key sectors of activity, whilst in other cases there may be a lack of suitable private partners. This may work to the multinational's advantage and permit slightly more manoeuvrability in market strategy. For parastatals are often inefficient (as noted in Chapter 6) and are likely to be less familiar with any one industry than would be a private partner. But, by the time they have failed to live up to their expectations, they have already become institutionalised forms of bribery for the functionaries of the party faithful. Only in those countries where parastatals are under scrutiny and more emphasis is being given to private enterprise is their future importance as joint venture partners in doubt.

Indigenisation means that a substantial part of the operation is owned by local interests, who are equity holders rather than active partners. It is a structure almost always adopted by necessity because if offers few advantages for the multinational. Whilst it may be acceptable to give a minority holding to a former agent to reward him or even buy goodwill from a local political, if a substantial amount of equity is held by local individuals the multinational's global market strategy is likely to be severely curtailed.

As noted in the last chapter several governments, notably in Andean Pact countries, Nigeria and India, have, through legislation, required multinational companies to sell off shares, often dictating prices and conditions, unless the multinational is bringing in significantly new technology or earning large amounts of foreign exchange. The multinational does have some room for manoeuvre in its possible responses. Some are dubious. Others border on law-breaking. Firstly the multinational can ensure that shares go into the right hands – that is, individuals who will protect the interests of the company, such as people with the right political connections. Secondly frontmen can be enlisted. These people, for a price, allow their names to appear as shareholders whilst ownership and control remains firmly with the multinational.

A complication may arise if shares fall into the wrong hands, such as a section of the community viewed with suspicion or disfavour by the host government. Examples include right-wing opponents of a left-wing government, or an unacceptable ethnic group such as the Chinese in Malaysia, where the government has been buying shares on behalf of the indigenous Malays who are reluctant to do so themselves. The result here has been the state creating what amounts to a parastatal on behalf of the Bumiputras.

Global market strategy is generally not possible and if more developing countries persist in enforcing this structure, the future existence of the multinational could be threatened. A multinational will, however, accept an indigenisation policy fairly readily if the developing country's domestic market can support an operation on a one-off basis (as a large, rich country can) and if the production facility cannot be integrated into a global plan.

Nevertheless, *a wholly-owned structure* remains the most favoured method of operation by the multinational in a politically stable environment, if financial resources permit this. It may be achieved by buying out a joint venture partner (usually unacceptable in most developing countries), buying over a local company (usually also resisted), or setting up a greenfield development (which may even be welcomed in many small, poor countries, especially if local talent is 'grown'). The major advantage is complete manoeuvrability. The multinational can dispose of its assets and markets as it wishes and operate on either a global market strategy, or an individual strategy, or both.

Although in reality there will usually be a compromise in *overall* strategy dependent upon the particular market and producer, it is fair to say that global strategy is possible with no ownership but a wholly-owned situation is the most likely to favour it. Since there are no local shareholders, complete freedom of action is possible. An individual market strategy can be adopted under any of the four ownership structures but it is virtually obligatory under joint venture or indigenisation since a multinational cannot switch production, markets or sourcing once local interests are involved. Because of this a multinational will often seek to move from a joint venture or indigenisation structure to a wholly-owned or even no-ownership one if trade marks can be safeguarded and distribution channels controlled. Sometimes a multinational can avoid joint venture or indigenisation legislation by continuously injecting substantial amounts of new technology or earning large amounts of foreign exchange. But generally this is difficult. A no-ownership structure allows political or ideological obstacles to be circumvented and it is likely that new ownership structures along these lines will develop.

(c) Marketing strategy in relation to both type of country and organisational structure

At present, however, a multinational may involve all four structures in different parts of the world. To a large extent it will be the developing country which determines which one is actually adopted within its boundaries. The likely ownership structure according to type of country is summarised in Table 8.2. A large, rich country is in the strongest position, when negotiating with a multinational, to insist on a joint venture or indigenisation structure, which means that an individual market strategy must generally be followed. The initial policy of the multinational under these conditions may be to introduce obsolescent products using equipment which is being phased out elsewhere, but if there is competition present, more modern methods will be introduced.

Table 8.2 Most likely ownership structures and market strategies according to category of host country

Category of country	Most likely ownership structure by the multinational	Most likely market strategy by the multinational
Large rich	Joint venture or indigenisation	Individual market
Large poor	No ownership	Global or individual market
Small rich	No ownership	Global or (more likely) individual market
Small poor	No ownership or wholly-owned subsidiary	Global

At the other extreme small, poor countries with the least bargaining power are likely to permit wholly-owned subsidiaries or favour a no-ownership structure. A global market strategy is generally followed. A large, poor country, with its highly unstable political situation, will tend to promote a no-ownership structure, under which a global market or individual market strategy is possible. However, multinational activity will be limited. Finally the small, rich country is likely to have an even smaller multinational presence; that which is involved being primarily concerned with turnkey projects. Under this no-ownership structure an individual market or global market strategy is possible, but with industrial projects an individual market strategy is more common.

(d) The relationship of the marketing mix and marketing strategy

Whether an individual market strategy or a global strategy is used, the multinational is unlikely to formulate its marketing mix in the conventional way suggested by the general marketing textbooks. Because of its spread of activity, its manoeuvrability and especially its inherent marketing advantages, such as trade marks, brand names and 'foreignness' (which is synonymous with superior technology and 'prestige' in most developing countries) the individual elements of the marketing mix receive a very different emphasis. Naturally, under the most favourable ownership structure, where a global market strategy can be pursued, the manoeuvrability is the greatest. But even under less favourable conditions, where an individual market strategy has to be adopted, a certain global perspective is often still reflected. Indeed the formulation of the marketing mix always tends to show a basic product-rather than market-orientation. Nowhere is this better demonstrated than in product policy and market research.

Having got beyond the first, and presumably most important, market for the new product, a multinational may be able to *impose* it on a new market. The savings involved in converting a market to a product rather than a product to a market are enormous. Thus the sort of product policy which is condemned if used by the inexperienced exporter – that is, selling a product designed for one market to another for which it is not designed – makes sense for the multinational.

Such global product policy can take three forms and can be used in any of the four ownership structures. Firstly the multinational can produce identical products throughout the world. This horizontally integrated approach is the most common method. A universal product is manufactured but is only relevant in economies where conditions are similar to those in the original market. Industrial equipment, consumer durables and cars are good examples. This is the maximum product-orientation, based on the assumption that there is one world market for which a no-ownership or wholly-owned structure is essential.

The second form is to build *apparently* identical products, but to different standards. Since these products will usually be for the host country market a joint venture or indigenisation structure is possible. Whilst in the advanced world products may have to be built to higher standards, perhaps due to health and safety legislation, in the developing world it is more likely that products will be designed to lower specifications. For in most developing countries lower purchasing power, less pollution and safety control, lower community health and fewer labour-saving devices are required. A multinational may therefore choose to produce a stripped-down version of a product. This suits an individual market strategy.

The third form of policy is to produce different products either on a specialisation basis, or different generalisations of the same product. If specialisation is opted for (such as producing gearboxes in one country, engines in another, for a car to be sold world-wide) a no-ownership or preferably a total ownership strategy is essential, since switching of production facilities and markets may be necessary. However, to build different generations of the same product, such as the Volkswagen Beetle in Brazil, joint venture and indigenisation structures can be used. This manufacturing of a product in a less important market once it has become obsolete in the major market is perhaps the most controversial form of global product policy.

The impact of adopting a global product policy on market research is profound. Conventional market research and test marketing become irrelevant in the secondary market. Instead the major objective is to determine what is the minimum adaptation that is required to be made to an existing product before it is accepted in the new market. Next there must be some investigation into when production facilties can be made available. For example, if a certain technology is being phased out in a major market, this may be a major criterion in choosing to set up in a secondary market. Finally political and technical intelligence in the proposed new market are essential. It must be established what the host government's policy towards the multinational is and what kind of operation will be permitted. Also the existing level of technology must be determined, so that the multinational can phase in a new production process with the minimum of problems.

In terms of promotion standardised advertising throughout the world may be possible for some products where a global market strategy is being pursued. But even where a standardised message world-wide is not possible a multinational can usually build on its 'foreignness' and 'prestige' to promote a product and perhaps change traditional attitudes in the process. For, as noted above, there are enormous cost savings if a multinational can change the market to suit the product rather than changing the product to suit the market. Thus spending on advertising is likely to be high, but if brand loyalty can be built up, the rewards too are high.

Other aspects of promotion such as packaging can also be standardised to varying degrees and used to promote corporate image. Kodak and Coca-Cola provide good examples of the most extreme approach. Because these products can be bought throughout the world, are easily recognisable and always available, consumers are more willing to buy them than local products and the convergence of consumer tastes is reinforced.

Multinational distribution and pricing strategies also have certain distinguishing characteristics. Frequently they are interrelated. It may be decided that certain plants should serve certain markets. The world is consequently divided into market segments of the multinational's making and distribution channels are set up accordingly. Where specialisation of production is followed there will be transfer of components between plants necessitating a distribution system within the multinational. Internal pricing systems are developed alongside, which gives the multinational tremendous manoeuvrability in the movement of financial assets. Transfer pricing can be used to reduce tax liabilities in a host nation and increase overall multinational profits. It can also be used to reduce commitments in a politically unstable host environment.

As far as price to consumers is concerned, a multinational can, if there are no host country restraints, operate a standardised pricing policy, reallocating costs on a global basis. But host governments sometimes intervene. This is particularly true of governments in large, rich countries where an import substitution strategy has been adopted. Although the multinational may be operating in a sellers' market, protected by tariffs on competing imports, the host government may also administer price – after some negotiation with the multinational. A black market often develops and profits are siphoned off by middlemen or corrupt government officials. Under such conditions the multinational may not be in the strongest position.

Generally, however, it is. Notwithstanding the ownership constraints, the multinational has the power and manoeuvrability to gain both from economic progress in developing countries or from the lack of it. If standards of living and tastes are converging more and replicating those in the developed world, the multinational can gain even more from mass production and marketing a product designed for no one market but acceptable in all. If there is still a gap in living standards the multinational has the option of extending the life of certain products and production processes once they become obsolete in markets for which they were designed. Not surprisingly, there are many arguments raging about the impact of multinationals in host countries.

The impact of the multinational on host countries in the developing world

Although the bulk of multinational investment is still in the developed world, that which exists in the developing world is growing significantly in absolute terms. More importantly, its significance is much greater.

Unfortunately there is no consensus as to what the impact has been or is. It is a fact that multinationals have played an important part in the development of many developing countries. At the same time there have been economic, social and political consequences which have given cause for concern.

Often these advantages and disadvantages are expressed in an extreme fashion. At one end of the spectrum the multinational and its supporters have argued that the multinational is essential in the development process since developing countries lack capital and expertise to undertake their own industrialisation. The multinational brings not only the necessary technology but also a broader package deal of jobs, foreign exchange, entrepreneurship and management and the rest, with the result that a multiplier effect is set in motion. At the other extreme the critics have argued that the multinational is an exploiter and neo-colonialist. Originally investing in extractive-type activity in order to acquire raw materials, it kept the developing countries at a disadvantage and dependent. Today they suggest, it has added to its sins by upsetting countries' political, social and cultural fabric.

The controversy surrounding Nestle's impact on the developing country exemplifies many of these points. The multinational itself claims it has not only helped to reduce the need for food imports in countries where it has located subsidiaries, but has also provided capital investment, technology and jobs, and stimulated further development. Indeed it could claim to have filled a gap that the state marketer should have identified and filled. Its first operation was in Brazil where, in 1920, a local condensed milk factory was bought over. A multiplier effect in the surrounding area was soon set in motion. As well as more jobs being created in the factory, technology (however primitive, since everything had to be developed from scratch) was diffused. A collection system for farmers' milk increased demand and, in turn, production. A technical advice service was established so that farmers were encouraged and convinced of the benefits of modern production techniques. Hygiene standards were raised. Veterinary specialists, agricultural economists and development officers were other aspects of the 'package deal'. Because Nestle was not competing with farmers (since it did not own land or farms) an atmosphere of confidence was established. Farmers, suggest Nestle, saw that prosperity, regular income and a secure market for their milk were all bound up with the commercial success of the company.

Nestle operations were extended 60 miles north of the original site of Araras and the interior began to be developed. Nestle has subsequently set up operations manufacturing powdered and condensed milk, instant coffee and chocolate drinks in numerous countries in Latin America, The Caribbean, Asia and Africa. In all it suggests its beneficial effect is obvious. Because its factories are generally in the poorest rural areas, usually with no electricity, poor communications and an uneducated workforce, Nestle has had to provide everything. Furthermore agriculture and industry have both been stimulated in a balanced way, basic industry developing hand in hand with better animal husbandry and agriculture. Demand has been created, diversification promoted and general standards of living have risen.

But whilst the multiplier effect is well demonstrated in the rural areas of production, the critics have pointed out that despite Nestle's stated policy of 'improved nutrition', immense damage has been caused by the company and others in this field. Medewar (1981) and his supporters have suggested that not only have unsuspecting consumers been exploited but malnutrition has been promoted. The infant formula – that is, an alternative to breast milk – has been 'agressively and insidiously' promoted in developing countries to people who do not need it, who cannot possibly afford it and are in no position to use it safely (Medewar, 1981, p. 101). Although it must be admitted that many of the problems have arisen because of lack of education and incorrect use of the product, the situation has been aggravated by the multinational depicting breast-feeding as undesirable and substitute products as superior. Because of poverty, compounded by ignorance, mothers overdiluted the powdered milk, which increased malnutrition. Worse, because of poor hygiene standards – resulting in non-sterilisation of bottles and teats and the use of contaminated water – deaths occurred in parts of Africa. Thus by heavy advertising in all the media, through hospitals, doctors and directly to consumers, bottle-feeding was promoted as 'up-market' and westernised. In this way, argue the critics, the multinational has changed traditional attitudes and became a neo-colonialist.

In reality it is difficult to generalise about the multinational's impact. Developing countries vary enormously in colonial experience, market size, politics, stage of economic development and culture and so on. Equally multinationals' strategies and structures are not uniform. Finally governments' attitudes to and expectations of multinationals still differ widely. It seems fair, however, to say that some tension still exists between the multinational and host government. By listing and considering the major issues a little further it is easy to understand why.

Table 8.3 shows that for each major advantage brought by the multinational, there is a counter-argument on the negative side. Each is considered below.

Table 8.3 Arguments centred on the impact of the multinational

Positive impact of the multinational in relation to	Negative impact of the multinational in relation to
1. *Technology* Industrialisation initiated and promoted. Knowledge and skills transferred.	1. *Technology* Inappropriate technology brought. Key sector domination. R & D remains in home country. Knowledge and skills not transferred on a large scale.
2. *Jobs* Directly created in the multinational. Indirectly created by stimulating entrepreneurship and efficiency.	2. *Jobs* Wrong type of jobs provided. Economic and social inequalities promoted. Jobs destroyed through local competition being killed.
3. *Competition and complementary activity* Competition stimulated to improve. Entrepreneurship in complementary activity promoted. Overall efficiency improved.	3. *Competition and complementary activity* Local competition eliminated. Oligopolistic industrial structure promoted.
4. *Management* Effective management promoted.	4. *Management* Inappropriate management techniques introduced. Destruction of local culture.
5. *Foreign exchange* Earned or saved by host nation.	5. *Foreign exchange* Lost through transfer pricing and other means.
6. *Attitudes* 'Modernising' attitudes promoted.	6. *Attitudes* Materialistic attitudes stimulated and local culture destroyed.
7. *Demand* Increased consumer and industrial demand.	7. *Demand* Demand distorted. Social inequalities promoted.
	8. *Politics* Interference by the multinational in the host nation's politics.

1. Technology

The multinationals and their supporters would argue that they are absolutely essential in a developing country's industrialisation, since first and foremost they bring the necessary technology which could not be developed by the host country itself. As well as promoting manufacturing capacity, knowledge and skills, particularly management skills, are transferred.

The counterclaims centre on the type of technology, the terms under which it is transferred, and the control of it. It is often argued that inappropriate technology is implanted. If intermediate technology is used this may be considered obsolete and a ploy to keep the developing country at a permanent disadvantage. It has also been suggested that labour-intensive practices may not be more economical in some instances. Where skilled labour is scarce it may be preferable to use capital-intensive methods rather than train and supervise labour, however cheap. Conversely, the argument goes, if very sophisticated technology is introduced employment is not created and the balance of payments worsens because of the need to import expensive capital equipment.

Horizontally integrated manufacturing by multinationals brings in reasonably sophisticated technology and establishes important industries, such as cars and textiles, in developing countries. But, where there are restrictions imposed to prevent profit repatriation and profits must be ploughed back into the local economy, a host nation will often begin to complain after a time that key sectors are foreign-dominated.

Next a host nation may encourage licensing but then complains about the prices charged and the conditions attached. Furthermore it has been suggested by many developing countries that technology is never completely transferred, because the multinational continually innovates and keeps vital processes at home in order to maintain its lead. Indeed, R & D facilities tend to remain in the home country, but this seems justifiable from the multinational's point of view, since vast amounts of finance have been spent to develop a process, whilst lack of adequate skills and a small market size may not justify transferring R & D activities.

Finally, since technology involves more than just a production process, the multinational trains manpower and skills can then be diffused. There have been many examples of multinationals promoting training benefits beyond the initial process. For example, Heinz, Del Monte and Dole provide training for fruit and vegetable growers and also supply seeds, fertilisers and insecticides. Nestle provides another good example, as noted above. However this argument too has been questioned. Germidis (1976) noted that this did not happen on a large scale, especially in terms of skilled workers or senior executives.

2. Jobs

Indeed the next major benefit the multinational claims to bring, jobs, is a very controversial area. It is also closely associated with the issues of entrepreneurial development, competition, complementary activity and management. The multinationals and their supporters argue that not only are jobs created directly at both the managerial and blue-collar level but they are also stimulated indirectly. For through the multiplier effect backward and forward linkages are promoted and new entrepreneurs appear to fill the demands for inputs of goods and services created by the multinational, whilst others appear to cope with the increased output from the multinational.

Closely related is the additional advantage of training that the multinational provides in order that its requirements can be met. Technical, financial and marketing expertise is passed on and confidence is therefore built up in other sectors of the economy. Multinational employees can in time move into their own business and other entrepreneurs are stimulated to upgrade their products, expand their markets and develop more backward and forward linkages themselves.

There have been many accounts of such development. For example Vernon (1971) argued that the Mexican mining and railway building boom of the nineteenth century helped to establish a new entrepreneurial class composed of traders, bankers, provision providers, contractors and small manufacturers. Others have pointed out the positive correlation between the growth of an entrepreneurial class and increases in foreign investment in the most successful newly industrialised countries, such as Hong Kong, Malaysia, South Korea and Taiwan.

The reverse side of the coin is the argument that the multinational brings the wrong type of jobs. Highly capital-intensive jobs, as well as being inappropriate in some contexts, may also lead to a very small multiplier effect. At the same time economic and social inequalities may be promoted, since only a few local people benefit from higher wages and an enclave of wealth among a sea of poverty is said to result. Sometimes ethnic stratification too is promoted, as has happened in Malaysia where the multinationals have tended to collaborate more with the Chinese. Furthermore their effect on consumption patterns and life styles promotes the conspicuousness of inequality, since only the rich can afford the consumer durable goods introduced.

3. Competition and complementary activity

An oligopolistic market structure may also develop from highly capital-intensive multinational activity, for the technology is orientated to high demand and the developing country's domestic market is usually too small to provide this. It has even been argued that jobs are actually destroyed, since the multinational operating on this basis kills local competition and stifles entrepreneurial development. For the multinational possesses the advantages of superior technology, more financial resources for advertising and, above all, those important visible trade marks and brand names which assure it of consumer loyalty and thus large markets. The entrepreneur's position is therefore undermined and any potential new competitors are discouraged. On top of this there is a psychological barrier to be faced by the local competitor. Since a nation is often referred to as 'underdeveloped', 'backward' and so on, it is often assumed that he too falls into this category and cannot hope to be as efficient, innovative or successful as the multinational. Figures have been produced to back up the claim that, once a multinational is established, there is a corresponding decline in small, local or family enterprises. In Peru this was documented in 1976 by the International Labour Organisation which went on to suggest that the local entrepreneur had two choices – to collaborate with the multinational or face extinction.

4.   Management

The next major advantage brought by the multinational is management. This has been said to be absolutely essential to the unlocking of any potential a country possesses and the provision of its organisation. Management techniques are demonstrated, nationals are trained and skills are passed on to all sectors of the economy. Before any of the previous or subsequent advantages listed in Table 8.3 can be maintained management must be provided, and the multinational remains perhaps the most important factor in introducing it. However the critics argue that even this may have a negative impact, since culture is not sufficiently taken into account. Consequently inappropriate techniques are introduced and local cultural values are destroyed.

5.   Foreign exchange

Although there is no argument that most developing countries need foreign exchange, there remains controversy over the extent to which multinational activity provides it. The multinationals and their supporters argue that their impact in this area is extremely positive. The host country either saves scarce foreign exchange through the multinational manufacturing products formerly imported, or earns foreign exchange through the multinational exporting its manufactured goods. Sometimes both are possible and the multinational, with its global perspective, is usually more successful at earning foreign exchange than are the local competitors. At the same time income within the nation is raised, which leads to domestic savings which can be ploughed back to generate more income.

The critics, however, argue that the financial benefits of multinational activity are kept to a minimum by the multinational and may even be considered to be negative if a wider conception of wealth, which takes into account the social distress, disruption and increased income differences promoted by the multinational, is used. Although there is always likely to be some loss of foreign exchange through profit repatriation, interest, service charges, consultancy fees, royalties or patents and payments for materials and equipment, the critics argue that too much is channelled back home under dubious circumstances – notably transfer pricing. For the prices of goods and/or services sold from division to division within the corporation can be varied to achieve many results which will further the overall financial strategy of the firm. Profits can be shifted from a subsidiary in a host country to another one elsewhere or to the parent plant by creating costs in one or more of the legitimate measures listed above.

6. & 7.   Attitudes and demand

These two advantages the multinational claims to bring are perhaps the most controversial, since they are centred on people's attitudes and consumption patterns. In a previous chapter it was noted how Myrdal (1968) suggested that certain 'modernising' attitudes, such as diligence, punctuality and preparedness to change, were essential before economic development was possible. In the last chapter these non-economic obstacles were referred to as a major handicap for the governmental marketer. The multinational, however, provides the means of introducing the necessary attitudes and consequently reducing the associated non-economic barriers to development. At the same time, because people see what is available and what can be achieved, demand is stimulated and a multiplier effect set in motion. The multinational therefore brings in products and processes which are wanted but would not be available otherwise.

The critics argue that not only is local culture destroyed but the demand that is stimulated is distorted, with social inequalities being promoted instead. There are various levels of hostility. The mildest argue that the multinationals change values because they spread the idea that happiness and fulfilment will be greater the more goods people possess. Consumption therefore becomes the measuring instrument of both the developed and developing worlds.

The more hostile critics have argued that the cultural identity of developing countries is undermined because of these values, beliefs and lifestyles which are *imposed* by the multinational. Indeed some have suggested that the multinational is a neo-colonialist, dominating and destroying national culture, so that the developing country is dependent upon the multinational. For, although the innovators who initially purchase the new products and services brought by the multinational come from upper socio-economic classes, once a product is seen as successful people with lower incomes start to use it. There are many examples put forward.

Soft drinks are consumed widely in Mexico and Brazil, people buying four bottles per week and the multinational accounting for 75 per cent of the market. But these, as Ledogar (1975) points out, is a country where there is a shortage of protein and vitamins in people's diet. Baby foods are another example, as seen in the Nestle reference. Kellog's have successfully encouraged people to buy breakfast cereals while traditional, cheaper, and often more nutritious foods rot on local markets (Girling, 1976). This changing of tastes for the worst, argue the harshest critics, is not only immoral but is destroying a way of life. The multinational's global market strategy is pointed to as the underlying cause. The multinational has no incentive to produce goods satisfying the basic needs of the majority since it is more profitable to introduce products which are well known and for which the multinational possesses the technology. Effective demand is easily created, argue the critics.

8. Politics

These arguments have perhaps fuelled the argument that multinationals interfere politically in the affairs of the host nation. But although it is sometimes suggested that multinationals refuse to let a subsidiary trade with countries at odds politically with the company's home government, but not necessarily at odds with the country in which the subsidiary is located, it is really as an agent of Western imperialism that the multinational receives most criticism.

An evaluation of the debate

Most of the above points of view need to be treated with caution. There are many half-truths in the arguments on both sides and to ensure that the multinational brings benefits rather than negative effects the government must be quite clear in its objectives and understanding of the multinational – as discussed in Chapter 7. Some of the arguments, however, can be evaluated to a certain extent individually.

The multinational is undoubtedly a useful agent in the transfer of technology. Although there have been cases of the multinational making mistakes in the level of technology introduced, it has often been the host government's insistence on the wrong sort of technology which has resulted in inappropriate technology. Equally the jobs issue is complex. The type of job provided directly by the multinational is tied up with the technology introduced. Those host governments which have clear objectives, understand the production process and have worked out what they require from the multinational in terms of types and numbers of jobs are likely to see the most positive impact.

However the indirect creation of jobs is more difficult to assess. To a large extent whether a multinational stimulates or stunts entrepreneurial development is likely to be influenced by such factors as:

(a) the level of industrialisation in the country;
(b) the sectors of activity in which the multinational is operating;
(c) the policies of government towards entrepreneurs;
(d) the autonomy of the entrepreneur.

Where there is already some progress towards industrialisation, the establishment of multinational activity can inhibit further entrepreneurial development. If the multinational is simply processing raw materials, which does not require many backward or forward linkages, its effect will be marginal. But if the government is prepared to protect local enterprise and support it, if directly competing with the multinational, its development will continue. At the same time the government should not provide too much protection, or the multinational could be driven away. Finally some autonomy by entrepreneurs is essential. For if they are too dependent upon the multinational they cannot play a significant role in the country's industrialisation process.

There have also been attempts to look at entrepreneurial development through time in those countries which have had long-established relationships with the multinational. Vernon (1976) suggests a certain progression can be seen. Up to World War II entrepreneurs dependent upon multinationals in Latin America, Asia and North Africa were simply 'adjuncts and partners of foreign enterprises'. World War II marked a turning-point, since local entrepreneurs had to become self-reliant, as they were cut off from their overseas sources of supplies and markets. Since World War II these local enterprises have started asserting their independence.

Thus it is possible to see how the multinational affects local enterprise differently as a country industrialises. Certainly there will always be some entrepreneurs who remain dependent upon the multinational and usually in a junior position in relation to sophisticated technology, capital investment and access to foreign markets. But there are some sectors in developing countries, such as banking, mining and petroleum, where entrepreneurs have successfully dislodged the multinational's predominance, often helped by government's nationalisation programmes. Finally there are usually some entrepreneurs who are indifferent towards the multinational and unaffected by it, since their interests do not coincide. It may be that entrepreneurial developments in complementary activity to the multinational's are stimulated, whilst those in competitive activity are stifled unless there is some government assistance.

The issue of management is more easy to resolve. Undoubtedly some managerial ability is essential but Western management practices and principles may not be relevant in some cultures. This is discussed later in this chapter.

In relation to foreign exchange, it seems clear that the multinational is generally good at exporting and earning it. At the same time it is inevitable that, because the multinational is accountable to its shareholders at home rather than local interests, and because it is so powerful, there may well be a significant loss of foreign exchange too. Transfer pricing does occur to a significant degree despite the fact that it has become more complicated with floating exchange rates in recent years.

In the 1960s transfer pricing to avoid tax liabilities was possibly the most significant. But more recent work by Kim and Miller (1979) would suggest that transfer pricing is now considered most significant in relation to profit repatriation and exchange controls. Perhaps this is not surprising, since exchange controls are being imposed in more and more developing countries. The third factor identified by the firms surveyed (342 United States multinationals with subsidiaries in Korea, Malaysia, the Philippines, Taiwan, Brazil, Colombia, Mexico and Peru from which a 15.1 per cent response rate was achieved) was joint venture constraints. Many developing countries impose some limitation on foreign ownership but tend to be lenient with regard to transfer of funds through royalty and fee payments for managerial and technical skills, especially where sophisticated technology is being acquired. Therefore multinationals may receive very favourable treatment when negotiating royalty and fee payments which present good opportunities for transfer pricing.

As for the multinational's impact on attitudes, demand and politics, it may be fair to suggest that to a large extent the multinational is simply an agent of change bringing what is desired. As such, if it promotes inequalitites it does so unconsciously. Certainly the multinational's marketing is largely based on the concept of mass markets for relatively standarised products. Whilst it often does seek to change the market to suit the product, nevertheless nations still have the choice of whether to accept Western standards or not. Japan and South Korea are excellent examples of countries which have benefited from multinationals and incorporated some of their qualities, but have not had their culture destroyed. A different sort of case is some of the Arab nations such as Iran where it has been decided that industrial society's standards cannot be accepted.

In other instances, however, the adoption of the Western life-style and the materialism brought by the multinational have been actively promoted by many of the elites in developing countries who regard the multinational as a necessary transmitter of 'modern' values, and the only way of achieving a similar economic and political set-up as that at present enjoyed by Western developed nations. Generally, though, there is usually change in any society (except the most pre-industrial stagnant kind) and the multinational simply demonstrates what is available. It is therefore less of an active neo-imperialist wishing to impose a certain way of life and more an agent of change. and often only half understood by the host nation.

It is true, however, that the multinational may unconsciously promote ethnic stratification within a society and thus promote social inequalities. For in many developing countries one (or more) ethnic group has come to occupy a dominant position and the multinational reinforces this, which sometimes leads to complications. For example, in Malaysia, because the Chinese have the business experience, entrepreneurial attitude and technical skills, the multinational has in the past been happy to collaborate with them. But this became unacceptable to the government, who, through their New Economic Policy, sought to redress the balance in favour of the indigenous Malays. Because the latter have not in the past had the same business acumen multinationals have become more reluctant to enter into joint ventures with them and foreign investment has declined. In order to attract it back the rules have recently been changed, thus undermining one of the pillars of the New Economic Policy. But this demonstrates how the problem is inherent in Malaysia's society rather than of the multinational's making.

Finally the accusation that a multinational interferes politically in the affairs of a host nation is largely unjustified. Usually the multinational is very loath to interfere in politics and prefers to adopt a low profile, neutral policy. It may, however, be convenient for a host government to use this accusation if multinational assets are about to be nationalised!

In reality, it is very difficult to measure the impact of the multinational on a host nation. One can attempt to do so by considering:

(a) financial flows in and out of the country;
(b) the country's real income;
(c) externalities e.g. social benefits, sub-contracting;
(d) distortions, e.g. via protection;
(e) attribution – i.e. how much the multinational is responsible for government policy;
(f) alternative scenarios.

But the problems are enormous. For example, financial flows in and out of a country are logically unrelated – profits reflecting previous investment – and therefore all items of the balance of payments should be considered. And it would be virtually impossible to resolve (f), i.e. what would have happened to the economy without multinational activity. Wells (1977) suggests that the cost of the multinational's investment and the efficiency of the utilisation of resources employed by the multinational can be considered. If the cost is higher than some ideal figure, then multinational activity may be harmful, while resources can be said to be being used inefficiently if they could have been used elsewhere more effectively (Wells, 1977). Again, to arrive at an accurate answer would be impossible.

It is, however, possible to ask policy makers what they think the costs and benefits of multinational activity within their countries have been. Jain and Puri (1981) surveyed policy makers in 73 countries. From 84 usable completed questionnaires from 35 of these countries it was found that multinationals were seen as beneficial in (i) bringing in capital, (ii) helping capital formation locally, (iii) using capital efficiently and acting as an example to local firms, (iv) bringing in new products and processes and (v) achieving higher productivity. Major problem areas identified centred on a clash of interest between the host nation's and the multinational's objectives. This resulted in disappointment for those who had considered the multinational as a problem solver in the national economy. Also the parent company wa seen to interfere in the subsidiary's operations to the detriment of the host country. Expectations of policy makers were high. A rate of return on investment of 10–20 per cent was expected from multinationals whilst it was felt by two-thirds of the respondents tha 40–60 per cent of their profits should be reinvested.

To a large extent, however, the fact remains that the multinational's impact will be the most beneficial where the host nation knows what it wants from the multinational and can ensure that the product or service supplied and the technology imported serve the national interest. The host country has a responsibility in devising the right package of tax incentives, import protection, rebates, administration facilities, protection against expropriation and so on and promoting a stable environment for the multinational. If policies are poor and luxuries from cosmetics to cars are introduced to cater for the demands of the bourgeoisie rather than essential products, a dependent state is likely to result and many of the negative aspects of multinational activity will be present in their most extreme form. If, however, the multinational is allowed in on the host country's terms and there is careful selection of what to accept in terms of social and political change, the benefits of multinational activity can be great. Japan provides the classic example. Less than forty years ago a developing country, today it is a first rank nation. This was largely achieved through the multinational – on Japan's own terms. Furthermore its culture has not been destroyed. Many of the Newly Industrialised Countries are following in Japan's footsteps, making multinationals work for them without destroying their national systems. And this despite the fact that many are captive producers with technology based on world markets which, when in recession, cause them serious problems.

It has been argued (Hill, 1981) that multinationals do increasingly realise the problems of developing countries and have sympathy for their national goals (which often seek to maximise net social benefits of multinational activity). Multinationals are increasingly prepared to accept joint ventures, indigenisation structures and the employment of local personnel. Some developing countries, too, would seem to be more understanding of the multinational's position as well as more confident and competent in negotiating. If these trends continue it is likely that the impact of the multinational on these host countries will become increasingly beneficial, and the accusations currently levelled at multinational activity will decrease in number and ferocity.

The transferability of western management techniques

One area, however, which is not easy to resolve is the question of the appropriateness of management techniques introduced by the multinational. Drucker, in 1958, and others since have pointed out how essential efficient and effective management is if a developing country is to organise efforts and unlock any existing potential, and the multinational has been a major agent in introducing the management. The problem which arises, however, is that the multinational is largely a creation of Western culture. The only substantial exception so far is the Japanese version. But as multinationals move increasingly into developing countries with different cultures it is useful to consider the issues of the transferability of Western management techniques.

This section examines two main questions: to what extent can tried and tested management principles, practices and know-how be transferred effectively to developing countries and at what cost, and to what extent is the overall process and effectiveness of management constrained by cultural variables?

(a) The two schools of thought

There are two major schools of thought. The first is that efficient and effective management is based on universal principles, practices and general know-how. All managers perform the same basic function of planning, decision-making, controlling, organising, staffing and supervision. The second school of thought argues that management is a philosophy and/or process that is essentially culture-bound (Richman, 1977).

The first school of thought was promoted to the greatest extent by the Americans who simply and unthinkingly applied their management techniques elsewhere, regardless of local conditions. To a large extent this reflects America's history of wishing to Americanise all people who came to the United States by suppressing their original culture. And because of the enormous prestige given to businessmen and the business elite in America (there being no aristocratic or other elite) it was only natural, especially at the peak of their advance in the 1950s and 1960s, that this should be the approach.

Indeed American techniques were regarded as a means of eliminating social obstacles to economic development in many parts of the world. It was largely assumed (and to some extent still is) that the multinational can transcend national boundaries and, with its forces of uniformity, promote functional loyalties by people of all nations to one or more corporate bodies. The idea is that, as technology spreads and skills rise, employees are given responsibility and occupation takes the place of class. Thus hindering ideologies, beliefs and dogmas surrender to economic pragmatism and the performance of the high achiever takes the place of nepotism or other methods indigenous to the culture.

However, whilst some convergence of managerial practice can be seen in very broad terms around the world, on the micro level, where managers communicate, motivate, make decisions and the rest, this apparent convergence is much less marked. Furthermore in the last few years there has been a certain cultural reaction to the typical ethnocentric American approach of wishing to Americanise everyone. It has been stimulated further by the spectacular plunge in America's economic performance and by alternative management techniques, for example, Japanese, German and even Korean, which have been noted as highly effective. Especially interesting have been developments in many of the Far Eastern newly industrialised countries, such as Hong Kong, Singapore and the Philippines, which are unusual in that they represent bicultural and multicultural societies which have drawn heavily on the West and Japan, but are different from both the older industrial societies and from each other. None has unthinkingly accepted all aspects of Western management's practices and principles. Conversely, in other developing countries where American manufacturing techniques were adopted wholesale, their inappropriateness has become apparent.

This has given more credence to the second school of thought which argues that what is accepted practice and behaviour in Western societies may be much less attractive elsewhere. Not surprisingly this school of thought is gaining ground. For in reality there are many management styles. These may be:

(i)   dictatorial –   i.e. absolute authority.
(ii) paternalistic –   i.e. similar to a feudal system, with both managers and the managed having reciprocal rights and duties.
(iii) constitutional –   i.e. managerial rights being only part of the overall picture.
(iv) democratic –   i.e. the legitimate authority of management subject to the rights of those who express their views and attempt to influence management's thinking and action.

Equally if management elites exist in a society they can be subdivided into categories such as patrimonial (executives being found among relatives), political (where political connection is all important) or professional (where competence acquired by training is the main requirement).

Management style and characteristics of management elites will depend largely upon cultural heritage, for no one can escape his religious background, language heritage or political and family ties (Cateora and Hess, 1979). All individuals are born into a sea of culture. As any individual matures and gains experience of the world, he builds a system of personal standards of judgement and points of reference that allow him to make decisions. These are always intertwined with culture and have been called self-reference criteria. Rarely can an individual of one culture develop complete sensitivity to another.

This is a particular problem for the multinational locating in a developing country, especially one whose culture has never given much status to management or industry. For example, in parts of Latin

American one is born into high or low social class and because of an established aristocracy, late industrialisation and strong centralised government, managers are in short supply. Under such conditions the multinational enters into a seigniorial role alien to its operations in more advanced countries.

Yet at the same time multinationals are increasingly under pressure by host governments to adopt a policy of employing nationals. Indeed, trends now in evidence show that home country specialists are being sent overseas on shorter-term arrangements and there is a reduction in the number of junior jobs available. Expatriate staff are being regarded more as fire-fighters.

There are many advantages from the multinational's point of view in employing local nationals. Firstly, because such people are familiar with local culture, it is likely that they bring with them some knowledge of the local market and thus can tailor the marketing of goods more accurately and maximise buyer acceptance. At the same time they understand local ways of doing business so that problems can be minimised. Secondly, they are often cheaper for the multinational to employ. But the problems resulting from the multinational introducing management principles and practices founded on Western assumptions about the scientific under-standing of reality and designed to solve problems in a Western context can be enormous. In addition to a possibly complete lack of familiarity with Western management techniques, nationals having been intro-duced to them may not be able to perform their duties satisfactorily because of certain attitudes, such as an unwilliness to delegate authority.

(b) The influence of culture

Culture, therefore, is an all-pervasive influence which will affect a variety of attitudes. These include attitudes to authority, personal involvement, material gain, bribery, truth, politeness or directness in speech, people as persons or as part of an organisation with a specific function, the terms of work, formality, contact level, risk-taking, change, decision-making, achievement, reward, ethical standards, willingess to adopt the scientific method and time.

In numerous developing countries existing attitudes are likely to constrain what is considered to be 'effective and efficient' in Western eyes. Weinshall (1977) has considered some of the above attitudes under the headings of sociological and educational constraints. He shows how major functions and methods of management are affected.

Sociological constraints, he suggests, manifest themselves in attitudes, values and beliefs which in turn affect the motivation, behaviour and performance of individuals. Attitudes towards the following in particular will be affected:

authority and subordinates;
business management;
achievement;
wealth and material gain;
the scientific method and risk changing;
change;
leadership;
class structure and individual mobility.

Educational constraints will affect such aspects as:

literacy levels;
amount of specialised vocational and technical training;
higher and advanced education;
management training;
attitudes towards education.

These in turn will affect productivity levels, type and quality of human resources available to the multinational. Specifically he lists:

1. Ease or difficulty in obaining personnel with the right skills.
2. Ease or difficulty in motivating employees – both managers and workers – to perform their jobs efficiently and to improve their performance.
3. Degree of identification between individuals and departments and the firm itself.
4. Degree of frustration, absenteeism and turnover of emplopyees.
5. Degree of co-operation and conflict between employees.
6. Degree of information distortion and ineffective communication within the enterprise.
7. Amount of time spent bargaining.
8. Ease of difficulty of introducing change within enterprises.
9. Degree to which the scientific method is applied.
10. Degree of organisational flexibiity in relation to changing conditions.

In turn the techniques involved in management, particularly the planning and *modi operandi* will be affected. Specifically, this includes:

methodologies, techniques, tools used in planning;
time horizons of plans;

types of performance and control standards used;
degree of centralisation or decentralisation;
degree of work specialisation;
span of control;
grouping of activities;
extent and use of committees;
selection and promotion criteria used;
nature and extent of formal company training programmes;
degree of participation or authorisation of management;
communication structure and techniques;
methods of motivating personnel;
nature and extent of employee welfare services.

In the West efficient planning for the future using a scientific method is most important. Change is accepted and innovation welcomed. Individual achievement is highly valued and efficiency is the main measure of this. Material gain is regarded as the logical reward. But in some developing countries such attitudes and objectives may be inappropriate, unacceptable and difficult if not impossible, or even immoral in some instances, for the multinational to impose. For example, Western management philosophy teaches that efficiency is all-important, the inefficient needing to be eliminated, irrespective of personal attributes or connections. But in many developing countries nepotism and political connection are much more important than how well an individual performs his job.

Equally the master–servant relationship and the concept of rights and duties may be different. In the West there is no longer a master–servant relationship. It has been replaced by an employer–employee one. The break was promoted by trade unionism, whose survival depended on worker loyalty. The erosion of employer–employee relationship has reached the point in the West where it is simply concerned with cash. But in many developing countries a master–servant relationship still exists. Again it may be quite feasible that it should *not* be broken down. The Japanese have industrialised and maintained their culture, while Korean multinationals still maintain loyalty among their employees to a much greater extent than any Western multinational.

Differing attitudes to innovation cannot be accommodated so easily. In the Western world the frontier approach and the Protestant ethic explain the innovator's being acclaimed a hero. While such positive attitudes may be equally appropriate in Latin America and some African countries, flexibility may be lacking elsewhere. Instead, due to a fixed social system and religious doctrines, approved standards are rigorously adhered to and there is a deep respect for tradition. Innovation is consequently regarded with suspicion.

Attitudes to authority and decision-making are equally varied. Brazil provides a good example of a country where absolute control by one man is the norm. Related to the semi-feudal attitude that land is power, family members are likely to dominate business decisions, with middle-management decision-making being played down and workers being trained to do the job, but not sufficiently to usurp the superior's power. Rather than disagree with instructions, the employee will take evasive action. Generally, however, the negative aspects of this type of authoritarianism are moderated by paternalism. At the other extreme is committee decision-making which exists in the Far East. Here the emphasis is on group participation and harmony and in order to avoid discord one makes points without winning arguments so that adversaries do not lose face.

Attitudes to achievement are perhaps the most significant and closely associated with attitudes to wealth and material gain. Religion, education and child-rearing are often stated as being the three principal sources of achievement drive, but it is perhaps religion which predominates. If attitudes to achievement are considered as a continuum, those influenced by Hinduism and Buddhism are at the other, for these religions with their emphasis on salvation through withdrawal from the world regard achievement as antithetical to religion. Between the two extremes, Judaism favours high achievement, stressing individual and self-reliance whilst Catholicism is said to be more biased towards spiritual rather than worldly goals. Views of material gain and wealth are supposed to follow a similar pattern. In the West, where the Protestant ethic prevails, material gain is viewed as the 'just' reward of hard work. In Hindu and Buddhist countries, the goal of nirvana tends to promote more static aspirations.

Attitudes to time often coincide with achievement motivation. In many traditional societies time is perceived of as a circle, suggesting repetition and another chance – the idea that if time is lost today, it will return tomorrow, In the West, on the other hand, mechanical time and the development of science and industry have resulted in time being dissociated from natural events, which have been replaced by a sense of urgency, time-consciousness and the future being the temporal focus of life. The discipline associated with schedules, split-second decisions and rigid deadlines is deplored and regarded as distasteful by managers in those countries where spiritual satisfaction in life is sought. Emphasis on leisure, contemplation and an unhurried way of going about things, with little thought of the future, are common in many developing countries. In Ethiopia time required for a decision is directly proportional to its importance and in the Arab East time depends on the personal relationship, relatives taking priority.

Finally attitudes towards risk-taking, often closely correlated with general levels of education, business experience and social risks, determine the degree of willingness to accept change and therefore progress. In animistic societies innovators may risk ostracism, or even death, by violating a taboo. Reformers in Moslem societies face assassination. Another attitudinal factor related to the measuring of a society's openness to change is its place on the optimism–pessimism scale (also related to willingness to adopt the scientific method). Whereas the developed world is generally optimistic, traditional societies in developing countries tend to be fatalistic.

Hall, as long ago as 1960, suggested that there are certain unspoken languages which incorporate many of the above examples and which must be clearly understood by the multinational. These are the languages of time, space, things, friendship and agreement. It is easy to see how important these constraints are on Western management practices and principles if specific examples taken from Africa, Latin America and Islamic areas are used.

(c) Management in different parts of the world

Whereas Western multinational management considers time important, with little flexibility allowed, punctuality expected and personal relationships regarded as unimportant, the reverse is often true to the African. Time is flexible. Anyone in a hurry is regarded with suspicion and inflexible time schedules are difficult to impose. People come first, trust, confidence and friendship ranking very highly. In the larger cities some change is under way and punctuality is becoming more important. But elsewhere a relaxed, easy-going manner is the norm. Closely associated is the typical lack of task-orientation, which is usually regarded as 'foul-play' or a desire to demonstrate superiority if adopted by an American. If seen in this neo-colonial role there is little chance of success for a Western multinational insisting on such a principle. Finally, whereas age is generally considered unimportant in Western management, in Africa age is an asset, the older a man is, the wiser he is judged to be.

Many parts of Latin America display distinctive characteristics. No one rushes into business. Appointments are not kept on time and American punctuality is regarded as eccentric. Instead the concept of 'manana', which to a Latin American means an indefinite future, is important. Consequently it is contended that 'a clock runs in the United States but walks in Latin America' (Smedley and Zimmerer, 1986). Decisions are taken at the top and in person rather than in a letter or on the telephone. Machoism is important. Translated into business this means that management must demonstrate forcefulness, self-confidence and leadership with a flourish. Authoritarianism is strong. The owner is manager and master in his own domain. He does not allow for questioning by subordinates. However, because of instability in many Latin American countries, speculation, manipulation and gambling to get rich quick are important. There is also a significant amount of fatalism, since most people are convinced outside forces govern their lives.

However, nowhere are the cultural constraints more clearly demonstrated than in Islamic areas. Wright (1981) considered multinationals operating in such regions and concluded that because of lack of understanding of Moslems, many frustrating, highly unproductive situations had arisen when Western management dealt with subordinates, co-workers and supervisors.

In addition to the general characteristics of Arab executives examined later in Chapter 9, Wright (1981) identified nine areas where attitudes and behaviour tended to differ significantly. The first was the way in which the organisation was perceived. The Westerner regarded a multinational as a subsystem of a broader environment, but the Moslem regarded it in a deital way, as part of an all-embracing total system stemming from Islam.

Secondly superior–subordinate relationships were very different, the Westerner evaluating a person on his strengths and weaknesses, the Moslem regarding his subordinate as a person first and an employee second. For loyalty was found to be more important than personal competence and this would determine promotional prospects. Thirdly the Western employee perceived the organisation as a means of providing money for basic necessities whereas the Moslem employee was more dependent upon God, the job being insignificant. Not surprisingly, whereas a Westerner associates himself with a multinational for prestige purposes, the Moslem considers himself first and the organisation second. Next, whereas in the West authority is generally expected from top management in return for accountability, the Islamic approach is to demand accountability from subordinates, yet without any authority, which remains at the top.

Power within the organisation was another area identified as very different. Whereas a Western executive wants power but does not usually show it and those who have it use it discreetly, the higher levels of management in the Moslem situation flaunt their power and are quite happy to force their wills on the organisation. Not surprisingly, team work within a multinational is more difficult to achieve, for the Islamic employee is reluctant to modify his behaviour to belong to any group. And simply because the approach to management is through personalisation rather than departmentalisation with group work within, the Islamic corporate entity is always charismatic. Finally the time orientation is very different. The Western executive's concept of the organisation is futuristic. But most Moslems believe in predetermination and therefore an element of fatalism creeps in, with the emphasis in time being on the past.

The above examples would seem to suggest that Western management practices and principles cannot be transferred to developing countries, but that instead management is culture-bound. However, whilst it is essential for the multinational fully to understand cultural constraints, it may well be that there can be some meeting of the two sides.

Certainly there are still strong advocates of the first school of thought. Wenlee Ting (1980) looking at several Asia-Pacific newly industrialised countries, all non-westernised in culture, concluded that since many Asian managers who had been 'nutured and nourished' by Western business school education and management training at home and abroad were performing better than others who had not, management practices and principles can be successfully transferred. Despite the Oriental environment with its much talked of 'workaholicism', group-orientated thinking, cheap labour, government–business partnerships and so on, the explicit, linear, deductive approach of modern Western planning operating and control was significant and applicable.

However the Japanese approach has clearly demonstrated that there is a successful alternative centering on consensus, group-loyalty and the concept of seniority. Notwithstanding recent redundancies in some Japanese companies, employment in many Japanese multinationals is still for life and progression within the corporation is through a spiral staircase of job rotation through the various functions of accountancy, marketing, personnel and so on. The result is that very experienced generalists, rather than experts in specific areas, are produced, and it has been argued that because there is no power struggle within the company individual ambition is subordinated to the interest of the company. Loyalty is promoted, efficiency increased and all competitiveness is directed outside to the market place. Allied to this is a two-way communication system rather than orders being passed down from the top; yet the respect for one's senior is not weakened.

The Japanese system may be described loosely as a feudal pattern of rights and duties, the worker seeing himself as a life member of a company which is like a surrogate family to which he owes loyalty, but which also offers him protection and companionship. Group performance is more important than individual gratification and rather than fit a person to a job description, the job description may be written for the competence and abilities of the person chosen for a job. With its emphasis on emotional sensitivity, consensus, group spirit, harmonious personal relationships and a paternalistic approach by the organisation, the Japanese system has demonstrated well that it is not essential to accept Western management practices and principles.

It is interesting to note that parts of Asia, such as Taiwan, South Korea and the Philippines, have made efforts to imitate some aspects of the Japanese system. The trading company or sogo shosha has been considered as a model for these countries, the assumption being that Japanese success is simply a matter of organisational pattern and all that is necessary to duplicate that success is to adapt the structure. But the Japanese trading company grew out of a total relationship within the economy between the banks, industry and common will, which may not exist elsewhere. It may be that the trading company which evolved in this monolithic culture is unique to it and may not be relevant elsewhere. This has been found to be the case in Malaysia, where companies modelled on the sogo shosha have failed. It remains to be seen whether this will happen elsewhere.

What is not in doubt is that non-Western, non-Japanese societies in developing countries can be *selective* in what they import. It could be that they can use some of the Western multinational's management practices and principles and use them within their own cultural frameworks. In terms of technology many East Asian countries have already done this. They have learnt modern ways of the West, taken and copied technology. But they have also separated these aspects from Western politics and religious institutions, which has allowed them greater flexibility than less selective people. Not only has the impact of multinational marketing on these countries been less traumatic and negative than elsewhere but it is now becoming evident that the same approach can be adopted in relation to management techniques. Group loyalty, solidarity, team work and so on can still be used alongside other aspects of Western management techniques.

Daewoo provides an excellent example. This multinational has combined monthly reports and goal setting (unusual for a Korean company) with oriental traditions such as loyalty and the sacrificing of individual, personal goals and desires for those of the company. This is clearly demonstrated by Daewoo's trading and construction division holding a rally at 8.0 a.m. one September morning, at which the employees decided to have no holidays or Sundays off until the export target of $3b was reached. But the loyalty is not just one-way. Daewoo has shown how Korean culture holds its workforce and business generally in high esteem. People are regarded as an important natural resource. $6m per year is spent on training in the Daewoo group, and by 1990 there should be 1000 Ph.D.s (*Financial Times*, 31 Oct. 1985).

Management systems and work methods of multinational subsidiaries in host countries are a matter of increasing concern to both business and government in developing countries. Although the more fixed cultures pose the greatest problems, it would seem that there is some room for compromise. The host country for its part can be selective in choosing carefully what it wishes to adopt. The multinational, on the other hand, can examine, attempt to understand as far as possible and respond to local cultural conditions. The imposition of Western management techniques as the only way to achieve efficient, effective management may not be essential. At the same time management may not be completely culture based. It would seem that there is no one set way forward, but many. However the significance of cultural differences for management techniques cannot be underestimated.

The significance of the cultural environment for multinationals

In addition to the constraints on multinational management, culture poses many additional problems. Although there will be a great range of cultural conditions in all developing countries, some of which are likely to be more restrictive than others, in any developing country it is necessary to consider certain aspects which are likely to affect the multinational's operations. Some of these have been touched on in previous chapters, but their relevance in relation to the multinational is such that there is justification for repeating them.

Firstly it is necessary for the multinational to establish whether there is an elite, and if so, what is the attitude towards business. Usually there is some type of elite but if it regards business unfavourably this is likely to result in available management being of a low quality and in many other handicaps for the multinational. Conversely, it may be regarded as prestigious or politically acceptable to work for a multinational. The quality of management may not be any higher, but the bureaucratic obstacles are likely to be much fewer.

The next fundamental question to be asked concerns society's aspirations. Although a certain amount of political stability is required in a host country, sometimes the most politically stable country goes hand in hand with a certain amount of fatalism, which is unlikely to be the most favourable operating environment for the multinational. An extremely stable society, where the *status quo* must be preserved and where aspirations are extremely low, is often more restrictive than a revolutionary society. In the latter situation change is at least welcomed and the multinational may be able to channel this drive.

Attitudes towards materialism and 'the good life' and class structure are other areas which must be closely examined. As well as affecting consumer demand and the importance given to status symbols, these aspects will also affect managerial and all other staff. Where there is an immobile class structure, the multinational must be careful in selecting the appropriate class for the appropriate status and in not promoting people out of their class.

Perhaps more important is the attitude held towards the family. Where an extended family system exists there is likely to be some moral obligation to the family. This may well result in nepotism in selection procedures and 'tipping' being widespread. there may, however, be advantages for the multinational. Where family takes precedence over society as a whole, pollution and other environmental controls are likely to be few, while the societal marketing concept is hardly likely to be essential.

Certain characteristics are generally present in the majority of developing countries, although they vary in intensity. Usually the administrative machinery is not the most efficient, especially at middle or lower levels. Together with the fact that the civil servants are often held in high esteem, which encourages an attitude of indifference, arbitrariness and even arrogance, the speed of decision-making is extremely slow. This is especially the case where key posts are held by political nominees and their relatives. Under such circumstances objectivity in decision-making is likely to be in doubt.

However the biggest, and often closely related problem is bribery and corruption. Bribery, a factor in international business which cannot be ignored or underestimated, is almost impossible to define. What is a bribe to one culture may be extortion to another (although some have attempted to make a distinction between bribery, where two people co-operate, and extortion, where one person compels). There has been world-wide attention and condemnation (much of which is hypocritical) but where bribery is endemic (and it exists in most countries to some extent), it is extremely difficult for the multinational to avoid. A 'tip' may be essential to encourage the least action and where this is the case the influence of the extended family can clearly be seen.

Many parts of Africa provide good examples. For her it relates to the tribal responsibility which individuals carry with them to the city. The enhanced status of city life means an increased responsibility for assisting tribal brethren. Consequently the pressure is enormous and financial demands often outstrip income. Because the official can not resist the pressure of society he will seek to augment his income by means that other cultures would regard as corrupt. Hence, as long as there is a disparity between income and what is required for the extended family, it is likely that the bribe system will continue.

In India a similar situation prevails but it is possibly much more ingrained. For despite all Mr Gandhi's attempts to stamp out bribery and corruption in India, nothing has really changed (*Financial Times*, 31 Oct. 1986). India is still characterised by self-seeking webs of interlinking vertical power structures where influence and prestige depend on caste, religion, who one knows and to whom one is related. Businessmen are claiming now that enhanced life-style ambitions have been fuelled by Mr Gandhi's policies, which largely assume the existence of effective Western-style delegation. The result is that the demand for small backhanders of up to a few hundred rupees by thousands of bureaucrats has increased, whilst kickbacks of up to 5 per cent of contract prices are still being sought from the multinationals, even if in a less systematic way than previously.

Such political payments, defined by Jacoby et al. (1977) as 'any transfer of money or anything of value with the aim of influencing the behaviour of politicians, political candidates, political parties or government officials and employees in their legislative, administrative and judicial action', are institutionalised facts of international business in many parts of the world. Bribing lower level government officials may be necessary to process goods through customs, acquire work permits for personnel, gain permission to build, approve repatriation of profits and so on. Such lubricating payments are not subject to a going rate but are determined by what the traffic will bear. Larger payments are usually made through a middleman – perhaps a professional fixer, but more often a member of the same family as the higher level recipient. Political payments are so common in many parts that most languages have words for them, such as 'baksheesh' in Egypt, 'hatchien' in Hong Kong and 'dash' in Nigeria.

Although the extent of the problem around the world is difficult to measure, bribery can be examined in terms of scale, and in terms of possible responses by the multinational. Small 'tips' to facilitate action are often regarded as 'acceptable' or certainly as a light grey area. Covert payments to a functionary or politician are usually seen as unacceptable or even immoral, and certainly the most risky. Between there are areas which are extremely difficult to evaluate. For example, excessive commission to an agent, perhaps an officially-appointed agent, is generally regarded as wrong. But what is acceptable depends on a variety of factors, such as the competitive situation and conventional mark-up, all of which may be difficult to determine.

There are various ways in which payments can be made. Currency in an envelope given to a recipient at an agreed rendezvous is perhaps one of the simplest. At the other extreme is a significant amount of money paid into a numbered Swiss bank account. Gifts of property, watches, jewellery, oil paintings and so on are other common methods. Selling property to the payee at deflated prices or buying from the official at inflated prices and overbilling are routes which offer the multinational a most satisfactory way of making a payment legally and satisfying accountants at home in the head office.

But whilst bribery may be essential to (i) reduce political risks, (ii) avoid threats and harassment, (iii) reduce inflated taxes, (iv) obtain or retain business, or just (v) induce government officials to perform their duties, the multinational still has a choice in its stance towards bribery. Firstly it can refuse to compromise. This is certainly a 'blameless' approach, but business is likely to be lost where 'tips' and the rest are the order of the day. Next a multinational can respond to approaches but not initiate them. If the competition is responding, this approach may be defensible. Finally a multinational can take the initiative, a very dangerous option. Whatever the position adopted, it is desirable that the multinational should have developed some policy towards bribery for, if not, it may find itself at a disadvantage when requests for payments are made.

But as well as having some policy towards the company's moral position, there is a need for internal consistency of ethical beliefs within the organisation. If all employees, particularly the management, are of the same culture, conflicts are likely to be reduced. But where people of different cultures are working together problems are likely to be greater. Sometimes there is the difficulty of ensuring consistency between top management and middle management. The latter is subject to more frequent reviews of performance, and is therefore under more pressure to make sales, cut costs and so on. The temptation to yield to unethical pressure is consequently greater (and is often helped by the outside world believing malpractice is the norm in the business world). Top management can help by preventing unethical practice lower down, but if top management is corrupt, the problems can be enormous. Again guidelines are desirable. Some multinationals are more advanced than others in this respect. Caterpillar Tractor, for example, have put considerable emphasis upon stating their company's ethical beliefs and have issued formal codes of practice.

To some extent it is possible to estimate what the likely constraints will be, depending on the category of country and its location. For example, large, rich countries are likely to be characterised by rapid inflation and corruption in the administration, especially if wealth was suddenly achieved through the discovery of oil. With the infrastructure under great strain payments to 'oil the wheels' in distribution channels, for example, getting goods through customs, are normal. On the other hand some of the oil-rich small Arab states, although possessing more efficient distribution systems and less corruption, may present a much more hostile cultural environment, since the culture a Western multinational is used to does not exist, and is not acceptable.

As noted in Chapter 2 the more variable the culture, the more complex, the greater the cultural hostility, heterogeneity and cultural interdependence in the host country, the more problems for the multinational. Nevertheless if the culture is understood (notwithstanding the problem of self-reference criteria) the chances of minimising the constraints are likely to be much higher, for 'managing relationships between an organisation and its cultural environment is largely a matter of accurate perception, sound diagnosis and appropriate adaptation' (Terpstra, 1978 p. xxiii)

Wider issues in the multinational operating environment

However, to a large extent, the multinational's operating environment is increasingly difficult. Firstly, and in many ways related to cultural and moral issues, there is the problem of counterfeiting, which is immense and growing. The result is that 'a wealthy Nigerian or Saudi Arabian can today enjoy many of the comforts and obtain many of the essentials of modern living without buying a single product from the legitimate manufacturer' (*Financial Times*, 1 Sep. 1986, p. 10).

This worldwide industry in counterfeit products is today worth $60b per annum and includes everything from designer clothes to cassettes, videos, French handbags, pharmaceuticals, expensive perfumes and watches, to games of Monopoly. Workshops of the Far East, Latin America, Southern Europe and some Eastern European countries find *any* wealthy market tempting. But this is no cottage industry. It is very sophisticated and showing evidence of control by organised crime.

Third World counterfeiters are estimated to cost the North American vehicle component multinationals £2.7b per annum, while pharmaceutical companies are another badly-hit sector. It may take ten years and a few million pounds to bring a pharmaceutical product to the market, but a chemist with an M.Sc. degree can often duplicate the product in sufficient quantities to pre-empt the legalised drug on the market. The situation is worse where poor counterfeit drugs are a danger to health.

The rise of the global brand has made life easier for the counterfeiter. Often appropriate packaging is really all that is needed. The multinational can do little. In many countries the law is inadequate to prevent counterfeiting. Patents granted in one country may be unenforceable in another. The breach of copyright of books, taped music or computer softwear has become endemic and when centres like Singapore, Hong Kong and Taiwan started to crack down the problem moved elsewhere, for example, to the Philippines.

Some multinationals have made attempts to do something about the situation themselves but the cost is enormous. Dunhill is spending one-quarter of a million pounds per annum to achieve some control and there have been many calls for an anti-counterfeiting code under GATT. The USA in particular, through its Intellectual Property Committee, is arguing that the situation is such that piracy is undermining their competitive position and distorting world trade. But although there are several conventions governing intellectual property rights, for example, the Paris Convention, 1883, the Universal Copyright Convention 1952, the Patent Cooperation Treaty of 1970 and the World Intellectual Property Organisation (WIPO) established in 1974, none are universal and, worse, they cannot be enforced.

Singapore, Taiwan, Indonesia, South Korea, the Philippines, Malaysia, Thailand, Brazil, Egypt and Nigeria have been identified by United States multinationals as places where most abuses of copyright occur (*Financial Times*, 8 Sep. 1986). But there has been very limited success in trying to persuade some governments to do more for, as noted in an earlier chapter, in some parts of the Far East intellectual property rights are not recognised.

Sometimes counterfeiting helps the multinational. For example, it has helped Micro Pro International become a market leader. Generally, the effect is extremely negative and expensive for the multinational. But what is not in doubt is the size of the problem. It has led some commentators to remark cynically, 'You could almost say that if your goods are not being counterfeited, you are not making the right product' (*Financial Times*, 1 Sep. 1986).

In addition to the counterfeiting problem, it has been claimed that the multinational is facing more political instability in its wider operating environment. Frank (1980) has suggested that this takes five forms. Firstly, until very recently, rapid economic growth has meant increased bargaining power for many host governments. For, if there is high GNP growth, there is also likely to be a rapidly growing domestic market. Where the country's population is large to begin with this means more negotiating muscle for the developing country. As other local industries develop and master technology it is likely that the incentives offered to multinationals will change, whilst ability to understand and scrutinise multinational activity will improve. Secondly national goals are often altered as economies develop. For example, an import substitution policy offering protection to the multinational may be switched to an export-orientated one with different incentives, as has occurred recently in the Philippines.

Thirdly there is the 'obsolescing bargain', which means that the multinational is encouraged to enter the market with the promise of long-term concessions. However these change once the production process is running. And when negotiations restart, both parties have different perceptions of what is a fair deal, the multinational usually coming off worst. This is particularly typical in the extraction of raw materials.

Fourthly 'scapegoating' is common where governments do not satisfy needs and aspirations of other people. Under these circumstances the multinational is accused of being the exploiter, upsetting local culture and so on, and this may go hand in hand with nationalisation.

Finally there is the 'succession of dilemmas' which the multinational has to face increasingly. If the company repatriates its profits it is accused of depriving the nation of newly created wealth. If it reinvests, it is accused of dominating the economy. If the multinational pays local wages it is accused of exploiting the labour force, whereas the payment of higher wayes attracts the accusation that it is siphoning off the best labour and promoting social inequalities. If the multinational brings in the latest technology it is seen as inappropriate. If intermediate technology is used the claim is that the multinational is shortchanging the economy. It is not surprising that the multinational often feels it is in a 'Heads, you win, tails, I lose' situation.

Some have pointed to the fact that in many economies foreign investment is in decline. For example, in Indonesia, it is running at less than half that desired – $4.2b, whereas the target was $11.8b in the current five-year plan. (Furthermore this is only *approved* investment. It may not be implemented). A similar picture is presented in Nigeria. Here the stock of foreign-owned capital grew at 15 per cent per annum between 1970 and 1982, but much of this (an estimated 80 per cent) was either involuntary – through unremitted profits and forced reinvestment – or in short-term commitments. New investment is running at less than N160m per annum.

Thus, whilst large, rich countries may have the most bargaining power, they are also likely to present the most difficult operating environment for the multinational. In times of world-wide recession the result is likely to be loss of foreign investment, for the multinational cutting back on foreign investment in such times is likely to concentrate its efforts on those nations which present more favourable conditions.

Conclusion

The growth of multinational activity in developing countries is significant. But not only have these nations become an increasingly important site for subsidiaries of Western and Japanese multinationals; they are now becoming a new source of multinationals themselves.

Whatever its country of origin, the multinational possesses great power and manoeuvrability. Having largely changed from extracting raw materials in developing countries to establishing manufacturing which is either horizontally integrated or vertically integrated through the export of technology, the multinational has formulated its own distinctive use of marketing. Whenever possible it has adopted a global perspective and has standardised its products. This is largely in response to the assumption that consumer tastes throughout the world are converging and there is only one market segment. While it is extremely profitable in terms of economies of scale, this may be criticised as a product-orientation in which markets are changed to suit the product, rather than the reverse as the marketing concept teaches.

In reality there are a variety of strategies which may be followed, with the global market strategy at one extreme, the individual market strategy at the other. And it has recently been suggested that, increasingly, multinationals are attempting to do both (standardising and tailoring) simultaneously, although this is 'easier to prescribe than perform' (*Financial Times*, 11 Feb. 1987, p. 12). To a large extent structure determines strategy and structure, in the form of no-ownership, joint venture, indigenisation or total ownership, is largely determined by the size and wealth of the host country. Large, rich and especially small, poor newly industrialised countries are attractive as sites of multinational activity, but the former have the power to insist on joint ventures or indigenisation, which in turn tends to require an individual market strategy. In small, poor countries, which have little bargaining power, a global market strategy is possible. Large, poor countries and especially small, rich ones, are less attractive as a site for multinational activity, but under a no-ownership structure either an individual or global market strategy can be followed.

Notwithstanding the ownership restrictions, mutlinationals can always use their intangible assets of international 'prestige', 'foreignness' and assumed technical superiority in their promotion, while their power and manoeuvrability is clearly demonstrated in their distribution and pricing strategies, particularly when a global market strategy is permitted. Under such circumstances market research takes on a much less important role and its objectives are largely to determine what the political attitude is, what technology can be absorbed, and when production processes become available. Although ownership structures may cause some restrictions, nevertheless the multinational can often use a developing country's development, or lack of it, to its own advantage.

Not surprisingly the multinational has been viewed as a neo-colonialist, changing local culture and making it conform to Western tastes, distorting demand and increasing social inequalities. Furthermore it has been accused of bringing inappropriate technology, the wrong kind of jobs and management, shifting local competition and promoting an oligopolistic industrial structure. Finally, as well as cheating the host country of foreign exchange, it has been said to interfere in the host nation's politics.

The reverse argument is that the multinational is absolutely essential in order to bring the necessary technology, jobs and foreign exchange, to stimulate competitive standards and entrepreneurship in complementary activity, to demonstrate effective management and to overcome resistant attitudes to change, as well as to stimulate demand and to set in motion a multiplier effect.

In reality there are many half-truths on both sides. Although there is no agreement on what the multinational's impact really has been, many of the negative effects can be minimised if host governments understand multinational marketing. Furthermore they must be clear in their objectives as to what is required of them. The multinational is both possible and beneficial.

An area which is difficult to resolve is the question of the appropriateness of Western management techniques in developing countries. While some efficient and effective management is essential in developing countries, it may be that the Western system is not the only one. For culture, as well as giving rise to certain management styles and management elites, determines attitudes which may make Western management systems very difficult to implement. Attitudes to innovation, decision-making, achievement and time are particularly significant, while the Japanese have clearly demonstrated that there are viable alternatives. It would seem that cultures can be selective in what they choose to adopt, while maintaining their own cultural environments. Thus to transfer Western management techniques in the belief that efficient and effective management is based on universal principles, practices and general know-how would seem to be largely undesirable. Equally it may be that management is not completely culture-bound but can incorporate some parts of other cultures. There is no one model.

Finally there is no more consistency in the broader marketing environment offered by host countries. The multinational must seek to understand the social systems, aspirations, extent of bribery and corruption and the rest. It can also attempt to formulate a moral code and decide how it is going to respond. In this way its chances of a more successful operation are increased. But there is less room for manoeuvre where counterfeiting and host government hostility exists, and some have argued that the operating environment for multinationals has become increasingly difficult in recent years.

The multinational marketer has, in the past, held the balance of power. In the future, with more understanding of multinational operations and developing countries themselves developing their own multinationals, manoeuvrability may be further curtailed. But, for the present, multinational marketing strategy, however product-orientated, remains largely successful from the point of view of the multinational. To ensure that the multinational's impact in the host country is most beneficial, multinational marketing strategy must be carefully assessed and monitored.

CHAPTER 9

Marketing by the Individual

Contents

Introduction

In Chapter 1 it was noted that there are relatively few indigenous marketers in developing countries if a 'marketer' is defined as someone who understands and applies marketing in order to create, build and maintain beneficial relationships with target markets. Conditions such as a sellers' market, poor distribution, constraining cultural factors, lack of marketing expertise and finance tend to encourage limited horizons. Yet there is a need for such people to become more creative at national and international levels, and governments are giving increasing emphasis to stimulating the private sector generally.

Within these broad generalisations, however, the situation is very much more complex. The range in *type* of indigenous marketer is enormous. Most manufacturing firms in developing countries are production-orientated, neglecting market research, seeing no need for promotion and being conrolled largely by the wholesaler and retailer in terms of pricing. Not surprisingly quick profits, rather than a well-devised long-term marketing strategy, are the objective. But whereas the manufacturers leave much to be desired, rural traders have been seen to be much more marketing-orientated and consequently have been extremely beneficial on a limited basis. Marketers in the retail sector have been difficult to assess, so great is their variety.

Indeed, once examples are considered throughout the world, the picture is even less clear. For, although the typical problems faced by all entrepreneurs world-wide are more extreme in developing countries, there are exceptions, such as small enterprises in Hong Kong, which are notably more marketing-orientated and internationally competitive than many in the United Kingdom or United States.

This chapter seeks to examine the above issues. The first section considers (i) the increasing awareness by governments and the relevance of small manufacuring firms in economic development, and (ii) the state of the art of marketing in such firms, bearing in mind the problems and constraints which the small firm has to face. The focus is manufacturing activity since, to a large extent, this is the only area of small firms considered to be of any significance by governments. The rural sector and retailing are examined next. In both these, but particularly in the rural sector, it is demonstrated that the indigenous marketer is often frustrated because of heavy state involvement and negative attitudes towards middlemen. Consequently his potential as a means of improving distribution specifically and furthering economic development generally is not fulfilled. Cultural issues which may hinder or help individuals' use of 'efficient' marketing are examined and examples of exceptionally successful entrepreneurs are quoted. Finally some pointers as to how marketing may be used to overcome the typical problems and uncertainties encountered by the indigenous marketer in the private sector are discussed.

The need for indigenous marketers and the state of the art in small manufacturing firms

In both the developed and the developing worlds, governments are turning more and more to small manufacturing firms in the private sector as a means of helping to solve economic problems. In the developed countries it has been assumed that small business (i) can preserve the present economic system (Bolton, 1971; Boswell, 1972), (ii) forms a seedbed of invention and innovation (Johnson, 1978; Bramley, 1978) and

(iii) is amenable to political authority and government control (Johnson, 1978).

In developing countries small manufacturing firms' scope is perceived as even greater. Table 7.2 in Chapter 7 summarises the ways in which small firms can redress the balance between industry and agriculture, create a more equitable distribution of wealth by helping to develop non-urban areas and thus aid the diffusion of modernisation so that the whole economy expands. For in the present increasingly competitive economic climate the amount of new foreign investment by multinationals has decreased world-wide and there is the additional impetus to revise industrialisation policies in many countries since it has been realised that emphasis on output, capital-intensive projects and heavy state involvement may not have been the correct approach. Small enterprises can help alleviate poverty and provide for the basic needs of a larger section of the population as well as creating jobs, increasing exports and helping to reduce imports.

The role of the individual marketer is therefore growing in importance. But the state of the art of marketing in small manufacturing firms leaves much to be desired and this is a serious problem for, if marketing is not being sufficiently carried out, small firms cannot hope to achieve their maximum potential beneficial effect.

Unfortunately the amount of research into the marketing function of the independent small firm in the developed world is minimal, and in the developing world it is practically non-existent. Several generalisations have been made. For example, it has been pointed out that small firms in the United Kingdom and USA lack a comprehensive marketing approach (Lamont, 1972; Ford and Rowley, 1979; Jackson, Hawes and Hertel, 1979), and tend to be established on the basis of technical proficiency, with marketing relegated to a simple selling function.

Little work has been undertaken on actual aspects of marketing, and what exists is often of an advisory nature. In terms of product policy Allen (1973) suggests that small firms should concentrate on products which: (i) do not require large amounts of capital per unit of output; (ii) do not require heavy retooling costs so as to be able to keep up with technical changes; and (iii) do not require heavy marketing and administrative costs relative to other costs.

It is generally agreed in the literature that small firms are more successful if they adopt a concentrated marketing segmentation strategy with products tailored and targeted accordingly (Brannen, 1980; Howell, Frazier and Stephenson, 1980).

Perhaps the greatest amount of comment in the marketing area has been in relation to trying to isolate small firms' strengths and weaknesses. Golby and Johns (1971) suggest that a small firm's strength often results from its ability to provide a specific service competitively. Davies and

Kelly (1972) continue this theme, stating that limited markets, too small to be considered by large firms, provide the biggest opportunity for small firms. Cleland (1955) offers labour co-operation and Johns (1976) suggests efficiency as alternatives.

Much less has been written about small firms' use of the marketing mix. Observations suggest that many small firms in developed nations underprice (Moreau 1980) whilst Stancil (1981) recommends that small firms should base their price on the customer's perception of the product's worth. Davies, Ryan and Noonan (1982) state that market research is frequently neglected because of lack of time and money.

Some attempt has been made to relate marketing to the use of planning and type of management. Research has tended to emphasise small firms' lack of planning and over-concentration on day to day problems, whilst inefficient management is also well documented (Boswell, 1972; Kaplan, 1948; Davies and Kelly, 1972; Woodruff and Alexander, 1958). Indeed there may well be a correlation between type of manager and success of the company. Many researchers have made a distinction between professional managers and the owner–managers (Ford and Rowley, 1979). The former were found to have more empathy with the marketing concept, whereas the owner–managers tended to set up through technical strength. As well as concentrating on the product rather than the market, they were more concerned with minimising personal risks and maintaining personal control. They used market segmentation and product positioning only to a limited extent. Furthermore they were conservative and committed to declining products.

Although it is generally agreed that small manufacturing firms world-wide are usually passive in their approach to marketing, in most developing countries the conditions are such that indigenous marketers have even less cause to be otherwise. A sellers' market, poor distribution systems, lack of finance and even less marketing expertise, as well as hostile cultural conditions in some instances, appear to justify the manufacturer's production-orientation, and certain caveats need to be taken into account in relation to the existing literature on small firms in developed nations.

For, first and foremost, domestic demand is generally greater than supply, which means that it is possible to operate a highly successful small business without emphasising the marketing function, let alone having a comprehensive marketing approach. Furthermore, with small amounts of capital available to the entrepreneur and the likely use of intermediate technology, a generic type of goods is often produced on a small scale. Such firms, often located in a few large cities, operate on a hand-to-mouth basis and are preoccupied with production problems. There is little analysis of the market or its growth rate and consequently market research is not used (not because of lack of finance, but primarily because of lack of perceived need). Products are not branded or promoted, this being considered unnecessary. However, despite the sellers' market which is likely to rule out the under-pricing noted by Moreau (1980), it may be that the wholesalers and distributors enjoy most of the market power and, consequently, control over pricing is lost, especially since the wholesalers often offer credit to the producer, which would be impossible elsewhere. Because the incentive in buying comes from the consumer, no selling efforts are necessary, nor is there much desire to open up new markets. Instead quick profits may be the objective, especially in conditions of rapid inflation, shortage of staple commodities and a random system of import controls.

Thus Allen's remarks on small firms needing to concentrate on products which do not require large amounts of capital per unit output, heavy retooling, administrative and marketing costs (Allen, 1973) still apply, but because competition domestically is likely to be less intense, targeting and tailoring of products to serve particular market niches at home are less essential. This is especially true where the level of economic development is not so advanced. Furthermore it may be that many manufacturing firms are less independent than those in developed countries. Many are tied to multinationals as contract suppliers and therefore the impetus to examine the final consumer and seek out new target markets is reduced.

Equally, although there is undoubtedly as much inefficient management and lack of planning in small manufacturing firms in developing countries, the distinction between professional managers and owner–managers cannot be made to the same extent, since the number of 'professional' managers, that is, those with some training and qualifications, is likely to be extremely low. Most managers will set up on technical strength and have a desire to minimise risk. But as well as their desire to grow often being constrained by culture, their poor financial resources and the fear of losing control of the firm, there are other uncontrollable factors in the operating environment which pose handicaps. For example, in many developing countries there may be insufficiently good infrastructure for a small company to expand its production. Where expansion is achieved, new premises are likely to be required. But it may be a distinct disadvantage to move out of town. Extra storage facilities may be a better solution. Other problems include poor power supplies and smuggling.

The Nigerian Weaving and Processing Company (NWPC) is an example of a local, small but profitable integrated textile mill. Owned 60 per cent by the Lebanese Debs family it produces material for shirts, safari suits, uniforms, and speciality prints for religious and other ceremonies. But it has had to invest in its own power supply and, despite improvements in recent years in the electricity supply, it had to use its own electricity for 20 per cent of its power between February 1985 and February 1986. Smuggling is another major problem, prices falling significantly when this occurs on a large scale (*Financial Times*, 24 Feb. 1986).

Another big handicap is that of government officials' attitudes to small firms in many nations. Despite the general increasing recognition of small firms, in several African states successful entrepreneurs are regarded as 'cowboys'. Yet the same officials may be responsible for assessing demand before grants for expansion are granted. Due to *their* lack of sufficient marketing knowledge they are not likely to make the best decisions. Furthermore training is often more relevant than financial assistance. Thus the ignorance or lack of marketing expertise and negative attitudes to entrepreneurs may be an added hindrance in some countries.

Finally there is always the possibility that there are multinational subsidiaries competing with the small firm. These are likely to have distinct marketing advantages and special skill and initiative is required by the competing entrepreneurs to survive.

In the longer term, however, once the economic development process is well established, and at the international level, the need for effective marketing by all small firms is essential for any degree of success. In this context many of the failings which have been noted in small firms' operations must be corrected. The advice offered in the literature, as discussed earlier in this chapter, must be applied. At present, because indigenous marketers are poor on quality control, they fare badly in international markets where more sophisticated buyers expect homogeneous quality. (Better quality control would also help at home, speeding the process of development and reducing dependence on multinationals, for variation in quality is one of the major reasons why foreign goods are preferred over domestically-produced ones.)

A comprehensive marketing approach must be adopted for long-term success. The strengths of small firms – that is, their flexibility, closeness to customers, ability to provide a specific service competitively (Golby and Johns, 1971) especially in a market niche (Allen, 1973) – still apply and are even more essential in economies where there is much multinational activity, and on international markets. There are already obvious market niches which depend upon good quality controlled craftsmanship, such as Thai silk dresses or Mexican Tasco silversmith goods. Under such circumstances a careful marketing strategy is essential and the marketing mix must be accurately formulated.

But the development of marketing expertise alone is not sufficient to create a favourable environment for growth. It must be complemented by efficient production, finance and personnel functions within the firm and, more importantly, by the right attitude from the government. For in most developing countries the incentive to use marketing is reduced by consumer rights not being well established. Sellers' markets mean that consumers are deprived of the right to choose. Instead quality fluctuations, misrepresentation, imitation and fraud are expected, while guarantees are usually unknown. Equally safety standards, even when regulations exist, may not be taken seriously by manufacturers who are unwilling to take such risks or to spend heavily on product improvements unless there is a payback within three years or less (Thorelli, 1981).

Governments can, if they desire, do much to promote an open market through more equality between buyers and sellers. They can enforce consumer standards, lead quality-consciousness campaigns, lay down minimum standards, inspect products, enforce health and safety standards, demand quality markings and so on. They can also ensure a spirit of enterprise and competition through legislation which (i) allows free entry into all business and professions, (ii) protects innovations and intellectual property and (iii) allows, through taxation, fast write-offs in new business investment, so rewarding risk takers. Furthermore they can run competitions to encourage the image of the businessman to become more favourable (Thorelli, 1981), guarantee a certain percentage of bank loans to new small businesses and stimulate competition through stamping out resale price maintenance where this exists and encouraging price marking. Finally they can provide better infrastructure to improve the small firm's marketing environment. And, if governments provide both the physical infrastructure and the impetus from the market place in the form of a consumerist movement, it is likely that the small firm's marketing will improve.

Fortunately the impetus to improve the small firm's marketing environment and encourage developments in this sector is appearing, particularly through international organisations. Rather than contributing to major capital-intensive industrialisation, communication or agricultural projects, the trend to 'small is beautiful' is being supported. For example the Swiss Foundation for Economic and Social Development (Fundes) is offering a new kind of aid – help in the most modest sectors of private enterprise.

Launched in 1984 by Dr Stephan Schmidheimy with Sw.fr.1m of his money it now also includes 20 more Swiss firms which have undertaken to provide Sw.fr.3m more. In the same year Fundes CH–Panama established a pilot scheme in Central America, beyond the Canal Zone where there is much poverty (and here Schmidheimy has no business interests, so he cannot be accused of furthering his own interests). Panamania Fundes guarantees loans of up to $20 000 for five years, and where entrepreneurs have no collateral this can save them interest rates of 40 per cent per annum. Many entrepreneurs have taken advantage of this. The major aim – to open up opportunities for new business – seems to be being achieved and Fundes has attracted more money, for example, from the Inter-America Development Bank in Washington and UNIDO (United Nations Industrial Development Organization) has also shown interest. A similar foundation has been set up in Costa Rica, whilst other countries, such as Guatemala, Ecuador, Colombia, Bolivia and even some Asian countries are examining the Fundes programme.

A trend is therefore becoming established which would appear to suggest that small businesses are being seen to have an important role to play in a country's development. The result is likely to be an improvement in the state of the art of marketing within small manufacturing firms. This is highly desirable, since without better marketing their full potential stimulus to economic prosperity cannot be fulfilled.

Marketing by the individual in the private sector in the rural economy

Whereas increasing attention is only now beginning to be paid to the small manufacturing firms, indigenous marketers in the rural sector have tended to receive even less priority. Although many governments have made attempts at agricultural planning, they have rarely stimulated more effective marketing by the farmer, whilst they have actively discouraged middlemen, on the assumption that the state should control basic commodities and their distribution.

Consequently the farmer's incentive to use marketing has been practically eliminated because of government interference and his dependence on the state. His problem, first and foremost, is in the pricing of output. Prices paid to him tend to be too low and are highly volatile and seasonal, while the wholesale and retail price is unknown. Much of the blame lies with governments which *impose* low prices on food products, often in order to placate city inhabitants. And, where marketing boards are established to help with exports, there may be a significant amount of cheating in the public sector. For example, in the 1970s the Thai government bought paddy field rice at extremely low prices from the farmer and sold it on export markets for a hefty profit. But the farmer received none of it – directly or indirectly – and it has been cynically referred to as a 'monstrous export tax' (Hoffman, 1982). Where such parastatal organisations, intended to serve farmers as 'export agents', have degenerated into fiscal bodies, they do nothing to stimulate farmers' marketing strategies.

In addition to fluctuations of price and ignorance of prices further down the long distribution channels, markets are often poorly organised. There is no recognition of difference in quality. Grading is unlikely to exist. Where traditionalism, tribalism and isolation occur the incentive to increase productivity is further reduced, while poor storage, distribution, hygiene and pest control are normal in most countries. In addition to all this low income levels give rise to a production strategy which accommodates the motives of food security and risk avoidance, reducing the scope for more effective decision-making.

The disturbing fact is that, whilst many governments have realised the need for rural development and effective marketing systems, they have not given credit to the private sector of traders which exists alongside the marketing co-operatives and other parastatal organisations. These people are often a considerable and undervalued source of dynamic marketing entrepreneurship. The Food and Agricultural Organisation writes 'One essential and underrated instrument of rural development is the dynamic small- and medium-scale marketing entrepreneurs who are consistently promoting sales and searching for new market outlets, as well as organising such other marketing operations as assembly, storage, processing, distribution, financing and pricing on efficient lines.' (Food and Agricultural Organisation, 1982, p. i).

One of the major reasons is that such people are ignored, hated or regarded as *middlemen* who are superfluous and who make an immoral profit at the expense of both farmers and consumers. It is the traditional attitude to middlemen, but in reality such people are a key element in rural development. Despite difficult conditions under which to work they have provided essential services to both producers and consumers at no direct cost to the public purse. They have in many parts (and the private sector still handles the majority of food products in developing countries) stimulated rural development through opening new marketing channels and extending established ones to cater for rising demand in urban areas.

They may take many forms. Firstly there are *hawkers* who distribute food from an area of surplus to one of demand. They provide a job or jobs, a service and often give part-time employment to others such as transporters. Furthermore they stimulate the development of a two-way trading system. Yet such people are often regarded as parasites and the authorities frequently attempt to eliminate them (often helped by the larger traders, who fear the competition).

Next there are *distributors* who buy commodities or produce from the farmers and set up buying agencies, transport and packaging for many markets. Small manufacturing firms are stimulated to produce packaging material, while the required transportation and the hiring of facilities, such as cold storage, provide more employment. The distributors therefore serve a particularly useful role despite the general poor transport and storage facilities and the lack of well organised wholesale and retail markets. As well as providing more jobs in related sectors they have the flexibility to react to demand or the problems of producers (an ability which parastatals with their heavy bureaucracies lack). More important, they buy produce from farmers at the going rate, which allows the farmers money to reinvest.

Processors are another category of indigenous marketers in the rural sector. Because they offer producers fixed prices, farmers develop more confidence in being able to sell their produce and their production therefore rises. Furthermore advice is given to the pickers on quality and packaging. Grading and packaging skills are developed and, again, extra employment is created for transporters. The processors also encourage changes at both ends of the channel. The farmers are provided with a means to an export market. Often this stimulates them to branch out into new crop production, such as vegetables, and to upgrade their quality. The consumer at the other end is provided with a bigger choice.

As well as the hawkers, distributors and processors, there are a number of market and export *traders*. The market traders are intermediaries who often provide finance as well as trust and personal contact to farmers, which is beyond the capacity of any state organisation. There are examples of traders, often dealing with fruit and vegetables, who have become millionaires with chains of retail stores, storage systems and regional buying offices. Although possibly regarded with envy, such people have nevertheless provided many jobs and set numerous multiplier effects into motion. The export traders provide grading and export services for small market gardeners.

From all the intermediaries mentioned above private businesses, consumers, farmers and the economy generally benefit. To start and maintain a business the private entrepreneur is likely to have the initiative, energy, skill, (and maybe luck) not possessed by the State. He is supplying a need which is not filled and as such is a good marketer. Willing to risk his savings and driven by individual ambition he provides employment for others and sets in motion a multiplier effect. Yet official policies often constrain rather than help these entrepreneurs in the rural sector. Instead of providing the most favourable environment a government official often measures 'success' by the extent to which he controls a large institution and employs many people over whom he wields power and authority. Occasionally an effective government agency is created but invariably, as noted in Chapter 6, excessive costs and inefficiency result.

Furthermore, if a commodity is considered important, the government steps in and attempts to exclude private traders. For example, in the marketing of export crops such as cocoa and coffee there is usually heavy government involvement and a state monopoly over export sales and foreign exchange earnings. Private business may, however, find limited room in assembling, storing and processing. In the area of basic foodstuffs there have been many attempts to reduce private enterprises' involvement. Monopoly marketing boards are often established but they rarely succeed in genuinely keeping supplies, prices and costs under control. The private sector then becomes the scapegoat. It is accused of hoarding, price speculation and exploiting producers and consumers. Only in the area of fruit and vegetable marketing does the private sector have a freer hand. Despite poor infrastructure and other problems, private enterprise has made a big contribution. Few governments have paid much attention to these products, especially when destined for domestic consumption, since they are of minor importance as well as being highly perishable. Where governments have attempted to take them over they have invariably failed. For fixed prices and bureaucratic procedures are inappropriate.

Overall, therefore, government interference has often been a hindrance rather than a help to private enterprise. Few governments have been successful in limiting inflation by controlling prices and trade margins. Instead farmers' returns have fallen and more private investment in agricultural trading has been discouraged. Not many traders are prepared to run the risks of operating in markets where prices are controlled. Equally the development of larger, more efficient private businesses incorporating more than one function have been restricted.

Thus, while the inadequacies of the parastatals with their swollen bureaucracies, centralised decision-making, lack of marketing skills and emphasis on capital-intensive schemes which cannot respond to local circumstances are maintained, the marketing skills of the small trader are stifled. To correct this unsatisfactory relationship government attitudes to the private trader must be changed. The relevance of entrepreneurial skills and abilities must be seen. For, if private traders and the government could work together more closely, many societies would be more prosperous. Private business would be more likely to become more socially responsible whilst government initiatives would undoubtedly be more effective.

It is highly desirable that governments see the private sector in a more constructive light, for then they can use traders as channels for extending information and technical services, collectors of information and joint planners. At the same time the government should regard itself more as having a major facilitating function – ensuring vehicle spares, promoting credit facilities and providing the same technical and other assistance offered to small scale manufacturers. It can help enormously by introducing measures and grading systems and improving local market and slaughter-house facilities, as well as building rural assembly centres and other physical facilities. It can assist in training to help entrepreneurs who wish to establish agricultural processing and trading businesses. In short, by providing a more favourable marketing environment, it can fulfil the potential of the indigenous marketer in the rural sector, at the same time narrowing the gap between the rural and urban sectors and enhancing the prosperity of the economy as a whole.

Marketing by private enterprise in the retail sector

As with the indigenous marketer in the rural sector, retailing by the individual in the private sector is not given much priority as an agent of development in a developing country. Indeed in some countries, such as the Dominican Republic, the official policy is aimed at discouraging investment in retailing. This is because unemployment forces a high rate of labour into retailing, which requires little capital to enter the system. But because there are many retailing units dividing up the market into segments too small to support the investment, high margins and discouragement to innovations in volume-selling techniques result. Lack of investment and inability to support the investment become a vicious circle (Adams, 1970). Often, too, there is a feeling of resentment and a desire to drive out ethnic groups which dominate retailing in some countries, for example, Asians in East Africa.

Because of the heterogeneity between and within developing countries and the resultant variety of types of market there are many sorts of indigenous marketer in retailing, ranging from speciality merchants selling in public markets in the traditional pre-industrial economy to the modern mass merchandiser in the urban sector. Between lie those owning or engaged in speciality stores, department stores, and street fairs.

However the dominant institutional form of urban food retailing is the small store. Typically the indigenous marketer here is passive or certainly less aggressive than more modern retailers, for he lacks a competitive attitude. He tends to regard the number of customers and the amount purchased as stable and inelastic, believing that the action of competitors will not affect him much. To a large extent this is true, for there is often a low outreach environment because of cultural and economic reasons which result in small quantities being bought, frequent shopping trips and low expectations (as noted in Chapter 6). Consequently there is a very fragmented retailing system, the trade area of stores being small and fixed, there being little comparative shopping by consumers or crossing of store boundaries.

Nevertheless some development by innovative indigenous marketers of small urban food stores can be predicted, according to Goldman (1974). Initially specialised retail institutions, such as grocers, bakers and so exist. All family-owned and small in size, they carry a limited product assortment. The innovative retailer can either add new stores of increase the sales volume of his store. The first option is limited since this poses a managerial problem to the family-type retailer. Consequently the second option is more popular. But the marketing environment of (i) high consumer loyalty to stores, (ii) lower movement of customers among stores and (iii) the smallness of stores' trading areas limits the potential for growth.

If, therefore, a retailer wishes to grow, he has to rely on regular customers spending more of their expenditure on food in his store. One major method is to begin to stock product lines traditionally held in other stores. Retailers will try to find new product lines which require small investment, are similar to existing lines, and are high in their divisibility, reversibility and recovery potentials. The divisibility potential of the commitment process relates to whether change can be undertaken gradually. The retailer prefers to change something on a limited basis, so that it may be continued if successful, rather than commit himself to an irreversible situation initially. A grocer might add canned goods, paper goods, dairy goods, baked goods and finally fresh produce and meats, since these need accurate estimation of demand and a relatively sophisticated ordering policy, which gives rise to new problems and risks. The reversibility potential relates to ability to return to the base situation. If reversibility to the original state is not possible in case of failure the retailer risks not only his investment but also his operating position. Recovery potential is closely related. For if a mistake has been made it will be possible to recover some money by seeking or returning fixtures and products if the recovery potential is high – as it is in the case of canned goods.

Such innovative marketers have to have growth as their objective, adequate supply arrangements and capital. Many move to higher outreach areas – that is, where the high- and middle-income consumer are to be found. But, as noted in Chapter 6, what tends to have developed is a step between the traditional foodstore and the supermarket. This stage is represented by stores smaller than supermarkets, carrying fewer lines and having partial self-service. They are mini-markets and draw away some middle- and upper-income consumers from the genuine supermarkets. And it has been argued that in the long run they will aid the modern large supermarket, since they promote the development of infrastructure which is necessary but lacking.

Many governments, however, have tended to concentrate their efforts on encouraging the setting up of supermarkets as known in the West. Such enterprises, for example, Unilever's Kingsway stores, Printana and Monoprix in West and Central Africa, Sears Roebuck in South America, all with capital and skilled management, may be relevant to the high-income groups but they are unlikely to provide a model to be followed universally by most indigenous marketers in the retail sector.

The impact of supermarkets in the retailing sector has been discussed in earlier chapters, where it was pointed out that there remains much controversy over whether a supermarket is the appropriate form of retailing outlet and to what extent it serves as a multiplier effect. If there is sufficient market demand a multiplier effect is set in motion and local indigenous entrepreneurs benefit. For the merchandising and promotional effort introduced by an aggressive retailing firm augments the demand for traditional and new products. Thus there is an indirect and direct stimulus to increase the level of output and the rate of research utilisation increases. Sears Roebuck in Latin America has assumed the marketing responsibility of its suppliers. It has also provided production and engineering advice to local manufacturers and stimulated the production of consumer goods such as clothing, rugs and shoes, which require smaller amounts of capital, skilled labour and technical knowledge. The indigenous manufacturer has also been encouraged to upgrade his product quality, making it more acceptable for international markets.

Generally, however, the conditions under which supermarkets developed in Western developed countries do not replicate themselves in developing countries. The low margin, high turnover principle developed in the USA in the depression years, and only survived subsequently because supermarkets had two advantages over the stores they replaced. These were: (i) they could perform the same tasks but more efficiently and offered a better price/quality relationship and (ii) they provided additional features such as variety, selection, cleanliness and convenience which were not available before. But, as noted elsewhere, in developing countries low margins may not be so easy to achieve because of lack of appropriate infrastructure and shopping habits, while variety and convenience are of little value to the majority of customers who cannot afford to travel the large distances or to buy in large quantities.

Thus, again, it would seem that the indigenous marketer in retailing has an important role to play. Although there are many abuses of the system, nevertheless the innovative retailers are agents of change, as shown by the development of mini-supermarkets which may be a result of the desire for growth or alternatively some outside force. For example in Puerto Rico there has been importer pressure on retailers to stock a wider range of goods and in Chile they were under government pressure to handle customers more quickly. Elsewhere the power of consumerism is growing, and in India the Fair Trading Practice Association is actively working to ensure a better relationships between buyer and retailer.

However the way in which change is occurring calls for a new look at the theory of the wheel of retailing. Traditionally, in the developed world, a new cycle is supposed to begin because innovations enter the 'low-status' end of the market. From these low-status, low-margin and low-price beginnings the successful eventuality become high-status, high-cost and high-price but also with a top-heavy vulnerability. In developing countries this theory may not be so relevant, since new forms of retailing, often encouraged by government, tend to be high-margin, low-volume (Kaynak, 1979) and are introduced at the top of the social and price scales. Initially serving the higher income groups they are later often downgraded. And where individual marketers in small store retailing wish to grow they are restricted from growing beyond a certain site, as seen above.

Naturally it is difficult to generalise, since the economic, political, social and business conditions will affect the retailing system. Furthermore, in the economically and socially advanced parts of countries, or even cities, more advanced retailing institutions exist. But where income levels, cultural attributes, consumer characteristics and the structure of channels dictate the market potential, the scale of retailing operations will be affected. This is well demonstrated by considering retailing in Guatemala City where there are three types of merchandising operations.

Firstly there are the 'mercados' or traditional markets, which are central food trading marts that concentrate hundreds of merchants selling a wide assortment of merchandise. Large modern buildings may have been created but traditional markets tend to be crowded and unsanitary. There are 21 of the latter group housing 10 000 retailers. Wholesale hours are 4–7a.m. retail hours 6.30a.m. to 3.30p.m. In such circumstances the retailer has to be persuasive in his selling efforts and effective in haggling with customers, for he runs the risk of spoilage if his produce remains unsold.

Secondly there are 'tiendas' which are small family-owned and operated shops. They sell mainly staple goods and cater for a few adjacent houses. Often in the form of one room in a house they survive because (i) no rent or utility costs are charged, (ii) labour costs are not considered, (iii) investment in equipment is almost nil and (iv) insurance, taxes and advertising are avoided. Consequently the gross margin is also the net profit. These small shops are convenience stores which open between 6.30a.m. and 10.00p.m. seven days a week. They carry a small selection of items, for most sales are concentrated on staples such as bread, cigarettes, beverages, sugar and so on. These small shops are also a form of disguised employment and entertainment.

Thirdly supermarkets, on the same conceptual lines as those existing in the most sophisticated countries, have emerged. Pulling in consumers through heavy mass-media advertising and organised for high volume, high turnover they are important for the middle and higher socio-economic groups but, outside such areas, the general lack of buying power makes them irrelevant.

Guatemala City would therefore seem to support many of the generalisations about retailing made above. However the fact remains that there is great scope for improvement in marketing by the individual retailier but the incentive to improve is reduced by operating conditions.

The implications of culture for effective marketing by the indigenous marketer

In relation to the multinational we have discussed in Chapter 8 how culture can hamper what in Western eyes is 'efficient and effective' management. But culture also has important consequences for indigenous entrepreneurs. Management styles are affected, as is attitude to methods of doing business and success internationally.

India provides a good example of the way in which the entrepreneur and the social system are closely interrelated. For here the system of management of indigenous business tends to be hereditary. It is well demonstrated by Harsh Goenke, the 27-year-old managing director of Ceat Tyres India and Sanjiv Goenke his younger brother (24 years old) who is deputy managing director of Dunlop India. Their father is R. P. Goenke, one of the country's most aggressively expanding tycoons. The whole family owns businesses which together total Rs14b in turnover. This represents the third largest business family after the Tatas and Birlas.

Although Goenke has a Harvard training, other jealous or cynical Indian business rivals put his success down to bribery, corruption and family connections. For Goenke was a close friend of Mrs Indira Gandhi and his expansion came in a series of controversial market raids and takeover bids which received the backing and approval of the government (*Financial Times*, 3 June 1985). Furthermore he belongs to India's 'famous aggressive and allegedly unscrupulous trading sub-caste, the Marwaris' (*Financial Times*, 3 June 1985 p. VIII).

Corruption has been a major reason for many entrepreneurs' successes in India, according to several authorities. Big business tycoon Dhirubhai Ambani is supposed to have used his friendship with Mrs Gandhi to secure licences and approval for some projects which have made his Reliance textile empire the country's fastest growing industrial giant. Reliance Textiles Industries came from nowhere to achieve sales of Rs6.114b (US$510m) in 1984.

The Arab indigenous marketer too is heavily influenced by society's structure, but corruption is much less important. Instead behaviour is heavily influenced by the values, norms and expectations of the Arab people as a whole. The link between business and personal or social life, as noted in the last chapter, is extremely strong and together with the

Islamic culture and limited multinational activity the differences in marketing between the individual in Arab nations and his counterpart in the West are likely to remain long-term phenomena.

The social structure involves strong kinship patterns. The clan is the basis of Arabic tribal society and the extended family is the foundation of rural and urban society. Thus throughout these three major communities there is a strong sense of loyalty to the clan or family. Arising out of this, the executive's role within his organisation is shaped by the expectations of relatives, friends and employees. The chief executive is like the head of a family, the employees being members of that family. But as well as society influencing his style of decision-making, management of conflict and interpersonal relations, the Arab executive is increasingly trying to influence his society. He has found it difficult to introduce modern and scientific methods and adapt them to a society which tries to retain its Arab identity and character.

Nevertheless the Arab executive himself cannot escape his culture. For each Arab feels he is a citizen of an individual culture which includes 160m people in 22 countries of the Arab League and has a common language, religion and history. Not surprisingly he is likely to have strong feelings of identity and commonality – a feeling of brotherhood and a common destiny. Socio-cultural pressures therefore have an enormous impact on his attitude and behaviour in relation to marketing and management, and despite his wishing to attempt some changes there are distinctive characteristics which will not be broken down easily or quickly. These are summarised in Table 9.1 and the implications for marketing can be readily seen.

Table 9.1　**The impact of the Arab culture on marketing management in private enterprise**

Socio-cultural factor	*Impact on marketing and management*
1. Fusion of social and business life.	Different way of conducting appointments and negotiating.
	Extra influences to be considered in marketing decisions.
2. Importance of reputation in the community.	Decisions based on social pressures rather than the scientific approach.
3. Patriarchal family structure.	Top-man syndrome.
	Individualistic approach – top-down management.

Table 9.1 – *contd.*

	No synergy within the firm's functions.
	Nepotism, with family connections rather than efficiency being all-important.
4. Low value given to time.	Strategic planning complicated.
	Targets and delivery dates unlikely to be achieved.
5. Lack of industrial logic; dislike of manual work.	Lack of functional sub-divisions within the organisation.
6. Religious taboos.	Restrictions on women in market research, advertising, door to door selling etc.

Firstly the strong kinship patterns of the Arab culture means that the executive is unable to separate business from his social or personal life. Work and leisure are no longer compartmentalised, which means that employees, clients, suppliers or government officials are likely to call on Arab executives at home or at the weekend to solve business problems. Equally family and friends are likely to drop in at the office and they will be given priority over outside business contacts. This different approach to conducting appointments and negotiating could, it might be argued, lead to inefficiency. What is clear is that extra influences must be considered in marketing decisions.

Closely associated is the second factor: reputation in the community. When making decisions it is likely that the opinion of family members and close friends and employees will be considered. With pressure to conform to such reference groups, decisions are taken in a less scientific manner.

The patriarchal family structure gives rise to many characteristics which are likely to have profound influences on marketing and management. Firstly it permits a top-man syndrome to develop, which means that an individualistic approach is followed. The top man is expected to be there when all decisions are made. This may be an unnecessary burden on time but it is believed that only the top man can get things done, trust and confidence lying in the *person* rather than the organisation. This puts enormous pressure on the head of the enterprise, since friends, family, colleagues and the rest all expect him to succeed in any new venture. Another result of the family structure is nepotism. Family and friends are likely to be employed and valued above their competence. Loyalty is considered the most important factor.

Although attitude to time may be changing, there still exists general disrespect for time. Procrastination is typical and appointments are unlikely to take place on time, especially if personal friends and relatives are waiting too. This approach complicates strategic planning as followed in the West, while the achievement of targets, delivery dates and so on is likely to be less successful. However it appears that in larger companies a three- to five-year planning horizon is increasingly used. The lack of industrial mentality and underlying dislike of manual work is likely to lead to less functional division within the organisation, the employment of immigrant labour and the leaning towards commerce and trading companies.

Finally religious constraints give rise to all sorts of restrictions within the function of marketing – such as lack of market researchers or inability to use women in advertising or to advertise to women.

It might appear that, with all these differences, inefficiency in marketing and management would result. However, as shown below, this is not the case. It may be that marketing management needs to be rewritten around the cultural conditions which give rise to a completely new system. Much is based on reciprocity. The family expects the executive to maintain family ties and help with personal problems, securing employment, pressuring government agencies and other institutions and offering financial assistance. In return loyalty is given by family and all employees. Equally, in relation to business associates and government officials, there are reciprocal obligations. Under such circumstances the interpersonal style of doing things may ultimately result in a different sort of marketing approach but one which is equally effective. Through family, friendship and personal relationships it is possible to get things done and personal ties rather than institutional ones are therefore of fundamental importance.

Nowhere are these characteristics better demonstrated than in Arabian trading houses. Although recently the recession has tested many nerves, resulting in staff being dismissed, service departments closed, prices slashed, inventory stopped and retrenchment (even at the expense of market share in some cases) the owner in most cases is still the only authority within the company. He initiates all new projects, authorises all expenditure, signs all cheques and has all decisions referred to him. Because of the interrelationship between personal and business life he mixes important meetings with minor details such as telexes and tends to rely on one major bank and one central budget for all functions under his control. Borrowing money is considered shameful, particularly among the older and middle-aged generation. Finally every opportunity offered tends to be grasped and once acquired there is great reluctance to discard a product, whatever the opportunity cost.

The most striking feature of the hundreds of businesses run in this way is that they have been extremely profitable (*Financial Times*, 23 Jan. 1985).

Perhaps the main reason is that the concentration of decision-making in the hands of the owners means that there are no extra costs for running different departments such as market research, personnel and the rest. Profits are consequently higher. However a major consequence is that growth potential is severely limited and turnover is likely to be restricted to a maximum of $200m (*Financial Times*, 13 Jan. 1985).

There are some Arab merchant families who have crossed this watershed by setting up decentralised decision-making and delegating authority. However, the number is small – about a dozen – and includes E. A. Juffali and Bros (the Saudi importer of Daimler-Benz trucks and the biggest merchant company in Arabia), the Olayan Group, important in manufacturing and services as well as trading, and Yusif bin Ahmed Kanoo, the Bahrain-based travel and heavy engineering and importing company.

But many owners find delegation impossible to stomach, especially since the recession. They saw the modern management system as something which could be bought. They enjoyed the prestige but would not change their behaviour and instead continually checked on managers' decisions and overruled them. The best known case is Yusif bin Ahmed Alghanim and Sons in Kuwait where the owner (Yusif) and his sons have interfered so much that there are continual management upheavals. Worse is perhaps the case of Mohammad Abdul-Rahman al Bahar's company, which is the Kuwait and Gulf agent for Caterpillar. In the 1970s it was taken over by his two sons Jassim and Issam. By 1980 Caterpillar and Volvo sales alone reached $200m, three quarters of the company's turnover. But this was achieved by delegation, and when, in 1980, Mohammad became concerned about rising overheads and declining control by the family, he reimposed his authority. He insisted on approving personally all Caterpillar orders, despite the fact that the system had been computerised. He closed and amalgamated support services, which he did not understand. The result was a major decline in sales and the company relinquishing its Volvo agency. Similar events have occurred elsewhere in the Middle East.

But, whereas the Islamic culture poses certain constraints in the direction and growth of the enterprise, many of the Far Eastern newly industrialised countries' cultures, notably the Chinese, have characteristics which make for very effective indigenous markets. High motivation, thrift allowing capital saving, industriousness, independence and a desire for property ownership have all been suggested by Hofheinz and Calder (1982) as the keys to a necessary modern attitude. In addition to possessing all these, tolerance, mutual adjustment, meditation to solve disputes, as well as helpful governments which provide backing in the form of credit, export market information and tax incentive are also typical.

Not surprisingly indigenous entrepreneurs tend to be extremely successful and export-orientated. Although the indigenous trading community always had lively commercial trading (in tea, handicrafts, vegetable oils, wood and so on) and an informal credit system through banks and pawnshops, and although 'putting savings to work' was always the philosophy, the industrialisation policies of these countries have also helped. For due to their export-orientated outward-looking strategy they have acquired the most up-to-date technology. And whilst, initially, indigenous entrepreneurs may have been or still are captive producers of multinational enterprises or buying houses, their educational system emphasising science and mathematics has encouraged invention and innovation, which has allowed them to adapt and apply the acquired technology elsewhere.

Hong Kong provides perhaps the best example of a success story of the indigenous marketer working within such conditions. Efficiency is high. Low cost production is promoted by cheap labour, government provision of low cost space for light manufacturing, the industrious nature of the culture and above all a marketing-orientation. In clothing factories, for example, there are no white elephants – that is, machines which are not suitable for the process and should never have been bought. Instead there is a large number of people and an appearance of total confusion. In effect this is illusory. The individual worker is intent upon his or her task, after which the product is moved by hand to the next section. All work is done on a piece-work basis and most equipment is simple – for example, cutting tables, sewing machines, button holes and scissors. Dextrous, careful female workers aged 15–25 are in high demand.

Yet almost all production is for export and the small shirt factories on How Ming Street sell on Main Street in thousands of United Kingdom and United States cities and towns, despite the physical and cultural distances between the two streets (Espy, 1972). Nothing is produced and then sold. Production is always against firm orders, and these are from buyers who represent manufacturers, wholesalers and retail chains in the Western developed world. The buyer designs the product and markets it, the Hong Kong manufacturer is simply a contract producer interested in getting orders large enough to permit economic production quantities and preferably repeat business. The foreign buyer is seeking solely a reliable economic source of production.

The link between the two worlds is therefore easy. Each has what the other needs and there are many small trading companies of 10–100 people which act as intermediaries. Many of Hong Kong's smaller manufacturers acquire all their orders from such export firms, many of whom have long relationships with overseas buyers. There are also some American retail chains with their own permanent buying offices in Hong Kong which may even offer technical and managerial assistance as well as long-term estimates of product requirements for assurances of the lowest prices.

Thus the indigenous marketers in Hong Kong have been extremely successful at matching up their strengths with the opportunities at the international level – so successful, indeed, that they are today facing all sorts of trade barriers. They have developed an outward-looking trading community of manufactures and servicing organisations and, although this has been stimulated by the outward-looking industrialisation policy of Hong Kong, nevertheless they provide excellent examples of the sort of approach many other indigenous marketers could adopt (even in the so-called 'developed' nations).

In many countries, however, notably the large, rich ones, the marketing environment, as discussed elsewhere, is not so favourable. The negative conditions described earlier in the chapter are present and the incentive to use effective marketing is reduced. However, even here there is great scope, for with the right approach enormous success can be achieved. Mr Joao Augusto do Amaral Gurgel in Brazil shows how.

Mr Gurgel is undoubtedly one of the most successful entrepreneurs that Brazil possesses. His achievement is based on a somewhat different approach to that of the successful entrepreneurs in Hong Kong. For he has selected a somewhat unorthodox, as yet, market segment – the less wealthy in the developing world, and 'keeping it simple' is his approach. He is currently developing an economical Third World car for the 1990s (Carro Economico Nacional, or CENA). This will carry four people at speeds of 75–100km per hour, using four litres of fuel per 100km. It will weigh a maximum of 500kg and have an engine size of 650 c.c. It is estimated that it will cost $2000.

Since 1970 Gurgel has sold 15 000 rugged jeeps and utility vehicles, taking three quarters of the Brazilian market (House, 1986). These vehicles (Gurgel X-12s) are used by a variety of people such as Catholic missionaries in the Amazon, tourists in the Caribbean and several Third World armies. His vehicles today sell in 40 countries and in 1985 his total sales increased by 53 per cent over the previous year. Now Gurgel is planning factories in Panama and Indonesia.

This successful entrepreneur previously worked for General Motors and Ford. He had no experience of running his own business (apart from a toy repair business as a ten-year-old) but saw a market niche which was being ignored by the multinationals using product standardisation policies. Thus, in 1968, ridiculed by the multinationals, he decided to set up his own car plant to produce super-simple cars. 'In an age dominated by sophisticated technology and First World products that are beyond the reach of the developing world, Gurgel is going back to basics' writes House (1986, p. 47). Gurgel aims at making the cheapest possible vehicle to match the earning power of the population.

His jeeps, which come in several sizes and models, are a combination of fibre glass bodies on Volkswagen engines and chassis. They have their own suspension and traction systems for off-the-road conditions. Therefore they are the same as a four-wheel drive at a fraction of the price.

Gurgel's success is well demonstrated by the recent agreement which allows him to sell Volkswagen technology overseas for the Carajas jeep which is his most sophisticated hard-top vehicle. In addition, the Fuki Motor Co. has signed an agreement for the future purchase of Carajas and its plasteel monobloc body-work technology to be adapted to Chinese-made engines. Cuba, which pirated one design (the X-12) now wants to make the vehicle under licence.

None of Gurgel's designs clash with the multinational's. It has been Gurgel's policy that they should not, since his market niche is the market segment with a limited income potential requiring economic cars as opposed to the elite buying multinational status symbols. For, although cars have been a leading agent of development in Brazil, their export accounting for over $1.2b per annum and 75 000 new cars per month selling domestically, these 'standardised' cars are only for the rich (0.5 per cent of Brazil's 130m). Furthermore his production methods are very different. Gurgel is using labour-intensive production methods, rather than following the trend towards more capital-intensive production. In 1973 he relocated to Rio Claro, 240km from Sao Paulo, where salaries are lower and weather conditions for fibre-glass are more favourable.

The value of both Gurgel's products and his production process has been seen. The government has given its approval for a new plant to produce 250 cars per day and the National Development Bank has offered idle factory buildings in the depressed north-eastern state of Paraiba. Equally many multinationals have approached Gurgel, hoping that he will sell out. But this successful entrepreneur will not. In the process he has demonstrated well that there is great scope for the effective innovative indigenous marketer who can identify consumer needs and wants. He has also shown that there is an opportunity to develop technology to suit basic needs rather than rely blindly on the multi-nationals imposing their standardised products.

How marketing can help the private sector indigenous marketer

Gurgel's success has a higher chance of being repeated in many more developing countries if the following guidelines are borne in mind. One of the major advantages of marketing is that, when correctly used, subjective values may be added to a product so that the consumer perceives it as superior to the competition and is therefore prepared to pay more for it. Consequently profit margins may be increased. But, as noted already, poor quality and lack of standardisation tend to be two of the major failings of indigenous manufacturers in developing countries, while generic products are often considered the only acceptable and economic type.

In order to move away from this situation the indigenous marketer must adopt the sort of planning procedure mentioned at the end of Chapter 6. All planning involves three simple questions:

1. Where are we now?
2. Where do we want to be?
3. How are we going to get there?

Because of the developing country context the diagnosis stage of finding out about the market, reading and interpreting trends and customer needs, assessing the firm's strengths and weaknesses and resources and noting the limitations of the domestic marketing environment is likely to take on greater significance. For only out of this can an effective strategy be formulated and an appropriate plan put into action. The selection of target market areas forms the foundation of marketing strategy for it is often the case that 20 per cent of a company's customers account for 80 per cent of its sales, and if this 20 per cent can be identified and served well, rather than attempting to serve all segments satisfactorily, maximum revenue will be achieved. The framework of marketing planning may be summarised as in Figure 9.1.

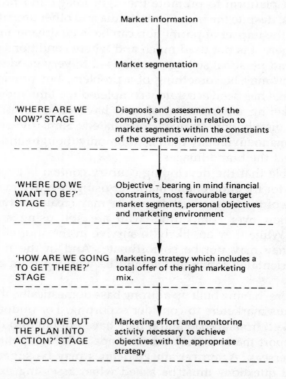

Figure 9.1 *The marketing planning framework*

Once feasible target markets with good growth and profit potential have been selected, strategy may be formulated. What should be remembered here is that two major advantages possessed by small firms is their closeness to customers and their flexibility, whilst two common mistakes made are attempting to offer too wide a range of products and service and competing in large markets where their size puts them at a disadvantage. But within these parameters the product may be made distinctive, with the correct marketing mix so that it offers more perceived value to customers than the competition's.

Even in a developing country the various product variables of quality, features, style and brand name, guarantees, and the rest may be used, just as promotion should aim at building the company's image. Indeed the scope is enormous. For the multinationals have demonstrated that brand names and trade marks are of great value and, provided that indigenous marketers' quality can be maintained, there is no reason why they should not follow suit. Branding helps to create 'exceptional value' in the eyes of consumers, provided that the company's products meet needs better than the competition's. The price/quality assortment, convenience, service and other elements of the marketing mix should all be used as a platform to promote the right image and promotion can reinforce this, despite the inadequate media and other limitations. It may well be that the impact of promotion can be even greater in developing countries where it is not used much and where conditions dictate sales promotion and personal selling can be used to very good effect.

Distribution may be something of a problem, but provided that the diagnosis stage has been accurately completed the limitations presented by the marketing environment should have been assessed and the appropriate distribution strategy formulated. Similarly price possibly offers more manoeuvrability than is commonly thought and it should be used to reflect the brand images.

It is possible that the developing country context is even an advantageous one for the indigenous marketer using effective marketing. For with the use of the correct techniques he may create for himself a very strong position over competitors who are still using a production-orientation. While they are likely to survive in the shorter term, in the long term they may not be so fortunate. And in the meantime the marketing-orientated individual should be working from a position of strength.

Furthermore, having built up a strong base domestically, it is important for indigenous marketers to consider exporting. For undoubtedly they will be attacked from abroad and if they have not built up their sales by acquiring export markets they cannot hope to be competitive either at home or overseas. Again certain guidelines may be suggested. Three fundamental questions must be asked when assessing export market opportunities. These are:

1. What is the market potential for my product(s) in (a) specific export market(s)?
2. What is the company's sales potential in that market?
3. On what segment(s) of the chosen market(s) should the company concentrate its efforts?

In order to answer such questions information is again required. and, since it is likely that the export market(s) will constitute a less familiar environment, the need for accurate information is greater. For some parts of the world (notably the rich Western developed markets) it may well be easier to locate and collect the necessary figures. Much can be acquired from secondary sources (commercial, institutional, official and from competing firms, as detailed in Chapter 4). For example, in order to answer the first question on market potential production, import and export figures are required and these will be found in international publications such as the United Nations Statistical Yearbook. The formula to be used is:

$$S_A = P_A + (M_A - X_A) - (I_i - I_{ii})$$

where S = total sales
      A = country in question
      P = production
      M = imports
      X = exports
      I_i = stocks at the beginning of the year
      I_{ii} = stocks at the end of the year

It is unlikely that a figure for stocks will be found and therefore production, import and export figures must suffice.

To estimate sales potential, a second formula is given:

company sales potential = market potential × penetration ratio.

The penetration ratio is a judgement made by the marketer and arrived at with the help of further information relating to trade restrictions, market structure, channel structure, characteristics of final customers and an honest assessment of the product's standing in relation to the competition. Some primary data may be required.

Equally, in order to define and select market segments to be focussed on, secondary data may not be sufficient. However all questions must take into account both external and internal parameters. The external constraints of culture, the legal, physical, technical, competitive and economic situation as well as the internal constraints of financial resources, company objectives, the role of the export market(s) under consideration in relation to other export markets and the domestic market can never be ignored.

Once the market opportunities have been assessed and the appropriate market segment(s) chosen, the indigenous marketer can formulate his strategy to provide that total offering required by the consumer which he or she will perceive as an offer that cannot be refused. Certainly there are many problems and uncertainties but at least such a method should promote a more favourable state of the art of marketing which should serve indigenous marketers well in the future.

Conclusion

The scope for the indigenous marketer in developing countries is enormous. But although more and more governments are recognising the importance of the private sector, especially in the present increasingly competitive economic climate which has restrained both multinational investment and state spending, there remain many inadequacies.

The state of the art of marketing in small manufacturing firms leaves much to be desired. In the developed world the limited research which has been done into the marketing function of small firms suggests that a comprehensive marketing approach is rarely adopted and instead too much attention is given to production. The typical conditions existing in most developing countries, such as excess demand, loss of control over products early in the distribution channel, poor infrastructure and an unhelpful government attitude, tend to encourage indigenous manufacturers to be even more passive in their approach to marketing. However, unless they do find appropriate market niches and develop good marketing strategies, their long-term future in the domestic market and their immediate viability in international markets are in doubt.

At the same time governments must promote a more favourable environment for growth through ensuring more equality between buyers and sellers and stimulating a spirit of enterprise and competition through appropriate legislation. Although some governments in developing countries have always encouraged small businesses, the most notable initiatives today would appear to be at the international level. The Swiss Foundation Fundes with its pilot scheme in Central America provides a good example, and one which is likely to be followed elsewhere.

Marketing by the individual in the rural sector, however, has received much less attention, although indigenous marketers here in the form of hawkers, distributors, processors and traders have served a very useful purpose by providing jobs, increasing producers' confidence and setting a multiplier effect into motion. Often considered as parasitic middlemen by governments which have maintained control of staple and export crops, their development has been constrained and their worth severely undervalued. Inflexible parastatals with swollen bureaucracies, central-ised decision-making and lack of marketing skills have continued to leave insufficient room for the indigenous marketer in this area to have the most beneficial impact. It would be preferable if governments could instead provide a more favourable marketing environment by working more closely with the individual and facilitating rather than limiting his development.

In the retail sector the picture is more complex. Resentment towards the individual may be equally high, especially if non-indigenous ethnic groups dominate retailing within a nation. Although it is difficult to generalise, the dominant form of urban food retailing is the small store, where a passive attitude tends to be maintained by the owner. The number of customers and the amount purchased are regarded as unchanging, except by the more innovative retailers who have tended to expand by stocking product lines traditionally held in other stores. Supermarkets, often promoted by the government, have been found suitable for the high– and middle-income areas but they are unlikely to provide a model or a substitute for the individual retailer. Furthermore the wheel of retailing theory needs to be re-assessed. The heterogeneity within developing countries often leads to a fragmented retailing structure with traditional markets, small family-operated shops and supermarkets being three distinct types of retailing institutions. The type of marketing required in each differs markedly.

If the broader picture of marketing by the individual is considered against the background of culture, many interesting examples emerge. India demonstrates well how corruption may be a major reason for entrepreneurial success, while the Arab context shows how the link between business and personal life is strong. Both situations call for a modification of marketing as it is described in Western-orientated textbooks. Other cultures, such as the Chinese in Hong Kong, have characteristics which make for very effective indigenous marketers on both national and international levels.

Finally there are always exceptions to generalisations about the lack of marketing expertise possessed by indigenous marketers. Gurgel's vehicles and his proposed Third World car shows how an entrepreneur who examines the market, selects an appropriate niche and produces what is needed and wanted can succeed despite the unfavourable operating conditions of many developing countries. By using the appropriate techniques and providing product offerings which are perceived as superior to the competition's, as well as fulfilling needs,

286 *Marketing in Practice in Developing Countries*

many other indigenous marketers can follow suit. And this is possible not only within the domestic market but also in export markets. It points the way to the future for marketing in developing countries, which is considered next in Part III.

PART III

ISSUES AFFECTING THE FUTURE OF MARKETING IN DEVELOPING COUNTRIES

The third and final part of the book examines the issues affecting the future of marketing in developing countries. In previous chapters the problems of marketing in a developing country context and the way in which marketing is carried out pointed to the need for (i) the better application of marketing, particularly by the state and individual marketers, and (ii) a broader perspective when using marketing.

However the prevailing economic crisis which, since the mid 1970s, has resulted in the world economy suffering from low real growth, periodic contractions of trade, record levels of unemployment, relentless poverty and more beggar-thy-neighbour protectionism, particularly in the advanced world, is not the most favourable background at the macro level. Equally there are some important changes occurring at the more micro level which must be identified, for in some instances they are potential stumbling blocks. Alternatively, they may provide interesting opportunities to be seized upon by the enterprising marketer.

By examining (i) the international scene, against which all developing countries must formulate their marketing strategies, (ii) individual trends such as convergence or divergence of culture, consumer tastes and political regimes and (iii) the rate of success of individual countries in their drive to secure economic development, some discussion of the problems and prospects of marketing in the future is possible.

PART II

ISSUES AFFECTING THE FUTURE OF MARKETING IN DEVELOPING COUNTRIES

CHAPTER 10

Problems and prospects for marketing at the macro level

Contents

Introduction

In Chapter 2 it was noted that the interrelationship between the organisation (whether public, private, commercial or non-commercial) and its ever-changing environment may be summed up by using an ecosystem analogy. On a broader scale it is possible to take this analogy further and look at the relationship between individual countries and groups of nations in a world system. But, although the concept of an interdependent world system had been postulated for some time earlier on a theoretical level, by such academics as Wroe Alderson (1968) in his functional approach, it was not really acknowledged by political leaders until the 1970s.

For previously, despite developing countries having searched for a new economic order for some time, military security, ideology and territorial ownership were assumed to be of greatest importance on political agendas. Since the 1970s, however, in addition to growing social concerns such as nuclear proliferation, population growth, food production, pollution and management of the oceans, the economic shocks of higher energy prices, inflation, exchange rate volatility, the emergence of new competitors and the rapid international transfer of technical progress through multinational marketing became important new forces of disturbance and disruption. Investment in basic industries slowed and public sector involvement in the form of subsidies, protection or other nationalistic measures grew. A large number of governments began to try and boost exports, limit imports and stimulate domestic job creation.

Such beggar-thy-neighbour deflationary policies which are still being adopted, according to some (Manley and Brandt, 1985), are unviable for the world as a whole and especially unjust for the developing countries which are hit the hardest. There is a need for redistribution as well as recovery and for the two to go hand in hand, for 'without an extension of global demand and a redistribution of expenditure and resources between industry and agriculture, social groups, and areas within the world economy, there is no prospect for global recovery and development' (Manley and Brandt, 1985, p. 16). The implications for marketing are enormous. Although it has been suggested that marketing strategies adopted by multinationals have exacerbated the problem (Hansen, 1979), governmental and indigenous marketers in developing countries must select their marketing response with great care.

In order that whoever uses marketing at whatever level is conversant with the international system at this unprecedented, dynamic, uncertain time, this chapter seeks to uncover many of the trends and tendencies which have occurred, are occurring, or are likely to occur in the future. It also examines possible responses. Firstly international trade theory and the international product life cycle are discussed. Against this framework the reality is matched, so that the extent to which theory is supported or questioned can be assessed. Finally the responses by developing countries on the individual level and as a whole in the form of the louder voice of the South, and North/South integrated marketing are noted. The three types of marketer are considered throughout. Multinational marketers are referred to particularly in relation to the international product life cycle whilst the implications of the broader international environment for the indigenous and state marketer and their responses are highlighted wherever relevant.

International trade theory

International trade theory (ITT) has limited utility for explaining the modern international business arena. But it remains an obvious starting point and continues to shape much business thinking as well as providing a rationale for many features of the broader global marketing environment.

The major objectives of ITT are to explain (i) why countries trade, (ii) what goods countries will export and import, (iii) how gains from trade are divided between trading nations and (iv) how adjustments are brought about when trade patterns are disturbed. Factors of production are assumed to be free to move within each country but are also assumed to be immobile between countries.

Adam Smith was one of the first economists to note how commerce of towns contributed to the improvement of the country. They provided a market. Commerce introduced order and good government while also improving the life of the peasant. On the international level it may be said that nations trade for economic, political and cultural reasons, but the principal economic basis is difference in price. For if a national can buy some commodity more cheaply from another nation than it can produce itself some basis for trade exists. Adam Smith used the example of England trading manufactured goods for Portuguese wine. He noted that although grapes could be grown under glass in England, this would lead to England having both less wine and fewer manufacturers than if it specialised in manufactured goods. Smith's conclusion was that the wealth of nations derived from the division of labour and specialisation. At the international level this meant trade rather than autarky.

Ricardo's law of comparative advantage refined Smith's argument by explaining why price should vary between countries. Prices differ because countries producing the commodity or goods under consideration have different comparative cost structures. Thus a country gains if it produces more of the goods in which it is relatively more efficient and exports these in exchange for those in which its absolute advantage is least. Thus the factor endowment of each country is all important and so long as each country is not equally efficient in all commodities a basis for trade exists. A country rich in natural resources but short of labour will tend to export land-intensive products. A country with high capital investment will export machine-orientated produce. Comparative advantage therefore provides a foundation for explaining trade patterns and the overall gains from specialisation and trade. And, if free trade is followed, global output is maximised.

The principles of the doctrine of comparative advantage may be summarised as follows:

1. Every region (country or firm) should specialise in producing goods in which it has the largest comparative advantage.
2. Every region (country or firm) should then trade those goods for others in which it has a comparative disadvantage.
3. A trade price will naturally evolve that will benefit both parties and motivate them to engage in trade.
4. All regions will have, as a result, a higher standard of living.

Source: Cundiff and Hilger, *Marketing in the International Environment* (New Jersey: Prentice-Hall 1984) pp. 73–4.

International Trade Theory and the law of comparative advantage assume away such aspects as tariffs, transport costs, protectionism, different political ideologies, special interest groups and cultural barriers. They also concentrate on commodities rather than manufactured products and branded goods. But they are useful to the extent that they help predict what products (and in what amounts) will be entered into international trade.

The international product life cycle

International trade theory examines why countries trade. But this is not sufficient to explain why the production of goods and services is transferred across national boundaries and why developing countries acquire technology at the expense of the developed nations, which then lose their competitive edge. It also failed to foresee the internationalisation of business, the use of marketing in the determination of needs and wants and the fact that it is business enterprises not governments which influence trade patterns to a very large extent, especially in the movement of manufactured goods.

The international product life cycle theory attempts to fill this gap. It derives from research by Vernon and Wells at the Harvard Business School and is a concept designed to show how technology is diffused from a developed country, such as the USA, which consequently loses its technological edge. The technology is lost to the developing countries (the multinational being a means of speeding the process) and ultimately it becomes more efficient for the advanced world to import the product back from developing countries.

In the first stage (Figure 10.1) there is a significant technological breakthrough in one of a small number of Western technologically-advanced societies. It is largely accident that determines which country has the breakthrough. In the typical example the mass production of motor cars is used. The USA started to manufacture them on a large scale first and consequently exports grew.

In the second stage the breakthrough spreads rapidly to other countries which have the necessary technological infrastructure (Western Europe in the mass production of motor cars). the enterprise which had the innovation may itself introduce it elsewhere, either through export or local production. It might also be licensed, pirated or simply adopted. Because other countries have started to manufacture exports from the USA (in the case of motor cars) start to level off.

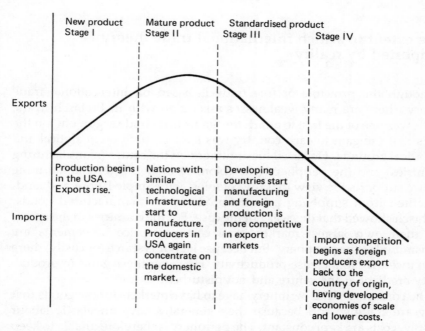

(Model based on the mass production of motor cars and the USA as the country of origin)

Figure 10.1   The international product life cycle

Source: Based on Vernon, R. (1966) 'International Investment and International Trade in the Product of the Life Cycle', *Quarterly Journal of Economics*, May 1966, p. 162; Wells, L. T. jr. (1972) 'International Trade: The Product Cycle Approach in Louis T. Wells (ed.), *The Product Cycle and International Trade*, Graduate School of Buisness Administration, Harvard University p. 15.

In the third stage the product becomes available in less developed countries – that is, those countries which do not possess the technological infrastructure to develop the process from the beginning, but can reproduce a process development elsewhere. Host governments are likely to encourage this, to build up domestic industry and cut imports. At first the quality of local versions may not be good but as the technology matures it improves, so that products are compatible. Exports from the USA (in the motor car example) begin to decline as these new production centres develop.

In the fourth stage the developing countries become more efficient sites of production. The tide of exports is turned and the less developed countries export back to the country of origin. This is quite acceptable if a brand name or trademark of a multinational which is already well established in the country of origin is used.

The extent to which international trade theory is supported by reality

Although the principle of free trade is based on international trade theory, there are many weaknesses associated with it. Prebisch in the 1950s was one of the first to attack the 'gains from trade argument' on the basis that the gain to each country was *unequal*, both on analytical and empirical grounds. He based his argument on the centre (manufacturing countries) and the periphery (the colonies) model. International trade theory supports the view that the colonies, with ample labour and land, benefited from supplying primary products for manufactured goods. Prebisch showed that this was not the case. For the countries of the centre are their own largest market. Any cost and price movements are transmitted to the periphery. But because labour is scarce (or costly) there is an incentive to increase productivity. However these gains in productivity are kept at the centre and not disturbed.

The countries of the periphery have to have markets for the goods that they are trading, and because they generally have an elastic labour supply, costs are kept constant. The periphery is therefore unable to keep any gains from improved productivity and these are passed on to the centre in the form of lower prices. Thus the periphery loses out to the centre.

Secondly there are divergent income elasticities of demand for primary products and manufactured goods. These are low for food and raw materials, high for manufactured goods. In the periphery, as income rises, expenditure on manufactured goods increases more then proportionally. On the other hand at the centre further income increases result in a less than proportional increase in food demands, while the search for, and development of, cheaper synthetic substances reduce the imports of primary products from the periphery. The income in the peripheral countries is thus held down. These nations cannot compensate by producing more, nor can they reduce their dependence on imports. Furthermore they are particularly susceptible to demand fluctuations, and despite OPEC having, until recently, been a relatively successful cartel, other attempts to control prices have failed. At present commodity prices are at an all-time low.

Prebisch also pointed out that the concept of international trade theory was based on Britain's case which, as workshop of the world, followed a policy of free trade. It grew wealthy and made the rest of the world a relatively wealthier place in the process. But this, he suggests, was an exceptional situation. Britain was deficient in raw materials and was willing to import freely. Today the situation is different. Firstly America, with vast resources of raw materials and a tradition of protectionism, encouraged the exploitation of its own resources and substitution wherever possible. The rapid expansion of such an economy was not of great benefit to other suppliers of raw materials. Elsewhere, such as in the EEC, agriculture has been encouraged and protected whilst the substitution of synthetics for raw materials has meant that the rich countries became richer while the poor were left behind.

Indeed Prebisch went further and argued that developments such as the General Agreement on Tariffs and Trade (GATT) are irrelevant except between nations which are of similar level of economic development. And the fact that developing countries continue to trade with the advanced world, which is now protecting its markets, has made the situation even more imbalanced.

Prebisch suggests that the only way to enable developing countries to advance is to change the rules so that the developed world allows the free movement of goods from the developing world. This is essential, since the scale of production today needs to be larger. No longer is it the case of one country (the United Kingdom) having the monopoly over technology and all markets. Instead many countries have the technology. But this means a need for a large market and this can only as yet be found in the rich developed countries. At the same time developing countries must be allowed to protect their home market. Under such conditions the developing countries have some chance of survival.

Prebisch has gone down in history as a person who helped to bring pressure to bear on the developed world in relation to its responsibility towards the developing world. And his thesis – that the nineteenth-century doctrine of international trade benefiting all (because the freer trade becomes the more the mutual benefit) was irrelevant and inaccurate

– would seem to be borne out by the existing situation today. The role of multinational marketing, the rise of protectionism in the advanced world and the fall in commodity prices associated with growing debt by developing countries are all factors which need to be closely considered.

(a) The role of the multinational

Conventional trade theory assumes (i) that capital and labour are immobile between countries, (ii) that trade is between different companies in different countries and (iii) that a competitive international market exists (where lower real wage costs in one country will give sufficient conditions for lower prices, increased competitiveness and greater exports). However in reality (i) capital investment is highly mobile, (ii) trade goes on increasingly between the same multinationals while (iii) lower wage costs in one country are insufficient to increase price competitiveness and exports.

The multinational's power and influence have been claimed to be major reasons for structural inequality in trade and production between North and South (Manley and Brandt, 1985). International trade theory must consequently be increasingly considered in association with the multinational. For no longer can direct investment be analysed in the classical manner as a flow of extra capital into a country where all else remains constant. Today large oligopolistic firms straddle international boundaries with the result that a high percentage of international trade in manufactured goods takes place within multinational corporations. With their horizontal linkages between production centres, vertical network linkages between various stages of production, other input and output linkages and the possibility of creating demand for their products, they can manipulate trade to a very large extent.

It is the small developing countries which do not have sufficient domestic markets to sustain a wide range of industries which are most heavily dependent upon export activities of multinationals. In some instances local raw material-processing may be undertaken, but often this is hindered by the tariff structure of the developed country or by the multinational processing the materials elsewhere. However, as noted in Chapter 8, the days of this sort of activity are numbered. More common are exports manufactured by labour-intensive methods, such as textiles, sports equipment, shoes and toys. Exports of components used within vertically integrated international industries are also common.

The latter (which form the third category of reverse vertically integrated manufacturing) have developed significantly in recent years. With semi-conductors, valves, electrical appliances, calculators, office and tele-communication equipment, bicycle parts, synthetic fibres and musical instruments as typical examples, these exports, which often originate from Hong Kong, South Korea, Singapore, Taiwan and Mexico, are likely to increase in the future. This is for several reasons. Firstly opportunities for earning foreign exchange in other ways are often limited. Secondly the export of such products and processes within multinational structures are less likely to be badly hit by protective measures since multinationals are powerful lobbies. Finally the multinational's incentive to source such products in these nations is increasing as income differentials between the North and South widen and as improvements in social conditions in developing countries result in a narrowing of the international differ-ences in labour quality and efficiency.

Thus the multinational will continue to play a fundamental role in the future development of manufactured exports from developing countries. And processing, assembling and component manufacture, typical of reverse vertically integrated manufacturing systems, are likely to become increasingly important in the future. The result is that the assumptions of international trade theory are too simplistic and do not sufficiently take into account the impact of the multinational.

(b) The fall of commodity prices and the rise of protectionism

According to the theory of comparative advantage many developing countries should be relying on commodities for export earnings. How-ever the prices of these began to fall at the end of the 1970s and collapsed to unprecedented levels in 1982. Few have recovered, many have fallen even further. This has meant loss of earnings, hitting the least-developed, low-income countries the hardest. Although international discussion started in 1973 on an integrated programme and there have been fifteen international commodity agreements, there has been little success and commodity prices have not stabilised. OPEC has remained (until recent-ly) the only successful cartel and even here its prices fell from $30 in late November 1985 to $15 in February 1986 and $10 subsequently. Most of the gain went to importing countries in both the advanced world and developing countries such as Brazil, South Korea, the Philippines, Turkey and Taiwan. The major losers were the oil exporters – Mexico, Nigeria, Venezuela, Algeria, Indonesia and Malaysia. Although there has been some recovery of oil prices the situation has not been helped by the fact that industrial production in the developed world has continued to witness smaller growth rates – 6 per cent in the 1960s, 2 per cent between

1973 and 1979 and − 0.4 per cent between 1978 and 1983 (*Financial Times*, 29 Aug. 1986).

And even where manufactured goods are produced and exported, theory falls down. For according to the theory of comparative advantage the reduction of direct wage costs and indirect social expenditure is critical to the prospect of developing countries gaining a global advantage in their export trade. But if this were the case, Bangladesh should have outstripped Japan. In practice the world's least developed countries with the lowest labour costs and the greatest labour reserves usually lack sufficient capital, management, labour skills or technology to be able to compete effectively as far as manufactured products are concerned.

Many of the inadequacies are explained by international trade theory being based on the United Kingdom case. When Britain industrialised there was no competition and really free trade. Subsequently other Western developed nations (European countries, North America and Japan) industrialised behind protective tariff barriers. Since their industrialisation there have been several rounds of trade liberalisation through GATT but this was mainly liberalised trade between the developed nations. In sectors crucial for exports from the developing countries, particularly traditional industry as well as agriculture, the North is almost as protectionist now as at any time in its own earlier industrialisation. And despite much pressure, protectionism is increasing and preventing the free trade assumed to exist in international trade theory.

World trade problems have worsened considerably since 1985 and the developing countries are the big losers. World trade as a whole grew only 2–3 per cent in 1985 compared with 9 per cent in 1984, and purchases from non-oil exporters of the Third World actually fell. Taiwan, Hong Kong and South Korea lost ground, as revealed by their total exports to the USA in the first half of 1985 (Westlake, 1986a), and this shows how protectionism by the North is becoming more effective and more discriminating against developing countries. In order not to infringe GATT regulations there has been a shift from border tariffs to quotas, voluntary restraint, bilateral agreements, orderly marketing arrangements, anti-dumping actions, and the imposition of health standards and bureaucratic customs procedures. Although still basically illegal under GATT, such non-tariff barriers have the advantage that they can be targeted against particular countries without a trade war developing. They are also sector-specific. Agriculture, mineral fuels, textiles, shoes, ceramic products, steel, various electronic goods and various household appliances, all of vital importance to developing countries, have been particularly badly affected.

These sectors of activity have all experienced limited growth in the North in recent years but have not reduced their employment accordingly. Consequently governments have protected and subsidised such industries. Bilateral agreements have also been regarded as means of protecting domestic producers in the developed nations. Often with multinational ratification (via GATT) they have been regarded as the best way of achieving national objectives while not interfering with the ideal of free trade by developed nations. Developing countries are not cut out but can negotiate with governments to acquire reciprocal arrangements.

But although bilateral agreements are deemed short-term, temporary measures, often they become long-term permanent instruments involving quantitative restrictions. The Multi-Fibre Agreement which started in a bilateral deal and developed into continued protectionism against textiles from developing countries is a good example. Begun as the long-term arrangement on cotton textiles in 1962 when the USA was concerned about Japanese cotton textile imports in the 1950s, it meant that Japan agreed to voluntary restraint. As a result, whereas Japan accounted for 63 per cent of all United States cotton textile imports in 1951, she accounted for only 26 per cent in 1960. However other countries such as Hong Kong began to take over, which shows the futility of such bilateral agreement. Therefore the United States sought relief under the auspices of GATT to ensure that cheap imports would not disrupt domestic consumption. Multilateral ratification was seen as the solution. But although it was initially assured that the agreement would be a temporary arrangement, not to be repeated, so that GATT ideals would still be adhered to, what in effect happened was that trade from developing countries was not inhibited (for synthetic and other fibres were produced to get round the agreement), and the framework was expanded into the Multi-Fibre Agreement in 1974.

Successive negotiations of this have shown how markets for developing countries can be limited. 1976 was a break point for the EEC which was receiving the brunt of imports but previously had only used specific agreements with individual countries. Its subsequent involvement with the Multi-Fibre Agreement has not been helpful to developing countries, whose clothing exports to the EEC, growing at 27 per cent per annum between 1973 and 1976, grew by only 18 per cent between 1976 and 1979. They are currently being further curtailed and recently the EEC extended its textile control to Bangladesh, the first least-developed country to be subject to such control. It has reportedly asked Pakistan, South Korea, Taiwan and China to moderate export of textiles and clothing to Japan.

Quantitative restrictions are easy for the advanced world to apply and pose a big threat to exporters from developing countries. Quotas are today having a significant impact on a wide range of product groups which now account for 30 per cent of developing countries' exports of manufactures to the developed world. Quotas are usually directed against the most successful exports, which leaves a margin for other entrants, but only in the short term since they too are discriminated against. Voluntary restraint is also becoming common. Although most obvious with the Japanese it seems likely that an increasing number of developing countries following the Japanese strategy of moving up-market will be affected.

Other measures such as anti-dumping rules have been used to create uncertainty in the minds of exporters and to discourage local companies from buying particular imported goods. This frequently occurs in the USA. Domestic competitors file anti-dumping petitions. Even if the case is lost other exporters may in the meantime have been discouraged.

The extent of non-tariff barriers is unknown but a recent UNCTAD – World Bank study estimates that approximately 34 per cent of goods bought from developing countries by sixteen leading industrialised nations were affected by non-tariff barriers between 1981 and 1983, compared with 21 per cent of trade between developed nations (West-lake, 1986a). UNCTAD has also estimated that if non-tariff barriers were removed from 150 key exports from the Third World, foreign earnings would rise by US$35b per annum (that is, two-fifths of the Third World's debt interest payments in 1985). Japan has perhaps been one of the worst offenders in not opening up its market to developing countries. Although claiming to be simplifying procedures and offering concessions, most measures taken have been aimed at lessening the United States' anger. The trade surplus of Japan with the Third World remains very high. It was equivalent to US$4.9b in Southeast Asia and $1.3b in Latin America in 1984.

The developing countries have agreed that there is little point in GATT's rules being extended to cover services, hi-tech products and counterfeit goods if a new pledge on all trade restrictions is not forthcoming. Indeed they have long argued that they get a raw deal out of the free-trade principles enshrined in GATT. In all negotiations they are condemned to the role of the weaker party.

But perhaps more important is the mobility of capital, which has fostered international investment flows and technological advance. For this process allows products to compete, not on the basis of comparative advantage, but more on the basis of product differentiation, style and marketing (Tussie, 1987). Many developing countries have seen nothing of these trends and, lacking both investment and technological resources, they have failed to develop those industries which have been in the forefront of international trade expansion. Eight per cent of world trade in manufactured goods still lies in the industrialised world. The developing countries are largely left to export traditional standard products such as steel and textiles where price is important but where there have been bitter trade disputes. Conversely such aggravation is less common in industries where style and technology are equally as important as, if not more important than price. Many developing countries have been squeezed out of an increasingly exclusive process dominated by the multinationals.

(c) Debt

Making the situation even more desperate for the developing countries is the problem of debt. This currently stands at $900b for all developing countries (Manley and Brandt, 1985), but some are much more badly affected than others. The highest debt is concentrated into a small number of nations which includes Mexico, Brazil, Venezuela, Argentina, the Philippines, Indonesia, Nigeria, Chile and Yugoslavia. For Latin America the debt crisis is particularly severe with the external debt standing at three times the value of exports and half of its GNP. In reality many countries are behind on their repayments but only a few so far have made unilateral declarations of default.

Under pressure from the IMF in Washington many have turned to export promotion policies but the fall in commodity prices and protectionism by the North has made for an inappropriate time to attempt this, and foreign sales declined faster in the first half of 1985 (supposedly a year of business recovery) than at the peak of the recession in the early 1980s. Exports from developing countries grew by 10.7 per cent in 1984 but only by 2.3 per cent in 1985 (*Financial Times*, 22 Sep. 1986) Furthermore, because of the deteriorating terms of trade, per capita income has fallen, while imports have been cut – by 25 per cent on average in Latin America but by 37 per cent in Mexico and 35 per cent in Ecuador. This has hit production and jobs but the greatest impact has been on the rural poor. Yet population in this continent continues to grow by 3 to 4 per cent per annum (Hurtado, 1986). Although many heavily-indebted countries of Latin America gained from the fall in the dollar interest rates this was offset by lack of demand for their exports. And even Asian countries which rely primarily on exports of manufactured goods saw a lower rate of growth compared with the previous two decades, Singapore even experiencing negative growth rates in 1985 for the first time in twenty years.

All the above factors call into question the validity of international trade theory. Many of the assumptions and much of the background against which the theory was developed have disappeared, while other new complications have presented themselves. Unfortunately much of the world's trading system and many of its institutions are still based on the reasoning of international trade theory.

The extent to which the international product life cycle is supported by reality

The international product life cycle suggests it is inevitable that there should be an adjustment in the global division of labour and the location of the world's industrial capacity. Although complicated by many of the above issues, its weaknesses are less severe than those encountered in international trade theory.

There are many examples which demonstrate how manufacturing capacity has been lost from the North to the South. Steel, ship-building and textiles have largely been transferred to developing countries, aided by the multinationals' eagerness to cut down on labour costs at home. The motor industry, the basis of the international product life cycle, has seen important developments in Brazil and South Korea. Brazilian output is impressive and likely to double by 1989, when it is estimated that it will be equivalent to Britain's output of one million cars per year. Many major multinationals are 'sourcing' in Brazil – Ford for Scandinavian, Austrian and Swiss markets, Fiat for its 127/147 and Uno models destined for Western Europe, and General Motors for its Scandinavian market. Exports are estimated to rise from 175 000 cars in 1984 to 272 000 in 1991.

Similarly South Korea is becoming a major car exporter in Southeast Asia and is taking over from the Japanese who are moving up-market in export markets where they are being subjected to voluntary restraint. For example, Daewoo now has an agreement to market its cars under the GM badge for 1987 while Hyundai has a sales and marketing headquarters in the United States and, when it launched its Pony car in Canada, had an instant success, exceeding the company's initial expectations four-fold.

Not surprisingly some change in the trade of manufactured goods generally can be witnessed. In the early 1950s all trade in manufactured goods was concentrated among the industrialised countries. Since the 1960s, however, there has been more participation by developing countries. Between 1963 and 1973 exports of manufactured goods from developing countries grew at an annual rate of 19 per cent so that by 1973 industrial products equalled two-fifths of all developing countries' sales abroad, demonstrating a basic shift from commodities to manufactured goods. The average growth rate for exports of manufactured goods from developing countries was 13.8 per cent on average between 1973 and 1980 and it has fluctuated markedly since but generally in a downward direction. The annual percentage growth was 8.6 per cent in 1981, 0.1 per cent in 1982, 10 per cent in 1983, 16.6 per cent in 1984 and 3.3 per cent in 1985 (World Bank, 1986).

The period from 1960 to 1973 was favourable for growth because of several factors. Firstly the trade regime of GATT was becoming more liberal. Secondly there were sizeable international flows of long-term capital and technology. Thirdly there was a stable framework of fixed exchange rates and fourthly many national development strategies in developing countries were altered to take advantage of the rapidly expanding world economy.

Since 1973 the situation has been very different. For the oil price rises of 1973 and 1974 altered the favourable wider marketing environment. Oil importing countries increased their external debt and shifted somewhat in their policies towards developing their own manufacturing industries. In the advanced world inflation and recession grew, not helped by floating exchange rates and greater trade conflict between developed countries. Protectionism in the North increased and has been referred to as 'the new protectionism' since, as noted above, despite the continuing adherence to free trade by GATT members, many non-tariff barriers have taken over from previous tariff ones.

Some regions of the developed world have proved more receptive to developing country imports than others. Europe has been the most receptive, followed by North America and Japan. At the same time some types of goods have been received by each region more readily than others. Textiles and engineering products are important imports in Europe; Japan has received textiles, clothing and engineering goods most favourably, while the United States remains the most diversified impor-ter. In global terms, however, the penetration of advanced world markets by developing countries in small. Developing countries accounted for 1.2 per cent of all manufactured goods consumed in the developed world between 1959 and 1960. By 1975 the figure had risen to 2 per cent. Today it is not much higher.

Once one begins to look at the countries and the sectors of activity which are involved a much more specific picture emerges. It shows how a few countries and sectors of activity have benefited much more than others. The most successful nations have been the 'Gang of Four' in East Asia, that is, Hong Kong, Taiwan, Singapore and South Korea. These countries, all characterised by export-orientated outward-looking policies and fully integrated into the world economy, accounted for 60 per cent of all developing countries' exports of manufactured goods in 1979. Another category of countries producing more manufactured goods than the first but only exporting a very small proportion comprises Brazil, Mexico and Argentina. Together these countries accounted for 12 per cent of all developing countries' exports of manufactured goods in the 1970s. A third category, all large economies in Asia, incorporates India and Pakistan. These countries accounted for 6 per cent of the total figure. Both, however, have failed to exploit their potential. The fourth group of countries includes Malaysia, Thailand, the Philippines, the Ivory Coast, Tunisia, Morocco, Colombia, Chile and Uruguay. Whilst none export much on an individual basis all have a pro-trade perspective and accounted for a further 9 per cent of all manufactured exports for developing countries in 1979 (Table 10.1).

Table 10.1   Exports of manufactured goods from developing countries in 1979

Group 1	East Asian newly industrialised countries	% Total
	Hong Kong	
	South Korea	60
	Taiwan	
	Singapore	
Group 2	Latin American large newly industrialised countries	
	Brazil	
	Mexico	12
	Argentina	
Group 3	Large Asian economies	
	India	
	Pakistan	6
Group 4	Selected second tier exporters	
	Malaysia Morocco	
	Thailand Colombia	
	Philippines Chile	9
	Ivory Coast Uruguay	
	Tunisia	
Other Developing Countries		13
Total		100 ($78 000m)

Source: Trilateral Commission, 1981.

In terms of *sectors of activity*, clothing, office and telephone equipment, household appliances and other consumer goods are manufactures produced in developing countries and very successfully exported to the advanced world. By 1980 60 per cent of all men's woven shirts and 49 per cent of women's blouses in the EEC were produced in the Third World. There has been some decline in the prominence of these sectors of activity due to trade diversification to avoid protectionist measures. Labour-intensive products are being abandoned for more sophisticated capital-intensive ones by those most successful NICs following the Japanese model. Nevertheless, globally, labour-intensive products still dominate the trade in manufactured goods from developing countries.

At present developing countries still import more manufactured goods than they export and, just as exports from developing countries are sectoral, so too are those from the advanced world. Basically the North still exports products characterised by skills and technology, for example, chemicals, power-generating machinery, other engineering products, road and motor vehicles. The South exports labour-intensive consumer goods, proving to a large extent that comparative advantage still applies in favour of the North, as Prebisch suggested.

It seems likely that the productive capacity of developing countries will grow more rapidly than that of the developed nations. Furthermore the margin of advantage now enjoyed by the North may narrow, so that exports will only be twice as high as imports (Trilateral Commission, 1981) although the absolute surplus will continue to increase. The argument by some developing countries that all marketing advantages will never be transferred and that only Western products will ever be acceptable has been disproved by several East Asian nations – firstly Japan and now the 'Gang of Four'.

But at the same time, whilst the international product life cycle is an attractive explanation of the transfer of an innovation, and thus a useful tool, it does have its limitations. A major weakness is that it uses a macro approach and considers broad industrial sectors rather than individual products. Next there is the danger that the analogy can be stretched too far. For example, not all developing countries will acquire a car industry. It seems that management skills (be these American, British, Japanese, Korean or Taiwanese) will be a major factor determining the winners, especially as more capital-intensive technology is used. There are several instances where the international product life cycle does not apply or where it may not work so well in the future.

Firstly it may be that a certain level of technology cannot be mastered by all developing countries. This could occur either in the case where technology is constantly changing or where a new production process is developed which makes mass production in a capital-intensive fashion more favourable than cheap labour-intensive methods. Alternatively it could be that after explosive growth the technology matures and it becomes preferable to use capital-intensive methods in the developed world rather than the previous hand assembly in developing countries. This is occurring to some extent with the computer industry at present. Some have even argued that it is also happening in the motor industry, since labour is playing a smaller part in costs. Production volumes are increasing and the strength of distribution channels and imaginative marketing also helps.

Secondly it may be that the multinational chooses to prevent the diffusion of technology. The Japanese preferred (for as long as they could get away with it) production at home based on a high technical input to the manufacturing process, rather than accept local production abroad. Only recently, when they have been forced to go international, have they modified this strategy. The USA or other Western developed countries could, theoretically, revert to the same policy in consumer durable goods, reinforcing the fact that the diffusion of all processes is not inevitable, nor must it always be in one direction – from the developed to the developing countries.

Thirdly there are some industries which require one-off production processes and are therefore not suitable, while fourthly there may be sufficient reluctance at home – political or otherwise – to prevent diffusion. Increasingly traditional industrial heartlands are suffering from 'a doughnut effect' – that is, they are losing heavy industry such as shipbuilding or heavy engineering to the developing countries but the high-tech and service industries which are replacing them are unlikely to create employment fast enough to accommodate the unemployed displaced from the traditional industries. Furthermore the sort of new jobs produced are unlikely to be compatible with the old ones. There is also a strong possibility that the new industry will not appear on a scale sufficient to avoid de-industrialisation. Thus a doughnut or ring of plant capacity is created abroad but the hole in the centre (the traditional heartlands) has insufficient employment to replace that lost. The pressure from trade unions and even governments may become so great that the process of transferring industry to developing countries is halted.

However, at present, the international product life cycle holds true in broad terms. But clearly there are issues on the more specific level which will affect what products can be transferred across national and cultural frontiers. The wider the gap in material culture terms between one society and another, the greater the potential problem of choosing which product can be transferred. Ultimately the issue of product suitability is only one aspect of a much larger question – are cultures and tastes converging or diverging? This is considered in the next chapter.

Possible responses by developing countries

There are various responses which can be made by all three types of marketers to the difficulties encountered in the broader international environment. This may be at the individual country level or at the more regional or international level.

On the individual level the multinational marketer, as usual, is in the best position to respond. Many protectionist measures can be avoided because of intrafirm trade flows and direct investment decisions. Indeed, because the multinational is largely to blame both for negating international trade theory and for determining to what extent the international product life cycle will apply, its manoeuvrability in responding to outside pressures is enormous.

(a) Encourage multinationals to locate

Not surprisingly some have suggested that developing countries only have one real hope – to shake free of the fear of domination by multinationals and encourage a fresh flow of foreign investment. But at the same time, as noted in Chapter 7, the government marketer must carefully consider the major advantages and disadvantages which result from multinationals locating in the nation and using it as an export base. The processing, assembly and components manufacture undertaken in the reverse vertically integrated type of multinational manufacturing may, if not carefully monitored, lead to dependence and structural imbalance in the economy. But where the impact of linkages and other dynamic influences are positive the government marketer should take the appropriate steps to encourage more multinationals to locate.

Simply to change the industrialisation policy from import substitution to export orientation has been found less than successful in many cases. For the supply of trained and educated labour may be lacking in countries which have attempted to build up their own domestic manufacturing by using intermediate technology. Equally large countries which can afford to adopt an inward looking strategy tend to be high-cost production sites and therefore their goods (especially if built primarily for the domestic market with less sophisticated technology) are likely to be uncompetitive on world markets. Thus a careful assessment of the conditions existing within the developing country, as well as a long-term marketing strategy for the country as a whole, needs to be devised before a decision to go down this path is taken.

(b) Adopt a protectionist stance

The reverse strategy – to become more protectionist – has been suggested by several writers. Westlake (1986a) suggests that developing countries could close their frontiers and begin to adopt inward-looking policies that were typical in the 1930s. This may seem rather extreme, but Spain has been doing this in relation to cars while using an export-orientated policy as well.

Even trade within regional groupings has been suggested as highly desirable by Tussie (1987). Although the Latin American Free Trade Area (LAFTA) failed this was because it was modelled on the old-fashioned idea of exchanging one good for another, rather than trading in products best suited to thriving international commerce, even if these are produced by the same industrial sector. This intra-industry trade (promoted by the multinational) has served the North well and must, according to Tussie, now be embraced by the South. However a careful assessment of this strategy needs to be made, for the problems associated with regional groupings are not easy to resolve.

(c) Adopt outward-looking policies and market aggressively overseas

Perhaps a more aggressive marketing response is for indigenous firms to develop and maintain export markets. For in most developing countries the size of the domestic market is too small to sustain modern industry. Therefore it is essential to export in order to increase the size of production and lower costs through economies of scale. Exporting and producing for the home market can only be maintained through marketing overseas. If this is not attempted foreign competition adopting this strategy will be able to undercut domestic producers in their home market. It may also be that competition is less intense in some export markets, the stage of the product life cycle may be different, or excess capacity can be put to good use.

The effect of trade barriers can often be minimised. For example, the impact of high *ad valorem* tariff barriers can be reduced by adopting marginal costing (although care must be taken not to be accused of dumping). Quotas are less easy to circumvent, but it is still possible to ask the following questions:

1. When does the quota year begin?
2. Is it applied on a first come first served basis or is it calculated on a historical basis so that each country's quota is known?
3. Will it be increased or decreased?

By considering the reason for the quota's establishment, the balance of payments situation, which industries are protected, what is happening on commodity markets and so on, some indication of the future application of quotas in particular export markets is at least possible. And other obvious and less obvious difficulties faced by export marketers, such as currency fluctuations, distance, political issues, culture, technology and credit-worthiness of both customers and countries, can be accommodated, provided that market research has been adequately used beforehand.

Individual and state marketers in the Far East have adopted outward-looking policies and marketed aggressively overseas very effectively for some time. They have at the same time managd to overcome increasing restrictions on their goods in the developed world. For example, protectionism has severely hit Hong Kong knitwear manufacturers. Their response the latest non-tariff barrier – the need for 'country of origin' labels in the United States market – has been to change their production process. Rather than continue to use Chinese-produced pieces of knitwear, they have, between May 1985 and May 1986 invested $HK300m (£25m) on the latest computer-driven machinery from Japan. It is ironic that Japanese exporters should benefit when they were the ones who originally triggered off protectionism against textiles. It is also sad that 50 000 jobs are likely to have been lost in Guangdong. But Hong Kong's persistent approach to the overcoming of any new barrier imposed is reflected in the fact that exports from Hong Kong in 1985 rose 11 per cent. This shows how trade barriers can be circumvented if determination exists.

Similar success can be noted for all four countries in the 'Gang of Four'. Their overall approach, encouraged by their government marketers, has been to move up-market. Just as Sony, Panasonic and Toyota were barely known in the 1960s and Japanese products were considered 'cheap and nasty', today Gold Star, Tatung and Samsung are not too well known in the West. Nor is the reputation of Far Eastern products particularly high. But these four countries' global marketing strategy is attempting to change all this. Although 40 per cent of the $93b exported in goods from these nations ended up in the USA, own labels such as Sears, Mattel and IBM were put on the products, covering their source of production. This situation is now starting to change, largely due to mounting pressure from China, Thailand and other lower-wage countries. The 'Gang of Four' need to move up-market, build a reputation for quality and widen their profit margins.

And to a large extent they are succeeding in doing so. Their products are challenging Sony and Zenith televisions, Head, Prince and Dunlop racquets, Eastman-Kodak cameras, and various designer-label clothes. Higher profile advertising is being used in New York. Gold Star televisions from South Korea are advertised on posters, Singapore Airlines on television commercials and Pro-Kennex Taiwanese tennis racquets in mail order advertisements.

Although all, except South Korea which has 42 million people, have extremely small domestic markets and consequently a smaller number of sophisticated consumers who can be used as a test market, these countries are aggressively using advertising in a Western fashion in the rich Western developed markets. Notwithstanding Tatung's meaning which is 'helping others' and other cultural differences between the Chinese and the West, Tatung is selling on quality, while Korean television makers Lucky Goldstar International Corporation and Samsung are selling on price.

Samsung is today being seen by American consumers as 'the sensible alternative'. Brand names have perhaps been more difficult to formulate in some instances. Taiwan's Kunnan Lo launched his own line of tennis racquets in the USA in 1977. But the brand name he chose, 'Kennedy', was not liked by the Republicans and therefore it was changed to 'Kennex'. Later he switched to Pro-Kennex to avoid confusion with Kleenex. Nevertheless he has already captured 15–20 per cent of the market for top quality racquets by responding quickly to the demand for mid-size graphic-composed racquets. In 1985 his sales in the USA were valued at $18m. Singapore's Tiger Beer, made by Malayan Breweries who redesigned the bottle, has not, however, been too successful, while many Hong Kong firms have found it preferable to buy out existing brands. The point remains however that 'made in Hong Kong' is no longer any disgrace.

To a large extent the Japanese have helped enormously. Sanyo and Sharp are now as acceptable in the USA as General Electric. They have managed to shake off the 'cheap and nasty' image and have broken down consumers' resistance to foreign goods. Today people are more ready to acquire Korean and other non-American products. Indeed few American consumers can tell whether Samsung is Korean or Japanese, while others associate good value and quality with certain names, so allowing manufacturers to broaden their range. At present Honda is selling vacuum cleaners and lawn mowers in the USA and 52 per cent of all United States sales in microwave ovens are accounted for by foreign manufacturers.

Thus it may be seen that the attitude 'foreign is superior', which is a threat to many developing countries trying to compete domestically with Western multinationals, can also apply in the advanced world in relation to products from developing countries. The 'Gang of Four' has shown that it is possible to produce good value, good quality products and to follow the Japanese strategy of moving up-market. Major marketing strategies used include selected market niches and offering a better service than domestic suppliers. If this is carried out on a global basis costs and quality levels can match those of leading competitors and with good reputation and image the chances of succeeding in a difficult international environment are undoubtedly better.

(d) Use countertrade more

However for many nations more dependent upon commodities or import substitution policies such possibilities are not available and other responses need to be found. For all types of marketers but particularly the state marketer and individual marketers countertrade provides one possible option. There are many forms of counter trading: (i) barter, where goods are exchanged for goods, (ii) counterpurchase, where a certain amount of payment is made in goods; (iii) product buyback, where payment is made in the goods produced by the capital equipment acquired; (iv) offset deals, where the exporter must make an investment in the client country to offset the cost of the goods sold.

Barter, one of the oldest forms of trade, is on the increase and likely to grow further. It always reappears in times of economic distress and the energy crisis gave respectability to such bilateral deals. For the government marketer countertrade provides several advantages. Firstly, for a country heavily dependent on an unstable commodity market, barter offers a firmer basis for planning. Secondly it may be used as a source of financial aid, with the effect that goods are acquired at minimal cost and thirdly, and very importantly, scarce foreign exchange is reserved. Often new markets and new sources of supply are established too. According to some (*Financial Times*, 21 Sep. 1986) the IMF has encouraged countertrade by forcing developing countries to cut their imports as part of their debt refinancing packages. Both oil-exporting countries which have seen their revenues cut and cash-poor countries which have had to scale down their projects or find some other funding have found countertrading useful.

It is estimated that by 1988 40 per cent of world trade will be in the form of countertrading (*Financial Times*, 21 Sep. 1986) and although oil price volatility, low commodity prices and major losses in two big European trading houses made 1986 a difficult year for the advocates of countertrading, it is still rising. Some countries, such as Brazil and Indonesia, have got the formula right whilst other nations – Zimbabwe, Nigeria and some other African states – have had their fingers burnt. Nigeria suffered when the oil price fell and found herself paying exorbitant amounts for Brazilian goods, all exacerbated by government officials exploiting the deal to their advantage. Although Babangida is basically opposed to countertrading Nigeria has had to start using it again since its debt servicing level was (in 1986) at 50–60 per cent of export revenue without re-scheduling.

For some countries in the Middle East, such as Iran and Iraq, countertrading is an indispensable ingredient in the trade-finance mix. Saudi Arabia recently bought 72 Tornadoes and 60 jet and turbo-prop trainer aircraft with spares, support and training for part cash and part crude oil. But this nation has also used offset deals. It bought a communications system for $3.5b to $4b from the USA and then insisted that 35 per cent of this was ploughed back into Saudi Arabia's economy through joint ventures and technology transfer (*Financial Times*, 27 Sep. 1985). Much of Asia is attempting to follow the Japanese sogo shosha system and increase the amount of countertrade. In China, too, countertrade amounts to 30 per cent of total trade.

For the government marketer a major problem often is lack of experience of countertrading. The other trading partner (if a developed nation or multinational), therefore, is likely to acquire the better deal. Secondly raw materials rather than semi-finished goods tend to be traded by developing countries, putting them in a weaker position. Finally official rules are fewer and more loose in developing countries.

For the individual marketer the costs of countertrade include (i) likely lower returns for goods, (ii) more risks involved handling unfamiliar products, (iii) the possibility of a longer time before payment is received and (iv) long and complex negotiations. At the same time there are benefits, such as that (i) excess capacity can be used, (ii) exports and employment may be maintained, (iii) there is the possibility of new sources of supply and (iv) good will is earned. In order that countertrade can be evaluated it is necessary to ask a series of questions:

1. Is it the only way the order can be won?
2. Is there a ready market for the goods acquired?
3. Can the countertrade position be kept to a minimum?
4. Is outside expertise necessary to dispose of the goods?
5. Has the contract price been raised sufficiently to cover the extra costs which may be involved in the countertrade deal?
6. Are the goods offered subject to import control?

If the individual marketer carefully assesses the situation, he may find that countertrading is a very useful method of adopting a more global perspective and circumventing many problems in the international trading environment.

(e) The louder voice of the South

However, on a group basis, government marketers have the opportunity of joining forces and using social marketing to their advantage in order to point out the inadequacy of the present international trading system and acquire a better deal.

Certainly the voice of the South is becoming louder, and this dates mainly from the fourth conference of the heads of state of the non-aligned countries which met in Algiers in 1973. Although the origins of the non-aligned nations go back to the 1950s, until the early 1970s there was little cohesion in evidence. Neutralism and non-alignment with the great powers struggling in the cold war was typical. In the 1960s anti-colonialism was the theme, and although the number of non-aligned states grew in this decade economic aspects of development were ignored. These were left to UNCTAD to express.

However in 1973 at the Algiers summit there was a coalition of UNCTAD and the non-aligned group which resulted in more voice, more power and a convergence of goals, strategies and programmes. At the same time there was the Arab/Israeli war, the oil embargo and the quadrupling of oil prices. The Algiers conference made various accusations against the North. It suggested, as Prebisch had done previously, that trade liberalisation via GATT was biased in favour of advanced world exports. Developing countries had gained little from the previous six rounds of tariff cuts between 1947 and 1967.

Since 1973, many economists have suggested that protective measures by the North in the form of quotas, health and safety regulations, nominal and effective tariff structures, variable levies and price support and the rest have cost the South billions of dollars. To make matters worse the North has dragged its feet on proposals to raise and stabilise prices of major commodity exports from the South. Together with the North's being largely unwilling to grant preferential tariff treatment for the South's manufactured goods, the terms of trade would seem to be continually moving against the developing countries.

Next the non-aligned group and others have argued that the volume and value of aid flowing from North to South is unjustifiably low. Again many northern writers agree on this, but there is always the caveat that much aid has gone to support the South's elite groups who were not really committed to equitable development strategies within their countries. It is estimated that ex-president Marcos managed to lodge up to $5b of his country's wealth in his own personal Swiss bank account (*Financial Times*, 25 Feb. 1987).

Finally the voice of the South has argued that multinational corporations have restricted their potential contributions to the South through (i) limiting tax liabilities via transfer pricing, (ii) limiting job creation by introducing capital-intensive methods and (iii) keeping a stranglehold on intellectual property rights as well as interfering in the South's politics. As noted in Chapter 6, this is not the whole argument. Indeed many of the above statements made by the South are not the whole truth. Nevertheless, if the inequality of present economic institutions and the fact that the international system favours the North are pointed out, the chances of a more favourable international marketing environment being achieved are much greater.

North–South integrated marketing and the prospect of a truly international trading system

Most countries have felt the cool winds of recession. Even South Korea's overseas construction and shipbuilding industries declined sharply in 1985, while Indonesia shows how oil exporters have been dramatically affected. After the first oil price rise of 1974 Indonesia entered a period when its vast and increasing population glimpsed the promised land. Then the price of oil began to fall, slowly at first but later with dizzy rapidity as energy-saving measures in the industrialised world began to take hold. Since 60 per cent of Indonesia's state budget reserve and 70 per cent of its export earnings are accounted for by oil and natural gas earnings every dollar drop in oil prices means that government receipts fall by more than US$300m (*Financial Times*, 10 Mar. 1986). Big projects have had to be scrapped and the annual budget was cut in 1986 for the first time in seventeen years. Overall spending has been slashed by 7 per cent and development spending by 22 per cent. Debt has risen.

But more important than this is the fact that the interdependence of developing countries within the world economy has been realised. If countries in the South cannot pay their debts and default unilaterally there will be unsustainable capital losses in the largest multinational banks and massive runs on deposits. A chain of bankruptcies and business failures in the North would follow. There is a need to accommodate the shift in manufacturing capacity to the South and their exports back to the North in the next ten years for stability of international relationships to be maintained.

To make matters worse, previous assumptions have been found to be untrue. Fears of shortages of resources are unfounded, for at present there are surpluses of many commodities and plunging prices. Better technology has extended both the life of reserves and agricultural productivity. Worse, the fall of the dollar has not imkproved the price situation – food prices in May and June 1986 falling to a third of their peak in 1974 and metal prices being less than a half (*Financial Times*, 29 Aug. 1986).

Although the rising dollar increased developing countries' debt and forced them to cut back on imports and push their exports, causing a weakening of prices, the falling dollar has not caused prices to rally. The 'economic recovery' of the North have become progressively weaker since the first oil shock, recording an average 5 per cent growth between 1971 and 1977, 4.2 per cent between 1976 and 1979 and 3.8 per cent between 1983 and 1985 (*Financial Times*, 29 Aug. 1986).

Indeed the North is suffering just the same from the unfavourable economic climate (some 'South' countries having weathered the storm even better), while beggar-thy-neighbour deflationary policies continue to exacerbate the situation. All this has caused many politicians to call for a change in the whole international trading system. It has been argued that the present system is unviable for the whole world and that there must be some redistribution and restructuring before there can be any hope of recovery (Manley and Brandt, 1985). These commentators suggest that global militarism and the power of the multinational must both be reduced, the energy crisis and ecological threats resolved and significant change made in the structure and management of the world economy.

Their argument is that a neo-Keynesian policy must be adopted, for it is obvious that the monetarist deflationary policies have set in motion a vicious circle. The drive by several countries to reduce domestic demand, to restrain imports and improve the balance of payments situation failed and instead caused more direct government intervention in the form of cuts in public spending. This in turn led to reduced domestic demand, increased unemployment, high interest rates to strengthen currencies and devaluations to increase competitiveness. But all was undermined because of the fall in global trade. Tax revenues therefore fell and unemployment increased. Governments borrowed more and debt servicing led to fiscal crises in many states. In turn fiscal crises encouraged governments to stimulate jobs through subsidies and tax cuts, which meant less money for government spending.

Global demand, and thus North–South integrated marketing, must be stimulated. But this is not sufficient. There is a need to reappraise the present protectionist measures and to liberalise manufactured exports for developing countries. If the advanced world does not change its policies in relation to the new comparative advantage of the developing countries there will be no overall advancement and the late-comers in the economic development race will be the most likely to suffer. There is also a need to respond to demands of welfare and social services in many developing countries where at present basic needs are not being met. This is a threat to world survival and the irregularities are a threat to world security. Differences in standards of living between North and South are bad enough but inequalities within countries themselves, with the richer part of the population developing stronger economic links with the richer parts of the other societies rather than the poorer part of their own countries, call for internal restructuring, regulation and distribution as well.

It may be that autonomous programmes may be pursued by countries of the South themselves rather than continue to rely on big institutions such as the IMF. But doubts have been expressed about the capabilities of a liberal market regime to continue without a dominant leader. Today it seems that a multipolar power structure exists and it has been argued that

North–South trade in manufactured goods poses a test to economic co-operation on a global scale.

It could be that, as industry is relocated to the developing countries, North–South dynamism will lessen protectionist pressures, especially as diversification in the South occurs and there is less concentration on labour-intensive activity and more intra-industry, intra-firm trade. Alternatively it could be that developing countries further behind in the economic development race, who step into spaces vacated by the more advanced, will be increasingly under attack.

The present eighth international round of negotiations of GATT in Uruguay (the location said by some cynics to have been chosen in order to allay fears that GATT is a rich man's club) which should have started in September 1986 but was delayed until February 1987 because of fears by some nations of the concessions they may have to make, has set out the most ambitious agenda yet contemplated by its 92 members. There are several contentious issues – such as the suggestion that South Korea and Singapore should move into a non-Third World category and start assuming the responsibilities of the industrial powers. The resentment of the North to counterfeiting of goods by the South and the possible protectionist measures which may be taken against those countries which do not trade fairly is another controversial issue. The United States already has the power to limit concessions under the generalised system of preference to developing countries which harbour counterfeiters. But many developing countries believe that intellectual property rights such as trademarks, patents and copyright are not a trade policy issue and should be dealt with in the framework of the World Intellectual Property Organisation (WIPO), a United Nations body. If GATT rules are established which permit retaliation, the access of foreign technology to developing countries may be threatened. Trade in services and the freedom of trade-related foreign investment are other contentious issues.

On the broader scale it is interesting to note that China formally applied to resume its membership of GATT and the USSR has also announced steps for improving its credentials so as to be seen as a serious GATT applicant. Many do not take the USSR seriously, whereas China has shown, via its open-door policy, willingness to take market forces into consideration. It remains to be seen what measures will be taken specifically to help developing countries. In 1984 the EEC was proposing measures to allow easy access into the European Market for developing countries' industrial and agricultural products under the generalised system of preferences. This might help Latin American and Asian non-member countries of the Lome convention. However inadequacies associated with previous measures have not yet been resolved. For example, funds still remain unspent from the days prior to Lome I (1975–80) and in March 1984 one year before Lome II expired, only one-fifth of aid funds had been spent. Lome III introduced in 1985 provides a range of measures to speed up aid and it is hoped that co-ordination of this will improve. If so, and new agreements can be reached for GATT members in the present rounds of negotiations, some advance towards more equal international trade may be achieved.

Another scenario, however, is one in which a regional division in international trade may occur, with the United States trading more with Latin America, there being more interchange between the EEC and Africa, while Japan trades increasingly with Southeast Asia. Already people are recognising that East Asia is a power in its own right if one includes Japan and China (Hofheinz and Calder, 1982). Independence, autocracy and self-determination have been isolated as goals of East Asian nations and since they are finding increasing restrictions against them in Western markets (50 per cent of Korean exports, 33 per cent of Taiwan exports and 43 per cent of Japanese exports to the United States are affected by some quota or trade barrier) they are seeking out new markets, mainly in developing countries. They are showing signs of greater symbiosis with the Third World generally and they may well be complementary, being short of resources. Most of these economies are not suffering from inflation, unemployment, or inability to compete as in the West, for they have innovated, adapted and are moving to higher value sectors so that Western developed country exports are being displaced. Their flexibility in dealing with uncertainty, their highly stable political system, export orientated policies and favourable cultural attributes have resulted in great success and exports in most East Asian newly industrialised countries account for 50 per cent of their national income.

Furthermore they are part of another region isolated as being 'where the future lies' (*Financial Times*, 20 Oct. 1986) – that is, the Pacific Rim. Countries such as Singapore, Hong Kong, the Philippines, Taiwan, South Korea and Indonesia are part of this region, which incorporates 34 countries and is seen as having great underlying strength and economic potential. It has been called a treasure trove of primary resources, entrepreneurial vibrancy and disciplines which are rooted in a rich and diverse cultural heritage (*Financial Times*, 20 Oct. 1986). The 34 countries contain one half of the world's population and half its total wealth. Although their political regimes are varied, individually and collectively these nations have caused a fundamental shift of power from the Atlantic. China is recognised as an awakening giant, but all Pacific Rim nations are becoming a natural regional grouping with individual economies shifting from a typical insular and highly regulated state a decade ago towards economic liberalisation and integration.

What is clear is that there is a need for a managed approach at the most international level possible so that high rates of growth are restored in the

North, national strategies are related to international trading opportunities and expansion of industries is encouraged in the South. Ideally this calls for an effective supranational marketing authority.

In reality those institutions which currently exist, such as GATT, the IMF and the International Bank for Reconstruction and Development (IBRC) have been biased in favour of the North. The only institution which has catered for North–South dialogue over the last twenty years has been UNCTAD. But, always regarded as unwieldly, unnecessary and ineffective by many countries of the North, it has only helped to clarify positions and has not succeeded in achieving treaty-like agreements. The international attempts to control multinationals provide a good example. UNCTAD along with the Organisation for Economic Co-operation and Development (OECD) and others has its 'code of conduct' which suggests how the multinational should behave in a host nation and how the host government should treat it. But because these codes are largely unenforceable they are ineffective. Countries do and will always break ranks. By 1972 UNCTAD had already lost much of its momentum and, apart from such commissions as that which led to the Brandt Report (1980), there is still no institution to respond to the present global challenge.

There remain various needs, such as better aid, perhaps in the form of grants rather than loans with lower interest rates which are related to export earnings, as well as an overall assessment of the relevance of projects before aid is given. Capital flight via the multinational must also be controlled and greater spending on socio-economic development rather than military projects should be encouraged. (Manley and Brandt, 1985).

Marketing can be used to ensure the best way of achieving these. Any multilateral institution must first understand the individual, state and multinational marketing perspective; the relevance of projects and the impact and practices of the multinationals may then be better assessed. Where greater co-operation between blocks of countries is seen as advantageous, social marketing may be used to promote this end, and notwithstanding the enormous difficulties, such as developing countries being at different stages of development, the three main trading blocks being at loggerheads with each other, threatening greater protectionism, and the privations imposed on developing countries to service their debt, if a marketing philosophy is adopted demand may be identified and stimulated, the appropriate response made and socio-economic development promoted. Recovery, restructuring and redistribution of global resources may then be achieved more easily.

Conclusion

The international marketing environment has become increasingly problematic for developing countries. Debt, beggar-thy-neighbour deflationary policies, the collapse of commodity prices and increasing protectionism are typical problems with which marketers at all levels must grapple.

International trade theory remains the foundation for much economic thinking but the assumptions upon which it is based need to be carefully explained. Prebisch argued as long ago as the 1950s that the 'gains from trade' argument was only valid between nations of the same level of economic development and that, if the nations at the periphery (the colonies) traded commodities for manufactured goods from the centre (the colonial powers), the gains from trade would always be unequal. The impact of the multinational promoting mobility of capital and intra-firm trade, the fall of commodity prices and the rise of protectionism have tended to support the argument that international trade theory is inadequate. With an increasingly competitive international environment associated with world recession, the developed world has become more effective in targeting its trade barriers against specific countries and sectors of activity, while not infringing GATT regulations. Quotas, voluntary restraint, bilateral agreements, anti-dumping actions, the imposition of health and safety standards and bureaucratic procedures have become increasingly common, and a high percentage of goods from developing countries are affected. The debt of developing countries has exacerbated the situation by causing many to cut back on imports and boost exports at the expense of their domestic populations.

The international product life cycle attempts to explain why goods and services are transferred across national boundaries and why developing countries acquire technology at the expense of the developed nations, which then lose their competitive edge. Based on mass car production in the USA, the model is supported to a large extent by manufacturing processes that have been lost to the developing world. Steel, shipbuilding and textiles are good examples. However in global terms the penetration of the advanced world markets by developing countries is small, with a limited number of countries (notably the 'Gang of Four' in the Far East) responsible for much of the trade. Equally certain sectors of manufactured goods – clothing, office and telephone equipment, household appliances and other consumer goods tend to dominate, and the multinational's influence cannot be denied.

The international product life cycle does have various limitations. Using a macro approach, it tends to consider broad industrial sectors too much and products not sufficiently. Also the analogy with the diffusion of man motorcar manufacture from the USA may be stretched too far. Not all developing countries can master all technology. Furthermore in some instances it may be preferable for the multinational to revert to capital-intensive production methods in the developed world. Alternatively the state may intervene. Finally some products may not be transferable for cultural reasons.

Having assessed the situation, there are various responses which may be made by developing countries on an individual or collective basis. Multinationals may be encouraged by government marketers to locate in host nations and export from them. Countries may adopt a more protectionist stance and/or trade within their own regional groupings. Some individual marketers have aggressively 'attacked' international markets and minimised protectionist pressure by modifying their products, and moving up-market. The 'Gang of Four' have been particularly successful here. For other nations countertrade has provided some slight respite from the unfavourable wider international environment. Collectively there is the option for developing countries to use social marketing to bring attention to their case and cause the system to be changed.

What is quite clear is that world interdependence is now not only obvious but also giving cause for concern. For it has been realised that international stability is threatened. The North is suffering economic recession, although to a lesser extent than the South and present monetary deflationary policies have been questioned. Numerous scenarios have been suggested but some recovery, restructuring and redistribution is required and it is desirable that some multi-lateral organisation co-ordinate efforts. Although this may be a somewhat idealistic notion, if marketing principles can be incorporated, the chances of success will be much higher.

But whatever occurs at the macro level marketers (individual, state or multinational) must be continually assessing the situation and attempting to be pro-active rather than reactive, for against this background there are also trends occurring at the more micro level which must also be considered. These are discussed in the final chapter.

CHAPTER 11

Problems and prospects for marketing at the micro level

Contents

Introduction

In addition to the issues in the global economic crisis on the macro level, there are other force at work which are likely to have a significant impact on individual countries. It has been claimed that 'the Third World's obsession with the Western way of life has perverted development and is rapidly destroying good and bad in traditional cultures' (Harrison, 1980).

Earlier chapters have made reference to the development of global products and lifestyles and the multinational's encouragement of these. It may well be that consumer tastes may converge even more in the future. But there are also some divergent tendencies in existence. The most extreme is perhaps the emergence of Islamic fundamentalism as a possible alternative to both Western capitalism and Eastern socialism. A more form of divergence may be witnessed through host countries' attempts to control multinationals by insisisting on some form of ownership and deciding the production process to be used and the products to be produced.

However convergence and divergence are, in many instances, not mutually exclusive. Both convergent and divergent tendencies may be noted is some countries. For example, there is still a high demand for Westernised consumer goods in Arabic states where Islam is strong. And to make matters more complicated there is always the possibility of the convergence of divergent political systems through collaborative links established by multinational enterprises. The transideological enterprise is becoming a reality as China opens its door and dilutes its ideology.

Indeed the issue of capitalism or socialism is one which is likely to affect many developing countries in the future. Until the recent world economic recession socialism was hailed as the logical alternative by many nations, especially those which were former colonies under capitalist regimes. State planning was important and, even though often costly, large bureaucracies and parastatal organisations proliferated, aided in the oil-rich nations by the rise of oil prices in the early 1970s. Today, as noted in earlier chapters, such strategies are running into difficulties and are being doubted as the only solution. Several nations, in order that their proposed schemes can go ahead, have now had to consider allowing private enterprise to take over. Other governments. although in the minority, are encouraging more capitalism of their own accord, and seeing the need to stimulate market forces. China is undoubtedly the country which has seen the most dramatic development and changes are not occurring easily. There are few governments, however, apart from some of the most successful newly industrialised countries of the Far East, which have encouraged consumer emancipation.

Generally the will to improve the state of marketing is not highly developed. But those countries which have used it to assess the trends in the external environment, respond to opportunities and counteract threats have been the most successful.

This chapter seeks to examine such trends which present marketing opportunities and stumbling-blocks at the more micro level. And through the consideration of individual countries' use of marketing, a greater insight into the problem and prospects of each is possible. Firstly the issue of cultural convergence or divergence is examined, particularly in relation to the multinational and governmental marketer. Next the possibility of the transideological enterprise is discussed. Thirdly the move towards more capitalism and the need for greater concern with consumer rights by government officials are considered, along with the stumbling-blocks to the elimination of socialism. Finally specific examples of countries are used to show different responses to the broader marketing environment. Some emphasis is given to the Far East and their policies are contrasted to oil-rich states elsewhere.

Cultural convergence or divergence? The issues

(a) Convergence

Many economists have suggested that developing countries all feel they must get into the development race as it iccurred in the West. In 1969 Landes wrote 'All the underdeveloped countries of the globe are converted to the religion of industry and wealth with a faith that surpasses that of their teachers' (Landes, 1969, p. 11). Indeed in the 1960s (and perhaps even in the 1950s) the Western way of life, particularly the American model of economic and cultural development, was seen as the one which should be followed. Advances in telecommunications permitted the shrinkage of international space with the result that people saw what was available on the other side of the world. Subsequently multinationals promoted this development, for, as noted in Chapter 8, they began to adopt a concept of mass markets and to standardise their products in certain fields, encouraged in the 1970s and 1980s by the meshing of the three major markets of Japan, Europe and North America. They have been responsible for introducing new technology and changing material culture in many developing countries.

The extent to which the multinational is responsible for the broad coverage of consumer tastes is a controversial point. Certainly the multinational is 'the single most important actor in the generation, application and global transfer of technology' (Terpstra, 1978, p. 175). And technology may be regarded as a force which culturally, psychologically, socially and economically shapes, or even regiments, society. But whether the multinational can be called a cultured imperialist which conquers 'not just the bodies but the souls of its victims, turning them into willing accomplices' (Harrison, 1980, p. 48) is not so certain.

However it would seem that to a large extent convergence of consumer tastes is increasing. Levitt (1983) goes so far as to say that technology has proletarianised communications and travel to such a degree that not only are 'isolated places and impoverished people eager for modernity's allurements' but also it is not possible to sell last year's model or lesser versions of advanced products any more in developing countries. Instead *all* people want products to lighten and enhance their work, raise living standards, divert and entertain, so that the world's needs and drives have been 'irrevocably homogenised' (Levitt, 1983, p. 211).

There are many examples of convergence in terms of both places and products. Traditional East Fijian society with its institutions of reciprocity and redistribution has been obliterated: 'Cash has driven out custom to a considerable extent and created a new economic order' (Knapman and Walter, 1980, p. 202). In India, where there are 740m people and one in two lives below the poverty line there is an estimated consumer market of 150m for products ranging from electronics to packaged noodles and other consumer goods. Previously advertisements and newspapers could only be used to reach 25 million people. But since the revolution in television ownership which dates from 1983, 70m may be reached immediately. This medium has also permitted the cutting across of traditional social boundaries, and the convergence of consumer tastes is accelerating. Fast foods are growing rapidly to respond to changing lifestyles. The $4m Wimpy investment in New Delhi serving lamburgers is hugely successful and it is likely that United Biscuits will set up a biscuit factory soon. Pepsi-Cola, after eleven years' deliberation, is attempting to establish a joint venture with Duncan Enterprises of Calcutta. If it succeeds this will be the first foreign company for years which has been allowed to bring a brand name into the country. Other proposed schemes include factories to manufacture soluble coffee, vegetable-based protein products and powdered drinks, which is an indication of the demand for fast foods.

Coca-Cola, which is also considering returning to India, is an excellent example of a product which epitomises the convergence of consumer tastes. It is sold in many countries and welcomed by all despite crossing 'multitudes of national, regional and ethnic taste-buds trained to a variety of deeply ingrained local preferences of taste, flavour, consistency, effervescence and aftertaste' (Levitt, 1983, p. 211). It would reach an even greater number of consumers if there were no artificial trade barriers.

It is not surprising that the Naisbitt Group, in its attempt to predict what opportunities lie ahead as leisure patterns change in the USA and Europe, has predicted that over the next ten years there will appear the 'global lifestyle'. They suggest that a 'new wave' generation, aged 21 and under, is emerging, which will reflect a shift in values from the liberal permissiveness of the 1960s to a 1980s conservation which is pro-technology, environmentally unconcerned and less inclined to worry about health and fitness (*Financial* Times, 9 Oct. 1986). The electric wonderland in the home will increase and there will be more technological wizardry in cars, ovens and other consumer durables. Western developed markets will require successful marketers to provide a balance between 'the known' and 'the new' and therefore brand loyalty is likely to be very important. And what occurs in the advanced world will undoubtedly spread to the developing world, for satellite television and global advertising will ensure that leisure lifestyles throughout the world will be similar.

(b) Divergence

But there are also some divergent tendencies which cannot be ignored. On the least drastic scale there is always the possibility that host governments attempting to control multinationals by insisting upon what production process of product is brought into the country will act as a catalyst for divergence. For under such conditions the multinational's manoeuvrability to adopt a global standardised product strategy is likely to be reduced. However, as noted previously, there are few large, rich developing countries and these are the ones which hold the balance of negotiating power. Unless more groupings of developing countries are established (and this seems unlikely) it would appear that, especially in today's economic climate, ownership in multinationals by host countries is not a big threat to convergence of consumer tastes. Indeed the reverse may be true in nations where the concept of intellectual property rights is not acknowledged and pirating of brand names and trademarks is not prohibited.

There are, however, always subcultures present within nations. Although developing countries' urban subcultures are a major force of convergence, and more akin to those in the developed world than those in the rest of the country, there may also be other ethnic groups, particularly in rural areas. These are often a force of divergence, particularly if social stratification is the norm.

Having much more of an impact, however, is the cultural reaction to the American model of cultural development. Since the 1970s there has been some loss of confidence in this. Alternatives have presented themselves in the advanced world. The Japanese approach has received much attention. In the developing world reaction has been more confused, except in some Islamic countries where Islamic fundamentalism may be seen as an extreme force of divergence.

In many countries in the Middle East in the last ten to fifteen years there has been a resurgence of Islam. Some have suggested it is because of a sense of failure. 'Wherever they have come into contact with Europeans Moslem societies have felt that they have been corrupted' (*Financial Times*, 10 Jan 1987). They have admired foreigners for their scientific knowledge and power but whenever they tried to copy them they felt as though they destroyed something of themselves. Although in all the Middle East Islam permeates people's lives in a way which it is difficult for Westerners to understand, it is Iran, with a population of 2.5 million, which is the most xenophobic towards the non-Arab world and which is the most 'fundamentalist'. With Islam as the focus of the non-Western identity the indigenous cultural system has led to a rejection of both Western capitalism and Eastern communism. The approach is to encourage qualitiative changes through education. Imigrant labour is not used and the transfer of technology is not assumed to imply development. But the problem of how to modernise traditional ways which are not satisfactory remains. It is not materialism which is rejected but materialism without spritualism.

Khomeni and his followers pose a threat to the Middle East, for Islamic fundamentalism here has taken over from the totally discredited philosophy of Arab nationalism (*Financial Times*, 14 Nov. 1986). It has also gained a strong foothold in Sudan, while Syria is another country where a theory of development based on religion and nationalism has emerged. Islamic fundamentalism is also trying to re-establish itself in Syria and is a major threat to President Mubarak in Egypt. Here special schools have been established in order to promote Islam. In Assiut, a city regarded as a centre of religious extremism, young children, dressed in green, prepare for school. The objective is to create a burgeoning Islamic infrastructure througout Egypt by encouraging a militant type of Islam from an early age. The demand for such schools in high, mainly because government schools are seen as poor in comparison. A poster advertising the school shows Mecca's holiest shrine flanked by American and Russian flags bearing crosses and the words 'Islamic: neither East nor West'. The process will take decades to realise but it nevertheless poses a threat to the established political system.

Generally, however, although the interrelated elements of Islam, Arabism and socialism suggest a divergence of cultural development, not all Middle Eastern states are going down the fundamentalist path. Many have 'bent with the wind'. The number of new mosques may have increased to an extent which is 'extraordinary and quite unnecessary' (*Weekend Financial Times*, 10 Jan. 1987, p. I) but fundamentalists may at the same time have been controlled. For example, in Bahrain the police treatment of the Shia community is controversial, while the more moderate Sunni elements have been co-opted into the official religious establishment so that they may be turned against the Shias. In this way the populist Islamic movement has been divided.

(c) Convergence within divergence

What is perhaps even more interesting is that, despite the growth of Islamic fundmentalism, the trend towards convergence in some fields is still obvious. Between 1973 and 1978 imports to the Middle East grew from $15b to $78b (out of a total of $1350b). Whereas in the early 1970s there had been some economic development, trading was essentially the same as it had been for thousands of years previously. But in the space of a few years the Middle East was exposed to modern industry and sophisticated consumer goods which have subsequently been absorbed. Even in the Iranian uprisings of 1979 men in fashionable French-cut trousers produced on a global market basis could be seen showing that, even where a culture is kept intact, standardised products are still used. Moreover the sophisticated people in the Moslem societies, including the royal family, do not behave in a proper Moslem fashion either in their own homes or abroad. So long as the ordinary people do not see the display of great private wealth, this is considered acceptable. The convergence of consumer tastes therefore is still maintained.

Similar apparently contradictory developments may be witnessed elsewhere. For example, in Brazil it is common to see televisions in crowded corrugated huts outside which stand battered Volkswagens, but people still make sacrificial offerings of fruit and freshly-killed chickens to Macumba spirits. In the Biafran war soldiers of both sides listened to transistor radios and drank Coca-Cola. Thus there may be convergence in terms of product tastes and people's behaviour while cultural identities may be maintained. The Naisbitt Group have accounted for this in relation to their proposed 'global lifestyle' by suggesting that, while people will welcome innovation, their traditions and/or ethnic cultures will be maintained at the same time. Thus people may eat globally-marketed products but the style of preparation will reflect local tradition.

It also seems that alternative models to the Western one will result in traditional products becoming globally acceptable. Already Korean food has made its debut in many Western cities, in the form of Korean barbecue – sliced, marinated beef, served with a side dish of spicy hot Kimchi vegetables and boiled rice, and called Bulgogi (*Financial Times*, 9 Apr. 1986). Like Chinese food, pitta bread, country and western music and jazz, all once peculiar to minority groups, it may be that other non-

Western products may become available in response to the convergence of consumer tastes.

What is clear is that there is no one trend which is occurring uniformly all over the world. There may be evidence of convergence in many countries and divergent tendencies in others. They may both exist within the same country. Several societies have adopted some products or institutions while maintaining their own cultural identity. Bali is a good example. This Indonesian island has an indigenous society whose religion is a variety of Buddhism and Hinduism and whose racial structure is dominated by four castes. Although each village today has a school, a medical service and often radio and television, not to mention tourists, the impact of these on culture has been light. The conclusion is that, whilst there are some broad trends which may be witnessed, they may affect individual nations differently.

The implications of convergence and divergence

For the multinational marketer working on the principle of convergence of consumer tastes, the future would seem bright. Sufficient evidence of convergence of consumer tastes exists for multinationals to persist in product standardisation strategies. The basic advantage of lower unit costs through economies of scale in production, distribution and marketing remains. Once a global producer lowers his cost and price internationally his patronage expands expotentially. He can reach distant markets and attract local consumers through lower prices. Thus the world market is satisfied but competitiveness at home is also increased. The multinational may have to take more account of methods of using standardised products in the future, if the Naisbitt Group is to be believed. But having taken into account this caveat, globally standardised products which are advanced, functional, reliable and low priced will be in great demand. And, as noted in earlier chapters, planning new products, product testing and conventional marketing research will continue to receive less attention and finance, while advertising will receive more. Nevertheless the multinational marketer must always bear in mind the threat of host countries imposing conditions which interfere with his product standardisation strategy.

For the indigenous marketer, convergence of consumer tastes indicates that the more he looks outwards, attacks abroad and attempts to follow the multinational's strategy, the greater his chances of success. For trouble in the long term is likely to face the company that lacks a global focus and remains inattentive to the economies of simplicity and standardisation. The companies most at risk are those dominating small domestic markets. For with transport costs disproportionately low, distant competitors will enter the now-sheltered markets of these companies and sell goods produced more cheaply under scale-efficient conditions. 'Global competition spells the end of domestic territoriality, no matter how diminutive territories may be' (Levitt, 1983, p. 213).

Although there are distinct problems in the local marketing environment for many indigenous marketers, problems such as poor distribution channels and no motivation to lower costs, in the long run, in order to survive and become successful world competitors, they must incorporate superior quality and reliability into their cost structures. To do this they must sell in all markets the same kind of product sold at home, or in their largest export market. Branding too is essential – again an aspect not sufficiently considered by indigenous marketers in developing countries, but, as noted in Chapter 6, if reliability and quality can be improved and value-added increased, the chances of success are higher. Ultimately it may be that the Japanese global strategy of developing high-quality, low-cost operations can be followed. Alternatively products developed solely for the Third World may be possible, as Gurgel is showing in Brazil.

The government marketer has to make decisions which have important moral implications. He must ask himself to what extent it is desirable that local culture should be subjected to a global lifestyle. The industrialisation problem inevitably involves alienation from rural family heritage, the relaxation of customs and the disappearance of the extended family in favour of the nuclear one. An industrial society discipline and greater affluence for the acquisition of non-essential items may be considered necessary but the matter needs careful thought. Equally the environmental costs of industrialisation must be weighed in the balance, but if a marketing approach is adopted the state marketer will, it is hoped, take into account both people's needs and wider society.

Where convergence of tastes is regarded as an opportunity to which to respond, government marketers can also help small firms by encouraging them to an outward-looking policy. They may help by improving the environment at home, for the indigenous marketer to develop a strong base from which he may attack global markets. And where undesirable divergent tendencies exist within a society the governmental marketer may use social marketing to change or reinforce certain attitudes and values.

Capitalism or socialism? The issues

Closely associated with the convergence–divergence theme is the question of what will happen to political regimes. Change certainly seems to be under way and this can be noted in relation to the transideological enterprise, the move towards capitalism and the need for more consumer emancipation.

(a) The transideological enterprise

The ultimate convergence of regimes could be manifested in the trans-ideological enterprise. Whereas culture means a body of economic, political and ethical beliefs which have historically evolved in a society, ideology refers to that systematic body of economies, political and ethical *doctrines* which are adopted by society or imposed upon it by the ruling establishment (Livingstone, 1975). 'Transideological' is a term coined by Perlmutter to describe those enterprises spanning Western societies and the communist world (theoretically, other ideologies could be involved, but this has not yet happened).

Although a few years ago such a concept was largely regarded as unrealistic, increasingly it is becoming more and more of a reality. The opportunities can be said to have begun in the 1970s, when there was some thawing of the cold war. Nevertheless in the USSR there is still much anti-West feeling and the problem of accommodating the principle of a foreign private enterprise making a profit within a Marxist state.

More recently, with China's open door policy and its new definition of socialism, the transideological enterprise is already a reality. The problems of ownership and financial characteristics in the form of profit, royalties and pricing are being overcome through redefinitions. The future may be frustated by an anti-marketing bias, ambivalence over how to justify Marxist ideas, or even a reversion to a stronger ideology; nevertheless the developments in China, which are taking over from the orthodox foreign trade organisations' transactions, turnkey operations and barter deals, point to what could be described as convergence in political regimes or at least some shift from a firm communist stand.

(b) The move towards capitalism

In the past socialism was often seen as attractive by developing countries, especially where an oppressive regime had dominated previously or where there was a strong desire to try something different from colonialism. Furthermore socialism and state planning were regarded as an essential means of forcing the gates to economic development and overcoming the lack of private capital and enterprise.

Unfortunately many developing countries have suffered from inefficient management and swollen bureaucracies. Key posts are often filled by political nominees and lower down family relations or specific cultural groups may be favoured. Training is generally lacking. The present problems of inflation, economic recession and debt have focused more attention on the planning and bureaucratic weaknesses. At the same time the present rash of privatisations in the West has been observed and recognised as a means of continuing where capital is in short supply.

Not surprisingly there are several countries which exemplify some move towards incorporating more capitalism. Several examples were quoted in Chapters 7 and 8 but two of the most unlikely are India and China.

Mr R. Gandhi has been criticised for speaking too bluntly and favourably about the private sector and productivity, admitting foreign technology on more favourable terms, allowing loss-making companies to die and taking a tough line with the inefficient job-protecting public sector. Many of the older generation would prefer to hear more about socialism, and planning. Mr Gandhi has tried to heal the rift by suggesting that socialism should not mean bureaucratic centralism but a policy to bridge the gap between rich and poor. Nevertheless a tough line would seem to be being taken with the inefficient administrative framework. Attempts are also being made to improve industrial growth, efficiency and international competitiveness through the relaxation of many industrial controls which inhibit managerial freedom to react to market conditions. Some parts of Indian industry are being forced to face foreign competition for the first time, instead of being able to produce poor quality, expensive goods for the previously captive domestic market. Although some trade protection will continue, the stock exchange is flourishing and banks are queuing to enter the country (*Financial Times*, 3 June 1985). This would suggest that the move towards more capitalism is having a beneficial effect.

Even more astonishing is China. Increasingly it is moving from the communist bloc and into the developing world category of countries. Despite continuing reliance on planning, many former Maoist principles have been overturned and several steps have been taken towards more of a market economy. Profit is no longer a dirty word.

The responsibility of production and quality has been put onto the shoulders of individual managers. Market forces have been introduced into wages and prices in both the agricultural and industrual sectors. As a result the peasant now owns his land and has a profit incentive. Suddenly there is much more efficiency than existed under collectivisation. There are more vegetables for sale and wealthier peasants. Indeed wages in some areas have risen fourfold as industry has been taken into the rural areas and it has been accepted that some people will get rich faster than others.

By the end of 1985 wage increases and more independent management had resulted in rapid growth. A head of steam was built up behind insatiable consumer demand. This was satisfied through imports, which resulted in soaring inflation and investment 44 per cent over the target. Global trade grew but imports grew by 88 per cent compared with exports which grew 1.5 per cent. A trade deficit resulted.

Since 1985 things have gone better on the economic front. The overheated economy was slowed down and the yuan was devalued by 15.8 per cent against major currencies in 1986 to help exports (which grew 14.8 per cent by volume from January to September 1986 to 21.4b yuan, with imports only rising by 5.1 per cent to 30.4 yuan). Thus the present five-year plan (1985–90) shows how previous mistakes are being taken into account. Supply and demand is to be balanced with industrial output planned to rise by 7.5 per cent consumption by 5 per cent. Equally the marketing environment is being improved. An appropriate infrastructure is being encouraged. Cheque books are available from some banks and capital markets are beginning to develop with the return of shares and bonds. A rudimentary form of the old Shanghai stock exchange has reopened while in February 1984 the first China-affiliated stockbroking firm (a joint venture) opened its doors for business in Hong Kong. In the past socialist China had no concept of dealing in shares, but this is now changing. 'We must learn to do business in a capitalist fashion and that includes share trading', said Mr Nelson Tsao, director of the Ching Mao and Sin Hua Trust. Since Hong Kong accounts for 80 per cent foreign investment in China, the Hong Kong stock market is being seen as an obvious place to raise funds for the development of China's economy.

Another interesting development is the Shanghai Advertising and Decoration Corporation which, although founded in 1956, now employs 900 staff and is the market leader (*Financial Times*, 19 Sep. 1985), which shows that advertising is developing. Recently Shanghai's municipal government overturned a thirty-year rule banning advertisements on buses and now it is estimated that 70 of them will serve as mobile hoardings. Posters and newspapers are also becoming accepted advertising media, which shows that in the space of a few years great progress has been made. In 1966 advertising was banned and slogans such as 'advertising is capitalism' coined against it. But by 1978 it had become respectable again (although at present an ideological debate is raging as the advertising industry grows). There is still some way to go. Advertisements tend to be comparatively backward in design (*Financial Times*, 19 Sep. 1985). Traditional advertisements have been linked to gold and silver medals awarded by the government (in order to incorporate the Communist Party and socialist ideology). A 'forever' theme is also liked, while a favourite graphic image is a monkey king who, legend has it, trekked across China to India, overcoming seemingly insurmountable obstacles en route. There is no fear of making people buy things they do not need or want, the Shanghai Advertising and Decoration Corporation argues, since people are not so rich in China and advertising is not so well developed.

Despite these advances, there remain many problems. Population is growing by 100m each year and there are many social inadequacies to be countered. A high level of corruption exists and investment tends to be channelled to areas where the returns are greatest – that is, the richest Eastern part of China – while 60 million are living in dire poverty and many more remain illiterate. But perhaps the biggest stumbling-block is the issue of ideology. True Communism proposes that individual wealth must be discarded for collective wealth and private enterprise must be replaced by planned development controlled at the centre. Not surprisingly many senior party members in the provinces do not understand why some reforms, such as bankruptcy laws, sale of public property to individuals and so on are necessary.

Indeed there are many different attitudes at the official level towards recent changes and the most conservative of these to some extent threaten China's future. Some officials are abiding by the changes because they consider it party policy. But there is also a 'new class of political opposition' which may be mobilised. For at present the situation is such that economic devices are being tested and, if successful, an ideological foundation will be laid *beneath* them. And this is unlikely to be acceptable to the doctrinaire party members.

The diplomats are aware that present policies do not have a clear theoretical base. Indeed they run largely counter to the ideological background and the problem is likely to worsen if Deng Xiaoping departs or retires. In order to try to appease the various factions China's government in late September 1986 produced a document *redefining* socialism and providing a basis for pragmatic policy reforms. The somewhat vague document called 'Resolution and Guiding Principles for Building a Socialist society with Advanced Culture and Ideology' aims at reconciling both the pragmatic leadership and the conservatism of some officials. It is seen by diplomats in Peking as a means of deflecting criticism by officials of loss of political direction at a time of growing material wealth, and of providing a foundation for further reforms (*Financial Times*, 29 Sep. 1986). It touches on some politically sensitive issues, such as the acceptance of some people growing rich faster than others and pornography and prostitution as side-effects of the open-door policy, but its main message is that the ideal communist should be guided by good education and self-discipline, not simply party ethics.

More recent developments would suggest that the document has not succeeded in papering over the cracks. The student protests in China in December 1986 and January 1987 show how the demand for democracy and freedom exists. Chineses academics travelling abroad and foreigners teaching in Chinese colleges and universities, as well as an increasing number of foreign television and radio programmes have raised awareness of what is available elsewhere. The desire for it (reflecting the relentless convergence of consumer tastes) is there. The Chinese leadership has had the problems of trying to counterbalance this trend with the criticism of conservative Marxists in Peking who have called it 'bourgeois liberalism'. The official People's Daily has commented on the 'vague and erroneous views of democracy which have recently become current' (*Financial Times*, 5 Jan. 1987) while a purge of Chinese academics took place in January 1987. The conservative Communist officials have suspended Zhu Houze, the propaganda chief, for mishandling the recent student protests and allowing the spread of 'bourgeois liberalism', and have demanded that enterprises given more power under the reforms now turn their 'full attention' to their responsibilities to the state (*Financial Times*, 23 Jan. 1987). The resignation of Hu Yaobang as China's party boss, now casts a shadow over China's ambitious modernisation programme. Deng Xiaoping has closed ranks with party conservatives, demanding an end to the talk of greater democracy, but the outlook for political stability is suddenly bleak, since Hu Yaobang was earmarked as Deng's successor.

A basic problem is lack of management skills and understanding of marketing or the need for marketing. The state of the art of marketing and management could be much improved, but first the conviction of its worth is necessary. The present contradictions between this and ideology threatens further reforms. There is no real sign that many of China's senior leaders recognise that a modern economy, and especially modern industry, require management skills different from those currently exercised by the Communist Party. Political leaders have traditionally been selected for their ideological zeal, while all individuals have been conditioned to accept group conformity. Enthusiasm, initiative and creativity were dampened, while the power structure in al types of organisation has tended to be hierarchical. Not surprisingly bureaucratic self-protection became endemic and local party officials remained conservative, since the traditional party system gave them all manner of perks and privileges. Now many are breathing a sigh of relief because they will be able to keep their bad old ways. However the objective of training 12 million managers by the year 2000, always rather ambitious, is now severely threatened and existing local managers of private enterprises will feel less free to take the bold decisions economic reform requires them to take.

Even before the present fraught political situation some problems were becoming obvious. Foreign investment fell by 50 per cent in 1986 from $6.3b to $3.3b as investors continued to be hindered by the country's foreign exchange shortage, bloated bureaucracy and the high cost of doing business. Lack of confidence in the long term political direction of the country has been isolated as a major stumbling-block, although the conflict of objectives – China wanting investment for export-orientated products, investors wanting to exploit the Chinese market – is another (*Financial Times*, 24 Feb. 1987). On a smaller scale the province of Guangdong, the most successful region in China, is experiencing difficulties. Despite being China's leading exporter and the major location of foreign investment (receiving 60 per cent of the total since 1978), the most agriculturally productive and affluent, it has had problems with (i) absorbing material wealth without destroying the socialist ethic, (ii) avoiding corruption and (iii) dealing with profiteering and smuggling. In addition it has experienced overheating of the economy and all sorts of infrastructural strains.

The implications of capitalism for socialism

On the surface it might seem that there is great scope for individual and especially multinational marketers. China's open-door policy suggests an increasingly large export market for individual marketers elsewhere and a growing domestic market for indigenous markets within China. It is especially attractive since it is a sellers' market and the most up-to-date model is unlikely to be insisted upon. Equally development of the transideological enterprise would seem to suggest great opportunities for not only Western multinationals but also those emanating from developing countries such as Singapore and South Korea.

However, without a more favourable marketing environment in any country moving towards capitalism, potential investors will be deterred and the country will not reach its maximum potential. In order that the right conditions are provided, it is essential that the governmental marketer understands and makes greater use of marketing concepts and principles. Whatever the extent of the move towards capitalism some planning is still likely to be essential and, as noted in Chapters 6 and 7, the need for marketing in this process is imperative. And where the economy is being channelled down a new path – as in India and China – social marketing can be used to change attitudes and inform, so that the change in direction is facilitated.

Clearly the need for more training in the better use of marketing is obvious. In 1972 Hoffman wrote 'One illusion is that you can industrialise a country by building factories. You don't. You industrialise it by building markets' (Hoffman, 1972). This has been realised by many nations as they incorporate more capitalism into their systems. Previous policies have been regarded as mistakes, but the extent to which they see that, to create open markets, one must start with the consumer is varied. The essential difference between a totalitarian state and a free enterprise state lies in the role of the market. In a communist or totalitarian state it is the government which decides what shall be produced and which companies will survive. In a free enterprise economy companies compete for the patronage of consumers. And in order to compete effectively on world markets a much wider understanding of the range of consumers' wants and expectations is necessary.

It has been strongly argued that a first step is for government officials to begin within their own countries and closely examine the needs and rights of consumers and promote their interests by enforcing their rights. But few developing countries have consumer policies and at present 'there is little reason to believe that the large private sector in most of the Third World is conducive to emancipation', since it is characterised by cryptocapitalism (Thorelli, 1981). This is like the capitalism of the guild system of pre-industrial Europe: that is, a sellers' market based on the idea of unchangeable demand and the preservation of 'fair' market shares for existing traders. Industrialists are unwilling to take risks and accumulated capital goes to banks overseas, land speculation or jewels and so on. Cheating in the market place and corruption at government level make the situation worse.

Undoubtedly government marketers require a very strong will to transform such a situation into a truly open market system. But it is essential to ensure a proper balance between the rights and obligations of consumer and producer and buyer and seller, for this will open up markets. It has already been shown that the most successful newly industrialised countries have an open market system which promotes consumer-led balanced development.

Consumer emancipation may be promoted in three ways: (i) consumer protection, (ii) consumer education and (iii) consumer information. Consumer protection means that consumer rights must be safeguarded so that product integrity is increased, product quality improved, deceptive practices stamped out, a complaints-handling procedure set up and health and safety enforced. There are various codes which already exist and can be applied in relation to the product. For example, in the United Kingdom the Trade Descriptions Act lays down the principle that no vendor shall make a factual claim unless prepared to verify it. The Federal Trade Commission of the USA offers a wealth of guidelines for identifying what is a deceptive and misleading statement, while the Code of

Fair Advertising Practice of the International Chamber of Commerce might be used for advertising standards. Legislation is also required to set up a framework for complaints by consumers. Conditions under which a refund, repair or replacement may be obtained must be specified. Guarantee legislation is necessary to define what is meant by warranties. For the right to complain is worth little if there is no framework to enforce it. Finally, health and safety is a big area but authorities must have the will to devise systems which give them the power to recall products endangering health, and even to ban products or brands involved. This is one area which, happily, is making some progress.

Secondly government marketers must ensure consumer education so that consumers know how markets operate and what the procedure is for complaining. Guides as to what consumers should expect must be distributed to *all* classes. These are especially relevant to problem areas such as family planning and powdered milk for babies.

Finally consumer information programmes are essential. Manufacturers must be required to give information. Certain labelling techniques are advisable, for example, colour for a quality code. Sellers can be encouraged to advertise price in order to reduce bargaining and increase competitiveness. Consumer associations, women's councils and other citizens' groups must be developed.

The burden on the government marketer is large, but if he is successful there is much to be gained. The high uncertainty, high-risk market environment which exists in many developing countries will be replaced by open market competitiveness and consumer-orientation among sellers. The consumer will be protected, educated and informed and will have the right to choose, be heard and be safe. More importantly consumer-led economic development will be promoted.

But as well as promoting consumer emancipation the government can do more. It must provide the necessary favourable wider environment in which an open-market economy can operate. As noted in Chapter 6, governments can improve all aspects of the infrastructure – roads, postage, telecommunications, electricity, warehouses, credit systems and so on. They can combat corruption and stimulate competition, thus reducing the emphasis on inefficient parastatals and co-operatives. Privatisation of various sectors, such as taxis and service stations can be encouraged. Price controls can be phased out wherever possible. Innovation, entrepreneurship and management can be stimulated through providing incentives and training. Finally social responsibility among businessmen and a Civil Service based on merit rather than political or personal connection can be promoted. As a result open-market systems and emancipated consumers will develop, which in turn should lead to faster economic development at home and greater competitiveness overseas.

The state of the art of marketing in developing countries

Previous chapters have demonstrated that, with the exception of one or two notable examples, the use of marketing in developing countries by government and indigenous marketers has been poor. Although few countries have spontaneously developed marketing training schemes, it would appear that the present unfavourable economic climate is causing more nations to reappraise their positions and recognise, if only indirectly, the relevance of marketing.

By considering the problems and prospects of individual countries or groups of countries some conclusions may be drawn which may prove useful to other developing countries contemplating such strategies. Although there is, unavoidably, some repetition of aspects considered in previous chapters, attention is focused on the trends at the macro and micro level indicated in Part III.

(a) Oil-rich nations

Many of the countries whose problems are numerous and prospects somewhat bleak are the oil-rich ones. Formerly very socialist, they tend to be introducing more capitalism into their economies as a necessity. Egypt's problems are typical of many large rich countries. They include debt, riots, rapid population growth (one million more every ten months), greater consumption than production, more imports than exports, expenditure higher than amount received and all manner of price distortions. Egypt's policy has been inward-looking, using import-substitution. The joint venture with General Motors (holding not more than 30 per cent of the equity) to build Ascona and Corsa cars in 1987 has been the centrepiece. But despite the 'open door' policy initiated 10 years ago, foreign investment remains patchy, while the present difficulties are causing some reassessment of potential investors. Only now is Egypt considering how attractive its marketing environment is from the point of view of the multinationals. Consequently it is relaxing many of its former stringent controls – foreign investors may now have 49 per cent of ownership in some projects, and Egypt is also trying to switch to more of an export orientation. Its prospects are not bright.

In the Middle East generally prospects are not as good as one would imagine, given their wealth in terms of per capita income. The small, rich nations have concluded that downstream activities of oil production are necessary to add value to the exported product. Thus the processing of both raw materials and wastes is being developed. But, as noted earlier, high cost production is normal. And problems have become more obvious as oil revenues have fallen. For example, in the United Arab Emirates they fell from \$19.4b in 1981 to \$11.7b in 1984. The UAE still have the highest per capita income in the world, standing at \$22,870, no foreign debt, zero or a negative rate of inflation which in the past led to the building of infrastructure, industry, apartment blocks and hotels, and the importation of 1000 immigrant workers who in turn generated more business. But with these workers gone, the problem is how to integrate local people into a much smaller economy, parts of which have no reason to survive (*Financial Times*, 21 Jan. 1986).

Oil rich countries elsewhere have called for more urgency in their industrialisation process, since the uncertainty of oil prices has forced them to look to non-oil exports. Brunei – although sitting on foreign reserves estimated to be \$20b or \$100 000 per capita – is to spend more on infrastructure and education. But the heart of the country's plan focuses on building up the private sector. However 'the question is whether the entrepreneurial drive will emerge among Brunei's citizens who have grown accustomed to a rather different sort of life-style – with subsidies for everything from rice to car loans' (*Financial Times*, 21 Jan. 1987, p. 3). To encourage the private sector to play a role the government has recognised that the financial system must make available sufficient funds and, although some critics have argued that the development plan is 'long on ideas and short on principles', nevertheless Brunei has not made the same mistakes as other oil-rich states and its prospects seem much better.

Nigeria, on the other hand, is a country whose prospects are much grimmer. Its over-dependence on oil and its lack of efficient management and planning, together with a complete disregard of marketing, have resulted in enormous problems. Initially much money from oil was squandered or siphoned off into external bank accounts, while in the excitement of oil discoveries agriculture was allowed to become moribund. Even big exports such as groundnuts (of which Nigeria used to be the world's biggest exporter fell and today Nigeria imports groundnuts. By 1985 only 2.7 per cent of all exports were in non-oil products and two-fifths of this was cocoa. The lack of forward planning and the failure to anticipate problems has meant that debt and unpaid trade bills (which stood at \$6b-\$7b in 1986) have become enormous. The inward-looking industrialisation policy encouraged the cutting of imports, but today manufacturing is operating at 20 per cent capacity since there is no money to buy imports, while to acquire an import licence has become a 'national obsession' (*Financial Times*, 3 Mar. 1986). Barter was used to alleviate the situation but, as noted in the last chapter, Nigeria had its fingers burned. In 1987, five years after the slump in oil prices, Nigeria's margins for manoeuvre are much reduced.

Because exports have fallen in value from $26b in 1980 to $12b in 1985 a programme of export incentives was introduced with the objective of raising non-oil exports to 15 per cent of the total. These include exporters being allowed to keep up to one quarter of their foreign exchange earnings, reduced import duties, preferential treatment in applying for import licences, tax holidays for three years if over 50 per cent of turnover is exported, export subsidies to encourage firms to buy locally, tax relief on bank financing and possible export credit guarantees, insurance and a free zone. But bureaucracy will not be easy, given the past policies which tend to suggest that marketing was insufficiently incorporated into the planning framework.

The need to make the marketing environment more attractive to foreign investment and to incorporate more of a capitalist approach has become obvious to many large rich countries. Indonesia's foreign investment fell 60 per cent between January and July 1986 and whereas it was valued at $395.4m in the first six months of 1985, in the same period of 1986 the corresponding figure was $139.3m; approved non-oil investment dropped from $2.7b in 1983 to $0.85m in 1985 (*Financial Times*, 29 Aug. 1986). High material costs, corruption and red tape have been identified as major weaknesses. Foreign debt is now $33b and tax has been increased by 65 per cent to offset this. The problems are obvious, but the will to improve the state of marketing remains in doubt. The only encouraging move in the right direction is that salaries of civil servants have not been increased (something which was expected prior to the election).

Malaysia has responded more positively to its problem. For fifteen years up to 1985 Malaysia's economy grew by 7.5 per cent per annum on average, on the strength of booming prices for tin, rubber, petroleum and palm oil. With the collapse of the price of commodities, Malaysia's economy is going backwards. Its response has been to implement new rules to attract foreign investment. Restrictions on ownership have been reversed and discrimination against the Chinese has been modified, but it is doubtful whether the government can restore sufficient confidence to this ethnic group. Between 1981 and 1986 many Chinese businessmen (recently joined by some indigenous Malays) channelled money out of the country. And foreign investment in the present depressed climate is unwilling to accept any restrictions on ownership, not to mention the stifling red tape and petty bureaucracy typical in Malaysia. Many plantation groups sold out in the late 1970s and went to Thailand, the Philippines and Indonesia, thus increasing Malaysia's competition. Some radical changes are required to improve this country's prospects.

(b) Outward-looking, export-orientated newly industrialised countries

The countries which have not interfered with market forces but have instead encouraged international competitiveness are those adopting outward-looking, export-controlled strategies. In the most successful of these, those of Southeast Asia, marketing is used much more. Although the multinational may be largely responsible for success in the international area, the government marketer has played his part, both in providing a favourable marketing environment and in using social marketing to reduce non-economic obstacles to growth. Equally the successful indigenous marketers, some themselves multinationals now, are making their mark using capitalist principles. To a large extent the unfavourable international climate has been combated, or at least circumvented, while other trends, such as the convergence of consumer tastes, have been seized upon as opportunities and therefore encouraged.

Various factors have been isolated as reasons for the success of Southeast Asia. The ability to export in a competitive environment, the right attitude to controlling population (Taiwan, Singapore and South Korea having halved their net reproduction rates since the 1950s), the low level of inflation and high government spending on infrastructure (Hong Kong and Taiwan spending eight times as much on projects such as roads, harbours and airports as on social services), the emphasis on education and reversing the braindrain by offering financial and psychological incentives for nationals to return home, the relatively few legal constraints, the way in which just technology rather than the whole system has been imported and the preparedness of industry to work with governments have all been highlighted as major strengths. The Chinese culture and its group consciousness, team-work attitude and ability to save and use capital is a somewhat more controversial aspect which has been identified as advantageous.

What is not in doubt is that the prospects for Southeast Asia newly industrialised countries, particularly the 'Gang of Four', are extremely bright. Although very dependent upon the rest of the world, their strategy of filling gaps rather than competing directly with western products wherever possible has proved highly effective. Well made, low-priced goods, especially in the sectors of cars, clothing, steel and electronics, were encouraged, although the strategy now, in such nations as South Korea and Singapore, is to move into high-tech industry niches. Yet at the same time protection of domestic industry was also typical in some countries. South Korea and Taiwan, both poorer than Ghana and Sudan in terms of GDP per head in 1960, in one generation raised their living standards to levels equivalent to parts of Europe through both the promotion of exports and tariff protection for domestic producers. Only now are these nations dismantling their protective tariffs.

South Korea may be singled out as a developing country which has successfully grown its own multinationals, taken advantage of the internationalisation of production (demonstrating the validity of the international product life cycle) and the convergence of consumer tastes and used the marketing mix, particularly advertising, to great effect. Although the Japanese (somewhat ironically) regard South Koreans as 'low cost imitators who could not hold an original idea in their heads') (*Financial Times*, 25 Apr. 1986), such names as Hyundai and Samsung are going from strength to strength. Hyundai's construction work in Jubail, Saudi Arabia, which involved everything from slipways to mosques, has been called one of the most massive civil engineering feats in the world. It put Hyundai on the map and aggressive salesmanship, tough workers and government support through inexpensive credit and diplomatic coverage have been pointed to as key strengths.

Today Hyundai is landing cars in the USA with the intention of becoming as large as Mazda or Nissan. Other manufacturers are waiting in the wings. For example, Chrysler may join with Samsung which is not involved with cars as yet. Some have suggested that by 1979 South Korea will be exporting one million units of cars and trucks to the USA. Considering that South Korea's front-wheel drive cars were only developed in 1984 the challenge seems daunting, but it may well be met.

The government is also encouraging high-tech industries and Samsung electronics is leading the way. Founded in 1969 and born out of the Samsung Group, whose activities range from jet engines to life insurance, it has experienced an annual growth rate of 60 per cent. Sales in 1985 equalled $1.5b with products ranging from rice-cookers to computer parts. It has achieved this position through licensing technology (mainly Japanese), importing 40 per cent of its raw materials and producing large volumes of inexpensive goods with reasonable quality and design by using cheap labour (one quarter of the cost of Japanese labour). Two-thirds of its products are exported, mainly to the USA, and, as noted in the last chapter, whilst companies in the past tended to stamp their brand name on Samsung products, today the company's strategy is to use its own name and promote it as 'the sensible alternative'. The intention is to improve production efficiency and manufacture overseas, to overcome trade friction with the west and improve access to Western technology. Thus the idea of an interdependent world is clearly recognised, as is the requirement to attack abroad and overcome the protectionist tide by moving up-market and manufacturing overseas. Samsung's push into more sophisticated consumer markets is reflected in (Table 11.1, which demonstrates how exports of inexpensive Korean televisions and radios are falling and their place is being taken by video cassette recorders and computers.

Table 11.1 Exports of electronics from South Korea

	1984	1985	1986 (est.)
Products	US$m	US$m	US$m
Colour TVs	443	392	400
Black & white TVs	263	216	180
Radios	544	499	520
Video cassette recorders	121	334	500
Computers	218	397	610
Telephone & communication equipment	87	109	125
Components			
Semi-conductors	1258	971	1300
Audio tape	170	238	300
Cathode-ray tubes	75	163	200
Microwave ovens	238	212	264
Total electronics output	4585	4730	5800
Ratio of exports: total output	74.6%	74.7%	75.8%

Source: Korean Electronics Industry Association, in *Financial Times*, 9 Apr. 1986, p. VIII.

Despite the fact that Korea too has suffered in the recession, especially in the sectors of overseas construction, shipping and shipbuilding, the government has helped soften the blow. It has encouraged retrenchment through cost-cutting, diversification and increased productivity in construction and shipping, while acknowledging the duty it feels towards these industries, which it previously helped to develop. More attention is now being given to high-tech industries as well as greater emphasis to small and medium-sized companies. Government and industry have great respect for each other and this is often pointed to in order to help explain South Korea's trade surplus of $4.2b with the USA in 1985. Whatever the underlying reasons, South Korea has been impressive in its development, and by examining its strengths and strategy, some pointers to the future marketing strategies for other nations may be found.

Singapore provides an even more interesting example. Lacking the 42m people South Korea has for its domestic market, Singapore until 1985 witnessed spectacular growth based on multinational activity. Its GNP trebled between 1975 and 1985, overtaking Greece in 1981, Spain in 1983 and Israel in 1984. In 1985 it experienced negative growth rates and people began to wonder whether the policy followed – to turn Singapore from an Asian sweatshop into a high-tech landmark – had not been a mistake, since Singapore seemed to be pricing itself out of the market (labour costs having increased 10.4 per cent between 1979 and 1984, productivity by only 4.6 per cent). Workers were laid off (previously unheard of), bankruptcies rose 20 per cent in 1985 and oil and shipbuilding were particularly badly hit. Various measures were taken, such as a two-year wage freeze, corporate tax was reduced from 40 per cent to 30 per cent and the employers' contribution to the Central Provident Fund (state pension fund) is to be cut by 15 per cent – from 25 per cent to 10 per cent of the employee's salary – for two years from April 1986 to 1988. It would seem that the clouds are now beginning to lift and 1–2 per cent growth for 1986 is expected to be recorded; this, although poor in comparison with the 8 per cent per annum recorded in the period 1970 to 1985, is much better than the decline of 1985. A similar growth of exports is expected, shipbuilding and the petroleum industry are improving and electronics expanded 25 per cent in the first quarter of 1986.

The lack of debt, good infrastructure, educated work-force and strategic location have undoubtedly helped, but much credit must go to the marketing-orientated framework of planning. The strategy of attracting multinationals to take advantage of its cheap labour and then actively encouraging wage levels to rise, so that more sophisticated technology, particularly in the electronics field, may be introduced has been described in Chapter 7. But it is interesting to note that Singapore's curious *dirigiste* style of government, based on capitalist principles, is not immune from making mistakes or against listening to advice. Initially there was overdependence on United States direct investment and an overblown construction sector. But Singapore has realised that it is enormously dependent on an interdependent world (having no hinterland, with 2.8m people and being heavily dependent on Indonesia and Malaysia which have suffered badly in the recent economic recession). And it is prepared to learn how to ride peaks and troughs. Its response to the recent downturn in world trade has been to lower labour costs and this seems to have been effective, helped further by the appreciation of the yen.

Many of the world's major companies involved in semi-conductor and electronic component manufacturing have production facilities in Singapore. Seagate has three factories and employs 6000, Siemens, Philips, AT and T, General Electric, Matsushita, Hitachi and other Japanese giants are all represented, and many electronic companies are expanding their operations. A multiplier effect, due to interlinkage in this sector, has been set in motion, while design and R & D are developing to take advantage of Singapore's relatively cheap supply of engineers. For the government, with its objective of making Singapore the brain centre of the world, this is something of a success, particularly since earlier wage rises threatened the strategy. The attitude towards multinationals – regarding them not as a danger but a necessity, and encouraging them on their own terms (100 per cent ownership, free to move out capital and handicapped by no restrictions) and also providing them with a favourable marketing environment – has worked well. Even though wages have risen they are still much lower than Japan's, while assembly work can be contracted out to neighbouring countries where wages are even lower.

The government seems to have got other things right too. For despite many criticising Singapore for 'imposing' a Western style of life and business on Singaporeans – English being the main language, British legal codes being used and Western lawyers, doctors, architects and bankers being welcome – this now seems to be an asset. The Japanese consumer company Aiwa has recently complimented the Singaporeans on being more 'international' in their outlook than the Japanese and having a better command of English (*Financial Times*, 3 Feb. 1987). For such a company so dependent on foreign markets, this is regarded as a big plus. Other advantages isolated by such companies include Singapore's superb telecommunication facilities, air and sea freight connections and other supporting infrastructure which counteract the rising cost of wages. It would seem that the government's efforts at improving the marketing environment are paying off handsomely.

Singapore's capitalist attitude is well demonstrated by the privatisation programme now under way, which corresponds somewhat to Britain's. Singapore Airlines is now privatised, although the government still holds 63 per cent of assets. The next main disposal is likely to be a company with no business record and which may be without tangible operations at the time of the sale. This is Singapore's Mass Rapid Transit (MRT) metro which is not due to open until 1988. Yet it may be privatised in 1987. Telecoms, the Port of Singapore Authority and Changi airport are other candidates (*Financial Times*, 3 Nov. 1986).

Yet at the same time there is an almost Fascist tendency to improve rules and regulations. Thrift and diligence are encouraged, ethnic minorities are broken up and heroin pushers are executed. In the past hippies have been thrown out and parents with only one or two children rewarded. Thus 'this tiny city state may have the most clearly defined and rigorously enforced public morality in the world' (Hofheinz and Calder, 1982). And Singapore's planners are not afraid to use social marketing to this end. In addition to the public information campaign on family planning and drug abuse, a courtesy campaign started in 1979 and is still running. The first slogan was 'Make courtesy our way of life'. In 1981 it beame 'It's so nice to be courteous' and in 1984 it was changed to 'Let's take the initiative to be courteous'. All social groups – even the less educated hawkers – have been included. Like Singapore generally, social marketing has a novel approach.

Singapore, as is the case with many other nations in Southeast Asia, has on its side a capacity for innovation, adaptability, flexibility and political stability. But more than this it has long-term objectives and

346 Issues Affecting the Future of Marketing

incorporates marketing. And in the game of national survival, especially
in a climate where countries are having to become more competitive,
marketing provides an increasingly important weapon and firepower.
The condition of East Asian newly industrialised countries may not be
replicated elsewhere, but the way in which these countries have made the
most of whatever they do possess provides valuable guidelines to others.

Conclusion

In addition to the broader issues contained in the global economic crisis,
there are additional forces at work which have implications for developing countries on a more micro level. Although it has been argued that
there is an obsession with the Western way of life and that eventually a
global lifestyle will emerge, this is not universally the case. Certainly the
multinational has speeded the transfer of technology and new products
to developing countries and, as a result, convergence of consumer tastes
is occurring as the world's needs and wants are 'homogenised'. But it can
also be shown that there are divergent tendencies at work in the form of (i)
host countries' insistence that multinationals manufacture products
specifically designed for other markets, (ii) subcultures which are present
in most societies and (iii) cultural reaction to the Western approach
which, in its most extreme form, has manifested itself in Islamic
fundamentalism. Yet even within such divergent trends there is a certain
amount of convergence also obvious, with Western products still
required. And the global acceptance of products once only associated
with certain ethnic groups shows that even specialities can be subject to
the force of convergence.

Obviously there are both convergent and divergent tendencies at work
and these present opportunities and threats. The multinational marketer
generally welcomes and encourages the convergence of consumer tastes.
The indigenous marketer should recognise the trend towards convergence and be seen to take advantage of it by following the multinational's
strategy and upgrading his product quality and reliability so that he may
effectively compete on world markets. The governmental marketer must
involve himself in moral decisions as to whether convergence or
divergence is desirable for his society as a whole. Where convergence is
regarded as acceptable he must encourage the indigenous markets to
attack export markets and reduce obstacles in his path.

Closely associated with the convergence or divergence there is the
issue of capitalism or socialism. The ultimate convergence of these two
political regimes might be manifested in the transideological enterprise,

and there has been some development along these lines in China. But even elsewhere socialist states are turning more to capitalist principles as they see the need for development along commercial lines, rather than rigid planning through costly, overstaffed bureaucracies. Mr Gandhi is making some changes in favour of the private sector in India, while China has gone even further. Many former, Maoist principles have been discarded, market forces have been introduced into wages and prices and one or two 'capitalist' institutions such as the Shanghai Stock Exchange have reappeared. The extent to which further change occurs is largely dependent upon the reconciliation of such developments with the communist ideology. But until there is greater acceptance and under-standing of marketing practices and principles from the top down, it would seem that China's future development hangs in the balance.

The implications of the convergence of socialism and capitalism in some instances and the greater acceptance of capitalism in others suggests, on the surface, many opportunities for individual and multi-national markets. The development of the transideological enterprise offers a wider sphere of operation for the multinational while the exporter has a huge potential market in China. Greater capitalism elsewhere offers enterprising individuals more scope. However, until the marketing environments of many developing countries are improved, such oppor-tunities are reduced. Thorelli (1981) has argued that consumer emanci-pation is an essential first step, so that markets can be opened up. But the government marketer can also do much to upgrade infrastructure and increase social responsibility among businessmen.

This may be something of a pipe-dream in the immediate future, since the art of marketing in developing countries as a whole is not highly developed, although the impetus to improve marketing training is becoming obvious in today's unfavourable economic climate. The coun-tries which have the biggest problems and poorest prospects are those which either have difficulty in attracting multinationals through their sheer wealth and small markets, such as the Middle East states, or have relied too heavily on socialist principles and inefficient state planning often associated with inward-looking import substitution strategies. The large oil-rich nations in particular are reappraising their past strategies and at least indirectly acknowledging the need for more marketing.

At the other extreme the countries which have encouraged market forces to operate naturally and multinationals to locate and export would seem to have much brighter prospects. Government marketers here have enhanced the marketing environment by building infrastructure and using social and educational progammes to control population and stimulate local entrepreneurship. They have accepted such trends as the convergence of consumer tastes and regarded these as opportunities to be seized. The result is that multinationals of their own have been estab-

lished and the objectives of specific sectors leading further development
have been achieved. Today South Korea is a major car exporter, while
Singapore is on target to become an important 'brain centre'.

Yet even within the most successful 'Gang of Four', no one formula can
be identified and universally applied. Just as it is not possible for all
nations to take the United Kingdom as a model and assume wealth will
result from industrialisation, so too the strategy of Singapore or South
Korea might be inappropriate. But those countries which are willing to
improve the state of their marketing and use it to assess their situation
and match their strengths with potential opportunities are likely to find
the best way forward, and ultimately to be successful in the economic
development race.

Appendix I: The World Bank classification of developing and other countries

DEVELOPED COUNTRIES

Low-income economies	Population (millions) mid-1984	GNP per capita ($) 1984
Ethiopia	42.2	110
Bangladesh	98.1	130
Mali	7.3	140
Zaire	29.7	140
Burkina Faso	6.6	160
Nepal	16.1	160
Burma	36.1	180
Malawi	6.8	180
Niger	6.2	190
Tanzania	21.5	210
Burundi	4.6	220
Uganda	15.0	230
Togo	2.9	250
Central African Republic	2.5	260
India	749.2	260
Madagascar	9.9	260
Somalia	5.2	260
Benin	3.9	270
Rwanda	5.8	280
China	1 029.2	310
Kenya	19.6	310
Sierra Leone	3.7	310
Haiti	5.4	320
Guinea	5.9	330
Ghana	12.3	350
Sri Lanka	15.9	360
Sudan	21.3	360
Pakistan	92.4	380

	Population (millions) mid-1984	*GNP per capita ($)* 1984
Senegal	6.4	380
Afghanistan	n.a.	n.a.
Bhutan	1.2	n.a.
Kampuchea	n.a.	n.a.
Lao PDR	3.5	n.a.
Mozambique	13.4	n.a.
Vietnam	60.1	n.a.

Middle-income economies
(Oil Exporters and Oil Importers)

(a) Lower middle income

Mauritania	1.7	450
Liberia	2.1	470
Zambia	6.4	470
Lesotho	1.5	530
Bolivia	6.2	540
Indonesia	158.9	540
Yemen Arab Republic	7.8	550
Yemen PRD	2.0	550
Cote d'Ivoire	9.9	610
Philippines	53.4	660
Morocco	21.4	670
Honduras	4.2	700
El Salvador	5.4	710
Papua New Guinea	3.4	710
Egypt	45.9	720
Nigeria	96.5	730
Zimbabwe	8.1	760
Cameroon	9.9	800
Nicaragua	3.2	860
Thailand	50.0	860
Botswana	1.0	960
Dominican Republic	6.1	970
Peru	18.2	1 000
Mauritius	1.0	1 090
Congo People's Republic	1.8	1 140
Ecuador	9.1	1 150
Jamaica	2.2	1 150
Guatemala	7.7	1 160
Turkey	48.4	1 160
Costa Rica	2.5	1 190
Paraguay	3.3	1 240
Tunisia	7.0	1 270
Columbia	28.4	1 390
Jordan	3.4	1 570
Syrian Arab Republic	10.1	1 620
Angola	9.9	n.a.

	Population (millions) mid-1984	GNP per capita ($) 1984
Cuba	9.9	n.a.
Korea, Democratic Republic	19.9	n.a.
Lebanon	n.a.	n.a.
Mongolia	1.9	n.a.
(b) Upper middle income		
Chile	11.8	1 700
Brazil	132.6	1 720
Portugal	10.2	1 970
Malaysia	15.3	1 980
Panama	2.1	1 980
Uruguay	3.0	1 980
Mexico	76.8	2 040
Korea, Republic of	40.1	2 110
Yugoslavia	23.0	2 120
Argentina	30.1	2 230
South Africa	31.6	2 340
Algeria	21.2	2 410
Venezuela	16.8	3 410
Greece	9.9	3 770
Israel	4.2	5 060
Hong Kong	5.4	6 330
Trinidad and Tobago	1.2	7 150
Singapore	2.5	7 260
Iran Islamic Republic	43.8	n.a.
Iraq	15.1	n.a.
High-income economies (Oil exporters)		
Oman	1.1	6 490
Libya	3.5	8 520
Saudi Arabia	11.1	10 530
Kuwait	1.7	16 720
United Arab Emirates	1.3	21 920
INDUSTRIAL MARKET ECONOMIES		
Spain	38.7	4 440
Ireland	3.5	4 970
Italy	57.0	6 420
New Zealand	3.2	7 730
UK	56.4	8 570
Belgium	9.9	8 610
Austria	7.6	9 140
Netherlands	14.4	9 520
France	54.9	9 760
Japan	120.0	10 630

	Population (millions) mid-1984	GNP per capita ($) 1984
Finland	4.9	10770
German Federal Republic	61.2	11130
Denmark	5.1	11170
Austria	15.5	11740
Sweden	8.3	11860
Canada	25.1	13280
Norway	4.1	13940
United States	237.0	15390
Switzerland	6.4	16330

EASTERN EUROPE
NON-MARKET ECONOMIES

Hungary	10.7	2100
Poland	36.9	2100
Albania	2.9	n.a.
Bulgaria	9.0	n.a.
Czechoslovakia	15.5	n.a.
German Democratic Republic	16.7	n.a.
Romania	22.7	n.a.
USSR	275.0	n.a.

Appendix II: Livingstone's classification of developing and other countries

I   DEVELOPING COUNTRIES

These may be subdivided according to:

Size: A country may be considered to be *large* if its population is 30m or over. This is simply an empirical cut-off point, blurred in the Third World by a rapidly rising population. But given a domestic population of 30m and with adequate and equitable per capita income, a country could sustain modern industry for its domestic market alone.

A country is considered to be *small* if it population is under 30m.

Wealth: A country is considered to be *rich* (or potentiall rich) if its earnings from the production and sale of raw materials are comparable (or, in prospect, comparable) with the income per head of an industrially developed country. It is often the internal political and cultural situation rather than the lack of exploitable resources which has thus far prevented many countries from achieving a standard of living comparable with industrial nations.

A country is considered to be *poor* if its earnings from the production and sale of proved raw material are well below, and not likely to achieve, the per capita income of an advance country.

This gives a classification as follows:

Large (potentially) rich countries, e.g. Nigeria.
Large poor countries, e.g. Bangladesh.
Small rich countries, e.g. Saudi Arabia.
Small poor countries, e.g. Malawi.

A subset drawn from large (potentially) rich, large poor and small poor countries constitutes the *newly industrialised* category. These countries are said to have broken out of the trap of underdevelopment and have achieved technological bases which enable them to produce a wide range of products. However some are very much more successful than others. Indeed some, such as Singapore, Hong Kong and Taiwan have moved into a situation broadly comparable with industrialised countries, which they are rapidly joining. Others are much further behind in their development.

II   WESTERN DEVELOPED NATIONS

North America, United Kingdom and the rest of Western Europe, Australia, New Zealand and South Africa (at least in respect of the dominant racial group).

III   JAPAN

(which although western developed is culturally distinct).

IV   MARXIST COUNTRIES

(Spanning the range from industrialised through industrialising to poor and backward).

References

Chapter 1

Alderson, W. (1968) *Men, Motives and Markets* (New Jersey: Prentice-Hall).
Baker, M. J. (ed.) (1983) *Marketing: Theory and Practice*, 2nd edition (London: Macmillan).
Baker, M. J. (1985) *Marketing: An Introductory Text*, 4th edition (London: Macmillan).
Baker, R. W. (1969) 'Marketing in Nigeria' in M. J. Thomas (ed.) *International Marketing Management* (Boston: Houghton Mifflin).
Baxter, N. (ed.) (1972) *Measuring Development: The Role and Adequacy of Development Inidicators* (London: Frank Cary & Co.).
Brandt, W. (1980) *The Brandt Report: North-South. A Programme for Survival*, (London: Pan Books).
Douglas, S. (1971) 'Patterns and Parallels opf Marketing Structures in Several Countries', *MSU Business Topics*.
Fisk, G. (1967) *Marketing Systems: An Introductory Analysis* (New York: Harper Row).
Kinsey, J. (1982) 'The Role of Marketing in Economic Development', *European Journal of Marketing*, 16 ,6, pp. 64–77.
Kotler, P. (1984) *Marketing Management: Analysis, Planning and Control*, 4th edition (New York: Prentice Hall).
Kotler, P. (1973) 'Defining the Limits of Marketing' in B. W. Becker and H. Becker (eds), *Combined Proceedings of the American Marketing Association*, p. 49.
Kotler, P. and Zaltman, G. 'Social Marketing: An Approach to Planned Social Change', *Journal of Marketing*, 35, July 3–12.
Livingstone, J. M. Professor and Head of the Department of Management, Queens University, Belfast.
Marcus, B. et al. (1975) *Modern Marketing* (New York: Random House).
Myrdal, G. (1968) *Asian Drama: An Inquiry into the Poverty of Nations* (New York: Pantheon).
Nurske, R. (1971) 'The Theory of Development and the Idea of Balanced Growth' in A. B. Mountjoy *Developing the Underdeveloped Countries* (London: Macmillan). pp. 115–28
Peterson, R. (1977) *Marketing: A Contemporary Introduction* (London: Wiley).
Rostow, W. W. (1962) *The Stages of Economic Growth* (Cambridge University Press).
Sears, D. (1969) 'The Measuring of Development', *International Development Review* 11, 4.
Thorelli, H. and Becker, H. (1980) *International Marketing Strategy* (New York: Pergamon Press).
World Bank (1986) *World Development Report 1986* (Oxford University Press).

pter 2

Baker, M. J. (1985) *Marketing: An Introductory Test* (London: Macmillan).
Beals, A. R. (1967) *Culture in Process* (New York: Holt Rhinehart).
Hall, E. T. (1960) 'The Silent Language in Overseas Business', *Harvard Business Review* May–June, pp. 87–96.
Harper, M. (1975) 'Advertising in a Developing Economy: Opportunity and Responsibility', *European Journal of Marketing*.
Hofheinz, J. R. and Calder K. E. (1982) *The Eastasia Edge* (New York: Basic Books).
Kotler, P. (1980) *Marketing Management: Analysis, Planning and Control* (New York: Prentice-Hall).
Terpestra, V. (1978) *The Cultural Environment of International Business* (Cincinnati: S W Publishing Company).
Tylor, E. B. (1871) *Primitive Culture* (London: Murray).

Chapter 3

Baker, M. J. (1985) *Marketing: An Introductory Text* (London: Macmillan).
Baker, R. W. (1969) 'Marketing in Nigeria' in Thomas, M. J. *International Marketing Management* (Boston: Houghton Mifflin).
Bates, J. A. (1981) 'Marketing Problems of Developing Countries', *EAARIM Conference*, March.
Bullock, H. A. (1961) 'Consumer Motivation in Black and White', *Harvard Business Review*, 39, May–June, pp. 89–104, and July–Aug, pp. 110–24.
Dichter, E. (1962) 'The World Consumer', *Harvard Business Review*, July–Aug, pp. 113–23.
Farmer, R. N. (1966), 'Organisational Transfer and Class Structures', *Academy of Management Journal*, Sept, pp. 204–16.
Financial Times, 19 Sept 1984.
Financial Times, 12 Jan 1985, 'Biscuit Factory May Follow Indian Wimpy Bar'.
Financial Times, 14 Feb 1987, 'Lightening India's Village Load' (J. Elliot), p. 3.
Girling, R. (1976) 'Mechanisms of imperialism: Technology and the Dependent State', *Latin American Perspectives*, 3, 4, pp. 54–64.
Harper, M. (1975) 'Advertising in a Developing Economy: Opportunity and Responsibility', *European Journal of Marketing*.
Harrison, P. (1979) *Inside the Third World* (Harmondsworth: Penguin).
Higler, M. T. (1980) 'Consumer perceptions of a Public Marketer in Mexico', *Columbia Journal of World Business*, Fall, 15, 3, pp. 75–82.
Hodder, B. W. (1978) *Africa Today* (London: Methuen).
Jefkins, F. (1982) *Introduction to Marketing, Advertising and Public Relations* (London: Macmillan).
Kumar, K. (1973) 'The Indian Consumer', *South Asian Review*, 8, Jan, pp. 215–21.
Kotler, P. (1984) *Marketing Management: Analysis, Planning and Control*, 5th edn (Englewood Cliffs, N. J.: Prentice-Hall).
Maslow, A. H. (1943) 'A Theory of Human Motivation', *Psychological Review*, 50.
Pinches, C. R. (1977) 'Economic Development: The Need for an Alternative Approach', *Economic and Development and Cultural Change*, 26, 1. pp. 139–47.

Reisman, D., Glazer, N. and Denney, R. (1950), *The Lonely Crowd* (Yale University Press)

Rogers, E. M. (1962) *The Diffusion of Innovations* (London: Macmillan).

Sommers, S. and Kernan, J. B. (1967), 'Why Products Flourish Here, Fizzle There', *Columbian Journal of World Business*, 2, March–April, pp. 89–99.

Thorelli, H. B. and Sentell, G. D. (1982) *Consumer Emancipation and Economic Development: The Case of Thailand* (Greenwich, Connecticut, JAI Press Inc).

Walter, H. G. (1974) 'Marketing in Developing Countries', *Columbia Journal of World Business*, 9, 4, pp. 29–30.

Chapter 4

Baker, M. J. (1985) *Marketing: An Introductory Text*, 4th edn (London: Macmillan).

Cateora, P. R. and Hess, J. M. (1979) *International Marketing*, 4th edn (Irwin). (Homewood Illinois.)

Davis, H. R., Douglas, S. P. and Silk A. J. (1981) 'A Hidden Threat to Cross National Marketing Research', *Journal of Marketing*, Spring, pp. 98–109.

Douglas, S. P. and Craig, C. S. (1983) *International Marketing Research* (Englewood Cliffs, N. J.: Prentice-Hall).

Douglas, S. and Shoemaker, R. (1981) 'Item Non-Response in Cross National Surveys', *European Research*, 9 October, pp. 124–32.

Frey, F. (1970) 'Cross-Cultural Survey Research in Political Science' in R. E. Holt and J. E. Turner (eds), *The Methodology of Financial Research* (New York: The Free Press).

Kracmar, J. Z. (1971) *Marketing Research in the Developing Countries* (New York: Pobger).

Lauter, G. P. (1969) 'Sociological, Cultural and Legal Factors impeding Decentralisation of Authority in Developing Countries', *Academy of Management Journal*, Sept, pp. 372–4.

Livingstone, J. M. (1977) *A Management Guide to Marketing Research* (London: Macmillan).

Loudon, D. L. (1976) 'A note on Marketing Research in Mexico', *Journal of Business Research*, 4, 1, pp. 69–73.

Chapter 5

Baker, M. J. (1985) *Marketing: An Introductory Text*, 4th edn (London: Macmillan).

Goldman, A. (1975) 'Stages in the Development of the Supermarket', *Journal of Retailing*, 51 Winter, pp. 49–64.

Goldman, A. (1981) 'Transfer of a Retailing Technology', *Journal of Retailing*, Summer, pp. 5–29.

Harper, M. (1975) 'Advertising in a Developing Economy': Opportunity & Responsibility', *European Journal of Marketing*.

Kacker, M. P.(1976) 'Distribution in a Developed Economy – Some Emerging Trends and Implications for Strategy', *International Journal of Physical Distribution* 7, 1, pp. 30–41.

Kaikati, J. G. (1976) 'Doing Business in Iran: The Fastest Growing Market Between Europe and Japan', *Atlanta Economic Review*, Sept–Oct, pp. 15–21.

Majaro, S. (1977) *International Marketing* (London: George Allen & Unwin).

Stock, J. R. & Lambert, D. M. (1983) 'Physical Distribution Management in International Marketing', *International Marketing Review* 1, 1. Autumn, pp. 28–41.

Chapter 6

Abbott, J. C. (1966) 'Marketing Issues in Agricultural Development Planning' in Moyer R. and Hollander, S. L. 1966, (eds) *Markets and Marketing in Developing Economies* (Illinois: Irwin).

Abbott, J. C. and Makeham, J. P. (1981) *Agricultural Economics and Marketing in the Tropics* (London: Longman).

Financial Times 20 Jan, 1984 'Kenya Tea: How the Smallholder is tasting Success', p. 33; 3 June 1985 *Rajiv's India*, Supplement; 3 Mar. 1986 *Nigeria* Supplement; 10 Mar. 1986 *Indonesia* Supplement; 12 May 1986 *India* Supplement; 4 Sep. 1986 'Food in the Wrong Places', p. 28; 6 Sep. 1986 'State of Siege', *Weekend Financial Times*, p.I.

Goldman, A. (1981) 'Transfer of a Retailing Technology to the Less Developed Countries: The Supermarket Case', *Journal of Retailing*, 57, 2, 5–29

Harrison, P. (1980) *The Third World Tomorrow* (Harmondsworth Penguin).

Hilger, M. T. (1980) 'Consumer Perception of a Public Marketer in Mexico', *Columbia Journal of World Business*, 15, 3, pp. 75–82.

Hodder, B. W. (1978) *Africa Today* (London: Methuen).

Kacker, M. P. (1976) 'Distribution in a Developing Economy – Some Emerging Trends and Implications for Strategy', *International Journal of Physical Distribution*, 7, 1.

Kotler, P. and Zaltman G. (1971) 'Social Marketing: An Approach to Planned Social Charge', *Journal of Marketing*, 35, 3–12.

Lewis. W. A. (1955) *The Theory of Economic Growth* (London: Allen & Unwin).

Nurske, R. (1953) *Problems of Capital Formation in Underdeveloped Countries* (Oxford University Press).

The Times 27 May 1986 'To end hunger set the peasants free', p. 12.

Chapter 7

Financial Times, 23 Apr. 1986 'Singapore puts brainpower behind thinking machines', p. 14; 8 May 1986 'Indonesia liberalises foreign investment and trade rules', p. 25; 13 Aug 1986 'Malaysia chooses common sense', p. 12; 23 Aug. 1986 'Master of Singapore', *Weekend Financial Times*, p.I; 1 Sep. 1986 'The War on

Product Pirates', p.10; 13 Nov. 1986 'Indonesian technocrats attack growing distortions in economy', p.8.

Harper, M. and Soon, T. T. (1979) *Small Enterprises in Developing Countries: Case Studies and Conclusions* (London: Intermediate Technology Publications Ltd).

Myrdal, G. (1968) *Asian Drama: An Inquiry into the Poverty of Nations* (New York: Pantheon).

Sarkar, N. F. (1978) *Social Structures and Development Strategy in Asia* (New Delhi: Peoples Publishing House).

Chapter 8

Barnet, R. J. and Miller, R. (1974) *Global Reach and the Power of Multinational Corporations* (New York: Simon & Silvester).

Cateora, P. R. and Hess, J. M. (1979) *International Marketing* (Illinois: Irwin).

Creamer, D. B. (1976) *Overseas R & D by US Multinationals 1966–75. Estimates of Expenditures and a Statistical Profile* (New York: The Conference Board).

Drucker, P. F. (1958) 'Marketing and Economic Development', *Journal of Marketing*, January, pp. 252–9.

Dunning, J. H. (1971) *The Multinational Enterprise* (London: Allen & Unwin).

Financial Times 3 June 1985 Rajiv's India F.T. Supplement p. I–XIV; 31 Oct. 1985 'Turning point of a South Korean Giant', p.18; 31 Oct. 1986 'See it in perspective', p.24; 1 Sep. 1986 'The War on Product Pirates', p.10; 8 Sep 1986 'A question of patent unfairness', p.4; 11 Feb. 1987 'A Balancing Act on the World Stage' (C. Lorenz) p.12.

Frank, I. (1980) *Foreign Enterprise in Developing Countries* (John Hopkins UP).

Germidis, D. (1976) *Manufacturing Firms and Vocational Training in Developing Countries* (Paris: UNESCO).

Girling, R. (1976) 'Mechanism of Imperialism: Technology and the dependent state', *Latin American Perspectives*, 3–4, pp. 54–64.

Hall, E. T. (1960) 'The Silent Language in Overseas Business', *Harvard Business Review*, May–June, pp. 87–96.

Hill, R. (1981) 'Are Multinationals Aliens in the Third World?', *International Management*, Jan, pp. 12–16.

Jacoby, N. H., Nehemkis, P. and Eells, R. (1977) *Bribery and Extortion in World Business* (London: Macmillan).

Jain, S. G. and Puri, Y. (1981) 'Role of Multinational Corporations in Developing Countries: Policy Makers' Views, *Management International Review*, vol. 21, no. 2, pp. 57–66.

Kim, S. H. and Miller, S. W. (1979) 'Constituents of the International Transfer Pricing Decision', *Colombia Journal of World Business*, Spring, 69–77.

Kumar, K. (1980) *Transnational Enterprises: Their Impact on Third World Societies and Cultures* (Boulder, Colorado: Westview Press).

Ledogar, R. J. (1975) *Hungry for Profits: US Food and Drug Multinationals in Latin America* (New York: IDOC).

Lee Kam-Hon (1981) 'Ethical Beliefs in Marketing Management: A Cross-Cultural Study', *European Journal of Marketing*, 15, 1, pp. 58–67.

Livingstone, J. M. (1975) *The International Enterprise* (Associated Business Programmes).

Medewar, C. (1981) *Insult or Injury* (Social Audit).

Miller, M. (1974) *The Baby Killer* (London War on Want Pamphlet).

Myrdal, G. (1968) *Asian Drama: An Inquiry into the Poverty of Nations* (New York: Pantheon).

Perlmutter, H. V. (1969) 'The Tortuous Evolution of the Multinational Corporation', *Columbia Journal of World Business*, vol. 4.

Richman, B. M. (1977) 'Significance of Cultural Variables' in Weinshall (1977) *Culture and Management* (Harmondsworth: Penguin), pp. 15–38.

Smedley, S. R. and Zimmerer, T. W. (1986) 'Doing Business in Third World Countries', *Business*, April–June, p. 53.

Terpstra, V. (1978) *International Marketing*, 2nd edn (New York: Holt, Rinehart and Winston).

Terpstra, V. (1978) *The Cultural Environment of International Business* (Cincinnati: South West Publishing Co.).

Ting Wenlee (1980) 'A Comparative Analysis of the Management Technology and Performance of Firms in Newly Industrialised Countries', *Colombia Journal of World Business*, 15, 3, pp. 83–91.

Vernon, R. (1971) *Sovereignty at Bay* (New York: Basic Books).

Vernon, R. (1976) Multinational enterprises in Developing Countries. Issues in dependency and interdependence in *The Multinational Corporation and Social Change*, edited by Apter, D. E. and Goodman, L. W. (New York: Praeger).

Vernon, R. and Wells, L. T. (1980) *Manager in the International Economy*, 4th edition (New Jersey: Prentice-Hall).

Weinshall, T. D. (1977) *Culture and Management* (Harmondsworth: Penguin).

Wells, L. T. (1977) 'More or Less Poverty? The Economic Effects of the Multinational Corporation at Home and in Developing Countries' in Carl H Madden (ed) *The Case for the Multinational Corporation* (New York: Praegar).

Wright, P. (1981) 'Organisational Behaviour in Islamic Firms', *Management International Review*, vol. 21, no. 2, pp. 86–94.

Chapter 9

Adams, K. A. (1970) 'Resource Utilisation by Meat Retailers in a Developing Economy'. *Business Perspectives*, 6, 2, pp. 10–17.

Allen, L. L. (1973) 'Factors Affecting the Profitability of Small Firms' in Carson (ed.) *The Vital Majority*, pp. 241–52.

Anderson, E. E. (1970) 'Retail Pull: A Source of Economic Stability and Growth for Developing Nations', *Journal of Retailing*, 49, 4, pp. 24–30.

Bolton, J. E. (1971) *Small Firms: Report of the Committee of Inquiry on Small Firms* (London: HMSO).

Boswell, J. (1972) *The Rise and Decline of Small Firms* (London: Allen & Unwin).

Bramley, G. (1978) *Local economic initiatives* WPI School for Advanced Urban studies, University of Bristol.

Brannen, W. (1980) *Successful Marketing for your Small Business* (Englewood Cliffs, New Jersey: Prentice-Hall Inc.)

Cleland, S. (1955) *The Influence of Plant Size on Industrial Relations*. Research Report Series No. 89, Princeton University.

Davies, J. R. and Kelly, M. (1972) *Small Firms in the Manufacturing Sector*, Research Report No. 3, Committee of Inquiry on Small Firms (London: HMSO).

Davies, J. R., Ryan, G. A. and Noonan, A. C. (1982) 'Marketing Research: Some Basics for Small Business', *Journal of Small Business Management*, vol. 20, no. 3, July, pp. 62–66.

Epsy, J. L. (1972) 'Some Notes on Business and Industry in Hong Kong', *Chung Chi Journal*, 11, 1, April–May, pp. 172–81.

Financial Times 23 Jan. 1985 'Retrenchment causes a bout of frayed nerves', *Arabic Trading*, p. 19 (M. Field); 3 June 1985 'India: Business Management Styles' (J. Elliott); 24 Feb. 1986 *Nigeria* Supplement, p. 15; 21 Oct. 1986 Swiss Fund for Panama Projects, p. 16 (J. Wicks).

Food and Agricultural Organisation (1982) *The Private Marketing Entrepreneur and Rural Development*, FAO, Agricultural Services Bulletin.

Ford, D. and Rowley, T. P. (1979) 'Marketing and the small industrial firm', *Management Decision*, vol. 17, no. 2, pp. 144–57.

Golby, C. W. and Johns, G. (1971) *Attitude and Motivation*, Research report No. 7, Committee of Inquiry on Small Firms (London: HMSO).

Goldman, A. (1974) 'Outreach of Consumers and the Modernisation of Urban Food Retailing in Developing Countries', *Journal of Marketing*, 38, October, pp. 8–16.

Goldman, A. (1981) 'Transfer of a Retailing Technology into the Less Developed Countries: The Supermarket Case', *Journal of Retailing*, 57, 2, 5–29.

Hoffman, O. G. (1982) 'A Policy Programme for the Mixed Economy' in Thorelli H. B. and Sentell, G. D. (eds) *Consumer Emancipation and Economic Development* pp. 267–84.

Hofheinz, J. R. and Calder, K. E. (1982) *The Eastasia Edge* (New York: Basic Books).

House, R. (1986) 'Keeping it simple for the Third World', *South*, February, p. 47.

Howell, D., Frazier, G. L. and Stephenson, P. R. (1980) 'Using Industry Data in Small Business Decision Making: Potential Problems', *Journal of Small Business Management*, vol. 20, no. 2, April, pp. 45–56.

Jackson, H. H., Hawes, D. K. and Hertel, F. M. (1979) 'Pricing and advertising practices in small retail businesses', *American Journal of Small Business*, vol. 4, no. 2, pp. 22–35.

Johns, T. (1976) 'Where Smallness Pays', *Management Today*, July, pp. 60–63.

Johnson, P. (1978) 'Policies towards small firms: Time for Caution', *Lloyds Bank Review*, 129, pp. 1–11.

Kaplan, A. D. H. (1948) *Small Business: Its Place and Problems* (New York: McGraw-Hill Book Company).

Kaynak, E. (1979) 'A Refined Approach to the Wheel of Retailing', *European Journal of Marketing*, 13, 7, pp. 237–45.

Lamont, L. M. (1972) 'Marketing Industrial Technology in the Small Business', *Industrial Marketing Management*, 4, pp. 38–96.

Moreau, J. F. (1980) *Effective Small Business Management* (Chicago: Rand McNally College Publishing Co.).

Nelson, R. E. (1984) 'Training Needs of the Small Enterprise Section in Asia, *Journal of Small Business Management*, vol. 18, no. 4, pp. 1–7.

Stancil, J. M. (1981) 'Realistic criteria for judging new ventures', *Harvard Business Review*, Nov–Dec, pp. 60–72.

Thorelli, H. B. (1981) 'Consumer Policy for the Third World', *Journal of Consumer Policy*, 3, pp. 197–211.

Thorelli, H. B. and Sentell, G. D. (1982) *Consumer Emancipation and Economic Development: The Case of Thailand* (Greenwich, Connecticut: JAI Press Inc.).

Woodruff, A. M. and Alexander, T. G. (1958) *Success and Failure in Small Manufacturing* (University of Pittsburg).

Chapter 10

Alderson, W. (1968) *Men Motives and Markets* (Englewood Cliffs, N.J.: Prentice-Hall).

Atkins, L. (1985) 'The Import Wave', *Dun's Business Month*, February 1985.

Bell, J. (1986) 'Focus on Barter', *South*, December, pp. 41–2.

Brandt, W. (1980) *The Brandt Report: North–South. A Programme for Survival* (London: Pan Books).

Cundiff, E. W. and Hilger, M. T. (1984) *Marketing in the International Environment* (New Jersey: Prentice-Hall).

Financial Times 27 Sep. 1985 'Britain agrees to boost Saudi trade as part of Tornado deal' (P. Bloom), p. 8; 10 Mar. 1986 Indonesia Supplement, pp. 1–16; 29 Aug. 1986 'An embrarrassing abundance' (M. Wilkinson), p. 14; 21 Sep. 1986 'Third World debt forces increase in countertrading' (P. Bloom), p. 7; 22 Sep. 1986 'The Third World struggles with debt' (P. Stephens), p. 5; 20 Oct. 1986 The Pacific Rim Supplement, pp. 1–VIII; 25 Feb. 1987 'Imelda's shoes inhabit a national shrine' (R. Gourlay), p. 5.

Fishlow, A. (1981) *Trade in Manufactured Products with Developing Countries: Reinforcing the North–South Partnership*, Trilateral Commission.

Hansen, R. D. (1979) *Beyond the North–South Stalemate* (New York: McGraw Hill).

Hofheinz, R. and Calder, K. E. (1982) *The Eastasia Edge* (New York: Basic Books).

Hurtado, M. E. (1986) 'The human cost of the debt burden', *South*, September, p. 37.

Jones, D. E., Gaffney, C., Debes, L. and Laxmi, N. (1985) 'The Four Tigers start clawing at Upscale Markets', *Business Week*, July 22, pp. 136, 138, 142.

Manley, M. and Brandt, W. (1985) *Global Challenge. From Crisis to Co-operation: Breaking the North–South Stalemate* (London: Pan).

Prebisch, R. (1959) 'Commercial Policy in the Underdeveloped Countries', *American Economic Review Papers and Proceedings*, May, pp. 251–5.

Prebisch, R. (1962) 'The Economic Development of Latin America and its Principal Problems', *Economic Bulletin for Latin America*, February.

Tussie, D. (1987) *The Less Developed Countries and the World Trading System* (London: Pinter Publishers).

Westlake, M. (1986a) 'The Protection Racket', *South*, February, pp. 33–6.

Westlake, M. (1986b) 'Impact of the Third Oil Shock', *South*, April, pp. 79–80.

World Bank (1986) *World Development Report 1986* (Oxford University Press).

Chapter 11

Financial Times 3 June 1985 'Rajiv's India', Supplement pp. I–XIV; 19 Sep. 1985 'Drawing the party line' (R. Thompson); 21 Jan. 1986 United Arab Emirates Supplement, pp. 17–22; 3 Mar. 1986 Nigeria Supplement, pp. 11–12; 9 Apr. 1986 South Korea Supplement, pp. I–XII; 25 Apr. 1986 'Samsung aims upmarket to secure its growth record', p. 22; 29 Aug. 1986 'Indonesia foreign investment falls 60 per cent', p. 6; 19 Sep. 1986 'China reaffirms stand on reform' (R. Thompson), p. 40; 9 Oct 1986 'Paradox of future lifestyles' (F. MacEwan), p. 26; 3 Nov. 1986 Singapore Supplement, pp. 19–24; 14 Nov. 1986 'The West and Iran' (R. Mathews), p. 22; 5 Jan. 1987 'China's student revolt', p. 12; 10 Jan. 1987 'Arabia keeps the Faith', *Weekend Financial Times* (M. Field), p. 2; 23 Jan. 1987 'Chinese academics and propaganda chief purged' (R. Thompson), p. 5; 29 Jan. 1987 'Brunei turns a leisurely eye to the future', p. 3; 3 Feb. 1987 'Singapore tunes in to the electronics boom' (S. Butler), p. 4.

Harrison, P. (1980) *The Third World Tomorrow* (Harmondsworth: Penguin).

Hoffman, P. G. (1972) *Time*, January 17.

Hofheinz, R. and Calder, K. E. (1982) *The Eastasia Edge* (New York: Basic Books).

Knapman, R. and Walter, M. A. H. B. (1980) 'The Way of the Land and the Path of Mondy: The Generation of Economic Inequality' in E. Fiji, *Journal of Developing Areas*, vol. 14, pp. 201–22.

Landes, D. S. (1969) *The Unbound Prometheus* (Cambridge University Press).

Levitt, T. (1983) 'The Globalisation of markets', *Harvard Business Review*, May–June, pp. 92–102.

Livingstone, J. M. (1975) *The International Enterprise* (London: Associated Business Programmes).

Terpstra, V. (1978) *The Cultural Environment of International Business* (Cincinnati: South West Publishing Co.).

Thorelli, H. B. (1981) 'Consumer Policy for the Third World', *Journal of Consumer Policy*, vol. 3, pp. 197–211.

Author index

Subject index